MASON'S MANUAL OF LEGISLATIVE PROCEDURE

The American Society of Legislative Clerks & Secretaries

in cooperation with the
National Conference of State Legislatures
1989

Additional copies of this manual may be purchased from the

National Conference of State Legislatures
1050 17th Street, Suite 2100
Denver, Colorado 80265

West Publishing Co.
St. Paul, Minn.

DEDICATION OF THE 1989 EDITION

This edition is dedicated to Paul Mason.
1898–1985

AMERICAN SOCIETY OF LEGISLATIVE CLERKS & SECRETARIES

Mason's Manual Revision Commission

Patrick E. Flahaven, Chair
Minnesota

Joe Brown
Florida

Edward A. Burdick
Minnesota

Grace Collins
North Carolina

Mark R. Corrigan
Pennsylvania

William C. Kandler
Michigan

Betty King
Texas

Mouryne B. Landing
Nevada

Gregory Gray, Vice Chair
West Virginia

Clyde W. McCullough, Jr.
Tennessee

Patrick J. O'Donnell
Nebraska

John B. Phelps
Florida

Robert L. Picher
Vermont

Jane Richards
Arizona

Donald J. Schneider
Wisconsin

Kenneth A. Wright
Illinois

Second Printing 1990.

Library of Congress Catalog Card Number: 88–63527

ISBN 1–55516–729–2

DEDICATION BY PAUL MASON
1979 EDITION

This book of rules is dedicated to the many legislators and members of other public decision-making bodies who devote their energies and often their life's work to making the decisions which so largely control the welfare and literally the lives of their fellow citizens and on whose integrity and judgment the protection of the interests of all the people depend.

May we provide for them the facilities to get the facts and make correct decisions, support them in making honest decisions even when unpopular, and provide the rules and procedure to enable them to make their decisions simply, directly, openly, expeditiously and accurately.

*

AMERICAN SOCIETY OF LEGISLATIVE CLERKS & SECRETARIES

The American Society of Legislative Clerks & Secretaries, the oldest of NCSL's staff sections, comprises the chief parliamentary officers and staff involved with the law-making and administrative processes of state legislatures. The Society undertakes special projects and surveys on aspects of legislative procedure, parliamentary rulings, data processing and staff training.

*

NATIONAL CONFERENCE OF STATE LEGISLATURES

The National Conference of State Legislatures serves the legislators and staffs of the nation's 50 states, its commonwealths and territories. NCSL is a nonpartisan organization with three objectives: to improve the quality and effectiveness of state legislatures; to foster interstate communication and cooperation; and to ensure states a strong cohesive voice in the federal system. The Conference has offices in Denver, Colorado, and Washington, D.C.

*

FOREWORD

In the foreword to the 1979 edition, Paul Mason wrote:

> This volume evolved from an exhaustive study of judicial decisions and legislative precedents and practice, guided by knowledge gained from many years of experience with legislative procedure and from specialization in constitutional law.
>
> A proper application of these rules of procedure will eliminate controversy, confusion and litigation and will make public bodies more efficient in their work and more pleasant to work in.

Prior to his death, Paul Mason assigned the copyright to his manual to the National Conference of State Legislatures (NCSL) with the request that the book continue to be updated and published. NCSL in turn asked the American Society of Legislative Clerks & Secrctaries (ASLCS) to proceed with a new edition of the manual. In 1984, the society created the Mason's Manual Revision Commission consisting of ASLCS members. The commission continued with the same members to provide consistency and continuity to the project. The members represented a broad cross section of state legislatures and brought many years of combined experience in dealing with questions of procedural theory and practice.

FOREWORD

The commission wishes to thank the legislators, legislative staff and the staff of the National Conference of State Legislatures, especially Jan Carpenter, Rich Jones, Bill Pound and Sharon Schwoch for their support and assistance in this effort.

Patrick E. Flahaven
Chair

Mason's Manual
Revision Commission

December 1988

INTRODUCTION

Principles of Parliamentary Law

An understanding of parliamentary principles will simplify the learning and application of parliamentary rules. Parliamentary procedure is based primarily on a group of principles which underlie the whole scheme of parliamentary rules. Some of these principles are set out below. Thought of in terms of principles instead of rigid, detailed technical rules, parliamentary law is essentially logical and simple.

Parliamentary Rules

Every deliberative body is bound to comply with all applicable rules laid down for it by the Constitution and laws, both statutes and court decisions and basic legal principles. These rules and principles govern whether adopted by the body or not, and they apply whenever group decisions are being made. Failure to conform to them invalidates any action taken or decision made.

Unless restricted by the Constitution, statutes or other superior authority, an organization can adopt its own rules of parliamentary procedure by a majority vote. Also by a majority vote, it can change, suspend or repeal the rules at any time it chooses. Failure to comply with its own adopted rules does not invalidate actions of the organization.

Every member of an organization is presumed to be the equal of each other member, and each has rights that must be respected. The rights of the minority and the majority both must be protected.

Ten Principles That Govern Procedure in Group Decision Making

Ten principles govern procedure in group decision making.

1. *The group must have the authority to take the actions it purports to take.* Jurisdiction must be given; it cannot be assumed. Groups sometimes assume powers that they do not have.
2. *There must be a meeting of the decision-making group.* When authority to make a decision is vested in any group, it is vested in the group collectively and not merely in the individual members of the group. To make a decision, the group must meet and make up its collective mind.
3. *A proper notice of the meeting must be given to all members of the group.* All members of the group are entitled to such a notice of the time, place and purpose of the meeting as will enable them to attend and participate. Failure to give such a notice will invalidate actions taken at the meeting.
4. *There must be a quorum present at the meeting.* A quorum is a sufficient number or proportion of the members as will qualify those present to act for the entire membership. A quorum is a majority of the members qualified to act, unless a lesser number is given that authority by proper authority

or a higher number is especially required. A member who is not entitled to vote on a particular question cannot be counted to make a quorum for voting on that question.

5. *There must be a question before the group upon which it can make a decision.* The question may be a motion, resolution or other proper form and may be oral or in writing and in most cases should be capable of being answered by an affirmative or negative vote. A member has the right to know what the question is and what its effect will be before voting on the question.

6. *There must be an opportunity to debate the question.* An opportunity to debate is necessary to enable the members of a group to reach a collective judgment. A member has the right to express personal opinions and hear the opinions of the other members.

7. *The question must be decided by taking a vote.* It is not enough to presume how a member will vote. A vote actually must be taken. It may be taken by an authorized and fair method.

8. *There must be a majority vote to take an action or decide a question.* In order to take any action or decide any question, there must be an expression of the will of the majority. This is usually a majority of the legal votes but sometimes is a majority of the entire membership or a two-thirds vote is required. A minority vote or a tie vote will not take any action.

9. *There must be no fraud, trickery or deception resulting in injury to any member.* A person is entitled to the protection of the courts from injury through injustice by a body making a group decision as in any other situation involving injury.

10. *To be valid, any action or decision of a body must not violate any applicable law or constitutional provision.* The decision-making procedures of any body must comply with the applicable provisions of any local, state or Federal law. It is governed by any statutory or court-made law, including provisions of constitutions and charters.

Principles Are Easier Than Rules to Remember and to Apply

Many parliamentary authors use a table to show how certain actions apply to a list of 40 to 82 motions. It is much easier to apply the governing principle than to memorize how the action applies to each of the 40 to 82 motions or to look up the answer each time in the table. For example:

Is the motion amendable? If the motion can be made in more than one form, it is amendable. If it can be made in only one form, it is not amendable.

Is the motion debatable? A main motion or other question presenting a matter of business to the body for its decision is debatable because debate is essential to enable the members to reach a meeting of the minds. The question is not debatable when it is a simple procedural motion that can be understood by the members without debate such as a motion to adjourn or to lay on the table.

May a speaker be interrupted? A speaker may be interrupted whenever the needs of the body require it, as the concern of the body outweighs the convenience of a member. A speaker may be interrupted by a question of privilege of the house that requires immediate attention, for example, or may be interrupted for a matter that has a definite time limit such as objection to the consideration of a question that is being presented.

Is a second required? Legislative bodies usually do not require seconds, but where seconds are used, motions require seconds. However, actions in which a member has the right to request or demand such as points of order, parliamentary inquiry or demands for a division do not require seconds. Only motions require seconds.

What vote is required? The rules of parliamentary law do not require the vote of more than a majority, but constitutions and statutes sometimes do and adopted rules often do. Unless there is a special requirement for a higher vote, a majority of the legal votes cast is sufficient.

How Can a Body Change Its Decision?

When a body is dissatisfied with its vote on a main motion or substantive question, it can cancel the vote by reconsidering it whether it was carried or lost. But if there is dissatisfaction with a vote on a procedural motion, if the motion was lost, the motion may be renewed. Whenever there is a change in the situation, or if the motion carried, the effect of the vote can be changed by a motion which will reverse the effect of the motion such as take from the table, change limits on debate, withdraw from committee or change the time of hearings. After an act is completed, it can be amended or repealed by another act.

Precedence of Motions

There is a principle that determines the precedence of motions. The closer a motion is to final disposition of the matter under consideration, the lower it is in the order of precedence. The furthest removed the motion is from final disposition of the matter, the higher it is in the order of precedence.

Rules Should Be Applied with Judgment

Any rule serves best when it is applied with judgment and fairness. Arbitrary, inflexible rules, rigorously applied to differing situations, often produce injustice.

TABLE OF CONTENTS

PART I

PARLIAMENTARY LAW AND RULES

TABLE OF CONTENTS

TABLE OF CONTENTS

TABLE OF CONTENTS

PART II

DEBATE

TABLE OF CONTENTS

PART III

RULES GOVERNING MOTIONS

TABLE OF CONTENTS

PART IV

RULES GOVERNING PARTICULAR MOTIONS

Division 1. Privileged Motions

Division 3. Subsidiary Motions

PART V

QUORUM, VOTING, ELECTIONS

TABLE OF CONTENTS

TABLE OF CONTENTS

Page

TABLE OF CONTENTS

PART VIII

RELATIONS WITH THE EXECUTIVE AND WITH THE OTHER HOUSE

PART IX

SESSIONS AND MEETINGS

PART X

INVESTIGATIONS AND PUBLIC ORDER

TABLE OF CONTENTS

*

KEY TO CITATIONS

For convenience, citations occurring frequently in this volume have been reduced to their briefest form. These citations, and the volumes to which they refer, are as follows:

Cushing's Legislative Assemblies—Cushing, Luther Stearns, "Elements of the Law and Practice of Legislative Assemblies in the United States of America—Lex Parliamentaria Americana," Boston, Little, Brown & Co., 1856 (usually available in the printing of 1874).

Cushing—Cushing, Luther Stearns, "Manual of Parliamentary Practice," new edition by Albert S. Bolles, The John C. Winston Company, 1928 (text unchanged in editions from 1907 to 1947, inclusive).

Demeter—Demeter, George, "Demeter's Manual of Parliamentary Law and Procedure," Boston, Bostonia Press, revised 1969.

Hatsell—Hatsell, John, "Precedents of Proceedings in the House of Commons," 3rd edition, London, 1756.

Hughes—Hughes, Edward Wakefield, "Hughes' American Parliamentary Guide," F.J. Heer Printing Co., revised 1926.

Jefferson—Jefferson, Thomas, "Jefferson's Manual," 1781, available as a document of the U.S. Congress; e.g., House Document No. 416, 93rd Congress, 2nd Session, published by U.S. Government Printing Office, 1975.

KEY TO CITATIONS

Mass. Manual—State of Massachusetts, Legislature, "Manual of the General Court of Massachusetts," 1947–48.

N.Y. Manual—State of New York, Legislature, "New York Manual" (Clerk's Manual), editions of 1936 and 1948–49.

Reed—Reed, Thomas B., "A Manual of General Parliamentary Law" (Reed's Rules), 1898; reprinted: State Printing Plant, Olympia, Washington, 1937.

Robert's—Robert, General Henry M., "Robert's Rules of Order, Newly Revised," 1970.

Sturgis—Sturgis, Alice Fleenor, "Standard Code of Parliamentary Procedure," New York, McGraw-Hill, 1950, and 2nd edition revised, New York, McGraw-Hill, 1966.

Tilson—Tilson, John Q., "Parliamentary Law and Procedure," Ransdell Incorporated, Washington, D.C., 1935.

Tilson's Manual—Tilson, John Q., "A Manual of Parliamentary Procedure," Oceana Publications, 1949.

U.S. House Rule—U.S. Congress: provisions of the U.S. Constitution and rules of the House of Representatives are cited from the "Manual of the U.S. House of Representatives."

Waples—Waples, Rufus, "A Handbook on Parliamentary Practice," Chicago, Callaghan, 1883.

PART I. PARLIAMENTARY LAW AND RULES

*

PART I

PARLIAMENTARY LAW AND RULES

CHAPTER 1

RULES GOVERNING PROCEDURE *

Sec. 1. Necessity for Rules of Procedure

1. It is necessary that every deliberative body be governed by rules of procedure in order that the will of a majority of its members may be determined and revealed in an orderly manner.

---

* Note Concerning Citations: A brief statement by Jefferson in the introduction to his manual describes the use of citations in this volume so accurately that it is repeated here as better describing the use of the citations in this book than could be stated by the author.

> "I could not doubt the necessity of quoting the sources of my information .... sometimes each authority cited supports the whole passage. Sometimes it rests on all taken together. Sometimes the authority goes only to a part of the text, the residue being inferred from known rules and principles. For some of the more familiar forms no written authority is or can be cited, no writer having presumed it necessary to repeat what all are presumed to know. The statement of these must rest on their own notoriety."

As far as feasible the text has been organized to facilitate the citation of authority. In order to leave the text unbroken the citations are carried as footnotes with reference to sections and paragraphs.

Sec. 1, Par. 1: Cushing's Legislative Assemblies, Sec. 498; French v. Senate of State of California (1905), 146 Cal. 604, 80 P. 1031, 69 L.R.A. 556; People *ex rel.* Gregory v. Strohm (1918), 285 Ill. 580, 121 N.E. 223; Landes v. State of Indiana (1903), 160 Ind. 479, 67 N.E. 189; *In re* Gunn (1893), 50 Kan. 155, 32 P. 470; Nevins v. City Council of City of Springfield (1917), 227 Mass. 538, 116 N.E. 881; Witherspoon v. State of Mississippi *ex rel.* West (1925), 138 Miss. 310, 103 So. 134; City of Sedalia *ex rel.* Gilsonite Const. Co. v. Montgomery (1904), 109 Mo. App. 197, 88 S.W. 1014; State of Nebraska v. Dunn (1906), 76 Neb. 155,

2. Any legislative body must have rules to promote the orderly and businesslike consideration of the questions which come before it for determination. These rules determine the priority and manner of consideration of questions and provide an orderly and methodical plan so that all business may receive proper consideration. Thus, confusion, waste of time and effort are eliminated.

3. Rules of procedure fulfill another purpose in protecting the rights of members. Individual members, for example, are entitled to receive notices of meetings and the opportunity to attend and participate in the deliberations of the group. Minorities often require protection from unfair treatment on the part of the majority, and even the majority is entitled to protection from obstructive tactics on the part of minorities.

4. Many rules of procedure are based upon fundamental rights such as the decision by the majority, but some rules are necessary only to avoid confusion by designating one course of procedure when more than one course might otherwise be followed. In some instances, as pointed out by Jefferson quoting earlier authority, it may be as important that there be a rule as what the rule is.

5. The great purpose of all rules and forms, says Cushing, is to subserve the will of the assembly rather than to restrain it; to facilitate and not to obstruct the expression of its deliberate sense.

---

107 N.W. 236; Wise v. Bigger (1884), 79 Va. 269; Taylor County Court v. City of Grafton (1915), 77 W.Va. 84, 86 S.E. 924.

Sec. 1, Par. 4: Jefferson, Sec. I.

Sec. 1, Par. 5: Cushing's Legislative Assemblies, Sec. 990; Dye v. State of Mississippi *ex rel.* Hale (1987), 507 So. 2d 332.

Sec. 2. Right to Regulate Procedure

1. Every governmental body has an inherent right to regulate its own procedure subject to provisions of the constitution, statutes, charters or other controlling authority.

2. A house of a state legislature has complete authority concerning its procedure so far as it is not limited by constitutional provisions.

3. The constitutional right of a state legislature to control its own procedure cannot be withdrawn or restricted by statute, but statutes may control procedure insofar as they do not conflict with the rules of the houses or with the rules contained in the constitution.

4. State legislatures and other bodies created by constitutional provision are controlled in their procedure by any provision of the constitution which directly, or by necessary implication, governs their procedure. Constitutions or statutes often authorize the bodies whose procedure they regulate to establish their own rules of procedure.

5. In general, state legislatures are governed in accordance with the recognized principles of parliamentary law subject to any special provisions of the

---

Sec. 2, Par. 1: Witherspoon v. State of Mississippi *ex rel.* West (1925), 138 Miss. 310, 103 So. 134; Jory v. Martin (1936), 153 Ore. 278, 56 P.2d 1093; Cushing's Legislative Assemblies, Sec. 792.

Sec. 2, Par. 2: Cushing's Legislative Assemblies, Sec. 792.

Sec. 2, Par. 3: Goodwin v. State Board of Administration (1925), 210 Ala. 453, 102 So. 718.

Sec. 2, Par. 4: Cushing's Legislative Assemblies, Sec. 793; Witherspoon v. State of Mississippi *ex rel.* West (1925), 138 Miss. 310, 103 So. 134; Atkins v. Philips (1890), 28 Fla. 281, 8 So. 429; Wheeler v. Commonwealth (1895), 89 Ky. 59, 32 S.W. 259; Boyd v. Chicago etc. R.R. Co. (1902), 103 Ill. App. 199.

state constitutions and any rules adopted by the body.

6. The powers and privileges which are necessary to the proper exercise, in all respects, of its appropriate functions, are inherent in the legislature and are to be ascertained primarily by reference to the common parliamentary law.

7. An act of the legislature is legal when the constitution contains no prohibitions against it.

Sec. 3. Each House Determines the Rules of Its Own Proceedings

1. Most state constitutions grant authority over procedure to each house of the legislature by substantially the following language: "Each House shall determine the rules of its proceedings."

2. The house and senate may pass an internal operating rule for its own procedure that is in conflict with a statute formerly adopted.

Sec. 2, Par. 5: Werts v. Rogers (1894), 56 N.Y.L. 480, 28 A. 726; Hodges v. Keel (1913), 108 Ark. 84, 159 S.W. 21.

Sec. 2, Par. 6: State of Washington *ex rel.* Robinson v. Fluent (1948), 30 Wash. 2d 194, 191 P.2d 241, *cert. denied,* Washington Pension Union v. State of Washington *ex rel.* Robinson, 335 U.S. 844, 69 S. Ct. 66, 93 L. Ed. 394.

Sec. 2, Par. 7: Diefendorf v. Gallet (1932), 51 Idaho 619, 10 P.2d 307.

Sec. 3, Par. 1: Cushing's Legislative Assemblies, Sec. 792; U.S. Constitution, Art. I, Sec. 5, Par. 1. State Constitutions: Ala. IV, 53; Alaska II, 14; Ariz. IV, II, 8; Ark. V, 12; Cal. IV, 7(a); Colo. V, 12; Conn. III, 13; Del. II, 9; Fla. III, 4; Ga. III, Sec. IV, 4; Hawaii III, 12; Idaho III, 9; Ill. IV, 6; Ind. IV, 10; Iowa III, 9; Kan. II, 8; Ky. 39; La. III, 7(a); Me. IV, Part III, 4; Md. III, 19; Mass. Part II, Ch. 1, Sec. II, 7, Sec. III, 10; Mich. IV, 16; Minn. IV, 7; Miss. IV, 55; Mo. IV, 18; Mont. V, 10; Neb. III, 10; Nev. IV, 6; N.H. II, 22, 37; N.J. IV, Sec. IV, Par. 3; N.Mex. IV, 11; N.Y. III, 9; N.Dak. IV, 12; Ohio II, 7; Okla. V, 30; Ore. IV, 11; Pa. II, 11; R.I. IV, 7; S.C. III, 12; S.Dak. III, 9; Tenn. II, 12; Tex. III, 11; Utah VI, 12; Vt. II, 19; Va. IV, 7; Wash. II, 9; W.Va. VI, 24; Wis. IV, 8; Wyo. III, 12.

Sec. 3, Par. 2: Coggin v. Davey (1975), 233 Ga. 407, 211 S.E.2d 708.

3. A state constitution is a limitation rather than a grant of legislative power. If not expressly or impliedly withheld, the whole legislative power of the state is committed to the legislature which may enact any law not forbidden by the constitution or delegated to the Federal Government or prohibited to the states.

4. The provision of the constitution that each house shall have the power to determine the rules of its proceedings is not restricted to the proceedings of the body in ordinary legislative matters, but extends to determination of propriety and effect of any action taken by the body in the exercise of any power, in the transaction of any business or performance of any duty conferred upon it by the constitution, as in proposing amendments to the constitution.

5. The constitutional rule that each house shall determine the rules of its own proceedings is authorization for the enactment of joint rules.

6. Under the power to determine the rules of its own procedure, each house of the legislature has the power to determine how it will handle conference committee reports including a minority report.

7. The fact that a house of the legislature acted in violation of its own rules or in violation of parliamentary law in a matter clearly within its power does not make its action subject to review

---

Sec. 3, Par. 3: Jory v. Martin (1936), 153 Ore. 278, 56 P.2d 1093.

Sec. 3, Par. 4: Opinion of the Justices (1949), 252 Ala. 205, 40 So. 2d 623; State of North Dakota *ex rel.* Spaeth v. Meiers (1987), 403 N.W.2d 392.

Sec. 3, Par. 5: Charleston National Bank v. Fox (1938), 119 W.Va. 438, 194 S.E. 4.

Sec. 3, Par. 6: Opinion of the Justices (1975), 295 Ala. 26, 322 So. 2d 107.

by the courts.

Sec. 4. Sources of Rules of Procedure

See also Ch. 6, Parliamentary Law, and Sec. 43, Indispensable Requirements for Making Valid Group Decisions.

1. Rules of legislative procedure are derived from several sources. The principal sources are as follows:

(a) Constitutional rules.

(b) Fundamental legal principles, *see also* Sec. 22, paragraph 3.

(c) Statutory rules or charter provisions (as to local bodies).

(d) Adopted rules.

(e) Customs, usage and precedents.

(f) Adopted parliamentary authority.

(g) Parliamentary law.

(h) Judicial decisions.

2. The rules from the different sources take precedence in the order listed above except that judicial decisions, to the extent they are interpretations of rules from one of the other sources, take the same precedence as the source interpreted. Thus, for example, an interpretation of a constitutional provision takes precedence over a statute.

3. Whenever there is conflict between rules from these sources, the rule from the source listed earlier prevails over the rule from the source listed later. Thus, where the constitution requires three readings of bills, this provision controls over any provision of

---

Sec. 3, Par. 7: State of Connecticut v. Savings Bank of New London (1906), 79 Conn. 141, 64 A. 5.

statute, adopted rules, adopted manual or parliamentary law; and a rule of parliamentary law controls over a local usage but must give way to any rule from a higher source of authority.

4. The term "parliamentary law" is sometimes used in two different senses. It applies to rules having two different priorities. Certain indispensable basic principles such as the requirement of a meeting, a quorum or a majority vote apply to all groups, in all instances and without adoption, superseding adopted rules and even statutes while other rules, sometimes also called parliamentary law, are mere custom and give way to adopted rules and apply only when the assembly has not adopted any contrary rule or practice. It is often necessary to determine in which sense the term is used.

5. There is a reason for every form of parliamentary procedure which has been long sanctioned by general usage. These procedures have been approved by experience, found useful and expedient in practice and have grown into general acceptance.

Sec. 4, Par. 5: Waples, Sec. 201.

CHAPTER 2

CONSTITUTIONAL RULES GOVERNING PROCEDURE

Sec. 6. Legislative Procedure Is Controlled by Constitutional Provisions

See also Sec. 3, Each House Determines the Rules of Its Own Proceedings.

1. The constitutional rules of procedure are principally contained in the state constitutions. These rules usually provide, among other things, that each house of the legislature shall determine the rules of its proceedings; that each house shall judge the qualifications, election and returns of members; that each house may choose its officers; that a majority of the house shall constitute a quorum; that each house may discipline or expel members and shall keep a journal.

2. A constitutional provision regulating procedure controls over all other rules of procedure.

Sec. 7. Constitutional Requirements Concerning Procedure Must Be Complied With

See also Ch. 64, Secs. 694–703, Journals and Records.

1. Being organic in character, constitutional provisions stand on a higher plane than statutes and are mandatory. Constitutional provisions prescribing exact or exclusive time or methods for certain acts are mandatory and must be complied with. Constitutional provisions which are general in nature and

not exclusive may be directory. Examples of mandatory and directory provisions are given below.

2. If Congress or a state legislature violates a constitutional requirement, the courts will declare its enactment void.

3. Under a state constitution, unlike the Federal Constitution, legislation not prohibited may be allowed. State constitutional provisions are not grants of power, but, instead are limitations on otherwise plenary power of the people of a state exercised through its legislature. A legislature may enact any laws that state or Federal constitutions do not prohibit.

4. Where there is no constitutional provision requiring that a legislature read a bill on three several days, a law to that effect is directory only, and an act passed without complying with the statute is not invalidated thereby.

5. A provision for recording the yeas and nays on the passage of a bill may be directory only and not mandatory.

Sec. 7, Par. 1: Capito v. Topping (1909), 65 W.Va. 587, 64 S.E. 845.

Sec. 7, Par. 2: State of Missouri v. Alt (1887), 26 Mo. App. 673.

Sec. 7, Par. 3: New Orleans, et al. v. Civil Service, et al. (1982), 442 So. 2d 402; Aquillard v. Treen (La. 1983), 440 So. 2d 704.

Sec. 7, Par. 4: Capito v. Topping (1909), 65 W.Va. 587, 64 S.E. 845; Schweizer v. Territory (1897), 5 Okla. 297, 47 P. 1094.

Sec. 7, Par. 5: People v. Chenango County Supervisors (1853), 8 N.Y. 317.

CHAPTER 3

STATUTORY RULES GOVERNING PROCEDURE

Sec. 10. Statutory Rules

1. It is usual for the form, organization and some of the more fundamental rules of procedure to be controlled by statutes.

2. When these statutes contain mandatory provisions, they must be complied with to give validity to the actions of the bodies. These statutes define jurisdiction and may prescribe rules governing meetings, notices, readings of ordinances, quorum and votes required for certain actions and other similar matters.

3. These statutory rules are often interpreted and applied by the courts.

4. If two statutes are in conflict, the statute that is more specifically directed to the matter at issue prevails as an exception to the statute that is more general in character.

Sec. 10, Par. 1: Zemprelli v. Scranton (Pa. 1986), 102 Pa. Cmwlth. 637, 519 A.2d 518.

Sec. 10, Par. 2: Zemprelli v. Scranton (Pa. 1986), 102 Pa. Cmwlth. 637, 519 A.2d 518.

Sec. 10, Par. 3: Zemprelli v. Scranton (Pa. 1986), 102 Pa. Cmwlth. 637, 519 A.2d 518.

Sec. 10, Par. 4: Bethard v. State, Through Bd. of Trustees (La. App. 1 Cir. 1983), 430 So. 2d 1122, *writ denied,* 435 So. 2d 430.

CHAPTER 4

ADOPTED RULES GOVERNING PROCEDURE

See also Ch. 28, Secs. 279–286, Suspension of the Rules.

Sec. 19. Right to Adopt Rules

1. A legislative body has the right to adopt rules of procedure.

2. It is customary for every legislative body to adopt rules which provide for its organization, for its officers and committees, and for special rules of procedure. In practice, most of the rules relating to procedure are based upon general parliamentary law, but they also may contain special rules of procedure applicable to the body which deviate from parliamentary usage.

3. The power of each house of a state legislature to make its own rules is subordinate to the rules contained in the constitution.

4. Either house of Congress or either house of a state legislature may make special rules for itself. Any other assembly may make regulations for its

---

Sec. 19, Par. 1: French v. Senate of State of California (1905), 146 Cal. 604, 80 P. 1031, 69 L.R.A. 556; Witherspoon v. State of Mississippi *ex rel.* West (1925), 138 Miss. 310, 103 So. 134.

Sec. 19, Par. 2: Cushing's Legislative Assemblies, Secs. 306–313; Hughes, Sec. 5; Tayloe v. Davis (1924), 212 Ala. 282, 102 So. 433, 40 A.L.R. 1052; Heimbach v. State of New York (1982), 89 App. Div. 2d 138, 454 N.Y.S.2d 993, *aff'd* 59 N.Y.2d 891, 452 N.E.2d 1264, 465 N.Y.S.2d 936, *appeal dismissed,* 464 U.S. 956, 104 S. Ct. 386, 78 L. Ed. 2d 331; Dye v. State of Mississippi *ex rel.* Hale (1987), 507 So. 2d 332.

Sec. 19, Par. 3: Tayloe v. Davis (1924), 212 Ala. 282, 102 So. 433, 40 A.L.R. 1052.

own government, and they may be partly or wholly different from those of the established parliamentary procedure.

5. Adopted rules of procedure need not be founded on custom, nor is it essential to their validity that they be reasonable, but they must not infringe upon the private rights nor contravene the laws in any way.

6. Adopted rules bear the same relation to the common law rules of order that statutes bear to the common law. They are of no effect when they are a mere repetition of common law rules. However, when they conflict with the latter, they supersede and override rules founded merely upon usage when they cover the same ground but provide different procedures.

7. Almost all of the rules of procedure which are adopted by deliberative bodies are rules of the common parliamentary law and need no adoption of which the courts will take notice to make them effective, whether written out and formally adopted or not.

Sec. 20. Joint Rules

See also Sec. 3, Each House Determines the Rules of Its Own Proceedings, and Sec. 4, Sources of Rules of Procedure.

Sec. 19, Par. 4: Waples, Sec. 209; Heimbach v. State of New York (1982), 89 App. Div. 2d 138, 454 N.Y.S.2d 993, *aff'd* 59 N.Y.2d 891, 452 N.E.2d 1264, 465 N.Y.S.2d 936, *appeal dismissed,* 464 U.S. 956, 104 S. Ct. 386, 78 L. Ed. 2d 331.

Sec. 19, Par. 5: Waples, Sec. 209; Heimbach v. State of New York (1982), 89 App. Div. 2d 138, 454 N.Y.S.2d 993, *aff'd* 59 N.Y.2d 891, 452 N.E.2d 1264, 465 N.Y.S.2d 936, *appeal dismissed,* 464 U.S. 956, 104 S. Ct. 386, 78 L. Ed. 2d 331.

Sec. 19, Par. 6: Waples, Sec. 209.

Sec. 19, Par. 7: Waples, Sec. 205 (5).

With few exceptions, state legislatures adopt joint rules which govern relations between the houses and other matters in which the houses have joint interests. The adoption of joint rules by a legislature is not incompatible with the constitutional provision providing that each house shall determine the rules of its procedure, nor does this rule preclude either house from adopting the same rules as the other.

Sec. 21. Rules Must Conform to Constitutional and Statutory Provisions

1. The right of any public body to determine its own rules of procedure must be exercised in conformity with existing laws.

2. A legislative body cannot make a rule which evades or avoids the effect of a rule prescribed by the constitution or statutes governing it, and it cannot do by indirection what it cannot do directly.

3. A third party cannot object to a breach of parliamentary rules. The members of the body alone have that right.

4. Rules adopted by a state legislature expire at the end of the session at which they were adopted.

Sec. 20: Tayloe v. Davis (1924), 212 Ala. 282, 102 So. 433, 40 A.L.R. 1052.

Sec. 21, Par. 1: Heiskell v. City Council of Baltimore (1886), 65 Md. 125, 4 A. 116.

Sec. 21, Par. 2: Crawford v. Gilchrist (1912), 64 Fla. 41, 59 So. 963; Canfield v. Gresham (1891), 82 Tex. 10, 17 S.W. 390; Tayloe v. Davis (1924), 212 Ala. 282, 102 So. 433, 40 A.L.R. 1052; Brennan v. Connolly (1919), 207 Mich. 35, 173 N.W. 511.

Sec. 21, Par. 3: People v. City of Rochester Common Council (N.Y. 1871), 5 Lans. 11; Corre v. State of Ohio (1881), 8 Ohio Dec. Reprint 715.

Sec. 21, Par. 4: Cushing's Legislative Assemblies, Sec. 792.

Sec. 22. Right to Change Rules

See also Sec. 24, Failure of a House of the Legislature to Conform to Its Rules Does Not Invalidate Its Acts, and Ch. 28, Secs. 279–286, Suspension of the Rules.

1. Legislative bodies have power to abolish, modify or waive their own rules of procedure.

2. A majority does not have power to make a rule which cannot be modified or repealed by a majority. If a majority of an official public body has authority in the first instance to pass a rule, it has authority to annul or repeal the same rule. Rules which can be adopted by a majority vote can be repealed or annulled by the same vote, even a rule which provides that no rule can be repealed or amended without a vote greater than a majority.

3. The power of a house of a legislature to determine its rules of proceedings is a continuous power. It can always be exercised by the house and is absolute and beyond the challenge of any body or tribunal if the rule does not ignore constitutional restraints or violate fundamental rights.

4. A legislative house cannot tie its own hands by establishing unchangeable rules. It may adopt and change procedure at any time and with no other

---

Sec. 22, Par. 1: Chandler v. Lawrence (1880), 128 Mass. 213; Rutherford v. City of Nashville (1935), 168 Tenn. 499, 79 S.W.2d 581; Holt v. Somerville (1879), 127 Mass. 408.

Sec. 22, Par. 2: State of Missouri v. Reichmann (1911), 239 Mo. 81, 142 S.W. 304; Richardson v. Union Congregational Soc. of Francestown (1877), 58 N.H. 187.

Sec. 22, Par. 3: State of South Carolina *ex rel.* Coleman v. Lewis (1936), 181 S.C. 10, 186 S.E. 625; Davis v. Thompson (Okla. 1986), 721 P.2d 789; State of North Dakota *ex rel.* Spaeth v. Meiers (1987), 403 N.W.2d 392.

notice than the rules may require.

5. Rules of procedure passed by one legislature are not binding on a subsequent legislature operating within the same jurisdiction.

6. No meeting of a legislative body can bind a subsequent one by irrepealable acts or rules of procedure. The power to enact is the power to repeal. A bylaw or rule requiring a two-thirds vote to alter or amend the acts of the body may itself be altered, amended or repealed by the same power that enacted it.

7. Rules of procedure are always within control of the majority of a deliberative body and may be changed at any time by a majority vote.

Sec. 23. Rules Can Be Suspended

See also Sec. 22, Right to Change Rules, and Ch. 28, Secs. 279–286, Suspension of the Rules.

1. The rules of the individual houses of the legislature are under their own control and may be suspended whenever in the judgment of that body suspension is required. This does not apply to rules of procedure imposed by the constitution.

Sec. 22, Par. 4: French v. Senate of State of California (1905), 146 Cal. 604, 80 P. 1031, 69 L.R.A. 556.

Sec. 22, Par. 5: South Georgia Power Co. v. Baumann (1929), 169 Ga. 649, 151 S.E. 513.

Sec. 22, Par. 6: Commonwealth v. Mayor of Lancaster (Pa. 1836), 5 Watts 152; Wardens of Christ Church v. Pope (Mass. 1857), 8 Gray 140; Richardson v. Union Congregational Soc. of Francestown (1877), 58 N.H. 187.

Sec. 22, Par. 7: Commonwealth *ex rel.* Fox v. Chace (1961), 403 Pa. 117, 168 A.2d 569.

Sec. 23, Par. 1: State of South Carolina v. Brown (1890), 35 S.C. 151, 11 S.E. 641.

2. During the same sitting, a legislative body may treat proceedings already taken as irregular or may reconsider the action, unless some right of a third person intervenes.

3. The purpose of rules is to aid a body to perform its duties more efficiently and with fairness to its members. Whenever the rules fail to serve this purpose and are not required by the constitution or other controlling authority, the rules may be suspended. Rules often require more than a majority vote for their suspension.

4. The rules under which a deliberative body will operate may be changed, suspended or waived at the body's pleasure where the rules of procedure are within control of the majority.

Sec. 24. Failure of a House of the Legislature to Conform to Its Rules Does Not Invalidate Its Acts

See also Sec. 73, Powers of Courts over Legislative Bodies Generally.

1. Violation of rules of procedure adopted by a house of the legislature for its own convenience and not required by the constitution will not impair the validity of a statute.

2. A legislative body having the right to do an act must be allowed to select the means of accomplish-

---

Sec. 23, Par. 2: Mansfield v. O'Brien (1930), 271 Mass. 515, 171 N.E. 487.

Sec. 23, Par. 4: Commonwealth *ex rel.* Fox v. Chace (1961), 403 Pa. 117, 168 A.2d 569.

Sec. 24, Par. 1: Tayloe v. Davis (1924), 212 Ala. 282, 102 So. 433, 40 A.L.R. 1052; Goodwin v. State Board of Administration (1925), 210 Ala. 453, 102 So. 718; State of Missouri v. Alt (1887), 26 Mo. App. 673.

ing such act within reasonable bounds.

3. A rule is virtually repealed for the occasion when it is disregarded by those who have power to control it; and the act of breaking it is at least a suspension of it. The body at its preceding meetings does not have the power to bind its successors or to put shackles on it that might be cast off only in a particular way.

4. Under a constitutional provision declaring that each house of the legislature shall determine the rules of its own proceedings, the fact that a house acted in violation of its own rules or in violation of parliamentary law in a matter clearly within its power does not make its action subject to review by the courts.

Sec. 25. Fraud Will Invalidate Acts

Where there is more than a mere technical violation of the rules of procedure, the violation may invalidate the act, and an act will be invalidated where there is fraud or bad faith.

Sec. 24, Par. 2: Attorney General v. Brissenden (1930), 271 Mass. 172, 171 N.E. 82.

Sec. 24, Par. 3: Commonwealth v. Mayor of Lancaster (Pa. 1836), 5 Watts 152.

Sec. 24, Par. 4: State of Connecticut v. Savings Bank of New London (1906), 79 Conn. 141, 64 A. 5.

Sec. 25: Robinson v. Nick (1940), 235 Mo. App. 461, 136 S.W.2d 374; Witherspoon v. State of Mississippi *ex rel.* West (1925), 138 Miss. 310, 103 So. 134; People v. Albany etc. Railroad Co. (N.Y. 1869), 1 Lans. 308, 55 Barb. 344; South Georgia Power Co. v. Baumann (1929), 169 Ga. 649, 151 S.E. 513.

CHAPTER 5

ADOPTED PARLIAMENTARY AUTHORITY

Sec. 30. Parliamentary Authority Is Usually Adopted

1. Most legislative bodies adopt a manual of legislative procedure as the authority to apply in all cases not covered by constitutional provisions, statutes or legislative rules.

2. In the absence of a statutory requirement that a particular manual be adopted, a local legislative body can choose and adopt its own rules of procedure.

3. Resort by deliberative assemblies to parliamentary manuals for light on relevant parliamentary usages is permissible.

Sec. 31. What Parliamentary Authority Contains

1. A manual of legislative procedure is a compilation of the usages and precedents of legislative bodies, usually stated in the form of rules and arranged for convenient reference. The principal advantage

---

Sec. 30, Par. 1: Cushing's Legislative Assemblies, Sec. 793; Sturgis, p. 210; Witherspoon v. State of Mississippi *ex rel.* West (1925), 138 Miss. 310, 103 So. 134.

Sec. 30, Par. 2: Commonwealth *ex rel.* Fox v. Chace (1961), 403 Pa. 117, 168 A.2d 569.

Sec. 30, Par. 3: Posner v. Bronx County Medical Society (1963), 19 App. Div. 2d 89, 241 N.Y.S.2d 540.

Sec. 31: Sturgis, pp. 210, 211.

of adopting a manual is to make available to the presiding officer and members a statement in concise form of the rules of legislative procedure, including rules based upon established customs and usages which could be found only on the most exhaustive research, except in a manual. A further advantage is that the manual eliminates uncertainties resulting from conflicting precedents.

2. A manual manifestly can state only general rules. Any special rules desired by the body should be stated in the rules adopted by the body. These special rules supersede the rules stated in the manual where conflict may exist, leaving the manual to govern only when no special rules have been adopted.

Sec. 32. Effect of Adoption of Parliamentary Authority

1. When a legislative body in its rules adopts a specified manual for the government of its procedure and no other provision is made on that subject in the rules, the manual specified controls the procedure of the legislative body.

2. A legislative body which has adopted a manual or parliamentary authority may abolish, modify or waive the rules therein contained the same as its own adopted rules.

3. The rules of an adopted authority can be suspended the same as the rules of the body. A motion

Sec. 32, Par. 1: People v. American Institute (N.Y. 1873), 44 How. Pr. 468; First Buckingham Community v. Malcolm (1941), 177 Va. 710, 15 S.E.2d 54.

Sec. 32, Par. 2: Wheelock v. City of Lowell (1907), 196 Mass. 220, 81 N.E. 977.

to "suspend the rules" for a certain purpose includes the rules in the adopted authority.

See also cases holding that rules can be suspended or waived, cited under Secs. 23 and 24.

4. An early case has held that when an authority has once been adopted the rules stated in the authority can be suspended only as authorized therein. Where there is no provision for suspension, the unanimous vote of all members present would be required. This statement, at least insofar as it relates to official public bodies, is clearly not the law.

5. When a manual or special rules of procedure have not been adopted by a deliberative assembly, its procedure is governed by general parliamentary law.

Sec. 32, Par. 4: State of Ohio v. Board of Education of Cleveland (1887), 2 Ohio Cir. 510.

Sec. 32, Par. 5: Witherspoon v. State of Mississippi *ex rel.* West (1925), 138 Miss. 310, 103 So. 134.

CHAPTER 6

PARLIAMENTARY LAW

Sec. 35. Parliamentary Law Defined

See also Sec. 4, Sources of Rules of Procedure.

1. Parliamentary law consists of the recognized rules, precedents and usages of legislative bodies by which their procedure is regulated. It is that system of rules and precedents which originated in the British Parliament and which has been developed by legislative or deliberative bodies in this and other countries.

2. Parliamentary law, like the common law, is an organized system of rules. It is built on precedents created by decisions on points of order or appeals and by decisions of courts. It has been guided in its development by the authority to make rules inherent in every deliberative body.

3. The common law of parliamentary procedure is founded upon well-established and reasonable usage. It does not rest upon mere custom but upon reasonable and equitable custom. "What is not reason is not law" may be said with reference to the common law of order in deliberative bodies, as well as to the common law of the land.

4. The parliamentary law is the rule of action for all deliberative bodies governing the introduction,

---

Sec. 35, Par. 1: Bouvier's Law Dictionary; Landes v. State of Indiana (1903), 160 Ind. 479, 67 N.E. 189.

Sec. 35, Par. 3: Waples, Sec. 200.

modification, discussion and decision of propositions.

Sec. 36. Parliamentary Law Not Determined by Any One Legislative Body

1. Parliamentary law is not determined by the procedure or rules of any single legislative body.

2. Parliamentary law as it is applied in this country today differs greatly from the practice of Parliament at the time deliberative bodies were established in the United States and also from the present practices of Parliament and of Congress.

3. Parliamentary law as it applies to deliberative bodies in America is not determined by the rules or practices of Congress or of the United States House of Representatives. The courts construe the acts of legislative bodies in accordance with general parliamentary law and not in accordance with exceptional usages of the United States House of Representatives.

4. The procedure of the two houses of Congress differs greatly. The procedure of each house is largely determined by its own rules designed to meet its own peculiar needs. The rules are suited to very large bodies of professional legislators, meeting practically full time, dealing with large volumes of legislation and acting largely through committees. The procedure in Congress is ill-adapted to other

---

Sec. 35, Par. 4: Waples, Sec. 200.

Sec. 36, Par. 3: People *ex rel.* MacMahon v. Davis (1918), 284 Ill. 439, 120 N.E. 326.

CHAPTER 7

PRINCIPLES OF PARLIAMENTARY LAW

Sec. 42. There Are Indispensable Requirements for Making Valid Group Decisions

Certain fundamental principles govern decision-making procedure. These principles are so fundamental as to be required to give validity to the decisions of a group. These requirements generally apply without being adopted and without the consent or the approval of the body. These principles are stated in Sec. 43.

Sec. 43. Indispensable Requirements for Making Valid Group Decisions

1. *The group must be so constituted and endowed that it has the power and authority that it purports to exercise.* A purported action must be within the power of the organization or the vote is ineffective.

See also Sec. 517, Action Must Be Within Power or Vote Is Ineffective, and also cases cited therein.

2. *There must be a meeting of the group at which the decision is made.* A decision of a group results from a meeting of the minds of the group. To provide a proper opportunity for such an agreement, there must be a meeting of the members. Decision-making powers of a group can be exercised only at a

---

Sec. 42: State of South Carolina *ex rel.* Coleman v. Lewis (1936), 181 S.C. 10, 186 S.E. 625.

legislative or administrative bodies.

5. The rules of parliamentary procedure applicable within a state are not controlled by the procedure in the state legislature. Even rules in the constitution governing the legislature do not apply to local bodies. For example, a requirement for three readings of bills in the legislature does not require three readings of municipal ordinances in that state.

Sec. 37. Parliamentary Law Governs When Other Rules Are Not in Effect

1. All matters of procedure not governed by constitutional provisions, adopted rules, including joint rules, or an adopted manual, are governed by the rules of the general parliamentary law. The rules constituting parliamentary law having their foundation in convenience and necessity have been uniformly received and acted upon in this country as the governing authority. Parliamentary law has been universally acknowledged as controlling the procedure of legislative and other governmental bodies.

2. Under parliamentary law, a legislative body, when established, becomes vested with all the powers and privileges necessary to a free and unrestricted exercise of its appropriate functions, except so far as it may be restrained by express constitutional provisions or laws pursuant thereto.

Sec. 36, Par. 4: Cannon, Clarence, Rules of Order: Encyclopedia Britannica (1964), Vol. 19, pp. 632B–634.

Sec. 36, Par. 5: Landes v. State of Indiana (1903), 160 Ind. 479, 67 N.E. 189.

Sec. 37, Par. 1: Briggs v. MacKellar (N.Y. 1855), 2 Abb. Pr. 30.

Sec. 37, Par. 2: *Ex parte* D.O. McCarthy (1866), 29 Cal. 395.

3. When special rules of procedure have been adopted by a deliberative body, its procedure is controlled by such rules only insofar as those rules apply and otherwise the body is governed by general parliamentary law.

4. The common parliamentary principles and rules may be resorted to in the absence of rules made by the organization itself in regulating its proceedings.

5. Where matters of procedure are not covered by bylaws or rules, the procedure should follow parliamentary principles. Gaps in the rules of procedure should be filled by the adoption of fair methods according to accepted parliamentary principles.

Sec. 38. Source of Parliamentary Law

See also Sec. 44, Parliamentary Law Is a Branch of the Common Law; Sec. 45, Parliamentary Law Is Based on Principles; Sec. 46, Differences Between Public Bodies and Private Organizations; Sec. 47, Parliamentary Law Is Applied Differently in Public Bodies and in Private Associations; and Sec. 48, Limitations on Powers.

Parliamentary law gets its name and basic principles from the Parliament of Great Britain. It was brought to the colonies with the common law and

---

Sec. 37, Par. 3: Witherspoon v. State of Mississippi *ex rel.* West (1925), 138 Miss. 310, 103 So. 134.

Sec. 37, Par. 4: Ostrom v. Greene (1897), 45 N.Y.S. 852; Mixed Local of Hotel and Restaurant Employees Union Local No. 458 v. Hotel and Restaurant Employees International Alliance and Bartenders International League of America (1942), 212 Minn. 587, 4 N.W.2d 771; Marvin v. Manash (1944), 175 Ore. 311, 153 P.2d 251.

Sec. 37, Par. 5: Mixed Local of Hotel and Restaurant Employees Union Local No. 458 v. Hotel and Restaurant Employees International Alliance and Bartenders International League of America (1942), 212 Minn. 587, 4 N.W.2d 771; Murdock v. Phillips Academy (Mass. 1831), 12 Pick. 244; Ostrom v. Greene (1897), 45 N.Y.S. 852.

Sec. 38: Cannon, Clarence, Rules of Order: Encyclopedia Britannica (1964), Vol. 19, pp. 632B–634.

other political institutions of England. Jefferson, as presiding officer of the Senate, looked to the procedure of Parliament as his guide and prepared his manual from English precedents. The state legislatures and local governmental bodies copied from Congress. But the procedure of the state legislatures, local legislative bodies and voluntary associations now differs greatly from the procedure of Parliament and Congress. While Congress is governed largely by rules adopted by the houses of Congress to meet their local and special needs, the state legislatures and particularly the more local bodies, both public and private, are governed by a branch of the common law based on court decisions and upon precedents and customs of deliberative bodies. There are some important differences between parliamentary law as applied in public bodies and as applied in voluntary associations.

Sec. 39. Precedents and Usages

1. When in a deliberative body a certain mode of procedure has been adopted in any case, it becomes a precedent for its government in every case thereafter of a similar character. Thus, in time, a succession of precedents is accumulated, forming together a regular system of procedure known as parliamentary law which, once established, is binding upon the body.

2. If precedents were not followed, the course of legislative procedure, instead of being known or capable of being ascertained, would be involved in the greatest uncertainty and lead to endless confu-

Sec. 39, Par. 1: Regina v. Paty (Eng., circa 1700), 2 Salk. 503.

sion. In a court of justice, a rule, when settled in an adjudged case, is binding thereafter upon the same court and upon all inferior tribunals so that the law may be known, instead of being left to the uncertain determination of every judge. Likewise, in a deliberative body, what has once been decided upon as a proper course of procedure is thereafter a guide in similar cases. This is to be understood, however, with some qualification. It has been the usage for legislative bodies to adopt rules for their own government. Adopted rules supersede custom and precedents.

3. Precedents, as distinguished from usages, are the decisions made by the presiding officer, or by the body upon appeal, when a question concerning a practice or point of procedure has been raised, as by a point of order.

4. A not inconsiderable part of parliamentary law is based upon the established usages of legislative bodies. The knowledge of the usages and customs of a legislative body are drawn from treatises on parliamentary practice, from the records of the body, insofar as the usages can be ascertained from them, and from the personal knowledge of the presiding officer and members.

5. When there is an established practice in a deliberative body or there has been a previous decision on a question, the practice or precedent may be said to govern. When there is no practice or precedent governing a question which has arisen, the presiding officer may consider the usages and prece-

Sec. 39, Par. 2: Briggs v. MacKellar (N.Y. 1855), 2 Abb. Pr. 30.

Sec. 39, Par. 3: Cushing's Legislative Assemblies, Sec. 780.

Sec. 39, Par. 4: Cushing's Legislative Assemblies, Sec. 778.

dents of other deliberative bodies. Precedents are not entitled to equal weight. The value of precedents depends partly upon the character of the proceedings by which they were created, partly upon the character of the body in which they were established and partly upon the time at which they occurred. The precedents of the other house of the same legislature are usually to be given the most weight. The precedents of other deliberative bodies of the same type and character are in general to be given more weight than the precedents of deliberative bodies of a different character. The precedents of deliberative bodies of a different type and character are to be given weight in the proportion that the conditions of the other deliberative body are similar to the deliberative body where the precedent is to be applied.

6. In the absence of rules, as immediately upon convening and before rules are adopted, the houses are governed by usages, custom and precedent and by the general parliamentary law. The best evidence of what are the established usages and customs is the rules as last in effect.

Sec. 39, Par. 5: Cushing's Legislative Assemblies, Sec. 783; Wood v. Town of Milton (1908), 197 Mass. 531, 84 N.E. 332.

Sec. 39, Par. 6: Cushing's Legislative Assemblies, Sec. 792; Hughes, Sec. 6.

meeting of the group. Any understanding or agreement made before, after or outside a legal meeting is not valid or binding.

3. *There must be a proper notice of the meeting so that all the members of the group have an opportunity to attend and participate.* The notice must be given to all of the persons entitled to attend the meeting, must advise the subject of the business to be transacted, state the time and place of the meeting and otherwise be such as to enable all members of the group to attend the meeting.

4. *There must be a quorum present at the meeting.* A quorum is a sufficient number that those present can act for the entire organization. Usually one half or more of the members of an organization with a definite membership are required to be present before the members present constitute a quorum and can act for the group. The power establishing an organization can require, in certain cases, more than a majority to act for the group or permit less than a majority to act.

See also Ch. 44, Secs. 500–506, Quorum.

5. *There must be a clear question before the group for decision.* The members of the group must have a clear question before them upon which they can make their decision by voting to approve or reject it. Members are entitled to know precisely what the question is and what effect their votes will have before they vote. The question should be in such form that it can be answered in the affirmative or the negative.

See also Sec. 140, Must Be a Definite Proposal for Consideration.

6. *Whenever a deliberative body is making decisions, the members must have an opportunity to debate the questions.* They have the right to express their opinions and hear the opinions of others to aid them to come to a meeting of the minds and reach valid joint decisions. The decisions of a deliberative body in exercising its responsibility must be the decisions of the membership of the body and not merely the opinions of the individual members.

See also Sec. 60, Right to Debate; Sec. 63, Debatability of Motions; Ch. 9, Secs. 80–85, What Is Debatable; and Sec. 90, Right to Debate Questions.

7. *In order for a deliberative body to make a decision or take an action, a vote must be taken.* An expression of opinion is not a vote and is of no effect. It cannot be assumed how or even if a member will vote and until a vote is cast nothing has happened.

See also Sec. 520, A Vote Is Required to Decide a Question.

8. *To make a decision or carry a proposition, there must be a vote in the affirmative of at least a majority of the votes cast.* The constitution or statutes sometimes require more than a majority vote for certain purposes. Parliamentary law requires only a majority vote but organizations may require by their rules more than a majority vote for certain purposes, as amendment or suspension of their rules.

See also Sec. 50, Majority Control; Sec. 510, Majority of Legal Votes Is Required; Sec. 511, More Than Majority of Legal Votes Cast May Be Required.

9. *There must be no fraud or trickery or deception causing injury.* As in other situations a person is liable for damage or injury intentionally or negligently caused to another.

See also Sec. 25, Fraud Will Invalidate Acts.

10. *Decisions must not be in violation of laws, rules or decisions of a higher authority.* Existing enactments or decisions of any rule-making authority supersede enactments and decisions of authorities of a lower rank. Under the U.S. plan of government, sovereign authority is vested in the states under the state constitutions. Certain powers were granted to the Federal Government by the Federal Constitution and other powers were denied to the states. In the other direction, powers have been granted to the local governments—counties, cities, districts and agencies by the state constitutions and by the legislatures. Whenever authority has been granted and exercised at any level, any attempt to act contrary to it by any organization not having higher authority is void.

Sec. 44. Parliamentary Law Is a Branch of the Common Law

See also Ch. 6, Secs. 35–39, Parliamentary Law.

1. Parliamentary law is a part of the common law. It developed in the same manner and is subject generally to the same rules. Parliamentary law developed precedent by precedent as decisions were made in legislative bodies and in courts in the same manner as common law developed through judicial precedents. Both have been guided in their development by the power of legislative bodies to make rules and to enact laws.

2. Parliamentary law differs somewhat from the other branches of common law in that it is based in an important measure upon precedents of legislative and administrative bodies. But particularly in

America, where the courts have the power to make final decisions on all constitutional questions, the law has been evolving upon the basis of court decisions, and a considerable volume of judicial precedents has accumulated. The application of parliamentary rules to new situations is subject to the same rules of reasoning as the application of established common law rules to new legal situations.

Sec. 45. Parliamentary Law Is Based on Principles

1. Parliamentary law is a system of principles, not a group of haphazard rules. It is based upon reason and was developed over a long period of time as individual questions were determined upon the best reasoning of the legislative bodies, of their presiding officers and of the courts.

2. Individual rules should be interpreted in the light of basic principles. It is only as a part of a field of law that the true meaning of individual rules becomes clear.

3. With the principles in mind, the detailed rules will be easy to remember and to apply.

4. Ordinarily from a knowledge of the principles, the rules become evident. In any event the correctness of any rules should be checked against the principles, and if there is no conflict the rule cannot be far wrong.

Sec. 46. Differences Between Public Bodies and Private Organizations

1. Parliamentary law, while developed primarily in legislative bodies, applies to all groups of persons

meeting as equals to study questions or make decisions.

2. There is a basic difference, however, in some phases of parliamentary law in its application to official public bodies and to private voluntary associations. In a public body the powers do not reside in the members themselves. State legislatures exercise the powers which are delegated to them by the people. County, city and township governments exercise, in general, powers delegated to them by the legislatures or by the people through their constitutions. In some instances powers may be granted to cities directly by the people of the cities through a system of home rule charters.

3. The organization and powers of a public body cannot be changed by its members. Any change must be made either by or in the manner prescribed by the authority which created it.

4. The powers of voluntary associations arise from the agreement of the members. They are governed by contract. The principal elements of the contract are embodied in the constitution or bylaws.

5. The members of a private association speak for themselves. They represent no one. They are controlled by no outside power. Members can join and leave according to the plan agreed to by the group, and generally as each individual pleases.

Sec. 47. Parliamentary Law Is Applied Differently in Public Bodies and in Private Associations

1. It follows that while private associations are governed by parliamentary law, there are extensive

differences in parliamentary law as applied to them, and parliamentary law as applied to official public bodies. Many of those differences will be pointed out under the various rules.

2. While the basic rules of parliamentary law are the same, the situations under which they are applied are substantially different. The more technical functions of public bodies require more technical rules and a more technical application of those rules.

3. The principal differences in the parliamentary rules which must be applied to official public bodies arise from the following facts:

(a) In public bodies the executive has important functions relating closely to the legislative body, and rules must be available to enable the executive and the body to function together without conflict or confusion.

(b) All of the state legislatures, except Nebraska, are bicameral, and the relations of the two houses in the enactment of legislation must be closely coordinated. This is particularly important with reference to conference committee procedure to enable the houses to reconcile their differences concerning legislation.

(c) Public bodies are governed to a considerable measure by constitutional and statutory rules over which the members have no direct control.

(d) Public bodies, due to their greater volume of work and more technical functions, require many rules to meet the particular situations of their own bodies which are entirely unknown to private associations. In the larger legislative bodies, a large measure of their procedure is regulated by their own rules.

(e) Public bodies perform their functions to a considerable measure through committees, and committees become a more essential part of the body and are governed by a body of rules particularly applicable to them.

(f) Legislative sessions are restricted in time which imposes special burdens and special problems in procedure.

(g) A legislature is largely made up of experienced members who devote a considerable part of their time to their legislative functions, and consequently are more skilled in procedure.

(h) Particularly in the enactment of legislation, a technical accuracy is required which is entirely beyond that which is necessary, or even appropriate, to private voluntary associations.

Sec. 48. Limitations on Powers

1. If Congress or a state legislature violates a constitutional requirement, the courts will declare its act void.

2. Constitutional provisions prescribing exact times and methods are mandatory.

3. When there is a limit imposed on the powers of a body, it must conform to those limits and when it acts under a delegation of power, it must act

---

Sec. 48, Par. 1: State of Missouri v. Alt (1887), 26 Mo. App. 673; Cross v. Alexander (La. 1986), 498 So. 2d 740.

Sec. 48, Par. 2: Capito v. Topping (1909), 65 W.Va. 587, 64 S.E. 845.

strictly within the limits of the powers conferred upon it by the authority which created it.

Sec. 49. Right to Act for a Body—Quorum

See also Ch. 44, Secs. 500–506, Quorum.

1. All members of a large group cannot always meet together to make decisions. There must be some rule to determine when a group is sufficiently represented at a meeting that its members present can speak for its entire membership. From the very earliest times, it has been recognized as a general rule that a majority of a group is necessary to act for the entire group.

2. The power or authority which establishes a public body also may determine what number constitutes a quorum. In a public body with a definite membership, that number is never less than a majority but a larger number may be required for the body to have authority to act for any purpose or only for certain purposes.

Sec. 50. Majority Control

See also Ch. 45, Secs. 510–518, Vote Required.

1. A fundamental and seemingly universal principle is that at least a majority of the vote cast is required to make decisions for a group.

2. If powers were given to a minority, the question immediately would rise as to what minority. In any group there can be but one majority, but there may be many different minorities.

Sec. 48, Par. 3: Hannibal & St. Joseph R.R. v. Marion County (1865), 35 Mo. 294.

3. To require more than a majority to reach any decision confers on less than a majority the power to block or prevent a decision.

4. The requirement of a majority to take an action is not in any sense an arbitrary rule but is a fundamental principle.

5. The only situation where there may be a deviation from the requirement of an absolute majority vote is the case of elections where rules authorize a plurality vote. This is a situation where there are more than two candidates running for the same office in the same election and the rule provides that the one who gets the highest vote will be elected though that candidate may not receive a majority of the legal votes cast. Also where there are several persons running for several identical offices, for example, there are three offices of director to be filled and six candidates for the office to be elected, the rule may say that the three candidates who receive the highest votes are elected, but the rule also may provide that only those who receive a majority vote are elected.

6. The power that establishes a public body can require the vote of more than a majority to take certain actions, but unless more than a majority vote is clearly required a majority vote can take any action which the body has the power to take.

Sec. 51. Delegation of Powers

See also Sec. 518, A Legislative Body Cannot Delegate Its Powers, and Sec. 512, paragraph 6.

1. A public body cannot delegate its powers, duties or responsibilities to any other person or groups, including a committee of its own members.

However, a legislative body may delegate by rule such procedural powers as appointment of members of standing, special and conference committees as well as the power to refer bills to committee to a constitutional presiding officer not a member of the body.

2. Where duties or responsibilities are imposed on a public body as on a state legislature, that body is bound to exercise those duties and responsibilities and cannot divest itself of them by delegation to others.

3. Legislatures may delegate to administrative agencies the power to promulgate rules necessary for the proper exercise of the laws. The delegation of some law-making authority is a necessary feature of modern government because the current degree of regulatory activity can be performed only by administrative agencies. An administrative agency's authority allows it to fill in details necessary for the proper execution of the laws.

4. Because the legislature may delegate some of its law-making authority to administrative agencies, it may properly condition the exercise of the delegated authority. However, the condition imposed by the legislature may not contain a grant to any branch of government to function in a manner prohibited by the constitution.

5. When delegating rule-making authority to administrative agencies, the legislature must declare a

---

Sec. 51, Par. 1: Dye v. State of Mississippi *ex rel.* Hale (1987), 507 So. 2d 332.

Sec. 51, Par. 3: Opinion of the Justices (1981), 49 Md. App. 300, 431 A.2d 783.

Sec. 51, Par. 4: Opinion of the Justices (1981), 49 Md. App. 300, 431 A.2d 783; State of Alaska v. A.L.I.V.E. Voluntary (1980), 606 P.2d 769.

general policy and prescribe standards for administrative action.

6. The duties and responsibilities vested in a group are of necessity to be exercised by the majority unless granted subject to other conditions. Such a body cannot delegate its essential powers to a minority even of its own members. A provision in the rules, for example, that a two-thirds vote is necessary to take a particular action, would delegate to any minority of more than one-third of the members the power to prevent the action being taken and grant to that minority the power to control the determinations of the body. The powers of the body to that extent would be delegated to a minority.

Sec. 52. Equality of Members

See also Sec. 120, Equality of Members in Debate.

In public bodies the equality of members is presumed. It would seem that for any democratic group to be able to operate, acceptance of the principle of equality of members is essential. Unless that equality is recognized, there is no basis upon which it can be determined who or what number has authority to speak for the group and to make its decisions. Equality seems essential also to secure the acceptance in good faith of decisions of the group.

Sec. 53. There Should Be a Definite Rule

In order for a group to work efficiently together, there must be an accepted manner of doing things.

Sec. 51, Par. 5: State of Louisiana v. Broom (1983), 439 So. 2d 357; Opinion of the Justices (1981), 49 Md. App. 300, 431 A.2d 783.

Even where the same thing reasonably might be done a number of different ways, it is necessary as a matter of convenience that everyone do the same thing in the same way. Just as it is necessary that the drivers of vehicles on a highway all turn the same way when meeting on the highway to avoid collisions, so it is necessary that people undertaking to do the same thing undertake the action in the same way in order to prevent confusion and disagreement.

Sec. 54. Use of Technical Rules

1. An important purpose of parliamentary law is to provide an orderly procedure of conducting the business of an organization and to prevent confusion.

2. Purely technical rules are to be applied only when they will aid in the deliberations of the body. They are not to be applied merely because they are available for use in case of need.

Sec. 55. Most Direct and Simple Procedure Should Be Followed

In the interest of saving the time and effort of the members and avoiding confusion, the most direct and simplest means of accomplishing a purpose should be followed. Simple procedural motions such as the motion to recess or lay on the table or postpone are acted upon when they arise. They cannot, for example, be postponed or referred to committee or laid on the table, which would only add complications and consequent confusion, but if these motions are not needed at the time, they are voted down and they may be made again when needed.

Sec. 56. One Proposition at a Time

An important practical principle is that only one proposition can be considered at a time. It is the responsibility of the presiding officer to promote efficient consideration of business by permitting only one proposition to be considered at a time and to limit discussion to that one proposition.

Sec. 57. The Immediately Pending Question

1. While a general subject remains before the group for discussion, a particular phase of that subject should have the complete attention at one time. Thus, if a motion is under discussion and someone proposes an amendment to the motion, discussion shifts from the original question to the amendment because the original question cannot be intelligently discussed until the proposed change in the question has been disposed of. When the amendment is voted upon, whether adopted or lost, discussion shifts back to the original proposition.

2. There are many incidental or subsidiary questions which may arise during the discussion of a question which require decision before the main question. When a resolution is under discussion, it is possible that some member may propose an amendment, another may move to refer the resolution to committee, another may move to cut off debate by the previous question, or a motion may be made to lay the whole matter on the table. While these are pending, a motion may be made to ad-

journ. In this case, discussion would shift successively to each new question as proposed. As each question is decided, consideration shifts back to the question pending immediately prior, until discussion reverts to the original question. Discussion, however, should be limited strictly to the immediately pending question, that point which must first be decided before consideration can be given to other questions.

Sec. 58. Precedence of Motions

See also Ch. 18, Sec. 187, List of Motions.

The order in which various questions claim the attention of a body cannot be left to any haphazard method nor can mere priority in the making of a motion give priority in its consideration. To follow this latter procedure would lead to endless confusion, waste of time and effort because of members attempting by various devices to secure prior consideration for their proposals. This can be eliminated only by recognizing a definite precedence of motions and fitting every motion into that order of precedence.

Sec. 59. Application of One Motion to Another

See also Ch. 17, Secs. 175–180, Classification of Motions, and particularly Sec. 178, Subsidiary Questions.

1. Motions are frequently applied to each other. Many motions, for example, are subject to amendment. Likewise, the motion to refer to committee, to postpone further consideration to a later date, to cut off debate or to lay on the table may be applied to a main motion.

2. There is a specific classification of motions and an order of precedence as to how they relate to one another.

3. The application of "procedural" motions serves an essential function in guiding the consideration of main motions.

Sec. 60. Right to Debate

See also Ch. 9, What Is Debatable; and Ch. 10, Right to the Floor; and particularly Sec. 90, Right to Debate Questions.

1. Before the members of any group can reach intelligent decisions, it is necessary that they understand the subject upon which they are making a decision and the effect of any decisions they are making. To accomplish these purposes, an opportunity is given for debate on all questions of business to be decided.

2. As an essential part of this free discussion, every person must have a right to present that person's own views for the consideration of other members of the group, to have the opportunity to persuade them to that person's way of thinking and to be able to listen to the arguments of others.

3. As a necessary part of this free discussion, the rule is well established that when authority is given to a group to make decisions, those decisions must be made at a meeting at which the matter can be discussed. Any decision made by the members individually is not binding on the body.

4. This right of debate does not take from a body the right to control its own procedure and it can restrict or cut off debate.

Sec. 61. Interruption of Members Speaking

See also Sec. 92, Interruption of a Member Who Is Speaking.

1. A member once recognized and having the floor is entitled to freedom from interruptions unless something arises which requires immediate consideration. A member cannot be interrupted merely to make motions having a higher precedence than the one under discussion. For example, the motion to adjourn cannot interrupt the speaker discussing a main motion. However, questions of privilege requiring immediate consideration must justify an interruption. A member can be interrupted and called to order if that person digresses from the subject, uses improper language or has exceeded a time limit on speeches.

2. It is also common practice to permit a member to be interrupted to ask questions concerning points made in a speech, if the interruption appears to be made in good faith and not for the purpose of heckling or harassing the speaker. Often much time is saved by settling a point at the instant it arises, and the presiding officer is justified in exercising discretion as to when a member can be interrupted by questions in the interest of expediting the work of the body.

Sec. 62. Seconds Not Required

See also Sec. 157, Seconds to Motions.

1. The origin of the requirement of seconds to motions is obscure, and while there were certain requirements for seconds in Parliament for a period of time, this requirement was discontinued more than a century ago.

2. The effect of requiring a second to a motion is to require that no business can be presented except by two persons, one who makes the motion and the other who seconds it. A member representing a constituency in a state legislature is entitled to present a matter for consideration of the body without having the support of a second, unless by law or by rule a second is required.

3. Although seconds are not required by standard legislative parliamentary procedure, they are sometimes required by rules. If seconds are required, they shall be required only on motions. The following questions not being motions never require seconds.

(a) Points of order.

(b) Parliamentary inquiries.

(c) Objection to consideration.

(d) Requests of any kind—as to withdraw a motion.

(e) Demands of any kind—as for a division.

(f) The exercise of any right or privilege given to any member.

Sec. 63. Debatability of Motions

See also Ch. 9, Secs. 80–85, What Is Debatable.

1. It is a fundamental right of members to engage in debate, to express their opinions and to hear the opinions of others before voting upon the determination of any general item of business. The right to debate in the interest of practical procedure is, however, subject to certain limitations.

2. A member does not have the right to debate a procedural motion. This rule is in the interest of economy of time and effort. A member is not entitled, for example, to debate a motion to adjourn or to lay a question on the table, nor is a member entitled to debate a motion to limit debate. These questions are questions of only temporary concern and the decision upon them is not final, as they can be revived and discussed later.

3. Members have a right to debate main questions subject to the right of the body itself to limit or restrict debate.

4. All main questions, amendments and appeals are debatable because they represent substantive questions requiring the judgment of the group. Motions to postpone indefinitely, to reconsider and to rescind are debatable because they finally dispose of the main question. They also open the main question to debate. Motions to refer to committee and to postpone definitely are debatable only as to the reference or postponement.

Sec. 64. Amendability of Motions

See also Ch. 38, Secs. 395–421, Motion to Amend.

1. Propositions are sometimes introduced in a form not acceptable to the body. It is essential therefore that it be possible to amend propositions in order that they state the common will of the group. There are limitations, however, on the right to amend, particularly with reference to certain procedural motions. There is a convenient rule by which it is possible to determine whether a proposal is subject to amendment. If it could properly have been submitted in a different form, it can be amend-

ed. If the proposition could not have been stated in a different form, it cannot be amended.

2. Certain propositions, as requests and points of order and committee reports, are not propositions of the body in the sense that their form is determined by the body. They can be accepted or rejected or accepted with exceptions or limitations but not amended.

Sec. 65. Finality of Actions

See also Secs. 451–457, relating to Reconsideration; Sec. 398, Decision on Amendment Is Final; and Sec. 159, Main Question May Be Considered Only Once at a Session.

1. When a final vote is taken upon any main motion, that vote is binding. It is necessary that it be possible to put an end to debate on controversial questions; otherwise a minority could continue to make motions concerning the matter and keep it under consideration to the exclusion of other matters and to the point that progress of the body would be seriously impeded. To prevent this possibility, since the earliest days in Parliament, the rule has been that when a vote is taken upon adoption of a main motion, that vote is binding subject to certain exceptions. This rule is applicable whether the proposition was approved or whether the proposition was defeated. This rule is applicable to substantive propositions, but it is not applicable to purely procedural motions. Thus, if a legislative body passes or refuses to pass a bill, that bill is disposed of for the session unless the vote is reconsidered. But if the bill is referred to committee, it can be withdrawn from committee. If the limitation is imposed upon debate, that limitation can be removed. If a question has been laid upon the table, it

can be taken from the table. If motions of this class fail to pass, they can be made again when the situation has so changed that the members might reasonably vote differently.

2. There are situations when the action taken is final and beyond the control of the body. Thus, if a motion results in a contract, that contract is binding and the body cannot reconsider or reverse the action taken. When any question has passed beyond the control of the body, no motion is permitted which would purport to change the action on it, as when the governor has signed a bill.

Sec. 66. Changing Actions Already Taken

See also Ch. 41, Secs. 450–474, Motion to Reconsider, and Ch. 42, Secs. 480–483, Motion to Rescind.

In spite of the desirability of finally disposing of questions when they are voted upon, it has been found necessary on occasion to reverse or alter the action previously taken and so the motion to reconsider became established. The U.S. courts hold generally that at least an official deliberative body has the same right to undo, change and reverse its actions as to take them originally. However, it is common practice to restrict the right to reconsider and, in many organizations, it may be essential to the progress of the business of the organization to restrict this right by rule.

Sec. 67. Renewal of Motions

See also Sec. 160, Procedural Motions May Be Renewed, and Sec. 161, Main Motions May Not Be Renewed.

1. A rule or a law should be interpreted in the light of its purpose. A rule against the renewal of

procedural motions is for the purpose of preventing waste of time and effort on discussion of questions which have already been decided. When such a rule prevents an organization from discussing or changing a rule that is preventing it from doing what it could properly do and wants to do, it is defeating the purpose of the organization and the purpose of the rule. To alleviate this problem, there is a rule that a procedural motion cannot be renewed until after other business has intervened and sometimes also that a decision has been made on that other business. In view of the frequency of an organization's changing its action on a procedural motion, the fact that procedural motions are quickly decided without debate and the inconvenience of the delay while other business intervenes, a logical and much more satisfactory rule would seem to be that procedural motions may be renewed whenever the parliamentary situation is such that the renewed motion reasonably might be expected to be adopted. The presiding officer should exercise discretion rather than wait for other business to intervene and be disposed of before accepting the renewal of a procedural motion which would probably be adopted.

2. The renewal of main motions is a different matter. Main motions are fully open to debate and should be decided only after mature consideration. They may be reconsidered and the motion to reconsider seems to be an adequate remedy.

Sec. 67, Par. 1: Sturgis, p. 32.

CHAPTER 8

POWERS OF COURTS WITH REFERENCE TO LEGISLATIVE PROCEDURE

Sec. 71. Courts Cannot Interfere with Rule-Making Powers of Legislative Bodies

1. The courts will not disturb a ruling on a parliamentary question made by a legislative or governmental body having authority to make rules for its government and acting within the scope of its powers.

2. A rule of procedure adopted by a legislative house pursuant to the constitutional provision authorizing each house to determine its rules of procedure cannot be impeached on the grounds that some other rule would be better or more accurate or more just, if the rule as adopted does not ignore constitutional restraints or does not violate fundamental rights and there is a reasonable relation between the mode or method of procedure and the result that is sought.

Sec. 71, Par. 1: Davis v. City of Saginaw (1891), 87 Mich. 439, 49 N.W. 667; State of Missouri v. Alt (1887), 26 Mo. App. 673; Wells v. Baine (1874), 75 Pa. 39, 15 Am. R. 563; Malone v. Meekins (Alaska 1982), 650 P.2d 351; Heimbach v. State of New York (1982), 89 App. Div. 2d 138, 454 N.Y.S.2d 993, *aff'd* 59 N.Y.2d 891, 452 N.E.2d 1264, 465 N.Y.S.2d 936, *appeal dismissed,* 464 U.S. 956, 104 S. Ct. 386, 78 L. Ed. 2d 331.

Sec. 71, Par. 2: State of South Carolina *ex rel.* Coleman v. Lewis (1936), 181 S.C. 10, 186 S.E. 625; Heimbach v. State of New York (1982), 89 App. Div. 2d 138, 454 N.Y.S.2d 993, *aff'd* 59 N.Y.2d 891, 452 N.E.2d 1264, 465 N.Y.S.2d 936, *appeal dismissed,* 464 U.S. 956, 104 S. Ct. 386, 78 L. Ed. 2d 331.

3. An interpretation by a house of a state legislature as to the extent of power conferred upon it by the constitution to determine the rules of its own proceedings is not binding on the courts, but should be accepted by them unless manifestly wrong.

4. Where no precise forms are prescribed, as in the removal of an official, a procedure may be adopted which incorporates the fundamentals of due process.

Sec. 72. Legislative Policy Is Not Within Control of the Courts

1. The propriety and wisdom of a statute are questions exclusively for the legislature. The wisdom, justice and expediency of an act of the legislature is not subject to review by the courts.

2. Before a statute can be declared unconstitutional, it must clearly and unavoidably appear to be beyond the power of the legislature. It is for the courts to decide whether or not there has been compliance with constitutional provisions and whether a bill of the legislature has become a law.

3. Where the constitution declares certain forms indispensable to the passage of laws, the courts will declare acts invalid unless passed according to those provisions.

Sec. 71, Par. 3: Witherspoon v. State of Mississippi *ex rel.* West (1925), 138 Miss. 310, 103 So. 134.

Sec. 71, Par. 4: Murdock v. Phillips Academy (Mass. 1831), 12 Pick. 244.

Sec. 72, Par. 1: City of Ensley v. Simpson (1909), 166 Ala. 366, 52 So. 61; *In re* Likens Petitions (1909), 223 Pa. 456, 72 A. 858.

Sec. 72, Par. 2: City of Ensley v. Simpson (1909), 166 Ala. 366, 52 So. 61; Neiberger v. McCullough (1912), 253 Ill. 312, 97 N.E. 660.

Sec. 72, Par. 3: Wells v. Missouri Pacific Railway Co. (1892), 110 Mo. 286, 19 S.W. 530.

See also Sec. 697, paragraph 1, Mandatory Requirements Must Be Complied With.

4. A court will go behind a statute to the legislative record to ascertain whether it has legal existence only when the attention of the court is called to a particular error.

See also Sec. 697, Journal as Showing Passage and Legality of Bills.

5. Under the constitutional provision of separation of powers, the courts are without jurisdiction to interpose judicial authority as against the exercise of legislative authority and power. However, an act violative of the constitutional provisions of separation of powers will be declared a nullity by the courts.

6. The motives of the governor, acting in the governor's legislative capacity in approving an appropriation bill, cannot be made the subject of judicial inquiry for the purpose of invalidating or preventing the full operation of the bill.

7. The rules of the general assembly are not reviewable by the judiciary except on constitutional grounds.

Sec. 72, Par. 4: State of Alabama v. Martin (1909), 160 Ala. 181, 48 So. 846.

Sec. 72, Par. 5: City of Bethany v. District Court of Oklahoma County (1948), 200 Okla. 149, 191 P.2d 187; Greer v. Georgia (1975), 233 Ga. 667, 212 S.E.2d 836; Alexander v. State of Mississippi by and through Allain (1983), 441 So. 2d 1329; Malone v. Meekins (Alaska 1982), 650 P.2d 351; Cross v. Alexander (La. 1986), 498 So. 2d 740.

Sec. 72, Par. 6: Lukens v. Nye (1909), 156 Cal. 498, 105 P. 593.

Sec. 72, Par. 7: Gewertz v. Joint Legislative Committee on Ethical Standards (1975), 132 N.J. Super. 435, 334 A.2d 64, *cert. denied,* 68 N.J. 156, 343 A.2d 444; *In re* Application of Lamb (1961), 67 N.J. Super. 39, 169 A.2d 822; Malone v. Meekins (Alaska 1982), 650 P.2d 351; Paisner v. Attorney General (1983), 390 Mass. 593, 458 N.E.2d 734; Moffitt v. Willis (Fla. 1984), 459 So. 2d 1018; People's Advocate, Inc. v. Superior Court (1986), 181 C.A.3d 316, 226 Cal. Rptr. 640.

Sec. 73. Powers of Courts over Legislative Bodies Generally

See also Sec. 24, Failure of a House of the Legislature to Conform to Its Rules Does Not Invalidate Its Acts.

1. Insofar as the judgment and discretion of a legislative body is uncontrolled by the law of the land, it is free from the control of the courts. But insofar as its acts are directed by law, it is subject to judicial authority.

2. While the people of a state have vested in them sovereign authority, their representatives in the legislature have only such authority as is delegated to them by the constitution.

3. The legislature cannot do by indirection that which it cannot do directly.

4. Where an alleged illegal ministerial official act has relation to legislative action, such action may be considered by the court in determining the validity or invalidity of the ministerial act. This is not an interference by the courts with the legislative department of the government.

5. An amendment to a state constitution otherwise validly proposed and adopted by the people is valid notwithstanding the fact the legislature may have failed to have the proposed amendment entered at length upon its journals as required by the constitution.

Sec. 73, Par. 1: Kerr v. Trego (1864), 47 Pa. 292; Martin v. Louisiana Stadium and Exposition District (1977), 349 So. 2d 349; Alexander v. State of Mississippi by and through Allain (1983), 441 So. 2d 1329; Pelligrino v. O'Neill (1984), 193 Conn. 670, 480 A.2d 476.

Sec. 73, Par. 2: Sherrill v. Pendleton (1907), 188 N.Y. 185, 81 N.E. 124.

Sec. 73, Par. 3: Brennan v. Connolly (1919), 207 Mich. 35, 173 N.W. 511.

Sec. 73, Par. 4: Crawford v. Gilchrist (1912), 64 Fla. 41, 59 So. 963.

Sec. 73, Par. 5: West v. State of Florida (1905), 50 Fla. 154, 39 So. 412.

6. The courts have jurisdiction to decide whether a house of a legislature has been organized in violation of the constitution. No warrant will lie to determine the title of the presiding officer to that person's office.

7. Illegality will not be presumed, but on the contrary, legality will be presumed until illegality is established.

8. The courts cannot declare an act of a legislature void on account of noncompliance with rules of procedure made by itself to govern its own deliberations and not involving any constitutional provision.

See also Sec. 24, Failure of a House of the Legislature to Conform to Its Rules Does Not Invalidate Its Acts.

9. Generally courts will decline to interfere, as long as the affairs of the organization are conducted in accordance with its laws and rules, leaving all internal questions to the constitution and rules adopted by the body.

10. Where a statute passed by the legislature has been submitted to referendum and approved, it is

---

Sec. 73, Par. 6: Werts v. Rogers (1894), 56 N.Y.L. 480, 28 A. 726.

Sec. 73, Par. 7: State of Minnesota v. Smith (1875), 22 Minn. 218; Bank v. Dandridge (U.S. 1827), 12 Wheat. 64; State of Iowa v. Vail (1880), 53 Iowa 550, 5 N.W. 741; McCarmack v. Berg City (1871), 23 Mich. 457; City of Greeley v. Hamman (1891), 17 Colo. 30, 28 P. 460.

Sec. 73, Par. 8: McDonald v. State of Wisconsin (1891), 80 Wis. 407, 50 N.W. 185; *In re* Ryan (1891), 80 Wis. 414, 50 N.W. 187; State of South Carolina v. Brown (1890), 35 S.C. 151, 11 S.E. 641; St. Louis and S.F. Railway Co. v. Gill (1891), 54 Ark. 101, 15 S.W. 18; Schweizer v. Territory (1897), 5 Okla. 297, 47 P. 1094; Ricarte v. State of Arkansas (1986), 290 Ark. 100, 717 S.W.2d 488.

Sec. 73, Par. 9: Brotherhood of Railroad Trainmen v. Williams (1925), 211 Ky. 638, 277 S.W. 500; Paisner v. Attorney General (1983), 390 Mass. 593, 458 N.E.2d 734; Moffitt v. Willis (Fla. 1984), 459 So. 2d 1018; People's Advocate, Inc. v. Superior Court (1986), 181 C.A.3d 316, 226 Cal. Rptr. 640; State of North Dakota *ex rel.* Spaeth v. Meiers (1987), 403 N.W.2d 392.

against public policy for the courts thereafter to declare it invalid because it did not receive the publicity required by law before the election.

Sec. 73, Par. 10: Allen v. State of Arizona (1913), 14 Ariz. 458, 130 P. 1114.

*

PART II. DEBATE

*

PART II

DEBATE

CHAPTER 9

WHAT IS DEBATABLE

Sec. 80. Purpose of Debate

See also Sec. 60, Right to Debate; Ch. 10, Right to the Floor; Ch. 11, Debate on Question; and Ch. 12, Conduct of Debate.

1. The purpose of legislative bodies is to reach their best joint judgment on the questions presented to them for decision. The decision is the decision of the group, not of the individual members. To reach the joint judgment of the body, the exchange of thought and the reasons of the members are essential. That exchange of thought is through debate. Every member has the right to present his thoughts and opinions and to argue and attempt to convince the other members of the group. Debate is one of the most fundamental characteristics of a legislative body.

2. As a general rule, the members of a deliberative body have the right to debate every substantive question presented to the body for determination, but debate upon purely procedural questions is not a right of the members.

Sec. 80, Par. 1: People v. American Institute (N.Y. 1873), 44 How. Pr. 468; Sturgis, p. 121.

Sec. 80, Par. 2: Sturgis, pp. 121, 122.

3. A deliberative body having the right to make its own rules can, by those rules, restrict or cut off debate.

Sec. 81. What Motions Are Debatable

1. All main motions are debatable because they present substantive questions for determination.

2. Amendments to main motions and other substantive propositions are debatable because amendments modify such substantive propositions. Amendments to procedural motions are not debatable.

3. Motions which present substantive propositions in any form are debatable. The most usual motions of this class are, in addition to the main motion, the following:

(a) Appeals, because they determine questions which are equivalent to making rules governing future procedure.

(b) Motion to reconsider, because it presents a main question for review.

(c) Motion to rescind, because it reopens the consideration of a main question.

(d) Motion to postpone indefinitely, because it finally disposes of a main question.

(e) Questions of privilege which present main questions. Many questions of privilege present main questions. They are privileged as to consideration only because they involve a question requiring immediate decision.

Sec. 81, Par. 1: People v. American Institute (N.Y. 1873), 44 How. Pr. 468; Sturgis, pp. 121, 122.

Sec. 81, Par. 2: Sturgis, pp. 26, 27, 121.

(f) Motions to approve, to concur, to confirm, to appoint, and similar motions, because they are only main motions in a different form.

4. Motions which adopt rules of procedure or amend such rules and rules which determine some future rule of procedure are main motions since they present substantive questions for determination by the body.

Sec. 82. What Motions Are Not Debatable

1. Motions of all kinds which relate to immediate procedure are not debatable. These usually are questions relating to how something is to be done. There is nothing so profound about these motions as to justify debate, and debate would only waste the time of the members. Recognition of the general application of this rule will eliminate much confusion.

2. The following motions are not debatable:

(a) Adjourn. (unqualified)

(b) Call of the house.

(c) Recess, when other business is pending.

(d) Parliamentary inquiry.

(e) Call for the orders of the day.

(f) Questions relating to the priority of business.

(g) Suspension of the rules.

(h) Objection to the consideration of a question.

(i) Other incidental motions.

(j) Lay on the table.

Sec. 81, Par. 3: Sturgis, pp. 27, 121.

Sec. 82: Sturgis, p. 27; Hughes, Sec. 715.

(k) Previous question.

(*l*) Motions to close, limit or extend the limits of debate.

(m) Amend an undebatable question.

(n) Amend titles of bills.

(*o*) Divide a question, when right is given by rule.

(p) Motion to lay aside or pass on calendar or file.

(q) Take from the table.

(r) Requests of any kind.

(s) A decision of the presiding officer, unless an appeal is taken from the decision.

3. It is commonly provided by rule that an appeal is not debatable when it relates to indecorum, transgression of the rules of speaking, or priority of business, or when made while an undebatable question is pending or after the previous question has been ordered. Such a rule follows congressional practice but is not a rule of parliamentary law.

Sec. 83. Motions Which Permit Limited Debate

1. On the motion to postpone to a definite time, the question of postponement is open to debate, but the main question is not. In Congress all debate is prohibited on the motion to postpone definitely, and this would seem to be the better practice.

See also Sec. 361, Other Means of Preventing or Limiting Debate.

2. The motion to commit or refer to committee is debatable as to the propriety of the reference, but

Sec. 83, Par. 1: N.Y. Manual, p. 463; Hughes, Sec. 316; Sturgis, p. 27.

the main question is not open to debate on this motion.

See also Sec. 388, Debate and Application of Subsidiary Motions to Motion to Refer.

3. The motion to discharge a committee or to withdraw a measure from committee is debatable as to the advisability of that action, but the measure is not open to debate.

See also Sec. 491, Withdrawing Bills from Committee.

Sec. 84. Motions Which Open the Main Question to Debate

1. The following motions open the main question to debate:

(a) Postpone indefinitely.

See also Ch. 39, Secs. 430–436, Motion to Postpone Indefinitely.

(b) Reconsider a debatable question.

See also Ch. 41, Secs. 456–474, Motion to Reconsider.

(c) Rescind, cancel or repeal.

See also Ch. 42, Secs. 480–483, Motion to Rescind.

(d) Ratify, approve, confirm, adopt or pass.

See also Sec. 443, Motion to Ratify.

2. It will be noticed that the above motions finally dispose of the main question. The motion to postpone indefinitely would prevent further consideration of the question while the purpose of the motion to reconsider is to defeat a question already approved or to revive a question otherwise defeated. The motions to approve and to ratify state the main question itself. The motion to rescind or repeal would reverse an affirmative action previously taken

---

Sec. 83, Par. 2: Hughes, Sec. 330; Reed, Sec. 120; Sturgis, p. 27.
Sec. 83, Par. 3: Hughes, Sec. 733.

and simply states the main question in a negative form, while the motion to adopt states the main question in its affirmative form. In this way, parliamentary law permits any main question to be debated before it is finally defeated.

Sec. 85. Questions or Suggestions Are Not Considered Debate

1. There is a clear distinction between debate and making suggestions or asking questions. It is permissible to ask questions or make brief suggestions concerning undebatable questions. A member is entitled to inquire as to the meaning or purpose or effect of an undebatable question. The presiding officer may permit the author or sponsor of the proposition to explain briefly, and without argument, the nature of the proposal or what it is expected to accomplish. It is also in order for the presiding officer to permit members to make suggestions as to the form of the proposition, its purpose or procedure concerning it. The presiding officer should be careful not to permit debate of an undebatable question and to put the question to vote without unnecessary delay.

2. The fundamental right of a member of a body to know what the member is voting on before being required to vote gives to the member the right to inquire concerning an unclear proposal at least to the extent of knowing the general purpose and intended effect of the proposal.

Sec. 85: Sturgis, p. 123.

CHAPTER 10

RIGHT TO THE FLOOR

Sec. 90. Right to Debate Questions

See also Ch. 15, Secs. 140–150, Proposals for Action.

1. Debate is the essential feature of a legislative body. It is the means by which the opinions of members are exchanged, questions deliberated, and conclusions reached on the business before the body.

2. It is a fundamental rule of parliamentary practice governing all deliberative assemblies that the opportunity to deliberate, and if possible convince their fellows, is the right of the minority, which right they cannot be deprived of by the arbitrary will of the majority.

3. To permit debate, there must be a debatable question before the body, and one member must have been recognized as entitled to speak. During debate various motions are in order, and if the question be not otherwise disposed of previously, it is brought to a vote at the conclusion of the debate and disposed of permanently or for the time being. Then another question can be brought before the body and, if it is debatable, debate follows on it.

4. A member who has just made a report or presented any matter to the house is entitled to be

---

Sec. 90, Par. 1: Sturgis, p. 121.

Sec. 90, Par. 2: Terre Haute Gas Corporation v. Johnson (1943), 221 Ind. 499, 45 N.E.2d 484, *modified,* 48 N.E.2d 455; Sturgis, p. 121.

Sec. 90, Par. 3: Cushing's Legislative Assemblies, Secs. 1177, 1178, 1183.

first recognized for the purpose of discussing that matter, but the member loses that right if that person does not claim it within a reasonable time.

5. Meetings are held under the U.S. democratic process for the purpose of discussion, argumentation and persuasion, and interested parties have the right to try to persuade the majority to accept their views and there can be no legal wrong from such an attempt.

6. Unless a proposal is of considerable length and must be read, the proposer should remain standing during the reading as notice to others of the intention to claim the right to first recognition.

Sec. 91. Recognition of Members

1. A member is not entitled to address a body nor to offer a motion or present a question or other business without first obtaining recognition, but may interrupt a speaker for the purposes listed in the following section.

2. When any member desires to speak or deliver any matter to the house, that person should rise and respectfully address the presiding officer. When the presiding officer recognizes the member by calling the member by name or by indicating recognition, that person is entitled to the floor and may address

---

Sec. 90, Par. 4: Hughes, Sec. 117; Reed, Sec. 214; Cushing, Sec. 204; Cushing's Legislative Assemblies, Secs. 1536–1541; Tilson, p. 46; U.S. House Rule XIV, Par. 3.

Sec. 90, Par. 5: Stansberry v. McCarty (1958), 238 Ind. 338, 149 N.E.2d 683.

Sec. 90, Par. 6: Tilson's Manual, Sec. 49.

Sec. 91, Par. 1: Jefferson, Sec. XVII; Sturgis, pp. 122, 123; Hughes, Sec. 181; Cushing, Sec. 46; Reed, Secs. 48, 213; Cushing's Legislative Assemblies, Sec. 1532.

the body or present a matter of business, but may not yield the floor to any other member.

3. The following rules should guide the presiding officer in determining whom to recognize:

(a) The first member rising and requesting recognition is entitled to the floor over others.

(b) When two or more members ask recognition at the same time, the one first rising is entitled to prior recognition.

(c) When two or more members arise at the same time, the one first addressing the presiding officer is entitled to be first recognized.

(d) The presiding officer has the authority to designate the member who is first to speak, subject only to points of order and appeals in case of flagrant or persistent unfairness.

4. In recognizing members, it is the custom for the presiding officer to alternate between those favoring and those opposing the pending question.

5. The presiding officer has the right to inquire for what purpose a member arises to ascertain whether the member proposes business which is in order or a motion which has a higher precedence.

Sec. 91, Par. 2: Jefferson, Sec. XVII; Sturgis, p. 122; Cushing's Legislative Assemblies, Secs. 374, 1212; Hughes, Sec. 117; U.S. House Rule XIV, Par. 1; Cushing, Secs. 46, 203; Reed, Sec. 102; Tilson, p. 43; Tilson's Manual, Sec. 66.

Sec. 91, Par. 3: Jefferson, Secs. XVII, XIX; Cushing's Legislative Assemblies, Secs. 375. 377, 1216, 1217, 1535; Sturgis, pp. 122, 123; Hughes, Secs. 117, 119, 120; Cushing, Secs. 67, 204; Reed, Sec. 213; Tilson, p. 45; 2 Hatsell 100.

Sec. 91, Par. 4: Sturgis, p. 123; Hughes, Sec. 117; Reed, Sec. 214; Tilson's Manual, Sec. 50.

Sec. 91, Par. 5: Sturgis, p. 123; Hughes, Secs. 26, 124, 735.

Sec. 92. Interruption of a Member Who Is Speaking

1. There are circumstances under which a member may interrupt a member who is speaking and present a question for action or decision. A member who is speaking may be interrupted only when some question requires immediate consideration.

2. A member who is speaking may be interrupted for the following purposes:

(a) Raise a question of privilege.

(b) Appeal from the decision of the presiding officer (if the appeal is made immediately following the decision and before progress in debate).

(c) Raise a point of order requiring an immediate ruling.

(d) Make a parliamentary inquiry, requiring an immediate reply.

(e) Make or give notice of a motion to reconsider.

(f) Object to consideration (must follow immediately after recognition).

(g) Call for the regular order, for the orders of the day or call attention to a special order.

(h) Call attention to disorderly conduct or to disorderly words in debate.

(i) Raise a question of "no quorum."

(j) Call for a division of a question.

(k) Call for a division of the house (must be made immediately following the vote).

(*l*) Vote when missed on roll call or change a vote when permitted. (It is too late to vote or change a vote after the vote is announced).

(m) To move the previous question, in some legislatures.

3. When a member is speaking and another member interrupts to request recognition, it is the right of the presiding officer to permit the one rising to state the reason for desiring the floor; and if the question that member desires to raise is entitled to precedence, the member originally speaking should relinquish the floor until the question having precedence is disposed of, but that member is entitled to resume the floor as soon as the privileged question has been disposed of.

Sec. 93. Place of Speaking

While speaking, members should remain standing at their seats or at the bar of the house, and when finished, should sit down. A member who is infirm or ill may be permitted to speak while seated. When a particular place has been set aside for speaking, members should speak from that place.

Sec. 94. Right of Member to Hold the Floor

1. When a member has been recognized, it is a breach of order for another to interrupt except for the purposes listed under Sec. 92, Interruption of a Member Who Is Speaking, and except to call the

Sec. 92, Par. 2: (a) Sturgis, p. 25; Hughes, Sec. 711, (b) Sturgis, pp. 25, 85; Hughes, Sec. 123, (c) Sturgis, p. 94; Hughes, Sec. 123, (d) Sturgis, p. 98; Hughes, Sec. 711, (e) Sturgis, p. 42, (f) Sturgis, p. 91; Hughes, Sec. 123, (g) Reed, Sec. 257; Hughes, Secs. 123, 711, (h) Sturgis, p. 125; Hughes, Sec. 709, (i) Hughes, Sec. 648; Sturgis, p. 102, (j) Hughes, Secs. 123, 711; Sturgis, p. 105, (k) Hughes, Secs. 123, 711; Sturgis, p. 105.

Sec. 92, Par. 3: Cushing's Legislative Assemblies, Sec. 1214; Hughes, Secs. 124, 176; Reed, Sec. 212.

Sec. 93: Jefferson, Sec. XVII; Cushing, Sec. 208; Cushing's Legislative Assemblies, Secs. 378, 379, 1550.

member speaking to order if that member should depart from it.

2. A member does not lose the right to the floor by the intervention of a privileged question, and when a member sits down while a paper is being read, that person does not thereby lose the right to the floor.

3. A member who had the floor or was entitled to the floor at adjournment or recess is entitled to the floor on the renewal of debate on the original question.

4. Where the right to close debate is recognized, a member who is in charge of a measure does not lose the right to close the debate unless the previous question is adopted, and in this case, the right to make a limited closing speech is often permitted by the rules.

Sec. 95. Yielding the Floor in Debate

1. A member having the floor in debate may, without objection, yield it for questions and explanations connected with the subject before the house. When yielding the floor temporarily upon request, members may protect their claim to the floor by indicating that they are yielding only temporarily; their claim to the floor is, however, a matter of

Sec. 94, Par. 1: Cushing's Legislative Assemblies, Sec. 1218; Hughes, Sec. 696; Cushing, Sec. 200; Sturgis, p. 126.

Sec. 94, Par. 2: Cushing's Legislative Assemblies, Sec. 1221; Hughes, Secs. 677, 681; Reed, Sec. 212.

Sec. 94, Par. 3: Cushing's Legislative Assemblies, Sec. 1543.

Sec. 94, Par. 4: Hughes, Sec. 677.

courtesy and not of right.

2. A member may propose an amendment to the question under discussion without yielding the floor, but loses the right to the floor when yielding it to permit another member to propose an amendment.

3. A member who yields the floor for a motion to postpone the matter under discussion, lay it on the table, or otherwise delay further debate to a later time is entitled to be first recognized when the discussion is resumed, but must promptly claim the privilege and be recognized.

Sec. 96. Right of Presiding Officer to the Floor

1. The presiding officer is not entitled to debate questions from the chair, although as a member the presiding officer may assign the chair to another member and speak from the floor.

2. The presiding officer has the right to speak on points of order in preference to members or, if a member, to other members, and to state the reasons for decisions on appeals, but may speak on no other subject from the chair except that, with the permission of the body, the presiding officer may state facts which are particularly within the presiding officer's own knowledge.

Sec. 95, Par. 1: Hughes, Secs. 677, 736; Reed, Sec. 217; Cushing, Sec. 205.

Sec. 95, Par. 2: Hughes, Secs. 117, 677.

Sec. 95, Par. 3: Hughes, Sec. 726.

Sec. 96, Par. 1: Reed, Sec. 40; Hughes, Sec. 74.

Sec. 96, Par. 2: Jefferson, Sec. XVII; Sturgis, p. 164; N.Y. Manual, p. 457.

CHAPTER 11

DEBATE ON QUESTION

Sec. 100. There Must Be a Question Before the House to Permit Debate

1. There can be no debate unless there is a question before the house.

2. Debate must always have relation to some definite question which is under consideration by the body. There must be a motion or question proposed to the body by the presiding officer for the purpose of ascertaining the will of the body.

3. When the subject appears clearly from the circumstances or speech, a member is often permitted to conclude the speech with a motion rather than being required to first make the motion. This is a particularly common procedure in making nominations.

4. If a pending matter is withdrawn, it precludes further debate on that subject.

See also Ch. 27, Secs. 272–276, Withdrawal of Motions.

5. Debate on a point of order is closed when the presiding officer makes a decision thereon.

See also Ch. 24, Secs. 240–246, Points of Order.

Sec. 100, Par. 1: Cushing's Legislative Assemblies, Secs. 1556–1581; Hughes, Secs. 676, 695; N.Y. Manual, p. 440; Sturgis, p. 122.

Sec. 100, Par. 2: Hughes, Sec. 676; Cushing, Sec. 198.

Sec. 100, Par. 3: Cushing's Legislative Assemblies, Sec. 1558.

Sec. 100, Par. 4: Hughes, Sec. 719.

Sec. 100, Par. 5: Hughes, Sec. 683.

Sec. 101. Debate Is Limited to the Question Before the House

1. Debate must be confined to the question before the body.

2. A member who resorts to persistent irrelevance or to persistent repetition after the attention of the house has been called to the matter may be directed to discontinue speaking by the presiding officer.

3. When a question has been entertained by the presiding officer and stated to the house, it is open to debate, and the presiding officer may properly put the question: "Is there any discussion?" or "Are you ready for the question?" in order to serve notice that the matter is open to discussion and may be closed if no one takes the floor.

4. Debate on a bill is confined to the bill under consideration and does not extend to criticism of other bills before the house or in committee, even though they relate to the same subject.

5. It is out of order to refer in debate to a bill or other matters not yet reported by a committee. Neither is it in order to refer to proceedings of a committee unless the committee has formally reported its proceedings to the house. Members may not allude to nor relate in debate what was done or said in committee or by any member of the committee,

Sec. 101, Par. 1: Jefferson, Sec. XVII; Sturgis, p. 124; Hughes, Sec. 728; Cushing, Sec. 209; Reed, Sec. 216; Cushing's Legislative Assemblies, Secs. 1617–1654; U.S. House Rule XIV, Par. 1.

Sec. 101, Par. 2: Hughes, Sec. 734; Sturgis, p. 124.

Sec. 101, Par. 3: Hughes, Sec. 675; Sturgis, p. 127.

Sec. 101, Par. 4: Hughes, Sec. 732; Cannon's Procedure in the House of Representatives, pp. 151–153.

except such as is contained in the written report made to the house by authority of the committee.

6. When a question is under debate and an amendment is proposed, the amendment then becomes the question under consideration. When an amendment is pending, the debate must be confined to the merits of the amendment, unless it is of such a nature that its decision practically decides the main question.

7. Debate begins with the statement of the question and ends when the question is put to vote and the vote announced.

Sec. 102. A Member Has a Right to Speak Only Once on a Question

1. No member has the right to speak more than once on the same question at the same stage of procedure, on the same day; or even on another day, if the debate be adjourned. But if a bill be read more than once on the same day, a member may speak once at each reading.

2. Members may be permitted to speak again to clear up a matter of fact, or merely to explain some material part of their speech, and while they do not have the right to discuss the question itself, they may be permitted to do so. When members have exhausted their right to speak, they may still make any

---

Sec. 101, Par. 5: Hughes, Secs. 694, 729.

Sec. 101, Par. 6: Reed, Sec. 216.

Sec. 101, Par. 7: Hughes, Secs. 676, 695.

Sec. 102, Par. 1: Jefferson, Sec. XVII; Cushing, Sec. 215; Reed, Sec. 215; Cushing's Legislative Assemblies, Sec. 1582; Tilson, pp. 29, 49; U.S. House Rule I, Par. 4, and House Rule XIV, Par. 6; 2 Hatsell 76.

motion having a higher precedence than the motion under debate.

3. When an amendment is offered, or any other motion is made, the amendment or other motion then becomes the question under consideration. In regard to the right to debate, such a question is treated as a new question. A member who has spoken once on the main question may speak again on an amendment. But when a question is not debatable, an amendment to that question is not debatable.

4. The rule providing that members shall not speak more than once on the same measure, at the same stage of procedure, applies to continued debate after adjournment or postponement.

5. In practice, a member is often given the privilege of speaking a second time on a question after others who desired to speak have spoken when that member can explain any point misunderstood and present facts to refute arguments by those opposed.

6. The rule that no one shall be permitted to speak a second time until all others who desire have spoken should not be so strictly enforced that someone who has spoken cannot clear up some question which has arisen in the debate.

Sec. 102, Par. 2: Jefferson, Sec. XVII; Cushing, Sec. 215; Cushing's Legislative Assemblies, Secs. 1585, 1592, 1602, 1603.

Sec. 102, Par. 3: Jefferson, Sec. XXXV; Sturgis, pp. 53, 54; Cushing's Legislative Assemblies, Secs. 1619–1633; Hughes, Sec. 719; Reed, Secs. 215, 216; Cushing, Secs. 215, 216.

Sec. 102, Par. 4: Jefferson, Sec. XXXIII; Hughes, Sec. 735; Cushing, Sec. 215.

Sec. 102, Par. 5: Cushing, Secs. 217, 218; Cushing's Legislative Assemblies, Secs. 1595, 1601.

Sec. 102, Par. 6: Tilson's Manual, Sec. 51.

Sec. 103. Member Sponsoring a Question Closing Debate

See also Sec. 90, Right to Debate Questions.

1. In many deliberative bodies, it is provided by rule or established by custom that the author or sponsor of a measure or a main question is entitled to close the debate after other members wishing to speak have spoken. Where this rule exists, a member may not be deprived of the right to close the debate, except by ordering the previous question, and sometimes the rules permit the author or sponsor a limited time to close debate even after the previous question has been ordered. Where the right of closing is not set out in the rules, the privilege is often granted by custom.

2. Usually when presenting a proposal, a member is recognized first to explain the proposal, and when the debate has been extensive, that member is called upon at the conclusion of the debate to close.

Sec. 103, Par. 1: Hughes, Secs. 677, 719; Tilson, p. 47; U.S. House Rule XIV, Par. 3.

Sec. 103, Par. 2: Tilson's Manual, Sec. 49.

CHAPTER 12

CONDUCT OF DEBATE

Sec. 110. Addressing Members or Presiding Officer

See also Sec. 124, Personalities Not Permitted in Debate.

1. All debate must be addressed to the presiding officer and not to the members.

2. To guard against the appearance of personalities in debate, it has long been the rule in legislative bodies that no member should refer to another by name in debate. The other member should be described by the district, seat, as the member who last spoke or by describing the member in some other manner.

3. The presiding officer of a house of a state legislature is always addressed as "Mr. or Madam Speaker," "Mr. or Madam President" or in committee, including Committee of the Whole, as "Mr. or Madam Chairperson."

4. The officers of a deliberative body should always be referred to by their official titles.

5. About 1972 presiding officers began to be called "Mr. Chairperson" or "Madam Chairperson" at conventions and political meetings.

Sec. 110, Par. 1: Reed, Sec. 212; Sturgis, p. 125; Cushing's Legislative Assemblies, Sec. 380.

Sec. 110, Par. 2: Jefferson, Sec. XVII; Sturgis, p. 125; Hughes, Sec. 679; Cushing's Legislative Assemblies, Secs. 381, 1671–1673; Reed, Sec. 212.

Sec. 110, Par. 3: Hughes, Sec. 705.

Sec. 111. Reference to Executive, to Other House, or Questions Before the Courts

1. It is unparliamentary and inconsistent with the independence of a legislative body to refer to the name or office of the executive in order to influence the vote. It is in order in debate to refer to the executive or the executive's opinions, with either approval or criticism when such references are relevant to the subject under discussion and otherwise conform to the rules.

2. It is irregular and unparliamentary for a member in one house of a legislature to quote or refer to the vote by which a measure passed the other house.

3. Any matter awaiting adjudication in a court should not be debated or discussed in a legislative body.

Sec. 112. Reading Papers

1. When papers which have not been printed are presented to the house or to a committee for action, a member has a right to have them read once before being compelled to vote on them. If there has been debate or amendment, a member may request that they be read again before voting upon them, but a motion or request for the reading of a bill or resolution is not in order after the roll call has been ordered.

Sec. 111, Par. 1: Cushing's Legislative Assemblies, Sec. 738; Hughes, Secs. 694, 737; Jefferson, Sec. XXXV; Reed, Sec. 224.

Sec. 111, Par. 2: Cushing's Legislative Assemblies, Sec. 739.

Sec. 111, Par. 3: Hughes, Sec. 680.

Sec. 112, Par. 1: Jefferson, Sec. XXXII; Cushing's Legislative Assemblies, Sec. 1472; N.Y. Manual, p. 448; Cushing, Sec. 155; Reed, Sec. 187.

2. Members do not have the right to have acts, journals, accounts, or papers on the table read independently of the will of the body. The delay and interruption which this might cause demonstrates the impossibility of the existence of such a right.

3. All members should have as much information as possible on every question on which they are to vote. When a member requests the reading of a paper for information and not for delay, the presiding officer should direct it to be read, but if any member objects, the presiding officer must put the question of reading to a vote.

4. If a member was absent from the chamber when the paper under consideration was read, even though absent on duty, that member cannot insist on its being read again, as the convenience of a body is of more importance than that of a single member.

5. Without the permission of the body, a member does not have the right to lay a book or paper on the table and have it read on suggesting that it contains matter infringing on the privileges of the body.

6. A member has no right to read, or have the clerk read, from any paper or book, or to use any electronic recording as a part of a speech, without the permission of the body. But this rule is never rigorously enforced except where there is an intentional or gross abuse of the time and patience of the body. It is customary, however, to allow members

Sec. 112, Par. 2: Jefferson, Sec. XXXII; Cushing, Sec. 156; Reed, Sec. 187.

Sec. 112, Par. 3: Jefferson, Sec. XXXII.

Sec. 112, Par. 4: Jefferson, Sec. XXXII.

Sec. 112, Par. 5: Jefferson, Sec. XXXII; Cushing, Sec. 157.

to read printed extracts as parts of their speeches, as long as they do not abuse the privilege.

7. Members do not even have the right to read their own written speeches, without permission of the body. This also is to prevent the abuse of time, and therefore should not be refused except where the privilege is abused. Members are entitled to speak from notes.

Sec. 113. Consideration by Paragraph

1. The natural order in considering and amending any legislative document is to begin at the beginning and proceed through it by sections or paragraphs.

2. When recurrences are permitted, they should be permitted only after the legislative document has been considered to the end, unless some good reason appears, when recurrences may be permitted by unanimous consent.

3. To this natural order of beginning at the beginning, there is a single exception found in parliamentary usage. When a bill is taken up in committee, or on the final reading, the consideration of the title is postponed until the other parts of the bill are finished. The reason for this is that on consideration of the body of the bill, alterations may be made which will also require the alteration of the title.

Sec. 112, Par. 6: Jefferson, Sec. XXXII; Cushing, Secs. 157–159; Reed, Sec. 187.

Sec. 112, Par. 7: Jefferson, Sec. XXXII; Cushing's Legislative Assemblies, Secs. 1553–1555.

Sec. 113, Par. 1: Jefferson, Sec. XXVI; Cushing, Secs. 95, 191.

Sec. 113, Par. 2: Reed, Sec. 130.

Sec. 113, Par. 3: Jefferson, Sec. XXVI; Cushing, Sec. 192; Reed, Sec. 130.

4. Should the presiding officer fail to take up the proposition by paragraph, any member may move that the proposition be considered by paragraph, or seriatim.

5. The usual method of procedure in acting upon a complicated report or a bill or resolution is as follows:

(a) Members submit the report of a committee, or a resolution or other proposal. They read the report or present the proposal or resolution, and move its adoption. Should they neglect to move its adoption, the presiding officer may call for such a motion, or may assume the motion and state the question accordingly.

(b) The member who submitted the report, or the secretary or clerk as the presiding officer directs, then reads the first paragraph, which is explained by the reporting member after which the presiding officer should ask, "Are there any amendments?" or "What is the pleasure of the house?" The paragraph is then open to discussion and amendment.

(c) When there are no amendments or no further amendments are proposed to the paragraph, the presiding officer then directs that the next paragraph be read. In a similar manner, each paragraph is read in succession and may be debated and amended, but is not adopted.

(d) After all the paragraphs have been considered, the report or bill or resolution is open to amendment as a whole, when additional paragraphs may be inserted and any paragraph may be further amended.

(e) When the report or measure is found satisfactory, or has been amended to the satisfaction of the house, the title or preamble, if any, is considered and may be amended, and then a single vote is taken on the adoption of the entire measure, report or resolution.

Sec. 114. Asking Questions of Members

Procedure on Asking Questions

1. If members desire to ask a question of other members, they may do so through the presiding officer, but it is discourteous and a strict violation of parliamentary rules to ask questions directly of a member. Unless some good reason exists, they should wait until the member has concluded speaking, but may interrupt with the consent of the member.

2. The procedure on asking questions is for the member to rise, and without waiting to be recognized, say, "Mr. or Madam President (or Mr. or Madam Speaker or Mr. or Madam Chairperson), I wish to ask the Senator (Representative, gentleman, lady or otherwise designating the member speaking) a question." The presiding officer then asks if the member will yield to a question. The member may consent or decline, replying through the presiding officer. If the member speaking consents, the member desiring to ask the question may then state the question and the member speaking may reply. If the first reply does not fully answer the question, it is the practice to permit a limited number of further questions to be asked.

Sec. 113, Par. 5: Cushing, Secs. 193, 194; Reed, Secs. 129, 130.

Sec. 114, Par. 1: Cushing's Legislative Assemblies, Sec. 1572; Sturgis, pp. 95, 96; Hughes, Sec. 700.

Sec. 114, Par. 2: Sturgis, p. 96.

3. In computing the time allowed for argument, the time consumed in asking questions must be considered. And if a member consents to the question, the time consumed by the interruption is taken out of any time allowed that member.

Limitations on Questions

4. Questions addressed to members may relate only to a question before the body.

5. A question should not be permitted which reflects upon the character or conduct of any member or upon the executive or other official. A question as to what course a member proposes to follow is not in order.

6. The purpose of a question is to obtain information and not to supply it to the body. A question may not contain statements of fact unless they be necessary to make the question intelligible and can be authenticated. Neither should a question contain arguments.

Questions Are Not Debate

7. Merely asking a question or making a suggestion is not debate. A member is entitled to inquire concerning the meaning or purpose or effect of an undebatable motion.

Sec. 114, Par. 3: Hughes, Sec. 431.

Sec. 114, Par. 4: Hughes, Sec. 706; Sturgis, p. 95.

Sec. 114, Par. 5: Hughes, Secs. 706, 707.

Sec. 114, Par. 6: Cushing's Legislative Assemblies, Sec. 1573; Hughes, Sec. 707.

Sec. 114, Par. 7: Sturgis, p. 123.

CHAPTER 13

DECORUM IN DEBATE

Sec. 120. Equality of Members in Debate

See also Sec. 52, Equality of Members.

The rights and duties of members of a legislative body are derived from and founded upon the absolute equality of the members. Every member has the same right as any other member to present questions for the consideration of the house and has the same right to be heard. Members must not be permitted by their conduct to deny to others that which they may claim for themselves. It is the duty of all members to conduct themselves so as not to obstruct the like rights of other members. Freedom of speech involves obedience to all the rules of debate.

Sec. 121. Breaches of the Order of the House

See also Sec. 101, Debate is Limited to the Question Before the House.

1. An ancient rule governing debate is that "no one is to speak impertinently, or beside the question, superfluously, or tediously."

2. A member who resorts to persistent irrelevance or to persistent repetition after the attention of the house has been called to the matter may be

---

Sec. 120: Cushing's Legislative Assemblies, Sec. 373; Cushing, Sec. 36; Hughes, Sec. 686; Sturgis, p. 121.

Sec. 121, Par. 1: 2 Hatsell 166; Jefferson, Sec. XVII; N.Y. Manual, p. 457; Cushing's Legislative Assemblies, Secs. 1676–1700.

directed to discontinue the speech by the presiding officer.

3. During debate, while the presiding officer is speaking, or the house is engaged in voting, no one is to disturb another in a speech by hissing, coughing, spitting, speaking or whispering to another, nor passing between the presiding officer and the member speaking, nor crossing the floor of the house, nor walking up and down, nor taking books or papers from the desk, nor writing there.

4. If, at any time, the presiding officer rises to state a point of order, or give information, or otherwise speak within the presiding officer's privilege, the member speaking must sit down until the presiding officer has been heard.

5. The reading in the house of any letter from a person not a member or any other communication calling in question acts of members or officials of the house or being abusive is out of order and should not be permitted.

Sec. 122. Procedure Under Call to Order

1. If repeated calls do not produce order, the presiding officer may call any member by name, who obstinately persists in irregularity.

Sec. 121, Par. 2: Jefferson, Sec. XVII, quoting Scob. 31, 32; 2 Hatsell 166, 168; Sturgis, p. 125; Hughes, Sec. 734.

Sec. 121, Par. 3: 2 Hatsell 171; Jefferson, Sec. XVII; Cushing, Secs. 37, 211; Reed, Sec. 212; U.S. House Rule XIV, Par. 7.

Sec. 121, Par. 4: Cushing, Sec. 207; Hughes, Sec. 724.

Sec. 121, Par. 5: Hughes, Sec. 708.

Sec. 122, Par. 1: Jefferson, Sec. XXIV; Cushing, Secs. 40, 225; Reed, Sec. 221.

2. When called to order by the presiding officer, the member must sit down until the question of order is decided. The member may not proceed without the body's permission. The presiding officer may state the offense committed, and the member may then be heard in explanation or justification, and may be required to withdraw while the body considers whether it will take any action against the member.

3. Although in control of debate on a question of order, the presiding officer may put to a vote the question of whether a member called to order during a debate should be allowed to proceed. A member who has been called to order in debate and decided out of order loses the floor and another may be recognized. When called to order for irrelevancy, a member may proceed in order unless the question was brought to a vote and the debate found irrelevant.

Sec. 123. Use of Disorderly Words in Debate

1. No person may use indecent language with reference to the body or its members.

2. When disorderly words are used by a member in debate, notice should immediately be taken of them by the member objecting, and if desiring the words to be taken down, the objecting member should repeat them exactly as that member believes them to have been spoken. If of the opinion that the words are disorderly, the presiding officer should

Sec. 122, Par. 2: Jefferson, Sec. XXIV; Reed, Sec. 223; Hughes, Sec. 690; Cushing, Secs. 40, 41, 228–232; Tilson, p. 47.

Sec. 122, Par. 3: Hughes, Sec. 693; Cushing, Sec. 214.

Sec. 123, Par. 1: Jefferson, Sec. XXXIII.

direct that the clerk take them down. If of the opinion that the words are not disorderly, the presiding officer may delay the order to the clerk to take down the words unless there is a demand by other members, when the presiding officer should order the clerk to take them down as stated by the objecting member, or a member may insist on the determination of the question by the house by putting the question in the form of a motion.

3. When words are taken down, they are then a part of the minutes, and when read to the offending member, that person may deny those words. When there is a dispute as to the words, before the question of disorderliness is voted upon, the presiding officer should first put the question: "Are the words written down the words spoken by the member?"

4. The question of whether the words are disorderly is then submitted to the body. If the body is satisfied that the words are not disorderly, no further proceeding is necessary. If the words are found disorderly, the member using them should be permitted to explain and apologize to the body, but if the member refuses to apologize, the presiding officer may censure the member or the body may choose to act in the case.

5. If the remarks of the member are decided to be improper, that member may not proceed if any one objects without the permission of the body ex-

Sec. 123, Par. 2: Jefferson, Sec. XXXV; Hughes, Sec. 709; Cushing, Secs. 227–232; Reed, Secs. 222, 223; Sturgis, p. 125.

Sec. 123, Par. 3: Jefferson, Sec. XXXV; Cushing, Sec. 229.

Sec. 123, Par. 4: Jefferson, Sec. XXXV; Hughes, Sec. 709; Cushing, Secs. 229, 230.

pressed by a vote, upon which question no debate is allowed.

6. When a member has been called to order for disorderly words, it is usual for a motion to be made to permit the member to explain and if the explanation is satisfactory, it is in order and customary for a motion to be made and carried that the member be allowed to "proceed in order." The motion should always be that the member be permitted to "proceed in order," and not merely to "proceed."

7. The procedure here given is the established formal procedure for dealing with instances of disorderly conduct or disorderly words.

8. Improper conduct of a member can be referred to a committee for investigation and report or for action and the notoriety which comes from discussion on the floor avoided.

9. When another member has spoken or any other business has taken place since the member spoke, it is too late to take notice of any disorderly words used for the purpose of censure.

Sec. 124. Personalities Not Permitted in Debate

See also Sec. 110, Addressing Members or Presiding Officer.

1. In debate a member must confine remarks to the question before the house, and avoid personalities.

Sec. 123, Par. 5: Cushing, Sec. 230; Sturgis, p. 125.
Sec. 123, Par. 6: Hughes, Secs. 720, 721; Reed, Sec. 223.
Sec. 123, Par. 8: Jefferson, Sec. XXXV; Cushing, Sec. 232.
Sec. 124, Par. 1: Sturgis, p. 125; Tilson, p. 44.

2. A member in referring to another member should avoid using the member's name, rather identifying that member by district, seat, as the member who last spoke or by describing the member in some other manner.

3. It is not the person but the measure that is the subject of debate, and it is not allowable to arraign the motives of a member, but the nature or consequences of a measure may be condemned in strong terms.

Sec. 125. Personal Disputes Between Members

1. Whenever there has been a dispute or an assault between members, the body may require the members to settle their differences and agree not to prosecute the disagreement further. The members may be put under restraint if they refuse to settle their differences or until they do.

2. In a dispute between members, of which the body takes official notice, both parties to the dispute should retire after being heard while the body decides what action, if any, it will take concerning the matter. It is not, however, necessary for a member objecting to disorderly words to retire unless that member is personally involved. Disorderly words to the presiding officer, or in respect to the official acts of an officer, do not involve the officer so as to require that person to retire.

Sec. 124, Par. 2: Jefferson, Sec. XVII; Cushing, Sec. 206.
Sec. 124, Par. 3: Sturgis, p. 125; Hughes, Sec. 705.
Sec. 125, Par. 1: Jefferson, Sec. XVII.
Sec. 125, Par. 2: Jefferson, Sec. XVII.

Sec. 126. Complaints Against the Presiding Officer

1. The presiding officer is subject to the same rules regarding disorderly words as members.

2. Complaint of the conduct of the presiding officer should be presented directly for action by the house, in which case the presiding officer should vacate the chair and call a member to preside until the matter is settled.

3. A question concerning conduct of the presiding officer should not be presented by way of debate on other matters. Allusions to, or critical reference to the presiding officer, are not in order. Such attacks are not conducive to the good order of the house.

Sec. 126, Par. 1: Hughes, Sec. 709.
Sec. 126, Par. 2: Hughes, Sec. 692.
Sec. 126, Par. 3: Hughes, Sec. 692.

CHAPTER 14

CLOSING DEBATE

Sec. 130. Bringing Question to Vote

See also Sec. 523, Putting the Question to Vote.

1. When the debate appears to be closed, the presiding officer should inquire, "Are you ready for the question?" If, after a reasonable pause, no one rises to claim the floor, the presiding officer may assume that no member wishes to speak, and put the question to vote.

2. Debate is not closed by the presiding officer stating the question, for until both the affirmative and negative are put, a member can rise and claim the floor and reopen the debate or make a motion, provided the member rises with reasonable promptness after the presiding officer asks, "Are you ready for the question?"

3. When the question is debatable, and no one rises to claim the floor after the question is stated by the presiding officer, the presiding officer should inquire, "Are you ready for the question?" After a moment's pause, if no one rises, the presiding officer should put the question to vote. When the question is debated or motions are made, the presiding officer should wait until the debate has apparently ceased, and should again inquire, "Are you ready for the question?" Having given ample time for any one to

---

Sec. 130, Par. 1: Sturgis, p. 127; Cushing's Legislative Assemblies, Sec. 1610.

Sec. 130, Par. 2: Cushing's Legislative Assemblies, Sec. 1610; Sturgis, p. 127.

rise and claim the floor, and no one having done so, the presiding officer should put the question to vote.

4. Should the privilege of reopening a question be abused by members not responding promptly to the inquiry, the presiding officer should act as in other cases of dilatory tactics or any other attempt to obstruct business and should protect the body from annoyance.

Sec. 131. Cutting Off Debate

1. A majority of the members may close the debate without allowing all the time desired by others. They can do so by ordering either the previous question or the closing of the debate at a certain time, or they can limit the length of the speeches and allow each member to speak only once on each question. Rules have been adopted by some legislative bodies requiring a two-thirds vote to limit or close debate but unless such a special rule has been adopted a majority vote only is required in legislative bodies.

See also Ch. 34, Secs. 345–352, The Previous Question, and Ch. 35, Secs. 355–361, Motions Closing, Limiting or Extending Limits on Debate.

2. By a majority vote, the body may lay the question on the table and thus temporarily suspend the debate. Debate can be resumed by taking the question from the table by a majority vote when no question is before the body at a time when business of that class, or unfinished business or new business is in order.

See also Ch. 33, Secs. 330–342, Motion to Lay on the Table, and Sec. 492, Motion to Take from the Table.

Sec. 131, Par. 1: Sturgis, pp. 64–66.
Sec. 131, Par. 2: Sturgis, pp. 70–72.

3. By unanimous consent, a body may limit the time for debate on any question.

4. When debate is limited and a member has spoken the allotted time, the presiding officer should call the member to order and notify that person of the expiration of the allotted time.

5. When debate has been limited, the time may also be extended by unanimous consent. And when unanimous consent to continue is not asked by another member, the member speaking may properly do so.

Sec. 132. Preventing Debate by Putting Questions to Vote Prematurely

1. The right of members to debate and make motions cannot be cut off by the presiding officer putting a question to vote so rapidly as to prevent a member securing the floor after the presiding officer has inquired if the body is ready for the question.

2. When a member arises and addresses the presiding officer with reasonable promptness after the inquiry, "Are you ready for the question?", the member is entitled to the floor. If the presiding officer gives ample opportunity for members to claim the floor before putting the question to vote, they cannot claim the right of debate after the question is put to vote.

Sec. 131, Par. 3: Hughes, Sec. 697.
Sec. 131, Par. 4: Hughes, Sec. 738.
Sec. 131, Par. 5: Hughes, Secs. 703, 704.
Sec. 132, Par. 1: Reed, Sec. 220.
Sec. 132, Par. 2: Cushing's Legislative Assemblies, Sec. 1616; Reed, Sec. 220.

Sec. 133. Debate Is Closed by Putting Question to Vote

After a question has been put and voting has commenced, it is too late to claim the floor for debate. In voting by roll call, the negative being put at the same time as the affirmative, and the vote on both sides beginning and proceeding together, it is too late, after one member has answered the roll call, to renew the debate.

Sec. 133: Jefferson, Sec. XLI; Cushing, Sec. 247; Reed, Sec. 220; Sturgis, p. 127.

PART III. RULES GOVERNING MOTIONS

Chapter **Page**

*

PART III

RULES GOVERNING MOTIONS

CHAPTER 15

PROPOSALS FOR ACTION

Sec. 140. Must Be a Definite Proposal for Consideration

See also Sec. 100, There Must Be a Question Before the House to Permit Debate.

1. Every question presented to a legislative or administrative body for its determination must be submitted as a definite proposition. Until such a proposal is submitted, there is nothing before the body upon which it can take any action.

2. A proposition is submitted in the form it is desired that the action be taken or question resolved. A motion states the order or decision it is proposed that the body make, and a bill states the law in the form that is desired if the law be enacted.

Sec. 141. The Moving Element in Proposals

See also Sec. 711, Motions Relating to Business Under Regular Order.

A motion is itself a proposal to act. The other forms of proposals embody the proposal but lack the moving element. Thus, a member presents a committee report and moves that it be approved, or presents a resolution and moves that it be adopted.

Sec. 140, Par. 1: Sturgis, p. 10.

Even a bill is presented with an actual or implied motion that it be passed.

Sec. 142. Form of Proposals

1. It is requisite that all proposals be in such form that they can be acted upon by approval or rejection.

2. Ordinarily any body can prescribe the form in which proposals are submitted. When no form is prescribed, language clearly signifying the intent is sufficient.

3. Constitutional or governing statutory provisions concerning form must be complied with.

4. State constitutions usually require that the subject be stated in the title of bills and prescribe the form of the enacting clause.

5. Titles of legislative proposals are frequently regulated by statute and constitutional provisions, particularly as to requiring the subject to be accurately expressed in the title and frequently providing that any subject not expressed in the title is unconstitutional or void.

6. Constitutional and statutory provisions also often make other general requirements with reference to the form of a legislative proposal, and may specify among other things that the bill shall be in the English language and how the proposal shall be divided into sections.

Sec. 143. How Questions May Come Before Body

1. Questions may come before a legislative body in any of several different ways.

2. The more usual ways in which proposals may come before a body are as follows:

(a) Motions.

(b) Resolutions, memorials or bills.

(c) Committee reports.

(d) Communications or petitions.

(e) Points of order and appeals.

(f) Requests or demands.

Sec. 144. Motions as Presenting Questions

1. A motion is a proposal submitted to a deliberative body that certain action be taken or determination made.

2. A motion is usually presented orally but if particularly long or involved, the presiding officer may require that it be presented to the secretary or clerk in writing in order that it may appear accurately on the record. Long and complicated motions should be submitted in writing.

3. The essential element of a motion consists of the proposal actually made and not of the precise words used.

4. In stating a question, the presiding officer is not bound by the exact words used by the person making the motion but the presiding officer has no right or authority to modify the purpose or effect of the motion without the consent of the person making the motion.

Sec. 144, Par. 1: Sturgis, p. 11.

Sec. 144, Par. 2: Waples, Sec. 1; Sturgis, p. 11.

Sec. 144, Par. 3: Sturgis, p. 13.

5. Motions are interpreted according to what is actually decided in the light of the situation rather than according to the particular words used. Thus, if a member moves to recess until the following day, the motion is to be understood as a motion to adjourn and may be stated by the presiding officer in that form.

Sec. 145. Resolutions, Memorials and Orders

1. A resolution is a form of written proposal. It may be recognized by the use of the word "resolved" in its acting or declaratory clause.

2. Resolutions are used for making declarations, stating policies, and making decisions where some other form is not required. For example, a statute cannot be enacted by a joint resolution or a concurrent resolution, though an amendment to a constitution may, in most states, be proposed by such a resolution.

3. A memorial is a written proposal sometimes used for an expression of sentiment of the legislature.

4. For particular types of resolutions such as concurrent resolutions or joint resolutions, a particular form of resolving clause is required. Where no particular form is specified, the word "resolved" is sufficient.

5. Frequently in a resolution introductory clauses are used, introduced by the word "whereas" and stating the reason or purpose of the resolution. Such clauses are not a part of the resolution technically, but are introductory clauses only, and are not essential to the use or validity of the resolution.

6. Orders are a form of written proposal used in some legislatures. The language giving effect to the proposal is the word "order" and from this word orders take their name. Orders are used in the same manner as resolutions for making determinations or laying down policies or directing actions. They are, in general, subject to the same rules as are resolutions.

7. Generally, a resolution does not prescribe a continuing rule of conduct for government or business.

Sec. 146. Bills

1. Bills are used for making statutory enactments. The term "bill" is ordinarily used for legislation enacted by state legislatures or Congress. The constitutions of practically all the states make provisions concerning the form and procedure regarding bills.

2. Since bills are the means of enacting legislation, they are often subject to rather complete control and restriction, and procedure concerning them is often specified in some detail by authority beyond the control of the body itself to change. Particularly, it is common to have extensive provisions as to titles and to procedural requirements such as three readings on separate days.

3. Bills or resolutions are not subject to change in statement by the presiding officer, nor can they be altered in any way except by amendment by the body itself.

Sec. 145, Par. 7: Dunlap v. Williamson (Okla. 1962), 369 P.2d 631.

4. The enacting clause is the very essence of any bill introduced into the legislature. A motion to strike out the enacting clause is a method used in some legislatures to kill bills.

5. What constitutes related matters which can be submitted to the vote of the people in one constitutional amendment is for the legislature to determine in the first instance.

6. An assembly may ratify any action which it had the power to authorize in advance and the ratification dates back to the action which was ratified.

Sec. 147. Committee Reports on Presenting Questions

See also Ch. 62, Secs. 663–678, Committee Reports.

1. Questions for determination are frequently presented to legislative bodies by reports of their committees.

2. Committee reports most often contain recommendations on legislation referred to the committee. Sometimes, in making studies referred to them, committees make recommendations or proposals which originate within the committee. These latter matters come before the body for its determination by the presentation of the committee report.

3. Any committee making recommendations on a question other than a written proposal referred to it

---

Sec. 146, Par. 4: Vaughn & Ragsdale Co. v. State Board of Equalization (1939), 109 Mont. 52, 96 P.2d 420.

Sec. 146, Par. 5: Keenan v. Price (1948), 68 Idaho 423, 195 P.2d 662.

Sec. 146, Par. 6: Harker v. McKissock (1950), 10 N.J. Super. 26, 76 A.2d 89, *cert. granted,* 6 N.J. 148, 78 A.2d 163, *modified,* 7 N.J. 323, 81 A.2d 480, *denied,* 8 N.J. 230, 84 A.2d 723.

should submit a formal proposal to the body. This proposal should be either in the form of a motion, resolution, or perhaps a bill upon which the body can properly determine the questions presented rather than attempt to secure a determination of the question by the adoption or the rejection of the committee report alone.

Sec. 148. Communications and Petitions

1. There are many instances where a question is presented to a legislative body by communications or petitions. The communications may come from the executive, judicial, local government officials or others. The right of petition is usually guaranteed in the constitution and presents a means by which questions can be presented to a legislative body.

2. If required, any decision on a communication or petition which would have more than a temporary effect should be made by the adoption of the resolution or other formal proposal embodying the determination or decision.

3. Communications and petitions may be disposed of by a deliberative body by reference to a committee for study and recommendation or by printing in its journal for the information of the members. Certain communications such as veto messages follow a prescribed course.

Sec. 149. Appeals, Points of Order, Inquiries

See also Ch. 23, Secs. 230–235, Appeals; Ch. 24, Secs. 240–246, Points of Order; and Ch. 25, Secs. 250–254, Parliamentary Inquiries and Other Requests for Information.

1. In conducting its business, a legislative body may have questions relating to policy or procedure

presented to it for decision on appeals from decisions on points of order. Appeals may involve important questions of policy and, therefore, appeals may take on all of the characteristics of a main motion and are subject, in general, to the same rules.

2. Points of order are presented to the presiding officer for determination. The decision of the presiding officer on points of order may always be questioned by the body on appeal and the question decided by the body itself.

3. A parliamentary inquiry may be directed to the presiding officer or an inquiry may be made from one member to another. While these may involve questions of concern to the members, they rarely present any question to be determined by the body.

Sec. 150. Scope of Terms, "Motions" and "Questions"

The terms "motion" and "question" are used in a broad sense to include all kinds or forms of propositions presented for action to a legislative body. In this sense, they include resolutions, bills, points of order, appeals, objection to consideration and all like proposals. Motions and questions are used in this sense when referring to main motions or privileged motions, or to the precedence of motions.

Sec. 149, Par. 1: Sturgis, p. 84.
Sec. 149, Par. 2: Sturgis, pp. 92, 93.

CHAPTER 16

PRESENTATION OF MOTIONS

See also Sec. 726, Introduction of Legislation.

Sec. 155. Time and Manner of Presenting Motions

1. One of the fundamental rights of a member is the right to present any proper proposal for the consideration of the body. Generally any member who has been recognized by the presiding officer may present a motion or other proposal to the body. A member secures recognition for the purpose of making a proposal in the same manner and subject to the same rules as when securing recognition to debate a question.

2. A proposal for consideration must be proposed at an appropriate time. A motion may ordinarily be presented at any time when the motion could be acted upon. A proposal may not be presented when business having higher precedence is under consideration.

3. Legislative bodies sometimes adopt special rules with reference to the presentation of bills. When there is no special provision, members may present their proposals at the desk, to the secretary or clerk, or from the floor in the appropriate order of business.

Sec. 156. Acceptance of Motion

1. It is the duty of the presiding officer to accept or to entertain any proper motion whenever it is in

order. A motion is in order when it is presented at an appropriate time, violates no rule and is not clearly dilatory.

2. A motion is entertained by the presiding officer by accepting it and stating it.

3. A motion is not in the possession of the body nor available for consideration until it has been stated by the presiding officer. When a proper motion has been made, the presiding officer should state it or if it is in writing, should order it read by the secretary or clerk, and it is then in the possession of the body. If it is debatable, the motion is then open to debate and is subject to such subsidiary or other motions as may be applicable to it.

4. When the motion appears to the presiding officer not to be in correct form or contrary to the rules or practice of the body, the presiding officer may state that fact and may suggest the proper form of the proposal to the author. When it is possible to state the motion in proper form, the presiding officer may do so rather than in the form and the language of the proposer. In a case where there could be any question as to whether the presiding officer is inaccurately stating the proposal, the presiding officer should inquire of the proposer whether the statement is correct before finally entertaining

Sec. 156, Par. 1: Sturgis, pp. 11, 12.

Sec. 156, Par. 2: Cushing's Legislative Assemblies, Sec. 1231; Hughes, Sec. 192; Sturgis, pp. 12, 13.

Sec. 156, Par. 3: Hughes, Secs. 181, 187, 192; N.Y. Manual, p. 450; Reed, Sec. 108; Cushing, Sec. 56; Tilson, p. 52; U.S. House Rule XVI, Par. 2, 82nd Congress.

Sec. 156, Par. 4: Sturgis, p. 14; Cushing's Legislative Assemblies, Sec. 1283; Reed, Sec. 103; Tilson, p. 51; U.S. House Rule XVI, Par. 1, 82nd Congress.

and proceeding with the motion.

5. If the presiding officer states a motion inaccurately, the language of the member making the motion controls in determining the meaning of the motion.

6. Whenever the presiding officer questions the form of a motion or the author on hearing the motion stated desires to correct it, the author may do so. It is also proper for other members to question the form of a resolution on introduction and to suggest corrections or improvements in the motion. These, the author may accept or reject. It is much simpler to have a motion stated correctly originally than to amend it after debate or after other motions have been applied to it.

7. After a motion has been finally stated, debate has begun or any subsidiary motions have been made with reference to the motion, it is too late to be corrected at the will of the author and it may be corrected only by amendments adopted by the body.

8. When a motion is made which is not in order but which is not otherwise objectionable, the presiding officer may submit the matter to the body in such form as "Is there objection to entertaining the motion?" If no one objects, unanimous consent has been secured to the consideration of the motion, and later objection may not be raised.

Sec. 156, Par. 5: Shoults v. Alderson (1922), 55 Cal. App. 527, 203 P. 209.
Sec. 156, Par. 6: Sturgis, pp. 13, 14.
Sec. 156, Par. 7: Sturgis, p. 14.
Sec. 156, Par. 8: Hughes, Sec. 485.

9. The house should be protected against dilatory or frivolous motions by the presiding officer's refusing to entertain such motions, or in case of doubt, submitting a question of whether motions are dilatory for decision by the body.

Sec. 157. Seconds to Motions

1. Parliamentary practice in American governmental bodies does not require seconds to motions, and in Parliament itself, where the practice of seconding motions originated, they have not been required for more than a century.

2. The old rule was that when a motion was made it was not to be debated or put to vote until it was seconded.

3. A second to a motion is not out of order, but its effect is only to disclose the fact that one or more other members may favor the motion made or proposal submitted. Unless the rules require, seconds may be ignored and the presiding officer may not refuse to put a question because it is not seconded.

4. Whenever a member submits a motion which is in order, the motion should be stated by the presiding officer without waiting for a second.

5. There would seem to be good cause for dropping the use of seconds to motions because of their lack of utility, convenience or necessity. Tilson says, "It would seem that nothing could be more

---

Sec. 156, Par. 9: Hughes, Sec. 218.

Sec. 157, Par. 1: Cushing's Legislative Assemblies, Secs. 1224, 1231; Hughes, Secs. 209, 210; Reed, Sec. 105; Tilson, p. 52.

Sec. 157, Par. 2: Cushing's Legislative Assemblies, Secs. 224–227.

Sec. 157, Par. 3: Hughes, Sec. 216; Tilson, p. 52.

Sec. 157, Par. 4: Hughes, Sec. 217; Tilson, p. 52.

nearly useless and unnecessary than for some unidentified voice from the midst of the assembly to boom out, I second it."

6. An even stronger reason for abandoning seconds is that they are not in accord with the present-day view of the rights and dignity of the individual. It is contrary to the theory of equality among the members. Parliamentary action is based on majority rule where each member should have one vote of equal weight. All members should have equal, individual, independent rights to propose to the assembly what they think it should consider.

7. A motion should not be suppressed because it is not seconded; neither should one be put to vote hastily without opportunity for debate.

8. It is still the practice in some legislative committees, based usually on adopted rules or adopted authority, to require seconds to motions.

Sec. 158. Only Motions Having Higher Precedence May Be Received During Consideration of a Question

1. It is a rule that a question before a legislative body must be disposed of before other business of the same class or rank of precedence can be considered. When a motion is under consideration, motions of a higher precedence are in order, but motions having a lower precedence are not. A main question, and the subsidiary and other questions

Sec. 157, Par. 5: Tilson's Manual, Sec. 95.

Sec. 157, Par. 6: Tilson's Manual, Sec. 98.

Sec. 157, Par. 7: Shattuck, Harriet R., The Woman's Manual of Parliamentary Law, Lee and Shepard Publishers (1896), Secs. 31, 35.

arising out of it, must be disposed of before another main question may be taken up for consideration.

2. The rules of some legislative bodies limit the motions which may be received when a question is under debate. These rules usually list all subsidiary motions and certain privileged motions as being admissible. The privileged motions usually listed are the motions to adjourn, to recess, a call of the house and sometimes the motion to reconsider. When a question is under debate, the presiding officer may refuse to entertain any motions except those specifically authorized, although from the nature of the situation it is doubted if these rules can always be strictly enforced.

Sec. 159. Main Question May Be Considered Only Once at a Session

See also Ch. 41, Secs. 450–474, Motion to Reconsider.

1. It was an ancient rule that when a bill was once passed or rejected, another of the same substance could not be brought in again during the same session.

2. The difficulties resulting from the application of this rule became so serious that the right to reconsider any main motion became established.

3. A rule of one house relating to further consideration of a question which was defeated has reference to a measure once acted upon by that house and does not prevent the consideration of the same

---

Sec. 158, Par. 1: Cushing's Legislative Assemblies, Secs. 1291–1296, 1441, 1442.

Sec. 158, Par. 2: Reed, Secs. 264, 265.

Sec. 159, Par. 1: 2 Hatsell 125; Jefferson, Sec. XLIII; Cushing, Sec. 250.

Sec. 159, Par. 2: Cushing, Secs. 254, 255.

subject matter when embodied in a bill or resolution coming from the other house.

4. A bill having precisely the same title and subject as one previously rejected by the house may be refused introduction.

5. When a decision has already been made on any question, the equivalent question, whether in the affirmative or negative, is not in order. Questions are equivalent when the negative of one amounts to the affirmative of the other and leaves no other alternative.

6. Indefinite postponement suppresses the subject during the session in the same manner as the rejection of the proposition.

Sec. 160. Procedural Motions May Be Renewed

See also Sec. 67, Renewal of Motions, and Sec. 209, Renewal of Motion to Adjourn.

1. Procedural motions such as motions to adjourn, to recess, to lay on the table, the previous question and motions to limit debate may be made again and again, provided there has been progress in debate or business so that the actual question presented is different and the members might reasonably decide the question differently.

Sec. 159, Par. 3: Leser v. Board of Registry (1921), 139 Md. 46, 114 A. 840; Leser v. Garnett (1922), 258 U.S. 130, 42 S. Ct. 217, 66 L. Ed. 505.

Sec. 159, Par. 4: N.Y. Manual, p. 419.

Sec. 159, Par. 5: Jefferson, Sec. XLVI; Hughes, Sec. 524; Cushing, Sec. 251.

Sec. 159, Par. 6: Hughes, Sec. 325; N.Y. Manual, p. 447.

Sec. 160, Par. 1: Hill v. Goodwin (1876), 56 N.H. 441; Reed, Sec. 106; Sturgis, p. 32.

2. If no objection is made to the renewal of a motion without intervening business, objection to the repetition of the motion will be deemed waived.

3. The motion to take from the table or a call for the orders of the day may be renewed after the business is disposed of that was taken up when such motion to take from the table or call for the orders of the day was lost. It is not a renewal when a subject which has been referred to a committee is reported back on the same legislative day or a subject that has been laid on the table is taken up on the same legislative day.

4. Minutes may be corrected regardless of the time elapsed and of the fact that the correction has been previously proposed and lost.

See also Sec. 700, Authority to Correct Journal.

5. It is the duty of the presiding officer to prevent the privilege of renewal from being used to obstruct business, and when it is evident that it is being so misused, should protect the house by refusing to recognize any motion which is clearly so used.

6. When the rules require that certain motions may not be renewed unless there has been intervening business, the intervening business constitutes motions and proceedings which can properly be entered in the journal, and unless such intervening business takes place, the motion may not be renewed.

Sec. 160, Par. 2: Hill v. Goodwin (1876), 56 N.H. 441.
Sec. 160, Par. 3: Sturgis, pp. 45, 46.
Sec. 160, Par. 4: Sturgis, pp. 118, 199.
Sec. 160, Par. 5: Sturgis, p. 32.
Sec. 160, Par. 6: Hughes, Secs. 146, 220; Sturgis, pp. 32, 40.

See also Sec. 67, Renewal of Motions.

7. Motions that have been presented and rejected, under certain circumstances, may be proposed again under the theory that a proposal made under one set of circumstances is not the same as the proposal made under a different set of circumstances. Generally it is held that the intervention of other business will justify the renewal of a privileged, incidental or subsidiary motion which is procedural and not substantive in effect. Debate is considered as intervening business as it may change attitudes and present new reasons for the desired action. The mere passage of time may result in a changed situation which justifies the renewal of a motion.

8. A main motion that has been defeated cannot be renewed but can be reconsidered. This includes all proposals that deal with substantive matters. An amendment to a main motion cannot be renewed because it changes the provisions of a main motion and a motion to postpone indefinitely cannot be renewed because it disposes of a main question. Questions of privilege generally relate to matters of substance and so cannot be renewed.

Sec. 161. Main Motions May Not Be Renewed

See also Ch. 41, Secs. 450–474, Motion to Reconsider.

1. Main motions or other substantive proposals, such as amendments to main motions which may be reconsidered may not be renewed. When an original main motion or an amendment to one has been

Sec. 160, Par. 7: Neely's Parliamentary Practice, The Abingdon Press (1914), pp. 124, 125; Eliot, Basic Rules of Order, Harcourt, Brace and Company (1952), Sec. 50.

Sec. 160, Par. 8: Demeter, p. 172.

adopted or rejected, or a main motion has been postponed indefinitely or an objection to its consideration has been sustained, neither it, nor substantially the same motion, can be again brought before the house at the same session, except by a motion to reconsider the vote.

2. The following motions, unless they have been withdrawn, may not be renewed on the same legislative day:

(a) To adopt or postpone indefinitely an original main motion.

(b) To adopt an amendment identical with one refused adoption.

(c) To strike out an amendment previously adopted.

(d) To divide a question.

(e) To reconsider, unless the question to be reconsidered was amended materially since previously reconsidered.

(f) To object to the consideration of a question.

The motion to suspend the rules for the same purpose is not in order on the same legislative day, although it may be renewed on another.

3. A point of order cannot be raised if an identical one has been raised previously, without success, during the same session, and after the presiding officer has been sustained in a ruling, the presiding officer need not entertain another appeal from a

---

Sec. 161, Par. 1: Sturgis, pp. 39, 40; N.Y. Manual, p. 464; Neely's Parliamentary Practice, The Abingdon Press (1914), pp. 124, 125; Eliot, Basic Rules of Order, Harcourt, Brace and Company (1952), Sec. 50.

Sec. 161, Par. 2: Sturgis, pp. 32–34.

decision on precisely the same question during the same session.

4. Main motions which deal with substantive matters as distinguished from procedural motions or motions which relate to procedural matters only and which are usually of short duration can be reconsidered but cannot be renewed.

Sec. 162. Demands by Members

Demands by Proportion of Membership

1. There are only a few situations in parliamentary practice where the demand of more than one person is required to place a matter before the body. There are constitutional provisions in several states requiring that a certain number of persons or proportion of a quorum may demand a roll call vote on any question and have the vote recorded in the journal.

2. Rules, in certain cases, require a demand by more than a single member to place the previous question before the body for its consideration.

Demands by a Single Member

3. The only instance where a member has a right to insist on anything is where that member calls for

---

Sec. 161, Par. 3: Hughes, Sec. 538.

Sec. 161, Par. 4: Demeter, p. 172.

Sec. 162, Par. 1: Hughes, Sec. 215; State Constitutions: Ala. IV, 55; Alaska II, 14; Ariz. IV, Part II, 10; Ark. V, 12; Cal. IV, 7(b); Colo. V, 13; Conn. III, 14; Del. II, 10; Fla. III, 4; Ga. III, Sec. V, 6; Idaho III, 13; Ill. IV, 8; Ind. IV, 12; Iowa III, 10; Ky. 40; La. III, 15(g); Me. IV, Part III, 5; Md. III, 22; Mich. IV, 18; Minn. IV, 15; Miss. IV, 55; Mo. IV, 26; Neb. III, 11; Nev. IV, 14; N.H. II, 24; N.J. IV, Sec. IV, 4; N.M. IV, 12; N.C. II, 19; N.Dak. IV, 13; Ohio II, 9; Okla. V, 30; Ore. IV, 13; Pa. II, 12; R.I. IV, 8; S.C. III, 22; S.Dak. III, 13; Tenn. II, 21; Tex. III, 12; Utah VI, 14; Vt. II, 9; Va. IV, 8; Wash. II, 21; W.Va. VI, 41; Wis. IV, 20; Wyo. III, 13.

the enforcement of the rules or for the execution of an existing order of the body. Any member has a right to insist that the presiding officer maintain order and enforce the rules or perform any other duty without debate or delay.

Calls for Action by Members from Their Seats

4. A call for adjournment, or for the question, by members from their seats, is not a motion. No regular motion can be made without rising and addressing the presiding officer. Such calls are themselves breaches of order, which a member who has risen to speak may regard as an expression of impatience of the house against further debate, but the member may proceed if choosing to do so.

5. There are certain demands which may be made or points which may be raised while a member has the floor. These demands and points are listed under Section 92, Interruption of a Member Who Is Speaking.

Sec. 163. Submission of Double Motions

1. It is not generally good practice to permit a member to submit more than one motion at a time and it may not be done without unanimous consent. There are three recognized exceptions to this rule:

(a) A member may offer a motion or resolution and move that it be set as a special order.

(b) A member may move to reconsider a measure and an amendment to the measure when desir-

---

Sec. 162, Par. 3: Jefferson, Sec. XVIII; Sturgis, p. 74.

Sec. 162, Par. 4: Jefferson, Sec. XX; Sturgis, p. 69.

Sec. 163: Cushing's Legislative Assemblies, Sec. 1284; Hughes, Secs. 196, 197; Cushing, Sec. 199.

ing to reconsider the amendment after the measure has been passed.

(c) A member may move that the rules be suspended and the action for which the rules are suspended be permitted.

In some bodies certain pairs of motions are permitted, as to move to reconsider and to lay that motion on the table.

2. A motion to suspend the rules often includes a series of actions such as to suspend the rules and reconsider a vote, or to suspend the rules and amend a resolution. Two coordinate motions of this type are treated as one motion. This is a particularly frequent occurrence in Congress.

Sec. 164. Consideration of Motions at a Future Time

A member may make a motion and then request that the motion be set as a special order for a particular time. Such a motion should be printed in the journal with the record of the special order and should likewise be carried on the calendar as a special order.

Sec. 165. Motions Not Always Required for Routine Business

1. When items of routine business, as bills on calendar, are presented in the regular order of business they may be understood to be presented with an implied motion to approve. The presiding officer may proceed as though the usual motion has been made, unless there is objection. If objection is

---

Sec. 164: Hughes, Sec. 227; Sturgis, pp. 62–64.

made, the presiding officer must wait for the appropriate motion.

2. A similar procedure is frequently provided by rule with reference to motions to reconsider.

See also Ch. 41, Secs. 450–474, Motion to Reconsider.

3. When a member desires to bring forward a question for consideration at some future date, it is the practice in Parliament and in Congress for the member to give notice of the intention to make a motion at the future time rather than to make the motion and have it set as a special order.

Sec. 165, Par. 1: Hughes, Secs. 134, 676.

CHAPTER 17

CLASSIFICATION OF MOTIONS

Sec. 175. Classification of Motions Generally

See also Sec. 158, Only Motions Having Higher Precedence May Be Received During Consideration of a Question.

1. The questions presented to and considered by a deliberative body may, for convenience in consideration, be divided into four classes as follows:

(a) Privileged questions.

(b) Incidental questions.

(c) Subsidiary questions.

(d) Main questions.

Motions stating the questions are divided into the same four classes.

2. *Privileged Motions:* During the deliberation, a recess or adjournment is sometimes necessary, or the measure may be made a special order, or a call of the house may be ordered or other privileged questions may arise.

3. *Incidental Motions:* The consideration of bills also brings before the house points of order, questions on precedence of measures, objections to consideration and other incidental motions which do not adhere directly to the main question, but which must be decided before the main question can be considered. These are incidental motions.

Sec. 175: Cushing's Legislative Assemblies, Secs. 1530–1609; Sturgis, pp. 15–20.

4. *Subsidiary Motions:* In the course of consideration of these questions, they are usually referred to committees, are often amended, and may be postponed, laid on the table or have other subsidiary motions applied to them.

5. *Main Motions:* Legislative bodies meet for the purpose of passing laws or of considering legislative proposals. The consideration and decision of main questions constitute the principal purpose of these bodies. These are main motions.

6. Different authors have classified motions in different ways, some carrying the classification much further than others. There are many ways that the motions could be classified as an aid in understanding and remembering the motions and their characteristics and rules. The classification used in this manual follows the one most usually adopted. It is based on precedence. The precedence of the classes of motions is as follows:

(a) Privileged motions.

(b) Incidental motions.

(c) Subsidiary motions.

(d) Main motions.

Sec. 176. Privileged Questions

Definition

1. Privileged questions are those questions which, by established practice or by rule, have been given a special privileged status. These questions relate generally to the house itself, or to its members or to

Sec. 176: Sturgis, pp. 21–24.

important matters which it has been found necessary to give a highly privileged status.

Precedence

2. Privileged questions, as a class, take precedence over the other classes of questions and have the following order of precedence among themselves:

(a) Call of the house when there is not a quorum present.

(b) To make, or give notice of, a motion to reconsider. (Reconsideration is incidental main motion.)

(c) To adjourn (when unqualified or when no provision has been made for next meeting).

(d) To recess.

(e) To raise a question of privilege. (A call of the house when a quorum is present is a question of privilege of the house.)

Not Subject to Debate

3. Privileged motions are not themselves subject to debate, but a question of privilege, being a main question, privileged only as to precedence, is, when taken up, subject to debate and to the subsidiary motions the same as other main questions.

Not Usually Subject to Subsidiary Motions

4. The privileged motions may not have any subsidiary motions applied to them, except that the motion to adjourn when no other provision for the next meeting has been made may be amended as to the time and the motion to recess may be amended as to duration. Questions of privilege are subject to all of the subsidiary motions.

See also Sec. 187, List of Motions.

Sec. 177. Incidental Questions

See also Sec. 184, Precedence of Incidental Motions.

Definition

1. Incidental questions are questions of a general procedural nature which arise out of the work of the body. They are questions affecting the business of the body which do not relate directly to nor adhere to any one main question. These questions relate usually to what may be considered and to the manner in which it is to be considered. They relate to the general business of the body in the same manner that subsidiary questions relate to the main questions to which they apply.

Precedence

2. In not adhering directly to any particular main question, incidental questions have a greater independence of the main question than have subsidiary questions. They require determination before main motions and the group of motions relating directly to the disposition of main motions and so take precedence over main and subsidiary motions.

See also Sec. 184, Precedence of Incidental Motions.

Priority

3. Incidental questions yield to privileged questions. These incidental motions, since they require immediate decision, rarely present any problem of precedence. They must always be decided before the questions out of which they arise. Should they arise out of the same question, the more common

---

Sec. 177: Sturgis, pp. 16, 17, 30, 31.

incidental motions take precedence among themselves as follows:

(a) Appeals.

(b) Points of order.

(c) Parliamentary inquiries or like requests for information.

(d) Orders of the day.

(e) Requests or motions to withdraw a motion or question which is under consideration.

(f) Suspension of the rules for some immediate purpose.

(g) Objection to the consideration of a question.

(h) Manner or order of considering questions.

(i) Motions relating to voting.

(j) Motions relating to nominations or elections.

(k) Motions relating to division of a question.

Debate

4. Incidental motions, except an appeal, are not debatable. It is sometimes provided by rule that an appeal cannot be debated when it relates to indecorum, transgression of the rules of speaking or to the order of business. Appeals are debatable in all cases unless prevented by rule.

Application of Subsidiary Motions

5. An appeal may have the subsidiary motions applied to it, but no other subsidiary motion, except the motion to amend, may be applied to incidental questions. Some incidental motions are not capable of presenting alternative propositions, and therefore, are not subject to amendment. The following incidental motions may, however, be amended:

(a) Motions relating to the manner or order of considering questions.

(b) Motions concerning voting.

(c) Motions concerning nominations or elections.

Sec. 178. Subsidiary Questions

See also Sec. 187, List of Motions.

Definition

1. Subsidiary questions are questions of a procedural nature relating directly to or adhering to main motions.

2. It is not usually possible for main motions to be immediately adopted or rejected upon presentation. In legislative bodies it is usually required that main motions be referred to committee and they may be amended. Debate may be limited to a certain time, or the consideration postponed from time to time. Procedural motions, by which main motions are guided through a legislative body, are a type of motion subsidiary to main motions and from this they acquire their name.

3. Subsidiary motions are most often applied to main motions, but the motion to amend may be applied to any motion which is capable of being stated in more than one form.

Precedence

4. Subsidiary motions, as a class, yield to privileged and incidental motions and take precedence over main motions. But a subsidiary motion may sometimes be applied to a privileged, incidental or

another subsidiary motion and it always takes precedence over the motion to which it is applied.

5. In their application to main motions, the more usual subsidiary motions take precedence among themselves as follows:

(a) To lay on the table (postpone temporarily).

(b) The previous question (vote immediately).

(c) To limit or extend limits of debate.

(d) To postpone definitely, or to a certain time.

(e) To refer or commit.

(f) To amend.

(g) To postpone indefinitely.

When any one of the motions listed above is pending, every motion above it in the table is in order, and every motion below it is out of order.

Application of Subsidiary Motions

6. Subsidiary motions may be applied to any main motion and, when duly made, must be considered and decided before the main question can be acted upon. The motion to amend may be applied to certain subsidiary and incidental motions, as well as to main motions. The previous question and motions relating to the limits of debate may, naturally, be applied to any debatable question regardless of its privilege. But the other subsidiary motions may not be applied to motions of these classes.

Sec. 178, Par. 4: Demeter, p. 64; Sturgis, pp. 22, 23, 25.
Sec. 178, Par. 5: Sturgis, pp. 16, 19, 30, 31; Demeter, p. 47.
Sec. 178, Par. 6: Sturgis, pp. 28, 29, 30, 31.

Amendment

7. Subsidiary motions, except the motion to lay on the table, the previous question and the motion to postpone indefinitely, may be amended.

Debate

8. The motions to lay on the table, the previous question and motions affecting the limits of debate are not debatable. Motions to postpone definitely and to commit are debatable as to the propriety of postponement or reference to committee. Motions to amend are debatable. The motion to postpone indefinitely, since its effect is to defeat the measure, opens the main question to debate.

Vote

9. Subsidiary motions require a majority vote. It has been stated by some writers that the motions limiting debate require a two-thirds vote for their adoption, but the practice in legislative bodies is to require only a majority vote to order the previous question or otherwise to restrict or limit debate.

See also Sec. 350, Vote on the Previous Question.

Sec. 179. Main Questions

1. All general questions of a substantive nature are main questions. The main question is usually stated as follows: to pass, to adopt, to approve, to ratify, to confirm, to concur, to appoint, to elect or to take other like action. The main question may sometimes be stated in such form as to reject, to

---

Sec. 178, Par. 7: Sturgis, pp. 27, 30, 31.
Sec. 178, Par. 8: Sturgis, pp. 26, 30, 31.
Sec. 178, Par. 9: Sturgis, pp. 28, 30, 31.

rescind, to repeal, to annul, to remove, to refuse to concur or in some other form disposing of some substantive proposition.

2. Main questions or main motions before a legislative body usually relate to the final disposition of bills or certain resolutions which, upon approval, become law and are usually found in the statutes of the session; while subsidiary, incidental and privileged motions are temporary in their purpose and their effect is exhausted in the process of legislation.

3. There is a group of questions which relates to procedure and still ranks in precedence with main motions. These questions relate to procedural questions not requiring immediate determination and not relating to any particular questions over which they take precedence. These motions are referred to as incidental main motions to distinguish them from substantive propositions of the same rank. Examples of incidental main motions are the motion to take from the table and the motion to fix a different time to adjourn when a regular time is fixed.

See also Sec. 187, List of Motions.

Sec. 180. Dilatory Motions

1. Any regular parliamentary motion, when improperly used for the purpose of delaying or obstructing business, is a dilatory motion. For the convenience of legislative bodies, it is necessary to allow some highly privileged motions to be renewed again and again after progress in debate or the transaction of business. If there were no provision for protecting the body, a minority could be constantly raising questions of order, appealing from every decision of the presiding officer, calling for a

division on every viva voce vote even when it was nearly unanimous, moving to lay motions on the table, moving to adjourn and offering frivolous and absurd amendments. By taking advantage of parliamentary tactics in this manner, they could practically stop business.

2. Every legislative body has the inherent right to protect itself from dilatory motions. Whenever satisfied that a member is using parliamentary tactics to obstruct business, the presiding officer should not recognize the member, but should rule that person out of order. After having been sustained upon an appeal, the presiding officer need not entertain another appeal from the same member while it is evident that the member is trying to obstruct business.

Sec. 181. There Are an Unlimited Number of Motions

1. Many of the motions have taken on a very definite form and may not be regarded as correct in any other form. In the above list of motions where they are listed by classes only, such as motions relating to the manner or order of consideration of questions, motions relating to voting and motions relating to nominations and elections, the possible variety of particular proposals that might be made for these purposes is much too extensive to attempt to list.

2. Even though the actual statement of a motion may vary rather widely, most motions can be classi-

Sec. 180, Par. 1: Hughes, Secs. 240, 241.
Sec. 180, Par. 2: Hughes, Secs. 240, 241; Tilson, p. 75.

fied according to purpose so that they fall definitely in the regular order of precedence.

Sec. 182. Use of Classification of Motions

1. There is no definite indisputable classification of motions. Classification is merely a device used as a convenient means of grouping motions according to some particular purpose. The more used classification, and the one used here, is based primarily upon the precedence of motions. Motions for a particular purpose have the same or a similar precedence.

2. Different authors at different times have used distinctly different systems of classification depending on the particular purpose sought to be accomplished. By using the classification according to precedence, the motions can be arranged within each class and the classes placed in such an order that the order of precedence remains reasonably consistent.

Sec. 183. Precedence with Reference to Main Motions

See also Sec. 187, List of Motions.

1. Most tables of precedence for motions are arranged with reference to the precedence of main motions. For example, when a main motion is under consideration, a motion to amend is in order; likewise, a motion to refer to a committee or a motion to lay on the table. While these motions are pending, a motion to suspend the rules for some immediate purpose is in order. After all of these

---

Sec. 182: Sturgis, pp. 15–20.

motions have been made, a point of order might be made and an appeal from the decision of the presiding officer might be taken. Without disposing of any of these matters, a motion to adjourn would still be in order. Here is an abbreviated table of precedence built upon the main motion.

2. There is another fundamental rule which should always be kept in mind. It is that a motion takes precedence when it relates to the subject under discussion at the time. For example, if a motion to adjourn is under consideration, which has the highest order of precedence in any ordinary circumstance, and an irregularity occurs, a point of order with reference to the motion to adjourn is in order and the decision of the presiding officer on the point of order can still be appealed. While a question of privilege has a much higher precedence than, for example, the motion to lay on the table, still it is in order to move to lay a question of privilege on the table. Much confusion will be avoided if it is always kept in mind that the ordinary lists of precedence are based only on their relationship to the main motion.

Sec. 184. Precedence of Incidental Motions

See also Sec. 187, List of Motions.

It is sometimes said that incidental motions as a group have no precedence among themselves, but as a group take precedence over subsidiary motions and yield to privileged motions. This statement is substantially accurate in practice, and the rule is a practical rule for ordinary purposes. When more

---

Sec. 183, Par. 1: Sturgis, pp. 30, 31.

than one incidental motion comes up at a given time, a convenient, practical rule which will rarely, if ever, result in unfairness is to decide each question in the order in which it may arise. However, due to the more complex procedure of legislative bodies, there may be important decisions in which different results would be obtained if this rule were applied instead of giving a definite order of precedence to incidental motions.

Sec. 185. Motions Change Precedence According to Use

When one motion is applied to another motion, the precedence is determined by the precedence of the motion to which the other motion is applied. For example, in most lists of precedence of motions the motion to amend is near the bottom above the main motion and the motion to postpone indefinitely, but when the motion to amend is applied to the motion to recess it takes precedence over the motion to recess and is near the top of the list of precedence of motions.

CHAPTER 18

LIST OF MOTIONS

Sec. 187. List of Motions

The following is a list of the more common questions or motions, arranged according to the usual classification, in the order of their precedence in relation to main motions, with citations to the sections of this manual relating to them.

Privileged Motions

1. Call of the house.

See also Ch. 19, Secs. 190–197, Call of the House.

2. To make, or to give notice of, a motion to reconsider (usual precedence established by rule).

See also Ch. 41, Secs. 450–474, Motion to Reconsider.

3. To adjourn.

See also Ch. 20, Secs. 200–210, Motion to Adjourn.

4. To recess.

See also Ch. 21, Secs. 214–216, Motion to Recess.

5. Questions of privilege.

(a) Privilege of the house

(1) Presence of members. (When a quorum is present, a call ranks as a question of privilege.)

(2) Organization of the house.

(3) Comfort of the members.

(4) Freedom from disturbance.

Sec. 187: Sturgis, p. 15.

(5) Disorderly conduct of members.

(6) Conduct of officers or employees.

(7) Conduct of reporters or the press or the accuracy of published reports.

(8) Accuracy of the journal and records of the house.

(b) Personal privilege

Questions relating to the reputation or conduct of members in their representative capacity.

See also Ch. 22, Secs. 220–226, Questions of Privilege.

Incidental Motions

6. Appeals.

See also Ch. 23, Secs. 230–235, Appeals.

7. Points of order.

See also Ch. 24, Secs. 240–246, Points of Order.

8. Parliamentary inquiry and like requests for information.

See also Ch. 25, Secs. 250–254, Parliamentary Inquiries and Other Requests for Information.

9. Orders of the day.

See also Ch. 26, Secs. 257–271, Orders of the Day and Calendar.

10. Requests or motions for leave to withdraw a motion or question which is under consideration.

See also Ch. 27, Secs. 272–276, Withdrawal of Motions.

11. Suspension of rules for some immediate purpose.

See also Ch. 28, Secs. 279–286, Suspension of the Rules.

12. Objection to consideration of a question.

See also Ch. 29, Secs. 293–300, Objection to the Consideration of Questions.

13. Manner or order of consideration of questions.

See also Ch. 30, Secs. 302–304, Order and Manner of Considering Questions.

14. Motions relating to voting.

See also Ch. 31, Secs. 306–308, Voting, Nominations and Elections.

15. Motions relating to nominations and elections.

See also Ch. 31, Secs. 306–308, Voting, Nominations and Elections.

16. Motions relating to division of a question.

See also Ch. 32, Secs. 310–316, Division of Questions.

Subsidiary Motions

17. To lay on the table (postpone temporarily).

See also Ch. 33, Secs. 330–342, Motion to Lay on the Table.

18. The previous question (vote immediately).

See also Ch. 34, Secs. 345–352, The Previous Question.

19. Close, limit or extend limits of debate.

See also Ch. 35, Secs. 355–361, Motions Closing, Limiting or Extending Limits on Debate.

20. Postpone definitely or to a certain time.

See also Ch. 36, Secs. 365–374, Motion to Postpone to a Certain Time or Definitely.

21. To refer or commit.

See also Ch. 37, Secs. 378–391, Motion to Refer or Commit.

22. To amend.

See also Ch. 38, Secs. 395–421, Motion to Amend.

23. To postpone indefinitely.

See also Ch. 39, Secs. 430–436, Motion to Postpone Indefinitely.

Main Motions

24. The main motion.

The main question presents a bill, resolution or other substantive proposition, for the passage, adoption, approval or rejection. The question is usually stated or assumed in the positive form as the final passage of a bill, the adoption of a resolution or the approval of an appointment, but the question can be put in the negative form as to reject.

See also Ch. 40, Secs. 440–445, The Main Motion.

Incidental Main Motions

The following motions, though they have procedural elements, have the principal characteristics of main motions and take precedence in the same order. These motions are usually called incidental or specific main motions to distinguish them from substantive propositions with which they rank in precedence. Any main motion or question is in order during the appropriate order of business when nothing is before the house. These motions take the same rank. No one is in order when another is before the house, and any one is in order in the proper order of business when no business is before the house.

25. To consider motion to reconsider.

See also Ch. 41, Secs. 450–474, Motion to Reconsider.

26. To rescind.

See also Ch. 42, Secs. 480–483, Motion to Rescind.

27. To dissolve or adjourn sine die when no hour has previously been fixed.

See also Sec. 781, Adjournment of Legislative Sessions.

28. To fix the time for final adjournment or adjournment sine die.

29. To fix a different time to which to adjourn when a regular time is fixed.

30. To fix the time at which or to which to recess.

31. To withdraw a bill from committee or discharge the committee.

See also Sec. 491, Withdrawing Bills from Committee.

32. To take from the table.

See also Sec. 492, Motion to Take from the Table.

33. To take from desk.

See also Sec. 493, Motion to Take from Desk.

34. To lay aside or pass on calendar.

See also Sec. 494, Motion to Pass on Calendar or File, Informally Pass or Temporarily Pass.

35. Motion to change the order of consideration of questions not then under consideration.

36. To withdraw papers not under consideration.

37. To suspend the rules with reference to business not immediately pending.

38. To close debate in committee of the whole.

39. To expunge.

See also Sec. 444, Motion to Expunge.

40. To consider petitions when no other provision for consideration of petitions is made by rules.

PART IV. RULES GOVERNING PARTICULAR MOTIONS

DIVISION 4. MAIN MOTIONS

PART IV

RULES GOVERNING PARTICULAR MOTIONS

DIVISION 1

PRIVILEGED MOTIONS

CHAPTER 19

CALL OF THE HOUSE

Sec. 190. Right to Compel Attendance of Members

See also Ch. 44, Secs. 500–506, Quorum.

1. The purpose of a call of the house is to compel the attendance of absent members.

2. The right of a house of a state legislature to compel the presence of absent members is usually guaranteed by a constitutional provision, even to ordering the arrest of members.

Sec. 190, Par. 1: Cushing's Legislative Assemblies, Sec. 264.

Sec. 190, Par. 2: Hughes, Sec. 666; Cushing's Legislative Assemblies, Secs. 256–259; State Constitutions: Ala. IV, 52; Alaska II, 12; Ariz. IV, Part II, 9; Ark. V, 11; Cal. IV, 7(a); Colo. V, 11; Conn. III, 12; Del. II, 8; Fla. III, 4; Ga. III, Sec. IV, 3; Hawaii III, 13; Idaho III, 10; Ind. IV, 11; Iowa III, 8; Kan. II, 8; Ky. 37; La. III, 10(A); Me. IV, Part III, 3; Md. III, 20; Mass. Amend. XXXIII; Mich. IV, 14; Minn. IV, 13; Miss. IV, 54; Mo. IV, 20; Mont. V, 20(2); Nev. IV, 13; N.H. II, 19, 36; N.J. IV, Sec. IV, 2; N.M. IV, 7; N.C. II, 2; N.Dak. IV, 12; Ohio II, 6; Okla. V, 30; Ore. IV, 12; Pa. II, 10; R.I. IV, 6; S.C. III, 11; S.Dak. III, 9; Tenn. II, 11; Tex. III, 10; Utah VI, 11; Vt. II, 14, 19; Va. IV, 8; Wash. II, 8; W.Va. VI, 24; Wis. IV, 7; Wyo. III, 11.

3. A legislature has power to punish, or even expel, members who fail, without sufficient cause, to attend when ordered by the house.

4. The absence of the power of a legislative body to compel the attendance of all members at all times would destroy its ability to function as a legislative body.

5. In Congress it has been held that a call is in order under the Constitution in the absence of any rule providing for a call of the house.

Sec. 191. Right of Less Than a Quorum to Compel Attendance

See also Sec. 208, Adjournment by Less Than a Quorum, and Sec. 506, Less Than Quorum Can Adjourn.

Until a legislature is organized it has no authority, unless granted by the constitution, to compel the attendance of absent members; but it can adjourn from day to day until a quorum can be secured and the body is organized. After organization a quorum has the unquestionable right to compel the attendance of other members, and less than a quorum is usually given that right by constitutional provision, the constitution or rules usually stating the minimum number who can exercise the right.

Sec. 192. Precedence of Call of the House

See also Sec. 187, List of Motions.

Sec. 190, Par. 3: Cushing's Legislative Assemblies, Secs. 264, 434; see also U.S. Constitution, Art. I, Sec. 5, Par. 1, Note 55 in House Manual.

Sec. 190, Par. 4: U.S. Constitution, Art. I, Sec. 5, Par. 1, Note 55 in House Manual.

Sec. 190, Par. 5: Hughes, Sec. 655.

Sec. 191: Cushing's Legislative Assemblies, Secs. 255–259, 264, 268.

1. When a quorum is not present, a call of the house takes precedence over all other motions.

2. When a quorum is present, a call of the house ranks as a question of privilege.

3. The reading of the journal is not in order in the absence of a quorum. In such a case a call may be moved before the reading of the journal.

Sec. 193. Who May Order a Call of the House

1. When a quorum is not present, a call is, in effect, demanded. Any member may raise the question of no quorum, and if a quorum is not present, the house must either order a call or adjourn.

2. When a quorum is present, a call may be ordered by a majority of the members present whenever any member is absent, provided the minimum number authorized to order a call is present.

See also citation to Sec. 190, paragraph 2.

3. It is provided in the state constitutions of many of the states that a certain number of the members of a house of the legislature may demand a call. Similar provisions will also usually be found in the rules.

Sec. 194. Motion or Demand for Call of the House

1. Rules sometimes prohibit the making of a call after the commencement of a vote if a quorum is

---

Sec. 192, Par. 1: Cushing's Legislative Assemblies, Sec. 437.
Sec. 192, Par. 3: Cushing's Legislative Assemblies, Secs. 269, 438.
Sec. 193, Par. 1: Hughes, Secs. 666, 671.
Sec. 193, Par. 2: Hughes, Sec. 658.
Sec. 193, Par. 3: Cushing's Legislative Assemblies, Secs. 255–259.

present. Unless some special rule prevents, a call is in order at any time.

2. A motion or demand for a call of the house is in order in any order of business but may not be permitted to interrupt a roll call unless authorized by the rules. Raising a question of no quorum, when a quorum is not present, compels the house to act on that question. The house may either order a call or adjourn.

3. When one call is in effect, another call is not in order, unless by a special provision of the rules.

4. When a quorum is present and a motion or demand for a call is lost, it cannot be renewed until after intervening business or a change in the parliamentary situation.

5. A motion or demand for a call is not debatable or amendable and may not be laid on the table, postponed, referred to committee or have other subsidiary motions applied to it.

6. The usual form of the motion is: "I move a call of the senate (or house)." The question of the presence of a quorum can be raised by raising a point of order that there is not a quorum present or by raising the question as: "Mr. or Madam President/Mr. or Madam Speaker: Is there a quorum

---

Sec. 194, Par. 1: Hughes, Sec. 655; N.Y. Manual (1948–49), p. 493.

Sec. 194, Par. 2: Cushing's Legislative Assemblies, Secs. 436–439; N.Y. Manual (1948–49), p. 416; Hughes, Secs. 666, 671.

Sec. 194, Par. 3: Cushing's Legislative Assemblies, Sec. 438.

Sec. 194, Par. 4: Cushing's Legislative Assemblies, Secs. 269, 438; N.Y. Manual (1948–49), p. 416.

Sec. 194, Par. 5: N.Y. Manual (1948–49), p. 417; Cushing's Legislative Assemblies, Sec. 270.

present?" or "Mr. or Madam Chairperson: I suggest the absence of a quorum."

Sec. 195. Bringing in Members Under a Call of the House

1. When a call of the house has been ordered, the doors are promptly closed, and the clerk calls the roll of members and notes the absentees. The list of the members not recorded as present may be verified by calling the names, and the list of the absentees is then given to the sergeant at arms with instructions to bring in the absent members. The original use of the call was to secure the attendance of members at the session and was accomplished by setting a particular day when the roll was to be called and when absent members would be sent for.

2. When members appear in the house during a call and present themselves to the presiding officer, the clerk is usually directed to record them as present and they are discharged. When a member is brought in by the sergeant at arms, that member may be required to pay any costs incidental to bringing the member in.

3. It is a common practice to permit members to enter and take their seats during a call and to take part in any business without being excused. The call may be removed when a count discloses that a quorum is present or that the members who were absent, and not excused, are present.

4. A call was not originally used to compel members to remain in attendance, but only to bring the

Sec. 195, Par. 1: Cushing's Legislative Assemblies, Secs. 264–266.
Sec. 195, Par. 2: Cushing's Legislative Assemblies, Sec. 265.

members into the chamber. In modern practice the doors may be kept locked under a call to keep the members in attendance during a session.

5. Members who have been granted leaves of absence should not be brought in by the sergeant at arms under a call. A leave of absence may be granted on the request of a member or upon the request of another member on behalf of the first. The body has the authority to revoke leaves of absence at any time and to require the members to attend.

Sec. 196. Proceedings During a Call of the House

1. After a call has been ordered, if a quorum is not present, no motion is in order except a motion to adjourn or to remove the call. If a quorum is present, the rules or the established practice may permit business to be conducted either generally or under certain limitations. The only necessary limitation is that another call cannot be ordered while one is in effect, unless specifically authorized by the rules.

2. A recess may not be taken, even by unanimous consent, during a call unless specifically authorized by the rules.

3. An adjournment puts an end to all proceedings under a call, except that if a quorum is present the house may, before adjournment, order members al-

Sec. 195, Par. 4: Cushing's Legislative Assemblies, Secs. 440–442.

Sec. 195, Par. 5: Cushing's Legislative Assemblies, Secs. 267, 435.

Sec. 196, Par. 1: Cushing's Legislative Assemblies, Secs. 438, 439; N.Y. Manual (1948–49), pp. 416, 417.

Sec. 196, Par. 2: Hughes, Sec. 449; N.Y. Manual (1948–49), p. 417.

ready brought into the house to make their excuse at a later meeting.

Sec. 197. Terminating a Call of the House

1. A call is terminated at any time by a vote to that effect or by the adoption of a motion to adjourn. The better procedure is not to admit the motion to adjourn during a call, but to require that the house first dispense with the call before the motion to adjourn is in order.

2. A motion to dispense with further proceedings under a call is necessarily in order at any time during the call. Proceedings under a call may be terminated at any time by a motion to that effect or by an adjournment. Proceedings under a call are from their very nature suppressed by an adjournment. The motion to dispense with further proceedings under a call requires a majority vote of the members present and voting for its adoption. The motion to dispense with further proceedings under the call or the motion to adjourn may be made by any member but, by courtesy, the member moving the call is usually permitted to make the motion to remove it.

3. If a quorum is present and the house desires to remove the call, the proper motion is "I move that further proceedings under the call be dispensed with." Upon the adoption of this motion, business is taken up in regular order at the point it was interrupted by the call.

Sec. 196, Par. 3: Cushing's Legislative Assemblies, Secs. 270, 439.
Sec. 197, Par. 1: Cushing's Legislative Assemblies, Sec. 439.
Sec. 197, Par. 2: Cushing's Legislative Assemblies, Secs. 270, 439.
Sec. 197, Par. 3: Hughes, Sec. 654.

CHAPTER 20

MOTION TO ADJOURN

See also Sec. 445, Motion to Adjourn Sine Die, and Sec. 781, Adjournment of Legislative Sessions.

Sec. 200. Precedence of Motion to Adjourn

See also Sec. 187, List of Motions.

1. A motion to adjourn, when it is unqualified, takes precedence over all other motions except a call when there is not a quorum present. Some bodies have by rule given higher precedence to other motions.

2. The motion to change the time to which to adjourn, to fix the time at which to adjourn, or the motion to adjourn when otherwise qualified loses its precedence as a privileged motion to adjourn. It becomes a main question, subject to debate and amendment, and to subsidiary motions.

Sec. 201. Adjournment When There Is No Provision for Future Meetings

When no provision has been made as to the time of reconvening, and the adoption of the motion to adjourn would have the effect of dissolving the body, the motion is in fact a motion to dissolve or to adjourn sine die, which is a main motion. It is subject to all of the rules applicable to main motions. In this situation, a motion to fix the time to

---

Sec. 200, Par. 1: Cushing's Legislative Assemblies, Secs. 1390–1392; Sturgis, p. 83; Hughes, Sec. 265; Reed, Sec. 168; Cushing, Sec. 137; Tilson, p. 57; 2 Hatsell 106; Robert's, p. 201.

Sec. 200, Par. 2: Sturgis, p. 80; Reed, Sec. 170; Tilson, p. 57.

which to adjourn takes precedence over the unqualified motion to adjourn, or the unqualified motion may be amended to fix a time of reconvening. This situation will rarely, if ever, arise in legislative bodies.

Sec. 202. When Motion to Adjourn Is in Order

1. A motion to adjourn is always in order, except:

(a) It may not interrupt a member who has the floor.

(b) It cannot be renewed when it has been defeated until after some business has intervened.

(c) It is not in order during the taking or verification of a vote.

(d) It is never in order for dilatory purposes.

2. A motion to adjourn may be made:

(a) After a roll call has been ordered and before the roll call has begun.

(b) After the previous question has been ordered but before voting has commenced.

3. The motion is not in order during committee of the whole. The motion to rise must first be carried before the motion to adjourn is in order.

Scc. 203. Adjournment When Time for Future Meetings Is Not Fixed

1. The houses of the state legislatures convene at the date fixed by the constitution and continue in

---

Sec. 201: Cushing's Legislative Assemblies, Sec. 254; Sturgis, p. 86; Robert's, p. 200.

Sec. 202, Par. 1: Jefferson, Secs. XIX, XXXIII; Sturgis, p. 80; Hughes, Sec. 267; N.Y. Manual, pp. 443, 444, 465, 466; Reed, Sec. 169; Cushing, Sec. 137a; Tilson, p. 57.

Sec. 202, Par. 3: Hughes, Sec. 267.

session until adjournment sine die. If such a house adjourns without fixing the hour of reconvening, it will reconvene on the next legislative day at the hour fixed in the rules, providing rules have been adopted which fix a regular hour for convening. When no time is fixed for reconvening, the houses reconvene on the next legislative day at the usual hour. If no hour has been established by custom, then the houses reconvene at the appropriate or usual hour for meetings of a similar nature. If no such hour can be ascertained then by ancient custom, they meet at noon.

2. The next legislative day is the next calendar day except when it falls on a day when the body does not ordinarily meet, such as Saturday, Sunday or a holiday. Meetings may be held on Saturdays, Sundays and holidays when specially ordered. The reading of a bill on a Sunday is not a nullity. The common law prohibits only judicial and not legislative acts on Sunday.

3. The sessions and hour of convening of legislative bodies are usually regulated by statutes or rules. There is usually also provision in the statutes or rules for calling special sessions.

Sec. 204. Right to Adjourn

1. Legislative bodies have the right to adjourn whenever they determine to do so. It is not neces-

---

Sec. 203, Par. 1: Cushing's Legislative Assemblies, Secs. 254, 368, 509–515, 1390–1393; Cushing, Sec. 139; Reed, Sec. 171; Tilson, p. 57.

Sec. 203, Par. 2: Cushing's Legislative Assemblies, Secs. 509–511; *Ex parte* Seward (1923), 299 Mo. 385, 253 S.W. 356, *error dismissed sub nom.*, Seward v. Brady (1924), 264 U.S. 599, 44 S. Ct. 335, 68 L. Ed. 869.

Sec. 203, Par. 3: Cushing's Legislative Assemblies, Secs. 254, 509.

sary that the work of a body be completed before it can adjourn.

2. The presiding officer cannot arbitrarily adjourn a meeting.

3. Neither the senate nor the house can constitutionally adjourn sine die without the consent of the other.

Sec. 205. Form of Motion to Adjourn

1. The usual form of the unqualified motion to adjourn is "I move that the senate (or house) do now adjourn."

2. When the rules authorize the body to fix the time of reconvening or fix a different time of reconvening, the motion may be in the following form, "I move that the senate (or house) do now adjourn until (stating the day and hour as) 10 o'clock tomorrow morning."

3. The rules in bodies having daily meetings usually provide that the body shall convene at a certain hour each day except Sunday, unless a different time is fixed by the body.

Sec. 206. Motion to Adjourn Is Not Debatable

While the unqualified motion to adjourn is not debatable it does not prevent a statement of the business requiring attention before adjournment. Be-

---

Sec. 204, Par. 2: Dingwell v. Detroit (1890), 82 Mich. 568, 46 N.W. 938; State of Oregon v. McKee (1890), 20 Ore. 120, 35 P. 292.

Sec. 204, Par. 3: In re Opinion of the Justices No. 115 (1950), 254 Ala. 179, 47 So. 2d 642.

Sec. 205, Par. 1: Sturgis, p. 79; Robert's, p. 207.

Sec. 205, Par. 2: Sturgis, p. 82; Robert's, p. 207.

Sec. 205, Par. 3: Reed, Sec. 281; Cushing, Secs. 137, 138.

fore putting the motion the presiding officer should be certain that no matters requiring attention that day have been overlooked. Any necessary announcements should be made before putting the motion to adjourn to a vote.

Sec. 207. Amendment to Motion to Adjourn

1. An unqualified motion to adjourn is not subject to any of the subsidiary motions, except when no time is fixed for the meeting, at which time the motion loses its privileged status. The motion is subject to any incidental motions which arise out of it such as a parliamentary inquiry, point of order or appeal. The motion can, of course, be withdrawn.

2. When the daily hour of meeting is fixed, the motion to adjourn may not be amended to specify that particular time, but when the hour of meeting is not fixed, or when fixed subject to the power of the house to change it, the motion to adjourn may be amended to state the time of reconvening.

3. The motion to adjourn to a certain time is subject to debate and to amendment as to the time.

4. As a matter of practice based upon convenience, it is not unusual in a motion to adjourn to state the time of reconvening although the hour may be definitely fixed by the law or rules. When this

Sec. 206: N.Y. Manual, p. 403; Reed, Secs. 170, 171; Cushing, Sec. 137b; Robert's, p. 198.

Sec. 207, Par. 1: Hughes, Sec. 264; Cushing's Legislative Assemblies, Sec. 1523; Sturgis, p. 83; Robert's, p. 202.

Sec. 207, Par. 2: Hughes, Sec. 267; Sturgis, p. 83.

Sec. 207, Par. 3: N.Y. Manual, p. 403; Sturgis, p. 83.

form of the motion is used simply as a matter of notice to the members, it may be treated as an unqualified motion to adjourn.

5. A motion to adjourn may not be reconsidered, but if lost, may be renewed after intervening business or a change in the parliamentary situation.

Sec. 208. Adjournment by Less Than a Quorum

See also Sec. 506, Less Than Quorum Can Adjourn.

It is a rule of parliamentary law applicable to all deliberative bodies that less than a quorum have the power to adjourn. In this respect the motion to adjourn differs from all other motions. It is, of course, necessary that a body finding itself without a quorum have a means of terminating its session. The constitutions of most of the states authorize the houses of the state legislatures to adjourn from day to day in the absence of a quorum, and statutes in the case of other legislative bodies frequently contain similar provisions. The right of less than a quorum to adjourn does not depend, however, on constitutional or statutory provisions, but exists in all cases by virtue of general parliamentary law and the necessity of the situation.

Sec. 207, Par. 4: Sturgis, p. 82.

Sec. 207, Par. 5: Reed, Sec. 204; Hughes, Sec. 268; Sturgis, p. 32.

Sec. 208: Reed, Secs. 20, 175; Hughes, Sec. 671; N.Y. Manual, p. 422; Cushing's Legislative Assemblies, Secs. 244, 254, 258, 1390, 1396; Choate v. North Fork Highway District (1924), 39 Idaho 483, 228 P. 885; Moore v. City Council of Perry (1903), 119 Iowa 423, 93 N.W. 510; Rolla v. Schuman (1915), 189 Mo. App. 252, 175 S.W. 241; Kimball v. Marshall (1863), 44 N.H. 465; O'Neil v. Tyler (1892), 3 N.D. 47, 53 N.W. 434; Smith v. Law (1860), 21 N.Y. 296; Duniway v. City of Portland (1905), 47 Ore. 103, 81 P. 945.

Sec. 209. Renewal of Motion to Adjourn

1. The motion to adjourn may be defeated simply to permit the completion of some business which is under consideration. The requirement of intervening business should not be as strictly construed in this case as in the case of other motions.

2. The motion to adjourn may be renewed after any business has been completed. That business might only be progress in debate, even though no question has been put in the meantime. Other examples might include:

(a) Calling of the roll.

(b) A decision of the presiding officer on a question of order.

(c) The receipt of a message from the other house.

(d) An announcement by a member.

These are sufficient to justify renewal of the motion to adjourn.

3. Where no objection is made to the renewal of a motion to adjourn without interposition of other intermediate questions as required by parliamentary rules, an objection to such successive motions to adjourn is deemed waived.

4. After a motion to adjourn has been voted down and a motion is immediately made to adjourn until a time certain, such motion is in order as being different from the motion previously voted down. This motion is not in violation of the parliamentary

Sec. 209, Par. 1: Sturgis, p. 32; Reed, Sec. 169.
Sec. 209, Par. 2: Sturgis, p. 32.
Sec. 209, Par. 3: Hill v. Goodwin (1876), 56 N.H. 441.

rule requiring intermediate business before a motion can be renewed.

5. The motion to adjourn is particularly subject to abuse and the presiding officer should refuse to entertain it when it appears to be made for obstructive purposes.

Sec. 210. Absence of Quorum Does Not Adjourn Body

See also Sec. 193, Who May Order a Call of the House; Sec. 208, Adjournment by Less Than a Quorum; and Sec. 506, Less Than Quorum Can Adjourn.

Where a roll call shows there is not a quorum present, it does not automatically adjourn the body. If a quorum is established prior to adjournment, the transaction of business can be continued.

Sec. 209, Par. 4: Hill v. Goodwin (1876), 56 N.H. 441.
Sec. 209, Par. 5: N.Y. Manual, p. 476.
Sec. 210: Pollard v. Gregg (1914), 77 N.H. 190, 90 A. 176.

CHAPTER 21

MOTION TO RECESS

Sec. 214. Distinction Between Adjournment and Recess

See also Ch. 20, Secs. 200–210, Motion to Adjourn.

1. The basic distinction between adjournment and a recess is that an adjournment terminates a meeting, while a recess is only an interruption or break in a meeting. After an adjournment a meeting begins with the procedure of opening a new meeting. After a recess the business or procedure of a meeting takes up at the point it was interrupted.

2. Breaks in the meetings of a day, as for meals, are usually recesses, but termination of meetings until a later day are adjournments.

Sec. 215. Precedence of Motion to Recess

See also Sec. 187, List of Motions.

The motion to recess takes precedence over all motions except a call of the house and the motion to adjourn.

Sec. 216. Rules Governing Motion to Recess

1. The motion to recess cannot be made while another has the floor, or during voting or the verification of a vote.

Sec. 214, Par. 1: Sturgis, p. 77; Hughes, Sec. 166; Robert's, p. 73.
Sec. 215: Sturgis, p. 83; Hughes, Sec. 448; Reed, Sec. 174; N.Y. Manual (1948–49), p. 379; Robert's, p. 197.
Sec. 216, Par. 1: Sturgis, p. 83.

2. A motion to recess may be unqualified or may be for a specified period as "for 10 minutes" or "until 1 o'clock." An unqualified motion to recess, when adopted and announced, places the house at recess until called to order by the presiding officer.

3. The motion to recess is not debatable. It is not subject to the subsidiary motions, except to amend, and may be amended only as to the length of the recess.

4. Adoption of motion to recess requires a majority of the legal votes cast.

5. A motion to recess unless otherwise specified takes effect immediately following adoption and the recess should be promptly announced by the presiding officer.

6. A motion to recess may be renewed subject to the same rules as the motion to adjourn.

See also Sec. 209, Renewal of Motion to Adjourn.

7. The motion to recess is not in order in the absence of a quorum. Either a call must be ordered or the body must adjourn.

8. A motion to recess is not in order during a call. The call must be terminated before a recess is in order.

Sec. 216, Par. 2: Reed, Sec. 174.
Sec. 216, Par. 3: Sturgis, p. 83; Hughes, Secs. 167, 449.
Sec. 216, Par. 4: Sturgis, p. 83; Hughes, Secs. 165, 167.
Sec. 216, Par. 5: Sturgis, p. 83; Hughes, Sec. 449.
Sec. 216, Par. 6: Sturgis, p. 83; Hughes, Sec. 166.
Sec. 216, Par. 7: Jefferson, Sec. L, and Note 586 in House Manual (1947); Hughes, Secs. 165, 166, 449.
Sec. 216, Par. 8: Hughes, Sec. 449.

9. A motion to recess when it relates to a recess at some future time takes precedence as a main motion and is subject to debate.

Sec. 216, Par. 9: Sturgis, p. 83; Hughes, Sec. 448; Reed, Sec. 174.

CHAPTER 22

QUESTIONS OF PRIVILEGE

Sec. 220. What Is a Question of Privilege

1. Questions which relate to the body or to its members in such a manner as to effect proper functioning of the body are questions of privilege. It is necessary that these questions be under the immediate control of the body. They relate to the rights and privileges of the body or to any of its members in their official capacity, or to the comfort and convenience of the body or its members in the performance of their official duties.

2. "Questions of privilege" should be distinguished from "privileged questions," which are a class of motions having the highest precedence.

3. Questions of privilege are of two types: They may relate to the privilege of the entire body, which are known as questions of "privilege of the house," and questions of privilege which relate to a member, which are known as questions of "personal privilege." In case of conflict, questions of privilege of the house take precedence over questions of personal privilege.

4. Some matters are so privileged that they put in abeyance whatever is under consideration and se-

---

Sec. 220, Par. 1: Sturgis, p. 74; Reed, Sec. 178; Robert's, pp. 191–193; Cushing, Secs. 136, 141.

Sec. 220, Par. 2: Cushing, Sec. 141.

Sec. 220, Par. 3: Sturgis, p. 75; Hughes, Sec. 546; Reed, Sec. 178; Cushing, Sec. 141; U.S. Constitution, Art. I, Secs. 5 and 9, and notes in House Manual (1947).

cure immediate attention. But no main motion is so highly privileged as to supplant all other business if it could abide its time for presentation when there would be nothing else pending.

Sec. 221. Privilege of the House

Some of the questions which are recognized as questions of privilege of the house are as follows:

(a) Questions concerning organization of the house.

(b) Questions concerning expelling or censuring a member or the member's capacity to serve.

(c) Call of the house when a quorum is present.

(d) Comfort of the members.

(e) Freedom from disturbance.

(f) Disorderly conduct of members.

(g) Conduct of officers or employees or the removal or censure of officers or employees.

(h) Conduct of reporters or the press or the accuracy of published reports.

(i) The journal and records of the house.

Sec. 222. Questions of Personal Privilege

1. Questions affecting the rights, reputation and conduct of members of the body in their representative capacity are questions of personal privilege.

2. Questions of privilege of members must relate to persons as members of the body or relate to

Sec. 220, Par. 4: Waples, Sec. 141.

Sec. 221: N.Y. Manual, p. 469; Sturgis, p. 75.

Sec. 222, Par. 1: Hughes, Secs. 548, 556; Reed, Sec. 178; U.S. House Rule IX; Sturgis, pp. 75, 76.

charges against their character which would, if true, incapacitate them for membership. They are not entitled to the floor on a question of personal privilege unless the subject which they propose to present relates to them in their representative capacity.

3. Persons raising questions of personal privilege must confine themselves to the remarks which concern themselves personally. When speaking under a personal privilege, members have no right to defend any persons other than themselves.

Sec. 223. Questions Not Constituting Personal Privilege

1. A charge in the public newspaper against a member is not a question of personal privilege as long as the charge, if true, would not incapacitate that person from membership.

2. A newspaper article merely criticizing a member's acts in a house does not constitute a question of personal privilege. Neither does a newspaper article charging a person with disreputable conduct before that person became a member, nor a like criticism of a member personally and not in that person's capacity as a member.

3. The fact that the presiding officer may have refused to grant recognition to a member would not constitute a question of personal privilege.

Sec. 222, Par. 2: Hughes, Secs. 556, 563, 567, 648; Sturgis, pp. 74, 75.
Sec. 222, Par. 3: Hughes, Secs. 556, 563, 567, 648; Sturgis, p. 75.
Sec. 223, Par. 1: Hughes, Sec. 560.
Sec. 223, Par. 2: N.Y. Manual, p. 469; Hughes, Sec. 560.
Sec. 223, Par. 3: Hughes, Sec. 558.

Sec. 224. Personal Explanation

1. A matter of personal explanation does not constitute a question of personal privilege. It may be received only by permission of the house.

2. Permission to make a personal explanation is not a transferable right and members making explanation must confine themselves to the matter personal to themselves. But a member having the floor for this purpose may not be interrupted as long as that person keeps within parliamentary bounds.

Sec. 225. Precedence of Questions of Privilege

See also Sec. 187, List of Motions.

1. Questions of privilege take precedence over all other questions except the motion to adjourn, the call of the house when no quorum is present and the motion to recess.

2. A matter of privilege, arising out of any question, such as a quarrel between two members, supersedes the consideration of the original question, and must be disposed of first.

3. Questions of privilege are privileged only as to the right to immediate consideration. When once stated and while before the house they are subject to debate and to all subsidiary motions in the same manner as main motions.

Sec. 224, Par. 1: Hughes, Sec. 564; Cushing's Legislative Assemblies, Sec. 1565; N.Y. Manual, p. 469.

Sec. 224, Par. 2: Hughes, Sec. 565.

Sec. 225, Par. 1: Sturgis, p. 77; U.S. House Rule IX; N.Y. Manual, pp. 467, 468; Reed, Sec. 179; Cushing, Sec. 141.

Sec. 225, Par. 2: Jefferson, Sec. XXXIII; 2 Hatsell 88; N.Y. Manual (1948–49), p. 445.

Sec. 225, Par. 3: Sturgis, pp. 75, 76; N.Y. Manual, p. 468.

4. The previous question applies to debate on questions of privilege the same as to any other questions.

5. When a question of privilege has been disposed of, the business is resumed at the point where it was interrupted.

Sec. 226. Manner of Raising a Question of Privilege

1. When a question of privilege is one affecting the house or any of its members and requires immediate action, it may be raised while a member is speaking.

2. It is in order to raise a question of privilege at any time. The presiding officer must decide whether it is a question of privilege and is of sufficient urgency to justify interrupting a speaker.

3. A member wishing to raise a question of privilege should rise and address the presiding officer and without waiting to be recognized, say, "I rise to a question of privilege of the house," or "I rise to a question of personal privilege." The presiding officer should then request the member to state the question of privilege.

Sec. 225, Par. 4: N.Y. Manual, p. 470.

Sec. 225, Par. 5: Cushing, Sec. 141; Cushing's Legislative Assemblies, Sec. 1501.

Sec. 226, Par. 1: Sturgis, pp. 74, 75; Cushing, Sec. 153; N.Y. Manual (1948–49), p. 445.

Sec. 226, Par. 2: Sturgis, pp. 74, 75; Cushing's Legislative Assemblies, Sec. 1500; N.Y. Manual, p. 468.

Sec. 226, Par. 3: Sturgis, p. 73.

*

DIVISION 2

INCIDENTAL MOTIONS

CHAPTER 23

APPEALS

Sec. 230. When an Appeal Is in Order

See also Sec. 245, paragraph 4.

1. The proper method of taking exception to a ruling of a presiding officer is by appeal. All questions of order are decided by the presiding officer, subject to appeal by any member. It is the responsibility of the presiding officer to rule on points of order in a fair and impartial manner.

2. An appeal from a decision of the presiding officer must be made promptly. It is too late to appeal after debate or other business has intervened.

3. When a presiding officer rules a motion out of order and refuses to present it to the house, the proper procedure is to appeal from the presiding officer's decision. It is not proper for a member to put a question to vote which has been ruled out of order by the presiding officer.

Sec. 230, Par. 1: Sturgis, p. 84; U.S. House Rule I, Par. 4; Hughes, Sec. 527; N.Y. Manual, p. 457; Tilson, p. 32; State of Connecticut v. Lasher (1899), 71 Conn. 540, 42 A. 636; Proctor Coal Co. v. Finley (1895), 98 Ky. 405, 33 S.W. 188.

Sec. 230, Par. 2: Sturgis, p. 85; N.Y. Manual, p. 410; Tilson, p. 30; Cushing's Legislative Assemblies, Sec. 1465; Hughes, Secs. 534, 719.

Sec. 230, Par. 3: Proctor Coal Co. v. Finley (1895), 98 Ky. 405, 33 S.W. 188.

See also Sec. 576, Refusal of Presiding Officer to Perform Duties.

4. An appeal from a decision of a presiding officer is in order while a member has the floor, if made promptly.

5. While an appeal is pending, a point of order on any other question is not in order but a point of order relating to the appeal may be raised. And if the determination of the appeal is dependent on this point, it may be decided by the presiding officer. This second decision is also subject to appeal. There is an early precedent in Congress that there can be no appeal from a second decision while the other appeal is pending, but that the correctness of the ruling can be brought up when no other business is pending. The presiding officer is subject to censure by the house if the ruling be irregular.

6. A second point of order on the same general subject, but not on the same point, is not in order while an appeal is pending. But when the first appeal is decided, laid on the table or otherwise disposed of, the second point of order is in order and is subject to appeal.

7. When an appeal has been taken from a decision of the presiding officer, the appeal must be disposed of before new business is in order.

8. An answer to a parliamentary inquiry is not a decision and therefore cannot be appealed.

Sec. 230, Par. 4: Sturgis, p. 85; Hughes, Sec. 541; N.Y. Manual, p. 410; Robert's, p. 220.

Sec. 230, Par. 5: Reed, Sec. 185; Cushing's Legislative Assemblies, Sec. 1470.

Sec. 230, Par. 6: Cushing's Legislative Assemblies, Sec. 1469.

Sec. 230, Par. 7: Sturgis, p. 85; N.Y. Manual, p. 457.

Sec. 230, Par. 8: Hughes, Sec. 542; Sturgis, p. 85.

Sec. 231. Form of Question on Appeal

1. When a member wishes to appeal from a decision of the presiding officer, the member should rise and address the presiding officer and, without waiting to be recognized, say, "I appeal from the decision," or "I appeal from the decision of the president (or speaker or chair)."

2. When an appeal is taken the presiding officer should clearly state the decision appealed from and may state the reasons for the decision.

3. If there is no debate, or when debate is concluded, the presiding officer may put the question in the following form: "Shall the decision of the president (or speaker or chair) stand as the judgment of the senate (or house)?"

4. In some states the ruling of the chair by tradition is given great weight, and appeals are not made lightly.

Sec. 232. Debate on Appeals

1. A decision of the presiding officer is not debatable unless an appeal is taken from the decision.

2. An appeal is debatable even though the question out of which it arose was undebatable, being governed by the same rules as debate on other questions.

Sec. 231, Par. 1: Hughes, Sec. 543; Sturgis, p. 84.

Sec. 231, Par. 2: State of Connecticut v. Lasher (1899), 71 Conn. 540, 42 A. 636; Sturgis, p. 85; Hughes, Sec. 543; Cushing's Legislative Assemblies, Sec. 1461.

Sec. 232, Par. 1: Sturgis, pp. 84, 85; N.Y. Manual (1948–49), p. 407.

Sec. 232, Par. 2: Croswell's Manual, Sec. 30; N.Y. Manual (1948–49), p. 407; Robert's, p. 220.

3. The question out of which an appeal arose is not subject to debate on appeal, but only the specific question involved in the point of order from which the appeal was taken.

4. Whether or not an appeal has been debated, the presiding officer, when making a decision on the appeal may state the reasons for the decision without leaving the chair.

5. It is sometimes provided by rule that an appeal is not debatable when the ruling relates to indecorum, to transgression of the rules or to the priority of business, nor if made while the previous question is pending, nor while the immediately pending question is undebatable.

6. An appeal from a decision of the presiding officer may be withdrawn by the person making it, but if it is so withdrawn, it may be renewed, by the same or other member, provided no other business has intervened.

Sec. 233. Amendment—Laying an Appeal on the Table

See also Sec. 231, Form of Question on Appeal.

1. An appeal may not be amended as the question on appeal is simply whether the decision of the presiding officer shall be sustained.

Sec. 232, Par. 3: Cushing's Legislative Assemblies, Sec. 1466; N.Y. Manual (1948–49), p. 410.

Sec. 232, Par. 4: N.Y. Manual (1948–49), p. 407; Sturgis, p. 85.

Sec. 232, Par. 5: Robert's, p. 220.

Sec. 232, Par. 6: Hughes, Sec. 544; Cushing's Legislative Assemblies, Sec. 1466; N.Y. Manual, p. 610.

Sec. 233, Par. 1: Sturgis, p. 86; Croswell's Manual, Sec. 30; N.Y. Manual (1948–49), pp. 407, 408; Hughes, Sec. 541; Robert's, p. 214.

2. An appeal may be laid upon the table but may not be referred to committee. Where the rules do not permit an appeal to be taken from the table, it is a common practice of opponents of an appeal to move that it be laid on the table, since this procedure has the effect of closing debate and sustaining the decision of the presiding officer.

3. When an appeal is laid on the table, it does not carry the main subject with it, but the question out of which the appeal arose is still before the body.

Sec. 234. Vote on Appeal

1. One-half of the legal votes cast, a quorum being present, sustains a decision of the presiding officer on appeal. A tie vote sustains the presiding officer since a majority is required to overrule the presiding officer's decision.

See also Sec. 513, Tie Votes and Casting Votes.

2. When a member of the house, the presiding officer may vote to sustain the presiding officer's own decision on appeal.

See also Sec. 582, Rights of Presiding Officer to Debate, Vote and Introduce Business.

Sec. 235. Reconsideration of Appeals

An appeal may be reconsidered, but when the subject matter upon which the appeal was taken has been disposed of, and it is impossible for the house

---

Sec. 233, Par. 2: Hughes, Sec. 542; N.Y. Manual (1948–49), p. 409.

Sec. 234, Par. 1: Sturgis, p. 86; Jefferson, Sec. XLI; Reed, Sec. 185; Robert's, p. 220.

Sec. 234, Par. 2: Hughes, Sec. 542; N.Y. Manual (1948–49), p. 409; Cushing's Legislative Assemblies, Sec. 1471.

to reverse its action, it is too late to move to reconsider the appeal.

Sec. 235: Hughes, Sec. 541; N.Y. Manual (1948–49), p. 409; Robert's, p. 220.

CHAPTER 24

POINTS OF ORDER

Sec. 240. Purpose of Points of Order

1. It is the duty of the presiding officer to enforce the rules and orders of the body without delay and without waiting to have the presiding officer's attention called to breaches of order. It is also the right of every member who notices a breach of order or of a rule to insist upon its enforcement. This is called raising a question or point of order, because the member puts to the presiding officer the question as to whether there has been a breach of order or of the rules. It is the duty of the presiding officer to maintain order and enforce the rules.

2. A point of order is the parliamentary device that is used to require a deliberative body to observe its own rules and to follow established parliamentary practice.

3. Any request for compliance with the rules is in effect a point of order and is subject to the same rules.

4. The presiding officer is not required to decide any point of order not directly presented in the proceedings of the body.

Sec. 240, Par. 1: Sturgis, pp. 92, 93; Hughes, Secs. 261, 527; Reed, Secs. 48, 111, 182, 183; Cushing, Sec. 151; Cushing's Legislative Assemblies, Secs. 1457, 1460; Robert's, p. 212.

Sec. 240, Par. 2: Hughes, Sec. 261.

Sec. 240, Par. 3: Hughes, Sec. 528.

Sec. 240, Par. 4: Sturgis, pp. 92, 93.

Sec. 241. When Point of Order May Be Raised

See also Sec. 149, Appeals, Points of Order, Inquiries.

1. A point of order must be raised before the irregularity or occasion for raising the point of order has passed. On procedural questions it is too late as soon as the particular point has been passed or the next business taken up. On substantive questions a point of order may be raised only when the bill or proposition is within the control of the body. When the question relates to a violation of the constitution or statutes, such as the requirement of three readings of bills, the question can be raised only when the measure is within the control of the body.

2. It is not in order to raise one point of order while another is pending. As soon as one point of order is disposed of another is in order. The overruling of a point of order does not preclude other points of order being raised against the same proposition.

3. It has been said that one point of order cannot be raised upon another since there would be two points pending at the same time. This would seem to be in error because a question on one point of order might well give rise to another. Unless prevented by the rules, one point of order can be raised upon another. The presiding officer should be careful that this procedure is not used for dilatory purposes.

4. A question of order may be raised when a member has the floor and may interrupt a speech,

---

Sec. 241, Par. 1: Cushing's Legislative Assemblies, Sec. 1465; Sturgis, p. 93; Hughes, Secs. 534, 719; Tilson, p. 30; Robert's, p. 215.

Sec. 241, Par. 2: Cushing's Legislative Assemblies, Sec. 1470; N.Y. Manual (1948–49), p. 458; Hughes, Sec. 268.

the reading of a paper or the making of a report when it arises out of the speech, paper or report.

5. A point of order must be raised at the time the particular question is pending. It is premature to raise a point of order against an amendment when an amendment of the amendment is pending or when a motion to recommit is pending.

6. The proper time to raise a point of order questioning the right of a member to vote because of a direct personal or pecuniary interest is after the vote has been recorded and before the result is announced.

See also Sec. 522, Members May Not Vote on Questions in Which They Have a Personal Interest.

Sec. 242. Limitations on Use of Points of Order

1. It is not the duty of the presiding officer to rule upon any question which is not presented in the course of proceedings. It is not the presiding officer's right to rule upon the constitutionality or legal effect or expediency of a proposed bill since that authority belongs to the house.

2. It is not within the province of the chair to decide as to the constitutionality of an amendment.

See also Sec. 401, Frivolous and Improper Amendments.

Sec. 241, Par. 4: Sturgis, p. 93; Hughes, Sec. 529; Tilson, p. 31; Robert's, p. 214.

Sec. 241, Par. 5: Mass. Manual, p. 669.

Sec. 241, Par. 6: Mass. Manual, p. 610.

Sec. 242, Par. 1: Hughes, Secs. 28, 270; U.S. Congressional Record, 35th Cong. 2d Sess., p. 680; U.S. Congressional Record, 46th Cong. 2d Sess., p. 1501; U.S. House Manual, 80th Cong., Rule I, Note 627; N.Y. Manual (1948–49), p. 443.

Sec. 242, Par. 2: Mass. Manual, p. 594.

3. A point of order may not be raised on the ground that a bill does not conform to the subject matter as stated in the title because this is a question which must be decided by the body.

Sec. 243. Form of Point of Order

See also Sec. 149, Appeals, Points of Order, Inquiries.

A member wishing to raise a point of order should arise and address the presiding officer, and without waiting to be recognized, say, "I rise to a point of order." The presiding officer should interrupt the proceedings. If a member is speaking that person should immediately yield the floor, and the presiding officer should then direct the member raising the point of order to state the point. The member should then state the point as briefly and concisely as possible, citing the authority for the point whenever possible, but should not presume to decide the question or argue the point. A point of order is not a motion and does not require a second, even where seconds to motions are required by rule.

Sec. 244. Consideration of a Point of Order

It is the duty of the presiding officer to immediately take notice of any point of order although the presiding officer's decision may be deferred. Before rendering a decision on any point of order, the presiding officer may request the advice or opinion of members. When the question is particularly complicated or important, it may require research or investigation for its determination. A ruling may be

Sec. 242, Par. 3: Mass. Manual, p. 662.

Sec. 243: Hughes, Secs. 273, 529, 531; Reed, Sec. 184; Cushing, Sec. 151; Sturgis, p. 92; Robert's, p. 216.

deferred by the presiding officer to give the presiding officer an opportunity to look into the precedents or to reach a decision.

Sec. 245. Submission of Point of Order to the House

See also Sec. 582, Rights of Presiding Officer to Debate, Vote and Introduce Business.

1. A point of order is decided by the presiding officer without debate unless in doubtful cases the presiding officer submits the question to the body for advice or decision. When the presiding officer submits a question to the house for its decision, the question is open fully to debate because the decision of the house is not subject to appeal. During debate, if the presiding officer rules on a point of order debate is closed but the decision may be appealed.

2. Whenever making a decision on a point of order, the presiding officer has a right, without leaving the chair, to state the reasons for the decision. In such cases the presiding officer may speak on points of order in preference to members, or if the presiding officer is a member of the house, in preference to other members.

Sec. 244: Jefferson, Sec. XVII; Hughes, Secs. 529, 541; Cushing, Sec. 152; Tilson, p. 32; Cushing's Legislative Assemblies, Sec. 1464; Sturgis, pp. 92, 93; U.S. House Manual, 80th Cong., Rule I, Note 627; Mass. Manual, p. 622.

Sec. 245, Par. 1: State of Connecticut v. Lasher (1899), 71 Conn. 540, 42 A. 636; Hughes, Secs. 541, 683; Croswell's Manual, Sec. 30; N.Y. Manual, p. 407; Cushing, Sec. 154; Cushing's Legislative Assemblies, Sec. 1462; Sturgis, pp. 93, 94; Robert's, p. 217.

Sec. 245, Par. 2: Cushing's Legislative Assemblies, Sec. 1471; N.Y. Manual (1948–49), p. 407; State of Connecticut v. Lasher (1899), 71 Conn. 540, 42 A. 636.

3. It is in order for a member to courteously request, but not demand, the presiding officer to reconsider the presiding officer's decision on a point of order.

4. It was the practice in the House of Commons not to permit debate on a point of order during division of the house, though informal consultation with members by the speaker was permitted. With the particular procedure used for division in the Commons to have permitted debate would have created too much confusion. For the same reason, appeals were not permitted on points of order while the house was divided and waiting to be counted. With the modern methods of voting, the reason for this technical rule has ceased to exist and points of order arising out of the procedure of voting are not now subject to any special rules or different procedure than if they arose out of any other situation or during any other procedure. Adopted rules, however, sometimes contain the ancient restrictions.

Sec. 246. Precedence, Subsidiary Motions and Debate of Point of Order

1. A point of order takes precedence over the pending question out of which it arises until the point of order is disposed of, and yields to motions having a higher precedence than the motion out of which it arose.

2. Neither a point of order nor a decision thereon can be amended nor have any other subsidiary mo-

---

Sec. 245, Par. 3: Hughes, Sec. 41.

Sec. 245, Par. 4: 3 Hatsell 143; Jefferson, Sec. XLI.

Sec. 246, Par. 1: Cushing's Legislative Assemblies, Sec. 1459; Sturgis, p. 95; Hughes, Sec. 541; N.Y. Manual (1948–49), p. 439; Robert's, p. 212.

tion applied to it, except that an appeal can be taken from a decision and that a point of order or appeal can be withdrawn.

3. A point of order is not debatable unless submitted to the house. The point can be debated on appeal if an appeal is taken from the decision.

4. If the presiding officer does not submit a point of order to the body for its decision, no vote is taken upon a point of order unless an appeal is taken from the decision of the presiding officer.

Sec. 246, Par. 2: Hughes, Sec. 527; Sturgis, pp. 94, 95; Robert's, p. 214.

Sec. 246, Par. 3: N.Y. Manual (1948–49), pp. 457, 464; Cushing's Legislative Assemblies, Sec. 1460; Sturgis, p. 94; Robert's, p. 214.

CHAPTER 25

PARLIAMENTARY INQUIRIES AND OTHER REQUESTS FOR INFORMATION

Sec. 250. Purpose of Parliamentary Inquiry

See also Sec. 114, Asking Questions of Members.

1. During the sessions of a legislative body, members may desire to obtain information concerning the procedure or business before the house. These requests are not technically motions but, for convenience, are classified with them. A parliamentary inquiry is a request for information from the presiding officer with respect to procedure concerning some question before the house or which may be immediately brought before the house.

2. The presiding officer should answer any questions on parliamentary law pertinent to the business before the house in order to enable the member making a parliamentary inquiry to make a proper motion or to raise a timely point of order. It is not, however, the presiding officer's duty to answer general questions concerning parliamentary law.

3. When not in possession of the information requested, the presiding officer may direct the question to a member who should be in possession of the information.

Sec. 250, Par. 1: Hughes, Sec. 521; Sturgis, p. 95; Robert's, p. 245; Demeter, p. 124.

Sec. 250, Par. 2: Sturgis, p. 96; Robert's, p. 245.

Sec. 251. Form of Parliamentary Inquiry

A member desiring information concerning a question before the body, or which may be immediately brought before the body, may rise, address the presiding officer and without waiting to be recognized, say, "I rise to a parliamentary inquiry," or "I rise for information," or "I rise to a point of information." The presiding officer should ask the member to state the inquiry, and if the question should appear to be pertinent to the business of the body, the member should supply this information. If another member is speaking and the question does not require an immediate reply, the presiding officer may delay replying until the other member's speech is completed.

Sec. 252. Rules Governing Parliamentary Inquiries

1. When a parliamentary inquiry relates to a question which requires immediate attention, it may be made while a member has the floor and may even interrupt a speech.

2. A parliamentary inquiry is not a motion but is simply a request for information and is, therefore, not debatable or amendable or subject to any other motion.

3. A parliamentary inquiry is an incidental question which yields only to privileged questions, appeals and questions of order and takes precedence over all other incidental motions, subsidiary and

---

Sec. 251: Sturgis, pp. 95, 96; Robert's, p. 245.
Sec. 252, Par. 1: Sturgis, pp. 95, 96; Hughes, Secs. 521, 522.
Sec. 252, Par. 2: Hughes, Sec. 522; Sturgis, p. 98.

main motions. The presiding officer may answer parliamentary inquiries even after the previous question has been ordered.

4. A parliamentary inquiry is never in order when made for dilatory purposes.

Sec. 253. Request for Information from Members

1. Occasions frequently arise when one member desires information from another. Requests for such information are not technically parliamentary inquiries but are generally subject to the same rules.

2. When the information is desired from a member who is speaking, or from any member other than the presiding officer, the member desiring the information should rise and say, "Mr. or Madam President (or Mr. or Madam Chairperson or Mr. or Madam Speaker), I desire to ask the Senator or Representative (identify member) a question." The presiding officer should inquire whether the member speaking, or other member, is willing to be interrupted or to answer the question, and if the member consents, the presiding officer directs the inquiring member to state the question. The presiding officer may then restate the question or merely request the other member to reply. The reply is made to the presiding officer and not to the inquirer.

Sec. 252, Par. 3: Hughes, Secs. 521, 522; U.S. House Manual, 80th Cong., Rule I, Note 627; Sturgis, p. 98.

Sec. 252, Par. 4: Hughes, Sec. 522; Sturgis, p. 97.

Sec. 253, Par. 1: Sturgis, p. 95.

Sec. 253, Par. 2: Sturgis, p. 96.

3. In committees and small groups the procedure of asking and answering questions may properly become quite informal. Questions from one member to another are more frequent in committees than in larger bodies.

4. A few questions to a member presenting a proposition will often clarify the points better than extended debate.

5. The presiding officer should never permit a speaker to be heckled by questions nor permit a member to present arguments under the guise of questions. A member should not be permitted to interrupt a speaker to ask questions of other members unless some urgent reason exists.

6. When the time of speeches is limited and a member consents to be interrupted by questions, the time consumed is taken out of the time allowed for the member's speech.

Sec. 254. Requests Other Than Parliamentary Inquiries

1. There are numerous other requests which should be distinguished from parliamentary inquiries. Examples are a request to withdraw a motion, a request to be excused from a duty or a request for some privilege. These requests are usually subsidiary in nature. They arise out of certain other questions and should be decided before those questions out of which they arise. Thus a request of a member to be excused from voting on a

Sec. 253, Par. 5: Sturgis, p. 97.

certain question would be in order when that question comes before the house for a vote.

2. Such requests are not subject to amendment or other subsidiary motions, but, if denied, may be followed by a motion to the same effect which may be subject to debate and subsidiary motions.

Sec. 254, Par. 1: Sturgis, pp. 74, 98.
Sec. 254, Par. 2: Sturgis, pp. 76, 98, 100, 103.

CHAPTER 26

ORDERS OF THE DAY AND CALENDAR

See also Ch. 66, Secs. 710–714, General Order of Business.

Sec. 257. Nature of the Call for Orders of the Day

1. A call for the orders of the day is a demand that the body conform to its order of business. Formerly, it was the practice to assign questions for consideration on a certain day and the questions set for a particular day were the general orders for that day. A demand for the orders of the day was a demand that the body proceed to consider those questions. It is the modern practice, at least in the larger legislative bodies, to have a calendar or file which is a list or file of measures arranged in the order in which they come up for consideration. This calendar or file takes the place of general orders. Under this latter procedure a demand for the orders of the day is a demand that the body proceed with the consideration of this calendar or file.

2. It is the duty of the presiding officer to announce the business to come before the house in its proper order. If the presiding officer always performs the presiding officer's duty, there will be no occasion for calling for the orders of the day. If the presiding officer fails to notice that the time set for a special order has arrived and the presiding officer

Sec. 257, Par. 1: Cushing's Legislative Assemblies, Secs. 1373, 1377.

has not interrupted a pending question or has permitted a digression from the calendar when consideration of the calendar is the proper order of business, it is in order for any member to call for the regular order or for the orders of the day, or to raise a point of order that the proper order of business is not being followed.

3. Any member may demand that the order of business be followed. The call must be simply for the orders of the day, since a call for any specified order would have no privilege.

Sec. 258. Precedence of Call for the Regular Order or for Orders of the Day

See also Sec. 187, List of Motions.

1. The call for the orders of the day takes precedence as an incidental motion and yields only to the privileged motions, and to appeals, points of order and parliamentary inquiries.

2. A demand for the regular order or a call for the orders of the day can be made at any time when no motion of higher precedence is under consideration and the order of business is not being followed. It may be made even while a member is speaking if the subject of the member's remarks does not conform to the regular order.

3. Under modern legislative practice, the order and manner in which the business of the body is

Sec. 257, Par. 2: Reed, Sec. 257.

Sec. 257, Par. 3: Jefferson, Sec. XXXIII; Cushing, Sec. 144; Cushing's Legislative Assemblies, Sec. 1401; Sturgis, First Ed., pp. 173, 192.

Sec. 258, Par. 1: Hughes, Sec. 157; N.Y. Manual, p. 499; Jefferson, Sec. XXXIII; Robert's, p. 187.

Sec. 258, Par. 2: Jefferson, Sec. XX; Hughes, Sec. 145.

considered is set out in the rules so that it follows a definite and predictable order. To vary from the plan provided for in the rules is a violation of the rules and permissible only under suspension of the rules. It is in order to insist upon a compliance with the rules any time there is a variation from the procedure required by the rules.

Sec. 259. Debate and Application of Other Motions

1. A call for the regular order or for the orders of the day is a demand that the body conform to its order of business and is not technically a motion. It therefore cannot be debated or amended, laid on the table, postponed, committed or amended, nor have any other subsidiary motion applied to it.

2. The modern practice is to permit the call for the regular order or for orders of the day to be renewed after intervening business or a change in the parliamentary situation. When the business in the regular order has been taken up, it is subject to the same motions and procedure as any other business in the same class. A call for orders of the day cannot be reconsidered.

Sec. 260. Effect of Call or Demand

1. When the regular order or orders of the day have been called for, the presiding officer should either announce the first or next business in the order of business, or put the question: "Will the

Sec. 258, Par. 3: Hughes, Secs. 145–152.
Sec. 259: Hughes, Secs. 141–160; Sturgis, First Ed., p. 175.

house proceed with the regular order (or calendar, or the orders of the day)?"

2. To refuse to proceed with the regular order or to the orders of the day, when it is the proper order of business, is a variation from the order of business and is equivalent to suspending the rules. It, therefore, requires the same vote. If under a special rule a two-thirds vote is necessary to suspend the rules, a two-thirds vote in the negative is necessary to defeat a demand for the regular order.

3. At the time fixed for consideration of the calendar or orders of the day or when they are called for, a member may move that the time for consideration of the pending question be extended for a certain time. Such a motion, since it changes the order of business, is equivalent to a motion to suspend the rules and requires the same vote.

4. Whenever the calendar or orders of the day have been disposed of, the consideration of the interrupted business is taken up at the point where it was interrupted.

Sec. 261. Consideration of Calendar or File

1. After an item on the calendar or an order of the day has been announced and is pending, it is debatable and may be amended or have any other subsidiary motion applied to it, the same as any other main question or proposal of that class.

Sec. 260, Par. 1: Jefferson, Sec. XXXIII; Reed, Sec. 257; Cushing's Legislative Assemblies, Secs. 1399, 1400.

Sec. 260, Par. 2: Hughes, Sec. 154.

Sec. 260, Par. 3: Cushing's Legislative Assemblies, Sec. 1398.

Sec. 260, Par. 4: Sturgis, First Ed., p. 175.

2. The items on the calendar or orders of the day, as a group, cannot be laid on the table nor postponed, but an individual item, after it has been taken up, may, by a majority vote, be laid on the table, postponed or referred to a committee. Thus, matters may be disposed of and the consideration of the question previously pending may be resumed.

3. By suspending the rules, any question may be taken up out of its regular order.

Sec. 262. Making Up the Calendar

Business takes precedence on the general calendar in the order specified in the rules. If there are no specific rules, business takes precedence in the order in which it was ordered or became business under that order of business. Thus, bills reported from committee take their place on second reading in the order in which the committee reports were read and the bills ordered to second reading, and bills take their place on third reading in the order in which they were read second time and ordered to third reading. This order may be changed in such manner as the rules provide, by unanimous consent or by suspension of the rules.

Sec. 263. General and Special Orders

1. Orders of the day may be divided into general orders and special orders.

2. All official business on the calendar or file which, by the regular rules of procedure, comes

---

Sec. 261, Par. 2: Sturgis, First Ed., p. 173; Reed, Sec. 257.

Sec. 262: Reed, Sec. 255.

Sec. 263, Par. 1: Hughes, Secs. 143, 156; Sturgis, First Ed., p. 174.

before the house for consideration under the proper order may be considered the general orders of the day. All measures or pending matters set for a special hour for decision or consideration, either by postponing them to that time, by setting them as special orders for that time or by adopting a special program or order of business, constitute special orders of the day for the time fixed.

3. When a special order has been set for a particular time, it has no special privilege until the time set for its consideration. If it is set only for a particular day, it can be brought up any time during that day.

4. In case of conflict, special orders always take precedence over general orders.

5. In a legislative body having a general order of business which makes provision for special orders, any business coming up for consideration in the usual order on the calendar or file is a general order. Any business set specifically for that day without specifying the hour is a special order and is in order in that part of the order of business designated as special orders.

Sec. 264. Motions to Set Special Orders

1. The purpose of a special order is to expedite important business and set a definite time for its consideration, which gives such a special order privilege over other business. Whenever the making of a

Sec. 263, Par. 2: Hughes, Secs. 141, 143, 150; Cushing, Sec. 142; Reed, Secs. 255, 256; Sturgis, First Ed., pp. 174, 192.

Sec. 263, Par. 3: Cushing, Sec. 145.

Sec. 263, Par. 4: Hughes, Sec. 157; Sturgis, First Ed., p. 174.

Sec. 263, Par. 5: Hughes, Sec. 143; Sturgis, First Ed., p. 174.

special order sets aside the general rules regarding the order of business, the same vote is required as would be required to specifically suspend the rules.

2. The usual form of the motion to set a special order is "I move that—(specifying the bill, resolution or other business) be made a special order for—(specifying the day and hour)."

3. The form of setting a general order is the same except that it is designated as an order or general order and that no hour is specified.

4. A motion to set a special order may be amended as to time. It is debatable only as to the question of setting the special order and does not open up the main question to debate.

5. A pending question may be made a special order for a future time by "postponing it and making it a special order for" a specified time. Such a motion is a form of the subsidiary motion to postpone definitely and it takes precedence as such.

6. If the question is not pending, the motion to make it a special order for a certain time takes precedence as a main motion.

7. A member may make a motion and request that the motion be set as a special order for a particular time. Such a motion should be printed in the journal with the record of the special order and should likewise be carried on the calendar as a special order.

Sec. 264, Par. 1: Hughes, Sec. 157; N.Y. Manual, p. 499; Sturgis, First Ed., p. 175.

Sec. 264, Par. 2: Hughes, Sec. 158; Sturgis, First Ed., p. 173.

Sec. 264, Par. 4: Hughes, Sec. 159; Sturgis, First Ed., p. 175.

Sec. 264, Par. 7: Hughes, Sec. 227.

Sec. 265. Special Orders Set for Same Day or Same Hour

1. If several orders appointed for the same time are made at the same time, then they take precedence in the order in which they were arranged in the motion making the general order.

2. When two special orders are set for the same day, without specifying the hour, the first one set must be disposed of before the second may be considered.

3. A series of special orders made by a single vote is treated as a program.

Sec. 266. Conflict Between Special Orders Made at Different Times

1. When special orders that have been made at different times come into conflict, the one that was first made takes precedence over all special orders made afterwards, although the latter were made for an earlier hour.

2. A special order does not interfere with one previously made unless it clearly indicates that it is intended to do so. It is presumed that a later order is not intended to affect an earlier order unless it so indicates.

3. When the presiding officer announces the hour set for a special order, any member can move to extend the time for considering the pending ques-

---

Sec. 265, Par. 1: Sturgis, First Ed., p. 174.

Sec. 265, Par. 2: N.Y. Manual (1948–49), p. 465; Reed, Sec. 255; Cushing, Sec. 144.

Sec. 266, Par. 1: Cushing, Sec. 144.

Sec. 266, Par. 2: Sturgis, First Ed., p. 174.

tion. Such a motion is not debatable, and must be decided before the new question can be taken up.

Sec. 267. Postponement of Special Order

1. A special order may be postponed by a majority vote when it comes up for consideration.

2. Where there is no rule to the contrary, a special order may be canceled or changed by a majority vote before it comes up for consideration. If there is a rule preventing such an action, it can be taken up by suspending the rule.

3. If a special order is not taken up at the hour fixed, it does not thereby lose its privileged character but may be called up at a later hour, but where a special order is set for one day and it is not considered on that day, it thereupon loses its privileged position. Likewise, when a special order is set for a particular legislative day, the special order may be called up at any time after the hour fixed on the same legislative day, even though several calendar days have elapsed.

Sec. 268. The Special Order for a Meeting

Sometimes a subject is made the special order for a meeting, in which case it is announced by the presiding officer as the pending business immediately after the convening of the meeting. This method is used when it is desired to devote an entire meeting, or so much of it as is necessary, to the consideration of a special subject. This form of special order

Sec. 267, Par. 1: N.Y. Manual, p. 499; Reed, Sec. 256; Sturgis, First Ed., p. 175.

Sec. 267, Par. 3: Hughes, Secs. 161, 162, 163, 167.

takes precedence over the other forms of special orders.

Sec. 269. Special Calendar or Program

1. Especially in the later days of a legislative session, a special calendar or program may be adopted for the consideration of certain matters. A program is in the nature of a special order.

2. While working under a program, when the time assigned to a certain subject arrives, the presiding officer puts any questions pending to vote and announces the subject set for that time. This is done because, under such circumstances, the form of the program implies that the period of time assigned to each subject or measure is all that can be allowed. But, if at the expiration of the time any member moves to lay the question on the table, to postpone it to a certain time, to refer it to a committee or to extend time for debate, the presiding officer should recognize the motion and immediately put it to vote without debate.

Sec. 270. General Orders Obsolete

1. The use of general orders of the day as the means of scheduling and controlling the flow of legislative business through the houses of the legislatures became impractical as early as 1818 and was abandoned. And the same course was followed in Parliament.

Sec. 268: Sturgis, First Ed., p. 124.
Sec. 269, Par. 2: Sturgis, First Ed., p. 174.
Sec. 270, Par. 1: Hughes, Sec. 62.

2. Under the calendar system of scheduling legislation for consideration by the houses the staff of each house prepares the daily calendar as directed by the rules of the houses or the joint rules. This is done as the bills are reported by the committees or otherwise come before the legislature. Bills stay on the calendar while they are before the house and are returned to calendar whenever they are again before the house. This is all done without wasting the time of the members of the legislature.

3. Special orders still have a use in setting bills for consideration at a special time. A member may ask that a bill be set as a special order for some appropriate time if it is controversial, has a special time limit for consideration, or has some other feature or condition that requires earlier or more full consideration than the usual bill. If unanimous consent is not given, the member may move that the special order be set. When a bill is brought up for consideration under a special order, it is subject to all of the usual rules of consideration.

Sec. 271. Legislative Day

1. A legislative day can be terminated only by an adjournment or some actual dispersing of the assembled membership amounting to the same thing.

2. If either house is in lawful session on a certain day, such date is considered a legislative day whether the other house meets or not.

Sec. 271, Par. 1: State of Florida *ex rel.* Landis v. Thompson (1936), 125 Fla. 466, 170 So. 464; Davis v. Thompson (Okla. 1986), 721 P.2d 789.

Sec. 271, Par. 2: Opinion of the Justices (1972), 288 Ala. 89, 257 So. 2d 336.

3. The meeting and action of a legislative committee on a day on which neither house is in session does not constitute a legislative day and should not be included among the legislative days of the session.

4. Committee meetings are an integral part of legislative work and some states consider days on which committees meet as legislative days, as well as those days when both houses are in session.

Sec. 271, Par. 3: Hainkel v. Henry (La. 1975), 313 So. 2d 577.

CHAPTER 27

WITHDRAWAL OF MOTIONS

Sec. 272. Right to Withdraw Motions

Until a motion is stated by the presiding officer to the body as a question for its determination, the mover may withdraw or modify it without asking consent of anyone. Upon presentation of a motion, objections may be made to its form or questions may be raised as to its effect, and the maker can modify or withdraw it. Although the motion may be repeated by the presiding officer during preliminary discussion, the motion remains in the possession of the proposer until the motion is stated by the presiding officer to the body for its action.

Sec. 273. When Consent to Withdraw Is Required

1. When a motion has been stated by the presiding officer or read by the secretary or clerk and presented to the body for determination, it is in possession of the body and can, thereafter, be withdrawn or modified only by consent of the body. But many state legislatures have provided by rule that a motion may be withdrawn without the consent of the house at any time before decision or amendment.

Sec. 272: Cushing's Legislative Assemblies, Secs. 1233, 1241; Sturgis, p. 99; Reed, Sec. 108.

Sec. 273, Par. 1: Jefferson, Sec. XXXIII; Cushing's Legislative Assemblies, Secs. 1232, 1235, 1237, 1240, 1241, 1477; Cushing, Secs. 56, 56A, 92, 161; Reed, Secs. 108, 189, 190; U.S. House Rule XVI, Par. 2.

2. The motion to reconsider cannot be withdrawn after it is too late to make the motion except by unanimous consent, and if the motion to reconsider is lost, it may be renewed only by unanimous consent.

See also Sec. 466, paragraph 1, Withdrawing and Renewing Motion to Reconsider.

Sec. 274. Request for Leave to Withdraw a Question

1. A request for leave to withdraw a question, or a motion to grant such leave, may be made at any time before voting on the question has commenced, even though the question has been amended. The request or motion to withdraw a motion may be made while motions incidental or subsidiary to the motion sought to be withdrawn are pending. These motions cease to be before the body when the question to which they are incidental or subsidiary is withdrawn.

2. The request or motion to withdraw a question or motion then under consideration is an incidental question which ranks below privileged questions and questions of order but takes precedence over all other incidental motions, subsidiary motions and main motions.

3. A request to withdraw a question may not be amended, debated, laid on the table, nor have any other subsidiary motion applied to it.

Sec. 273, Par. 2: Sturgis, p. 99; Hughes, Sec. 198.

Sec. 274, Par. 1: Cushing's Legislative Assemblies, Sec. 1241; Sturgis, p. 99.

Sec. 274, Par. 2: Reed, Secs. 181, 199.

Sec. 274, Par. 3: Cushing, Sec. 563.

4. When the mover requests permission to withdraw the mover's own motion, the practice is for the presiding officer to ask if there is any objection. If there is none, the presiding officer announces that the motion is withdrawn.

Sec. 275. Motion for Leave to Withdraw a Question

1. If anyone objects to granting leave to withdraw a motion, the presiding officer may put the question on granting the request, or a motion to grant the request may be made from the floor. The motion may be made by the author or any other member. A majority vote of the members present and voting is required to authorize the withdrawal of a question or motion when unanimous consent is refused.

2. The motion for leave to withdraw a motion takes the same precedence as a request, is not subject to debate, amendment or the other subsidiary motions, but differs from the request by submitting the question to a vote of the members.

Sec. 276. Effect of Withdrawal of Motions

1. When a motion is withdrawn, the effect is the same as if it had never been made. When permission to withdraw a motion is refused, the business proceeds as though the motion or request to with-

Sec. 274, Par. 4: Cushing's Legislative Assemblies, Secs. 1237, 1310, 1477; Sturgis, p. 99; N.Y. Manual (1948–49), p. 437.

Sec. 275, Par. 1: Sturgis, p. 99.

Sec. 275, Par. 2: Sturgis, p. 100.

draw had not been made.

2. Motions once offered and withdrawn may be again offered by either the same or a different member in the same or a modified form.

Sec. 276, Par. 1: Cushing's Legislative Assemblies, Sec. 1477; Cushing, Sec. 162.

Sec. 276, Par. 2: Cushing's Legislative Assemblies, Sec. 1310; Hughes, Sec. 200.

CHAPTER 28

SUSPENSION OF THE RULES

Sec. 279. Purpose of Suspension of the Rules

1. The purpose of suspending the rules is to give a deliberative body the liberty to follow whatever course it may choose, unhampered by any provision of its rules.

2. When a body wishes to do something that cannot be done without violating its own rules, but yet which is not in conflict with the constitution or with any controlling statutory provision, it "suspends the rules that interfere with" the proposed action. Suspension differs from amendment because it is limited in scope and in time. The object of the suspension must be specified, and nothing falling outside the stated limits of the motion to suspend the rules can be done under the suspension.

3. When desirable, a general rule of parliamentary law can be placed in the rules of the body. The rules are not subject to sudden changes, and may be considered as expressing the deliberate views of the body.

Sec. 280. Suspension of General Parliamentary Rules and Adopted Rules

See also Sec. 22, Right to Change Rules, and Sec. 23, Rules Can Be Suspended.

Sec. 279, Par. 1: Hughes, Sec. 574; Cushing, Sec. 165; Cushing's Legislative Assemblies, Secs. 1478–1486; Sturgis, p. 86; Robert's, pp. 223, 224.

Sec. 279, Par. 2: Cushing, Sec. 163; Cushing's Legislative Assemblies, Secs. 1478–1480; Sturgis, pp. 87, 88; Robert's, pp. 222, 223.

The phrase "suspension of the rules" is used in two distinct senses. In one case the term applies to the rules of parliamentary law and in the other case to the rules adopted to govern the body. The general rules of parliamentary law may be suspended according to the established parliamentary practice. The rules of either house or the joint rules of the legislature may be suspended as provided by the rules themselves.

Sec. 281. Right of Public Bodies to Suspend Rules

See also Ch. 2, Secs. 6–7, Constitutional Rules Governing Procedure; Ch. 3, Sec. 10, Statutory Rules Governing Procedure; Sec. 22, Right to Change Rules; Sec. 23, Rules Can Be Suspended; Sec. 285, Vote Required to Suspend the Rules; and Sec. 512, Two-Thirds Vote.

1. The right to suspend rules depends on the nature of the body and the manner in which it acquired its powers.

2. The rules which relate to priority of business, or to procedure, and would usually be termed rules of order can be suspended.

3. Rules which are required by, or which protect rights granted by, the federal or state constitutions cannot be suspended unless the constitution so provides.

4. A public body which has been given power and had duties imposed upon it is bound to exercise those powers and duties according to the conditions under which they were granted.

5. Any restriction or limitation on the authority granted must control its exercise. Provisions of the

---

Sec. 280: Reed, Sec. 191; Sturgis, pp. 87, 88.
Sec. 281: Sturgis, pp. 86–88.

constitutions, charters or statutes which grant powers may provide how those powers may be used.

6. It has been held that public bodies can adopt rules, even by a majority vote, which cannot be suspended or amended without a two-thirds vote, but it is also held by the courts that actions, taken in violation of procedural rules of parliamentary law and of adopted rules, are valid nevertheless, since failure to conform to the rules of this class suspended them by implication.

See also Sec. 22, Right to Change Rules; Sec. 23, Rules Can Be Suspended; Sec. 24, Failure of a House of the Legislature to Conform to Its Rules Does Not Invalidate Its Acts; Sec. 285, Vote Required to Suspend the Rules; and Sec. 512, Two-Thirds Vote.

Sec. 282. Motion to Suspend the Rules

1. The motion to suspend the rules may be made at any time when no question is pending, or while a question is pending provided it is for a purpose connected with that question.

2. A motion to suspend the rules may be made either under the order of business of motions and resolutions or under the order of business which relates to the matter proposed to be considered under suspension of the rules.

3. The more usual form of the motion to suspend the rules is "I move to suspend the rules that interfere with (stating the object of the suspension)," or "I move that the rules be suspended which prevent, etc."

Sec. 282, Par. 1: Sturgis, p. 88.
Sec. 282, Par. 2: N.Y. Manual, p. 459.
Sec. 282, Par. 3: Sturgis, p. 87.

4. A motion to suspend the rules should specify what rule or rules are to be suspended and, particularly, should state the purpose of suspending the rules.

5. A motion to suspend the rules yields to all:

(a) The privileged motions.

(b) Appeals.

(c) Points of order.

(d) Parliamentary inquiry.

(e) Calls for orders of the day.

(f) Other motions except incidental motions arising out of itself.

6. A motion to suspend the rules may not be:

(a) Amended.

(b) Debated.

(c) Laid on the table.

(d) Referred to committee.

(e) Postponed.

(f) Reconsidered or renewed for the same purpose on the same day, unless other business has intervened or there has been a change in the parliamentary situation.

A motion to suspend the rules may not have any other subsidiary motion applied to it.

Sec. 282, Par. 4: Hughes, Sec. 577; Sturgis, p. 88.

Sec. 282, Par. 5: Sturgis, p. 88; Hughes, Sec. 573; N.Y. Manual, pp. 451, 476, 478; Reed, Sec. 204; Cushing's Legislative Assemblies, Secs. 1487, 1488.

Sec. 283. Suspension of the Rules by Unanimous Consent

Instead of a formal motion to suspend the rules, it is not unusual for a member to request unanimous consent to consider particular business or to take a special action which would not be permitted by the rules. As soon as the request is made, the presiding officer should inquire if there is any objection, and if no one objects, the presiding officer may declare the rule suspended and direct the member to proceed as if the rules had been suspended by a regular vote.

Sec. 284. Suspension of Rules by Implication

Often actions taken by legislative bodies are in violation of general parliamentary rules, or rules adopted by the body or of an adopted authority without formally suspending the rules provided objection is not raised by any member. This may be regarded as implied suspension and the action taken in violation of the rules is valid as long as the body had the authority to suspend the rules violated. This does not apply to mandatory constitutional provisions.

See also Sec. 24, Failure of a House of the Legislature to Conform to Its Rules Does Not Invalidate Its Acts, and Sec. 280, Suspension of General Parliamentary Rules and Adopted Rules.

Sec. 285. Vote Required to Suspend the Rules

See also Sec. 22, Right to Change Rules; Sec. 23, Rules Can Be Suspended; and Sec. 512, Two-Thirds Vote.

Sec. 283: Cushing's Legislative Assemblies, Secs. 794, 1483.

Sec. 284: Cushing's Legislative Assemblies, Sec. 794; Hughes, Sec. 583.

1. A motion to suspend the rules of parliamentary law, adopted rules or rules of an adopted authority requires only a majority vote. When a body is specifically given the power to make or adopt rules having more than normal force, it can make or adopt rules of procedure which require more than a majority vote to suspend or repeal. It cannot curtail or restrict its essential powers by rules which require more than a majority vote to suspend or repeal. It cannot, for example, require a two-thirds vote to pass legislation which the constitution permits it to pass by a majority vote.

2. In many legislative bodies it is provided by rule that the standing rules may be suspended by a two-thirds vote. A notice may also be required for a motion to suspend the rules.

3. Rules required by the constitution or controlling statute are mandatory and cannot be suspended unless that authority provides for their suspension. When suspension of such rules is permitted the act must be taken in strict conformity with the rules.

4. Although rules of a prior legislative body, adopted temporarily until new rules are adopted, require a two-thirds vote for their amendment or suspension, new rules can be adopted by a majority vote.

Sec. 285, Par. 1: Cushing's Legislative Assemblies, Secs. 794, 1480, 1491; Reed, Sec. 53; Hughes, Sec. 572; Waples, Sec. 134.

Sec. 285, Par. 2: Hughes, Secs. 575, 580; Cushing, Sec. 164; Reed, Sec. 191.

Sec. 285, Par. 3: Capito v. Topping (1909), 65 W.Va. 587, 64 S.E. 845; State of Missouri v. Alt (1887), 26 Mo. App. 673.

Sec. 285, Par. 4: Armitage v. Fisher (N.Y. 1893), 74 Hun 167, 26 N.Y.S. 364.

5. Private clubs and associations almost always provide in their rules that they can be suspended by a two-thirds vote. So general is this practice that some writers have assumed that this is a rule of parliamentary law applicable to public bodies.

Sec. 286. Business in Order Immediately After Suspension of the Rules

If the motion to suspend the rules is carried, the business for which the rules were suspended is immediately in order. The presiding officer should recognize the member who moved to suspend the rules for the purpose of presenting the measure or business.

Sec. 286: Sturgis, p. 88; Hughes, Sec. 579.

CHAPTER 29

OBJECTION TO THE CONSIDERATION OF QUESTIONS

Sec. 293. Purpose of Objection to Consideration

The purpose of the objection to consideration is to bar from discussion or consideration any matter which is considered irrelevant, contentious or unprofitable, or which for any reason is thought not advisable to discuss.

Sec. 294. To What Can Objection to Consideration Be Made

1. Objection may be made only to the consideration of main motions.

2. Objection may not be made to:

(a) Matters pending before the house in their regular established order, such as reports of committees on subjects referred to them.

(b) Communications from any source entitled to file its communications, such as messages from the other house or from the executive.

(c) Matters incidental to the procedure of the house, such as proposed amendments to the rules.

Sec. 293: Sturgis, p. 89; Tilson, p. 54; Robert's, p. 227.

Sec. 294, Par. 1: Sturgis, pp. 90, 91; Demeter, p. 141; Reed, Sec. 110; Robert's, p. 63.

3. When the rules require that all bills when offered be referred to committee, or contain like provisions, the rules must be suspended before objection may be made to the introduction of a bill.

Sec. 295. Who May Raise Objection to Consideration

1. Objection to the consideration of a question may be made by any member. The presiding officer may personally decide it advisable to submit to the members the question as to whether any question will be considered.

2. Any question may be ruled out of order when the presiding officer considers the question entirely outside the scope of consideration and an appeal may be taken from the ruling.

Sec. 296. When Objection May Be Made

1. Objection to consideration must be made immediately following the statement of the question. It may be made when another has the floor but must be made before debate has begun and before any action has been taken or before any subsidiary motion is stated by the presiding officer.

2. An objection to consideration cannot be renewed, as it is too late to object after consideration has begun.

Sec. 295: Sturgis, pp. 90, 91; Hughes, Sec. 231.

Sec. 296, Par. 1: Hughes, Secs. 230, 233; Reed, Secs. 110, 112; Waples, Sec. 4; Sturgis, pp. 89, 90; Tilson, p. 54; Robert's, p. 63.

Sec. 296, Par. 2: Sturgis, p. 91; Reed, Sec. 112; Tilson, p. 54.

Sec. 297. Form of Question on Objection to Consideration

1. A member desiring to object to the consideration of a question should rise before debate of the question has begun and, without waiting to be recognized, say, "Mr. or Madam President (Mr. or Madam Speaker, or Mr. or Madam Chairperson), I object to the consideration of the question (further identifying the question when necessary)."

2. The form of the question on objection to consideration may be "Will the senate (house) consider the question?" or "Shall the question be considered?"

Sec. 298. Debate and Application of Subsidiary Motions to Objection to Consideration

An objection to the consideration of a question may not be debated, for to open the question to debate would defeat its purpose. Being a procedural motion in character, it cannot have any other subsidiary motion applied to it. It cannot be amended.

Sec. 299. Vote Required to Sustain Objection to Consideration

In legislatures there are few occasions when an objection to consideration may be properly made, but the legislative practice is to require a majority

---

Sec. 297, Par. 1: Hughes, Sec. 231; Sturgis, p. 89.

Sec. 297, Par. 2: Sturgis, p. 89; Hughes, Sec. 231.

Sec. 298: Sturgis, p. 91; Hughes, Secs. 233, 715; Reed, Sec. 110; Waples, Sec. 4.

vote to sustain an objection to the consideration of a question.

Sec. 300. Effect of Objection to Consideration

1. When objection to the consideration of a question is sustained, the whole question is dismissed for the session. When an objection is overruled, procedure continues as if no objection had been made.

2. A vote on an objection to consideration of a matter may not be reconsidered and the subject objected to cannot be again presented to the session unless the proposal or the situation is so changed as to present an essentially new question.

3. Objection to consideration of new questions or motions should not be confused with actions requiring unanimous consent and which permit the objection of any member to prevent action being taken.

Sec. 299: Jefferson, Sec. XLI; Hughes, Secs. 232, 234; Reed, Sec. 110; Sturgis, p. 91, referring to private associations, states that a two-thirds vote is required.

Sec. 300, Par. 1: Sturgis, p. 91; Reed, Sec. 110.

Sec. 300, Par. 2: Hughes, Sec. 230; Sturgis, p. 91.

CHAPTER 30

ORDER AND MANNER OF CONSIDERING QUESTIONS

Sec. 302. Order of Considering Questions

The order in which questions will be considered must be resolved prior to undertaking consideration of questions before the body. Motions dealing with the order of consideration have priority over the problems out of which they arise and, in general, take precedence as incidental questions immediately following objections to consideration.

Sec. 303. Manner of Considering Questions

After the order in which questions are to be taken up has been decided, it is frequently important to determine the procedures to be followed in the course of consideration. Among the questions which often arise and sometimes prove vexatious are:

(a) Should consideration be paragraph by paragraph?

(b) Should the entire question be discussed first?

(c) Which phases of the problem should be given prior consideration, if there are distinct phases of the problem involved in a decision?

Sec. 304. Debate and Application of Other Motions to Questions of Order or Manner of Considering Questions

1. The determination of the order or manner of considering questions presents simple procedural questions and is governed by the same rules which relate to other purely procedural matters.

2. These questions are not subject to debate, but, as in other cases, comments or suggestions may be permitted. Questions, however, are ordinarily so simple that to permit argument would be a waste of time.

3. Questions relating to order or manner of considering questions are not ordinarily subject to amendment. If, however, some member presents an entire program for considering measures, this program would be subject to amendment as it may be desired to change the items on the program or to change the order of their consideration.

4. These motions are not subject to other subsidiary motions as to postpone either temporarily, to a definite time, to refer to committee or to postpone indefinitely. The questions may not be reconsidered but may be renewed in an essentially different form or may be renewed after a change in the parliamentary situation.

5. Only motions relating to pending questions of order or manner of considering have priority. Questions regarding future consideration are main questions and subject to all of the rules of main questions. However, if the question presented involves

Sec. 304, Par. 1: Sturgis, p. 91.

the present consideration of any question, it is entitled to priority as an incidental question and is entitled to consideration and determination before the question out of which it arises.

6. Motions relating to the order or manner of considering questions must vary widely in form to meet varied questions which may require a decision. They are a family of motions which can be recognized by their purpose and use.

CHAPTER 31

VOTING, NOMINATIONS AND ELECTIONS

See also Ch. 46, Secs. 520–528, Rules Governing Voting; Ch. 48, Secs. 545–550, Nominations; Ch. 49, Secs. 552–556, Elections; and Sec. 531, Determining Manner of Voting.

Sec. 306. Motions Relating to Voting

1. The essential procedures of voting are established by parliamentary law and will in most cases prove entirely adequate. Special rules relating to voting may be contained in the rules of the body. There are still, however, occasions when it may be necessary or desirable at the time of voting to decide how the vote is to be taken or make other decisions with reference to voting.

2. If, for example, voting is ordinarily viva voce and some member feels that on a particular measure the vote should be by roll call or by ballot, that member is entitled before the vote is taken to propose the manner in which the vote may be taken. If the voting is to be by ballot, a member may propose such procedure as may be necessary to put into effect or further regulate the voting by ballot.

Sec. 307. Procedure Relating to Nominations and Elections

While the general rules relating to nominations and elections are determined by parliamentary law, it is frequently necessary or desirable to meet imme-

Sec. 306: Sturgis, p. 147; Demeter, p. 133.

diate problems by some particular decision or rule relating to a pending question of nomination or election. Prior to the nomination or election or at the time the decision becomes necessary, it is in order for a member to propose such procedure as that person thinks proper.

Sec. 308. Motions Relating to Voting, Nominations or Elections

1. Motions relating to voting, nominations or elections have a higher precedence than questions out of which they arise and must be decided before proceeding with the voting, nomination or election. These motions take precedence following motions relating to manner or order of considering questions and before division of questions.

2. Such motions are not debatable because they are simple procedural motions requiring immediate determination and are for the same reason not subject to subsidiary motions, except the motion to amend. Decisions on these questions are not subject to reconsideration and decisions are ordinarily promptly carried out. A motion which is voted down may be renewed as an essentially different proposition at any time if the subject matter is within the control of the body and when the situation is essentially different.

3. Because of the varied situations from which these motions arise, they may vary widely in specific purpose and form. They are to be recognized by their general purpose rather than by any characteris-

Sec. 307: Sturgis, p. 147; Demeter, p. 135.

Sec. 308: Sturgis, pp. 147–159; Demeter, p. 125; Robert's, pp. 141, 142.

tics of form. A qualified presiding officer should have no difficulty in recognizing and dealing with them.

CHAPTER 32

DIVISION OF QUESTIONS

Demand for Division, When Right Is Given

Sec. 310. Single Subject, When Mandatory

1. The constitutions of most states require that no bill shall contain more than one subject. Sometimes, they also contain other provisions, such as requiring, in an election, that candidates be voted upon separately. The purpose of these provisions is to secure the independent judgment of the members on each question and prevent members being required to vote for one proposition, which they may not approve, in order to secure the enactment of another.

2. Adopted rules often give the members the right to insist on a separate vote on each independent proposition.

3. In some jurisdictions this single subject principle is recognized in the absence of clear constitutional or statutory requirements.

4. When a resolution or other proposal is susceptible of separation into two or more parts, a member may call for its division so that each may be voted upon separately without being compelled to accept matters embraced in other parts of the measure. In such cases the propositions need not be incongruous or contradictory. It is sufficient if each is distinct and complete in itself and of such a nature that a

member might reasonably wish to vote for one and against another.

Sec. 311. When Division of Question Can Be Required

1. When the constitution, law or rule requires that each proposition have a single subject and a question contains two or more separate and distinct propositions, it is the right of any member to demand that the question be divided into separate propositions.

2. When there is a requirement that each question or candidate be voted upon separately, any member has the right to demand that any proposal containing more than one question be divided into its separate parts or that separate votes be taken upon each proposition or candidate.

Sec. 312. When Right of Division Can Be Suspended

1. When the requirement of a single subject or separate vote is contained in a constitution or controlling statute, it is binding on the body and cannot be suspended.

2. When the rule exists only as a rule adopted by the body it can be suspended as any other such rule, and where it is applied as a rule of parliamentary law it can be suspended as can other rules of parliamentary law.

Sec. 310, Par. 4: Waples, Sec. 83.

Sec. 311: Sturgis, pp. 100–103; U.S. House Rule XV, Par. 6 and notes following; Hughes, Secs. 403–405; Tilson, pp. 70, 193; Cushing, Secs. 81, 82; Cushing's Legislative Assemblies, Secs. 1342–1348; Reed, Secs. 151, 152.

Sec. 313. What Questions Can Be Divided

1. To be divisible, a question must include points so distinct and separate that, one of them being taken away, the other will stand as a complete proposition. A question not capable of being so divided may still be objectionable as containing more than one subject.

2. However complicated a single proposition may be, as long as it contains only one subject, no member has a right to insist upon its division. The member's remedy is to move that it be divided, if it is capable of division, or, if not, to move to strike out the objectionable parts and leave one clear proposition.

3. If a series of independent resolutions relating to different subjects is included in one motion, it must be divided on the request of a single member and wherever there are several names in a question they must, on demand, be put to vote separately.

4. When a committee reports a number of amendments to a question referred to it, one vote may be taken on adopting or agreeing to all of the amendments, provided no one objects. But if a member requests separate votes on one or more of the amendments relating to separate or distinct points, they must be voted upon separately. The others may all be voted on together.

Sec. 313, Par. 1: Jefferson, Sec. XXXVI; N.Y. Manual, p. 471; Tilson, p. 70; Cushing, Secs. 79, 80; Reed, Sec. 151; Sturgis, pp. 100–103.

Sec. 313, Par. 2: Jefferson, Sec. XXXVI; Sturgis, pp. 101, 102; Cushing's Legislative Assemblies, Sec. 1348; Reed, Secs. 151, 152.

Sec. 313, Par. 3: Jefferson, Sec. XXXVI.

Sec. 314. Precedence and Rules Governing Demand for a Division

1. A demand for a division takes precedence as an incidental motion but yields to privileged motions and all other incidental motions.

2. When a member has the right to demand a division, that person's demand is not subject to debate, amendment or other subsidiary motions.

3. Whether a proposition contains two or more subjects is a question to be decided by the presiding officer in the first instance but that decision is subject to appeal.

Division of Questions Where Single Subject or Separate Vote Rule Does Not Exist

Sec. 315. When Questions May Be Divided on Motion

1. Where there is no rule giving members the right to vote separately on each proposition, a member still has the right to submit a motion to divide a question when it contains two or more distinct propositions.

2. When a measure includes several distinct propositions but is so written that they cannot be separated without its being rewritten, the measure cannot simply be ordered divided. An order to divide a question must not require the secretary to do more than to mechanically separate the resolution into the required parts, prefixing to each part

---

Sec. 314: Sturgis, p. 103; Tilson, p. 70; Cushing's Legislative Assemblies, Secs. 1347, 1348.

Sec. 315, Par. 1: Sturgis, pp. 101–103.

the words, "Resolved, That," or "Ordered, That," dropping conjunctions when necessary, replacing pronouns by the nouns for which they stand whenever the division makes it necessary, renumbering divisions, and making like changes.

3. When a question is divided, each separate question must be complete and proper, irrespective of any action taken upon the other or any of the other questions.

4. The motion to amend by striking out certain words and inserting others is strictly one proposition, and therefore indivisible.

Sec. 316. The Motion to Divide a Question

1. When a proposition contains several parts, each of which is not capable of standing as a separate proposition if the others are removed, it can be divided by a motion to divide the question in a specified manner. The motion must clearly state how the question is to be divided. Any other member may propose a different division. These different propositions are alternative propositions and should be voted on in the order in which they are made, unless they suggest different numbers of questions, when the largest number is voted on first.

2. The motion or demand to divide a question can be applied to main motions and to amendments containing two or more distinct propositions.

Sec. 315, Par. 2: Cushing, Sec. 83; Cushing's Legislative Assemblies, Secs. 1342–1345; Sturgis, pp. 101, 102.

Sec. 315, Par. 3: Cushing, Secs. 80–83; Reed, Sec. 151.

Sec. 315, Par. 4: N.Y. Manual, p. 471; Tilson, p. 70; Reed, Sec. 141.

Sec. 316: Cushing's Legislative Assemblies, Secs. 1343–1353; Sturgis, p. 103; Reed, Sec. 151.

3. The motion or demand to divide a question may be made at any time when the question to be divided, or the motion to postpone the question indefinitely is immediately pending, even after the previous question has been ordered.

4. A member does not have the right to insist on a motion to divide when another member has the floor, but in the interest of saving time and more orderly consideration of business a member may be asked to relinquish the floor while it is determined whether a proposition should be divided.

5. The motion to divide a question takes precedence as an incidental question having priority over all subsidiary motions. A proposal to strike out extraneous matter or to rewrite a proposal containing more than one subject but not capable of division is a motion to amend and takes precedence as such. The motion to divide a question may be amended as to the matter of dividing the question, but it can have no other subsidiary motions applied to it. It is not subject to debate.

6. The formality of a vote on dividing the question is generally dispensed with, as it is usually arranged by general consent. But if this cannot be done, then a formal motion to divide is necessary, specifying the exact method of division.

*

DIVISION 3

SUBSIDIARY MOTIONS

CHAPTER 33

MOTION TO LAY ON THE TABLE

(Postpone Temporarily)

Sec. 330. Purpose of Motion to Lay on the Table

The purpose of the motion to lay on the table is to enable the body to lay aside the pending question in such a way that its consideration may be resumed at the will of the body and in preference to new questions competing with it for consideration. The motion to lay on the table, being undebatable and requiring but a majority vote, serves this purpose.

Sec. 331. Application of Motion to Lay on the Table

1. The motion to lay on the table may be applied to:

(a) Any main motion.

(b) Any question of privilege.

(c) Any order of the day after it is before the house for consideration.

Sec. 330: Jefferson, Sec. XXXIII; People *ex rel.* MacMahon v. Davis (1918), 284 Ill. 439, 120 N.E. 326; Cushing, Secs. 71, 171; Reed, Sec. 114; Cushing's Legislative Assemblies, Sec. 1449; Sturgis, p. 70; Tilson, p. 58; Robert's, p. 177.

(d) Any appeal.

(e) Any motion to reconsider when immediately pending.

(f) A bill of either house in any stage of its progress even after being returned from the other house with amendments.

(g) Only questions actually before the house.

2. The motion to lay on the table may not be applied to:

(a) Procedural motions.

(b) Privileged motions.

(c) Incidental or subsidiary motions relating to procedure.

(d) The disposal of business.

(e) Anything except a question actually before the house.

It is not in order to lay on the table a class of questions such as the orders of the day, unfinished business or reports of committees because only one main motion can be pending at a time.

Sec. 332. When Motion to Lay on the Table Is in Order

The motion to lay on the table is in order immediately after the stating of a question and before a member entitled to prior recognition has been recognized, or at any time thereafter while the question is still before the body, even after the adoption of the

---

Sec. 331, Par. 1: Sturgis, pp. 72, 73; Hughes, Secs. 274, 285; Robert's, p. 178; Waples, Sec. 50.

Sec. 331, Par. 2: Hughes, Secs. 278, 285; Sturgis, p. 71.

previous question. The motion can be made by any member who secures recognition.

Sec. 333. Precedence of Motion to Lay on the Table

The motion to lay on the table takes precedence over all other subsidiary motions and yields to privileged and incidental motions.

Sec. 334. Form of Motion to Lay on the Table

The motion to lay on the table may vary somewhat in form. The more usual forms are: "I move that the question be laid on the table," or "I move to lay the question (or motion, bill or resolution, etc.) on the table," or "I move that consideration (or further consideration) of the motion be postponed temporarily." The question cannot be qualified in any way, for if it is qualified it loses its status. A motion to lay the question on the table until a certain time is a motion to postpone definitely and takes a lower rank of precedence.

Sec. 335. Debate on Motion to Lay on the Table and Application of Subsidiary Motions

1. It is a matter of importance to a body that the consideration of a question may be put over to a later date without debate or delay. To permit debate

Sec. 332: Hughes, Sec. 278; Sturgis, p. 73.

Sec. 333: Reed, Secs. 117, 201; Cushing, Sec. 171a; Sturgis, p. 73; Robert's, p. 178.

Sec. 334: Sturgis, p. 71; Demeter, p. 98; Robert's, p. 184.

on the motion to lay on the table would defeat this purpose. This motion is therefore not debatable.

2. The motion to lay on the table is not subject to amendment.

3. No motion to amend or other subsidiary motions can be applied to the motion to lay on the table.

Sec. 336. Vote Required to Lay Question on Table

A motion to lay on the table requires only a majority vote even though the question is suppressed if not taken from the table.

Sec. 337. Effect of Laying a Question on the Table

1. The effect of the adoption of this motion is to place on the table, that is, in charge of the secretary or clerk, the pending question and everything adhering to it. According to the usual practice of legislative bodies in this country, a motion laid on the table may be taken from the table and proceeded with at any time, even on the same day it was laid on the table.

Sec. 335, Par. 1: Hughes, Sec. 274; Cushing, Sec. 171a; Reed, Secs. 117, 201; N.Y. Manual, p. 464; Cushing's Legislative Assemblies, Sec. 1523; Sturgis, p. 72.

Sec. 335, Par. 2: Sturgis, p. 72; Reed, Secs. 117, 164, 201; Hughes, Sec. 274; Waples, Sec. 55.

Sec. 335, Par. 3: Reed, Sec. 164; Waples, Sec. 55; Sturgis, p. 73; Hughes, Sec. 274; Robert's, p. 184.

Sec. 336: Sturgis, p. 73; Demeter, p. 95; Robert's, p. 179.

Sec. 337, Par. 1: Cushing's Legislative Assemblies, Sec. 1449; Sturgis, p. 72; Waples, Sec. 30; Cushing, Sec. 172.

2. As sometimes used in legislative bodies under a special rule a motion to lay on the table has the effect of final adverse disposition of the question. When this use is permitted, it has the advantage to the mover, over the question to postpone indefinitely, that it is not debatable and has a higher order of precedence.

3. A question laid on the table is not to be regarded as finally disposed of unless the rules clearly so provide, or unless the practice is established beyond question. The general rule is that the motion to table leaves the tabled measure open, to be thereafter taken up.

4. The practice of the House of Representatives of the United States and some states regarding the use of motion to lay on the table is different from that of general parliamentary law. In those bodies a motion to lay on the table is used only for the purpose of making a final unfavorable disposition of a matter.

5. Questions laid on the table remain there for the entire session unless taken up before the session closes.

Sec. 338. Matters Adhering to Question When Laid on the Table

1. When a question is laid on the table the principal motion, together with all of the incidental and

Sec. 337, Par. 2: Hughes, Sec. 285.

Sec. 337, Par. 3: Wright v. Wiles (1938), 173 Tenn. 334, 17 S.W.2d 736, 119 A.L.R. 456.

Sec. 337, Par. 4: People *ex rel.* MacMahon v. Davis (1918), 284 Ill. 439, 120 N.E. 326.

Sec. 337, Par. 5: People *ex rel.* MacMahon v. Davis (1918), 284 Ill. 439, 120 N.E. 326.

subsidiary motions connected with or adhering to it, is laid on the table with it.

2. When an amendment is pending to a question and the main question is laid on the table, the amendment goes to the table. A motion to amend being a subsidiary motion cannot be laid on the table by itself, but it is sometimes the practice to accept a motion to lay an amendment on the table since it carries the main motion with it. When either is taken from the table, the other comes with it.

3. A motion to refer likewise adheres to the main question and goes with it to the table.

4. When a motion to reconsider is laid on the table, the question proposed to be reconsidered goes with it, but when a motion to reconsider a vote whereby amendments of the other house were agreed to is laid on the table, the motion does not carry the bill with it to the table.

5. A question of privilege may be laid on the table without carrying with it the question which it interrupted.

6. An appeal from the decision of the presiding officer may be laid on the table and, when so disposed of, has the effect of defeating the appeal, and the decision stands. Neither the question out of which the appeal arose, nor any other matter, is

---

Sec. 338, Par. 1: Cushing, Sec. 172; N.Y. Manual, pp. 452, 472; Reed, Sec. 114; Cushing's Legislative Assemblies, Sec. 1449; Sturgis, p. 72; Robert's, pp. 178, 179.

Sec. 338, Par. 2: Hughes, Sec. 274; N.Y. Manual, p. 408; Reed, Secs. 114, 166; Cushing's Legislative Assemblies, Sec. 1449; Sturgis, pp. 71–73.

Sec. 338, Par. 3: Sturgis, p. 72.

Sec. 338, Par. 4: Hughes, Sec. 642.

carried with it to the table but the main question is unaffected and is still before the house.

7. Either a committee report or a "minority" report may be laid on the table without affecting the other report.

8. When a motion to instruct conferees is laid on the table, the bill does not accompany it.

Sec. 339. Renewal of Motion to Lay on the Table

1. A motion to lay a question on the table may be renewed after progress in debate or business, or after the amendment of the question.

2. When a motion to lay on the table has been lost, or a question has been taken from the table, a motion to lay that question on the table is not in order until there has been progress in business or debate, or unless an unforeseen urgent matter requires immediate attention. The house cannot be required to vote again the same day on laying the question on the table, unless there is such a change in the situation as to make it a new question.

Sec. 340. The Motion to Lay on the Table May Not Be Reconsidered

See also Sec. 450, paragraph 6, Right to Reconsider, and Sec. 451, What Actions Cannot Be Reconsidered.

Sec. 338, Par. 6: Hughes, Sec. 286; N.Y. Manual, p. 410; U.S. House Rule XVI and notes following.

Sec. 338, Par. 7: N.Y. Manual, p. 485.

Sec. 338, Par. 8: Hughes, Sec. 287; U.S. House Rule XVI, Note 785.

Sec. 339, Par. 1: Hughes, Sec. 274; Reed, Secs. 116, 201; Cushing's Legislative Assemblies, Sec. 1451; Sturgis, p. 32.

Sec. 339, Par. 2: Reed, Sec. 116.

The usual rule is that an affirmative vote on a motion to lay on the table may not be reconsidered because the proper procedure is to move to take from the table, and a negative vote on the motion cannot be reconsidered because the proper procedure is to renew the motion.

Sec. 341. Taking Question from the Table

See also Sec. 492, Motion to Take from the Table.

1. The motion to take from the table or to resume consideration of a question is a main motion and is, therefore, not in order when a question is under consideration.

2. When a question has been laid on the table because an urgent matter requires immediate attention, it may be taken from the table as soon as the urgent business is taken up.

3. In legislative bodies a question is laid on the table only temporarily with the expectation that its consideration will be resumed after the disposal of the interrupting questions or at a more convenient time. When taken up the question with everything adhering to it is before assembly exactly as when it was laid on the table.

Sec. 340: Hughes, Sec. 274; N.Y. Manual, p. 502; Reed, Sec. 204; Sturgis, pp. 45, 47.

Sec. 341, Par. 1: Hughes, Sec. 277.

Sec. 341, Par. 2: Cushing's Legislative Assemblies, Sec. 1449.

Sec. 341, Par. 3: People *ex rel.* MacMahon v. Davis (1918), 284 Ill. 439, 120 N.E. 326; Goodwin v. State Board of Administration (1925), 210 Ala. 453, 102 So. 718; Reed, Sec. 114.

Sec. 342. Postpone Temporarily

1. The motion to lay on the table is also sometimes called the motion to postpone temporarily. This name is more descriptive than the usual name since the real purpose of the motion to lay on the table is to postpone the question for an undetermined but usually brief period.

2. The same rules apply to the motion by whichever name it may be known.

3. The motion may be stated as: "I move that (identifying the proposition) be postponed temporarily."

Sec. 342: Sturgis, pp. 70–72.

CHAPTER 34

THE PREVIOUS QUESTION

(Vote Immediately)

See also Ch. 35, Secs. 355–361, Motions Closing, Limiting or Extending Limits on Debate; Sec. 131, Cutting Off Debate; and Sec. 132, Preventing Debate by Putting Questions to Vote Prematurely.

Sec. 345. Use of the Previous Question

1. There is a large and not well-defined group of motions which may be used to restrict, close or prevent debate. The previous question has an origin different from other motions having the same or a similar purpose and differs from the other motions in having a definite and distinct form and in several other particulars. This motion may be confused with other motions because its name is not indicative of the nature of the motion.

2. The previous question may be used to close debate on any debatable question. It may be applied to any question to which subsidiary motions may be applied, to prevent the making of subsidiary motions. The effect of the motion, if adopted, is to require that the question be put to vote immediately. It would be more aptly designated "vote immediately," and that term is in use.

3. The previous question applies to the immediately pending motion and adhering motions. A mo-

---

Sec. 345, Par. 1: Jefferson, Sec. XXXIII; Cushing's Legislative Assemblies, Sec. 1428; Reed, Sec. 126; Tilson, p. 82; Robert's, pp. 166, 167.

Sec. 345, Par. 2: Jefferson, Sec. XXIV; Cushing's Legislative Assemblies, Sec. 1428; Sturgis, pp. 67, 68.

tion to bring some particular question to vote is a motion to close debate even though stated as the previous question.

4. The previous question applies to questions of privilege the same as to other debatable questions, such questions being privileged only as to priority of consideration.

5. The previous question when applied to a motion to postpone or a motion to refer does not affect the main question.

6. The previous question may be moved on a series of resolutions, but this does not preclude a division of the resolutions for the purpose of voting on them separately.

Sec. 346. Motion or Demand for the Previous Question

The early practice was to require a demand of a certain proportion of the house before the previous question could be put to vote. The rules in some of the state legislatures still require that the previous question must be demanded by a certain number or by a certain proportion of the members. Where the rules do not specifically require that the previous question be demanded by a certain number or proportion of the members, it may be called for, or moved, the same as any other motion.

Sec. 345, Par. 3: Waples, Sec. 114; Sturgis, p. 68; Robert's, p. 168.
Sec. 345, Par. 4: N.Y. Manual (1948–49), p. 444.
Sec. 345, Par. 5: Cushing, Sec. 70a; Sturgis, p. 32.
Sec. 345, Par. 6: U.S. House Rule XVII, Note 806.
Sec. 346: Hughes, Sec. 291.

Sec. 347. Form of the Previous Question

1. The form of the motion for the previous question is "I move the previous question." It is also proper to state the motion as: "I call for the previous question," or "I move that we vote immediately." The use of the obscure and confusing designation for the previous question has often led in practice to the use of a more descriptive name. The term "vote immediately" has acquired recognition and is sometimes used in place of the old designation of "previous question."

2. The form of the previous question, as established by ancient parliamentary practice, and the form which is required by the rules of many of the states, is "Shall the main question be now put?" The motion in this form applies only to the question before the house and adhering questions.

3. The question on closing debate is frequently put to vote in the form: "As many as are in favor of ordering the previous question on (stating the question or questions), please say 'yea,' " or "All in favor of voting immediately on, etc." When the question is permitted in this form it is proper to specify the pending questions to which it is to be applied. This is really a form of the motion to close debate and should be governed by the rules applicable to those motions.

See also Ch. 35, Secs. 355–361, Motions Closing, Limiting or Extending Limits on Debate.

Sec. 347, Par. 1: Jefferson, Sec. XXIV; Cushing's Legislative Assemblies, Secs. 1280, 1427; Cushing, Sec. 170; Sturgis, p. 67; Robert's, p. 175.

Sec. 347, Par. 2: Cushing's Legislative Assemblies, Sec. 1433; Waples, Sec. 114.

Sec. 347, Par. 3: Sturgis, p. 67; Hughes, Sec. 292.

Sec. 348. Precedence of the Previous Question

1. The previous question takes precedence over the question out of which it arose, of all debatable questions, and of all subsidiary motions except the motion to lay on the table. It yields to all privileged and incidental motions and to the motion to lay on the table.

2. A question may be laid on the table after the previous question has been moved, after the previous question has been ordered on it, and until the last vote has been taken under the previous question.

3. A motion or demand to divide a question is in order even after the adoption of the previous question.

Sec. 349. Previous Question—Debate and Subsidiary Motions

1. The previous question is undebatable and cannot be amended nor have any other subsidiary motion applied to it. It may not be debated nor amended because the purpose of the motion is to prevent further debate and amendment and to bring the matter immediately to vote. The motion cannot be laid on the table, postponed, nor referred to committee because it is a subsidiary motion of such a nature that a decision is required before other action may be taken. The previous question requires an immediate vote on the main question and adhering subsidiary questions; if an amendment were permitted, it would change the previous question to a motion of

---

Sec. 348: Cushing, Sec. 174; Sturgis, p. 70; Robert's, p. 167.

some other kind. The form of the previous question is fixed by parliamentary usage and for that reason also it is not subject to amendment.

2. When the previous question is moved on the motion to reconsider, the previous question applies only to that motion.

Sec. 350. Vote on the Previous Question

1. A majority vote only is required for the adoption of the previous question in legislative bodies.

2. There is no more reason for requiring a two-thirds vote to order the previous question than to require a similar vote in deciding the main question, and such a requirement is at variance with the basic principle of majority rule.

Sec. 351. Effect of the Previous Question

1. The effect of ordering the previous question is to close debate immediately, to prevent the moving of amendments or other subsidiary motions, and to bring to vote promptly the immediately pending main question and the adhering subsidiary questions.

2. When the previous question is ordered, the presiding officer should immediately put the ques-

---

Sec. 349, Par. 1: Jefferson, Sec. XXXIII; Sturgis, p. 70; Hughes, Sec. 290; Reed, Secs. 164, 201; Cushing, Sec. 170; Cushing's Legislative Assemblies, Sec. 1523.

Sec. 349, Par. 2: N.Y. Manual (1948–49), p. 451.

Sec. 350, Par. 1: Hughes, Sec. 290; Cushing's Legislative Assemblies, Sec. 1428; Reed, Sec. 269; Tilson, p. 79. A majority vote only is required by the rules of many of the states.

Sec. 350, Par. 2: Tilson, p. 79.

Sec. 351, Par. 1: Jefferson, Sec. XXIV; Sturgis, p. 70; Cushing, Sec. 175; N.Y. Manual, p. 466.

tion, or questions, upon which it was ordered to vote until all the questions affected have been disposed of, or there has been an affirmative vote on a pending motion to lay on the table, to postpone definitely or indefinitely, or to refer to committee.

3. A rule of Congress provides that an appeal made after the previous question has been ordered and before its effect is exhausted is undebatable. This rule appears to have been rather widely copied. Where there is no such rule an appeal is debatable after the previous question has been ordered on the question out of which the point of order and appeal arose.

Sec. 352. Renewal of the Previous Question and Reconsideration

1. If the previous question is lost, the motion may be renewed after intervening business or after progress in debate or a change in the parliamentary situation.

2. The previous question may not be reconsidered.

Sec. 351, Par. 3: Tilson, p. 82; U.S. House Rule XVII, Par. 3.
Sec. 352, Par. 1: Sturgis, p. 32; Hughes, Sec. 290.
Sec. 352, Par. 2: N.Y. Manual (1948–49), p. 451.

CHAPTER 35

MOTIONS CLOSING, LIMITING OR EXTENDING LIMITS ON DEBATE

See also Ch. 34, Secs. 345–352, The Previous Question; and Sec. 132, Preventing Debate by Putting Questions to Vote Prematurely.

Sec. 355. Nature of Motions Limiting Debate

Motions closing, limiting or extending limits on debate are a group of motions used for the same general purpose and which are subject to the same rules. These motions are closely related to the previous question but that motion had a different origin, has a definite form, and is subject in part to different rules.

Sec. 356. Application of Motions Limiting Debate

1. Motions to close, limit or extend limits of debate may be applied to any debatable motion or series of motions. If not specified to the contrary, these motions apply only to the immediately pending question.

2. Motions to close or limit debate may be applied to a series of pending questions, or to a consecutive part of a series, when the matter immediately pending is one of the series affected. When debate is closed or limited on one or more questions, its effect adheres to these questions, preventing debate

---

Sec. 355: Sturgis, pp. 65, 66; Robert's, p. 161.
Sec. 356: Sturgis, pp. 65, 66; Cushing, Sec. 221; Hughes, Sec. 697; Robert's, pp. 161–166.

until they are finally disposed of or until the order is changed.

3. When a motion to limit or close debate is ordered on more than one pending question, its effect is not exhausted until all the questions have been voted upon, or the effect of those voted upon has been to refer the main question to committee or to postpone it definitely or indefinitely.

4. When it is voted to close or limit debate on a question, the order applies to all incidental and subsidiary motions and the motion to reconsider, subsequently made, as long as the order is in force. But an order extending the limits of debate does not apply to any motion except the one immediately pending and such others as are specified.

5. After the adoption of an order merely limiting the number or length of the speeches, or extending these limits on a particular question, it is in order to move any of the other subsidiary motions on the pending question.

6. The time for debate on any question may be limited by unanimous consent.

Sec. 357. Form of Motions Limiting or Extending Debate

Motions closing, limiting or extending limits of debate may take numerous forms. Illustrations of some of the more usual forms of these motions follow:

(a) To fix the hour for closing debate and putting the question, the form is similar to this: "I move that debate be closed and the question be put on the pending question at three p.m."

(b) To limit the length of the debate, the motion may be made thus: "I move that debate on the pending question be limited to twenty minutes." This motion may also contain the provision that the time should be allotted equally between the proponents and the opponents of the measure or any similar provision.

(c) To reduce or increase the number or length of speeches, the motion might be made in a form similar to the following: "I move that debate on the pending bill, and its amendments, be limited to one speech of five minutes from each member," or "I move that speeches be limited to five minutes each."

(d) To extend the limits of debate, the two following forms are perhaps the most common: "I move that the time of the speaker be extended five minutes," and "I move that the time for debate on the pending question be extended twenty minutes."

Sec. 358. Motions to Close, Limit or Extend Limits on Debate

1. Motions or orders to limit or to extend the limits of debate are undebatable, for to permit debate on these motions would defeat their purpose.

2. Motions to close or limit debate may be amended. When one of them is pending, another one that does not conflict with it may be moved as an amendment. After one of these motions has been

Sec. 357: Sturgis, p. 65; Cushing, Sec. 222; Robert's, p. 165.

Sec. 358, Par. 1: Cushing's Legislative Assemblies, Sec. 1428; Reed, Sec. 269; Hughes, Sec. 290; Sturgis, p. 66; Tilson, p. 79.

adopted, it is in order to move another one of them, provided it does not conflict with the one in force.

3. These motions yield to privileged and incidental motions, and to the motions to lay on the table and for the previous question. These motions take precedence over the other subsidiary motions, and any debatable motion out of which they arise.

4. Motions to close, limit or extend the limits of debate are not subject to subsidiary motions, other than the motion to amend.

5. These motions require only a majority vote.

Sec. 359. Effect of Closing or Limiting Debate

1. After the adoption of a motion limiting the number or length of the speeches, or extending these limits, it is in order to move any of the other subsidiary motions on the pending question since such motions do not dispose of the motions to which they are applied.

2. When debate has been limited, the time may be extended by unanimous consent or by the adoption of a motion to that effect.

3. When debate has been limited and a member has spoken the allotted time, the presiding officer should call to order and notify that member of the expiration of the allotted time.

Sec. 358, Par. 2: Sturgis, p. 66.
Sec. 358, Par. 3: Sturgis, p. 66.
Sec. 358, Par. 4: Reed, Sec. 269; Tilson, p. 79; Sturgis, p. 66.
Sec. 358, Par. 5: Reed, Sec. 269; Hughes, Sec. 697; Tilson, p. 79.
Sec. 359: Sturgis, p. 66; Hughes, Secs. 703, 704, 738; Mass. Manual, p. 667.

4. When consent to continue is not asked by another member, the member speaking may properly do so.

5. Adoption of a motion to close debate at a specified time does not shut off the opportunity of moving amendments, as would the adoption of the previous question.

Sec. 360. Renewal and Reconsideration of Motions Limiting Debate

The motions to limit or extend the limits of debate, if lost, may be renewed after there has been sufficient progress in debate to make it a new question. After motions closing or limiting debate are adopted, the limitations are often modified by motions to extend time or to extend debate without reconsideration of the original motion. A motion changing a limit or restriction on debate may be made whenever the situation is so changed that a different decision might reasonably be made by the house. Limitations on debate are also frequently modified by unanimous consent.

Sec. 361. Other Means of Preventing or Limiting Debate

1. A legislative body may lay a question on the table, and thus temporarily suspend the debate. It can be resumed by taking the question from the table when no question is before the house and at a time when business of this class or unfinished business or new business is in order.

Sec. 360: Sturgis, p. 32.
Sec. 361: Sturgis, pp. 89–91.

See also Ch. 33, Secs. 330–342, Motion to Lay on the Table.

2. A legislative body may prevent or stop debate at any time by the adoption of the previous question.

See also Ch. 34, Secs. 345–352, The Previous Question.

3. If it is desired to prevent any discussion of a subject, even by its introducer, this can be most effectively accomplished by objecting to the consideration of the question before it is debated or any subsidiary motion is stated.

See also Ch. 29, Secs. 293–300, Objection to the Consideration of Questions.

4. Debate may also be terminated for the time by postponement to a definite time or by reference of the question to a committee.

See also Ch. 36, Secs. 365–374, Motion to Postpone to a Certain Time or Definitely, and Ch. 37, Secs. 378–391, Motion to Refer or Commit.

Sec. 361, Par. 4: Sturgis, pp. 61–64, 57–60.

CHAPTER 36

MOTION TO POSTPONE TO A CERTAIN TIME OR DEFINITELY

Sec. 365. Application of Motion to Postpone Definitely

The motion to postpone to a certain time may be applied only to main motions. To permit it to be applied to privileged, incidental or subsidiary motions would be piling questions one on another, which is not allowed, and the same result may be accomplished more simply by voting down such subsidiary motions and renewing them at a later time if desired. A question of privilege being a main question is subject to postponement.

Sec. 366. Precedence of Motion to Postpone Definitely

The motion to postpone to a certain time or definitely takes precedence over the motions to commit, amend, postpone indefinitely and main motions. It yields to all privileged and incidental motions, to the motion to lay on the table, the previous question, and motions to close, limit or extend the limits of debate.

Sec. 365: Jefferson, Sec. XXXIII; Cushing, Secs. 168, 169, 180; Sturgis, pp. 61, 62; Hughes, Sec. 315; Robert's, pp. 150–160.

Sec. 366: Sturgis, p. 64; Reed, Sec. 118; Cushing, Sec. 70a; N.Y. Manual (1948–49), p. 474; Robert's, p. 151.

Sec. 367. Only Pending Question May Be Postponed

1. Business that is required by the rules to be attended to at a specified time or in a particular order cannot be postponed in advance to another time, but when the specified time arrives, it may be postponed to a later time or order of business.

2. It is not in order to postpone a class of business such as reports of committees. But as each question is announced or called for it may be postponed or the rules may be suspended and the desired question be taken up.

3. After an order of the day or a question of privilege is before the house for action, its further consideration may be postponed, or any other subsidiary motion may be applied to it.

Sec. 368. Form of the Motion to Postpone Definitely

1. The usual form of the motion is "I move to postpone consideration (or further consideration) of (describing the question) until (stating the time)," or "I move that the consideration (or further consideration) of (describing the question) be postponed until (stating the time)."

2. The motion should specify either the hour or the order of business to which the question is to be postponed, as "at ten a.m.," or "following second reading" on a certain day.

Sec. 367: Sturgis, pp. 62, 152.

Sec. 368: Sturgis, pp. 61, 64; Robert's, pp. 152, 159; Hughes, Sec. 317.

3. If it is desired to set the question as a special order, the motion might be "I move that the question be postponed and made a special order for (stating the time)."

Sec. 369. Limited Debate Permitted on Motion to Postpone Definitely

1. On the motion to postpone to a definite time the question of postponement is open to debate, but the main question is not. The merits of the main question must not be referred to any more than is necessary to enable the house to determine the propriety of the postponement. The theory upon which debate on the question postponed is prohibited is that the effect of the motion is merely to defer debate on the question. The purpose of the motion would be entirely lost if discussion of the merits of the bill were permitted at this stage.

2. The previous question and the motions closing, limiting or extending the limits of debate may be applied to the motion to postpone definitely, but these motions, when so applied, do not affect any other pending motions.

Sec. 370. Application of Subsidiary Motions to Motion to Postpone Definitely

Motion to Lay on the Table

1. The motion to postpone definitely or to a certain time may not be laid on the table. When it is

---

Sec. 369: Hughes, Secs. 316, 733; Sturgis, p. 64; N.Y. Manual, pp. 364, 463; Reed, Secs. 118, 201; Tilson, p. 64; Cushing, Sec. 70a.

pending the main question may be laid on the table, which carries with it and defeats the motion to postpone.

Reference to Committee

2. The motion to postpone definitely may not be referred to committee, but when the motion to refer or commit is pending and the main question is laid on the table, the motion to refer or commit is carried with it and defeated.

Amendment

3. The motion to postpone definitely may be amended as to the time, and also by making the postponed question a special order, but not otherwise.

4. The better procedure appears to be to regard proposals for postponement to different times as alternative propositions, putting the question on the longest time first.

Postponement

5. The motion to postpone definitely cannot itself be postponed either to a certain time or indefinitely.

6. A motion to postpone to a certain day having been voted down, the presiding officer may entertain a motion to postpone to a different day.

Sec. 370, Par. 1: Hughes, Sec. 316; Sturgis, p. 64.
Sec. 370, Par. 2: Hughes, Sec. 316; Sturgis, p. 64.
Sec. 370, Par. 3: Jefferson, Sec. XXXIII; Sturgis, p. 64; Hughes, Sec. 316; Reed, Secs. 118, 165, 201; Cushing, Sec. 176.
Sec. 370, Par. 4: Cushing, Secs. 176, 178.
Sec. 370, Par. 5: Hughes, Sec. 316; Sturgis, p. 64.
Sec. 370, Par. 6: Mass. Manual, p. 620.

Sec. 371. Vote Required on Motion to Postpone Definitely

1. The simple motion to postpone definitely requires a majority vote.

2. In legislative bodies the general rule is that special orders require only a majority vote. But if a motion to postpone also sets the question as a special order and, by rule, a two-thirds vote is required to set a special order, then a motion to postpone and set as a special order requires a two-thirds vote.

3. A majority vote only is required to amend the question to postpone, even though the amendment also sets the question as a special order, and under a special rule a two-thirds vote is required to set a special order. The vote on the original motion, as amended, would require a two-thirds vote.

Sec. 372. Reconsideration and Renewal of Motion to Postpone Definitely

1. The motion to postpone may be renewed after intervening business or progress in debate.

2. If a question has been postponed and it is desired to give it further consideration before the time to which it was postponed, it may be taken up without reconsidering the vote by which it was postponed.

Sec. 371: Hughes, Sec. 316; Sturgis, p. 64; Robert's, p. 153.

Sec. 372, Par. 1: Sturgis, p. 32; Cushing's Legislative Assemblies, Sec. 1376.

Sec. 372, Par. 2: Sturgis, p. 62.

Sec. 373. Postponed Question May Become an Order of the Day

1. The effect of postponing a question to a certain day and hour is to make it a general order of the day for the time to which it was postponed. If it is not then disposed of, it becomes unfinished business. Postponing a question to a certain hour does not make it a special order unless so specified in the motion.

2. When a question has been postponed to a certain time, it becomes an order of the day for that time.

Sec. 374. Definite Distinguished from Indefinite Postponement

1. The time to which a question is postponed must fall within the session. Neither the motion to postpone definitely nor an amendment to this motion is in order which would have the effect of an indefinite postponement, that is, to defeat the measure by postponing it until after final adjournment or until it is too late to act upon it, or until action would be ineffective.

2. When the motion to postpone is, in fact, a motion to postpone indefinitely, and that motion is in order at the time, the presiding officer may treat the motion as such at the presiding officer's discretion. However, it cannot be recognized as a motion to postpone definitely.

Sec. 373: Sturgis, p. 62; Cushing's Legislative Assemblies, Sec. 1377.
Sec. 374, Par. 1: Jefferson, Sec. XXXIII; Sturgis, p. 63; Cushing, Sec. 70; Robert's, pp. 103, 150.
Sec. 374, Par. 2: Demeter, p. 87.

CHAPTER 37

MOTION TO REFER OR COMMIT

Sec. 378. Purpose of Reference to Committee

1. The purpose of referring a question to committee may be:

(a) To secure a more thorough study of the question than the time of the larger organization would permit.

(b) To secure an investigation or to give time and an opportunity to conduct an investigation.

(c) To secure privacy for the consideration of a delicate question.

(d) To give a better opportunity for persons to appear either for or against the matter and to hear and question witnesses to an extent that would not be possible in the committee of the whole.

(e) To permit more informal consideration.

(f) To revise or redraft a proposal or a report and put it into better form.

(g) To keep the consideration more completely within the control of a particular group.

(h) To delay consideration of the question until a more favorable opportunity.

(i) To prevent action on the question or to delay action.

Sec. 378: Sturgis, pp. 57, 58; Jefferson, Sec. XXXIII; Cushing, Secs. 73, 181a, 183; Reed, Sec. 119; Hughes, Sec. 331; Robert's, p. 140.

2. In legislative bodies it is good practice to refer every main question to a committee for its consideration unless immediate action is required.

Sec. 379. Precedence of Motion to Refer

1. The motion to refer a pending question takes precedence over the motions to amend, to postpone indefinitely and main motions. It yields to all the other subsidiary motions and to all privileged and incidental motions.

2. The motion to refer to committee is in order at the time a question is brought up for consideration, or at any time during the consideration of the question.

3. The motion to refer, when made with reference to a question not pending, takes precedence as a main motion.

Sec. 380. Application of Motion to Refer

The motion to refer or commit may be applied to any main motion. Procedural motions concerning pending questions are decided by the body as they arise and not referred to committee. They do not require study by committees and may be made when they are needed.

Sec. 381. Reference of Bills to Committee

1. Bills or other measures may be referred to

Sec. 379, Par. 1: Jefferson, Sec. XXXIII; Hughes, Sec. 330; Cushing, Sec. 70a; Reed, Sec. 119; Sturgis, p. 60; Robert's, p. 141.

Sec. 379, Par. 2: Sturgis, pp. 59, 60.

Sec. 379, Par. 3: Sturgis, p. 60.

Sec. 380: Jefferson, Sec. XXXIII; Sturgis, p. 60; Hughes, Sec. 330; Reed, Sec. 10; Robert's, p. 142.

standing or special committees not yet appointed.

2. Where the rules require that all bills be referred to committee, a bill which has been introduced by a committee is not required to be referred back to a committee for further consideration.

Sec. 382. Correction of Errors in Reference to Bills

A bill which has been referred to the wrong committee may be re-referred as follows:

(a) By the presiding officer upon unanimous consent.

(b) Upon a motion from the floor.

(c) If the bill may be reported back by the committee to which it was referred with the recommendation that it be re-referred to the appropriate committee.

Sec. 383. Variation from Rule Regarding Reference of Bills

When the matter of reference of bills is covered by rule, any variation from this rule, made by a motion to refer, is, of course, equivalent to a suspension of the rules. The usual and better form of rule is to provide for legislation to be referred to particular committees subject to the right of the body to direct otherwise.

Sec. 384. Re-Reference of Bills

1. A bill may be re-referred to a committee which originally considered it or to any other committee

Sec. 381, Par. 1: Hughes, Sec. 840.
Sec. 381, Par. 2: N.Y. Manual, p. 416.
Sec. 382: Hughes, Secs. 49, 792.

including the committee of the whole. When re-referred without limitation the entire bill is open to consideration by the committee or when amendments are proposed to a bill the committee may be restricted to consideration of the amendments only.

2. After a bill has been reported by a committee it should be recommitted only in cases of importance and for special reasons. It is usually referred back to the same committee. When a measure is recommitted before the report has been considered or approved in the house, the whole question is again before the committee and the first report of the committee is disregarded.

3. It is advisable to refer a bill back to committee when numerous amendments are to be proposed or substantial revision of the bill is required.

4. When an amendment is adopted which causes a bill to have a fiscal impact some states require that the bill be re-referred to a standing fiscal committee for further consideration.

Sec. 385. Motions to Take from Calendar and Refer

A motion to take a bill from the calendar and refer it to a committee takes precedence over the main question. This motion is in order whenever the bill to which it refers is reached on calendar and is before the house. This motion requires a majority

Sec. 384, Par. 1: Hughes, Sec. 803.
Sec. 384, Par. 2: Jefferson, Sec. XXVIII.
Sec. 384, Par. 3: Hughes, Sec. 882.

vote of the members present and voting, but is usually approved by unanimous consent.

Sec. 386. Form of Motion to Refer

1. The motion to refer to committee may vary substantially in form. The most usual form is "I move that the (bill, resolution, etc.) be referred to the committee on (naming the committee)." Or, in case of the reference of a question to a special committee, the motion may be "I move that (the bill, resolution, etc.) be referred to a committee of five to be appointed by the president (or speaker or chair) with the following instructions. . . ." Details of the motion may be added or changed by amendments, although proposed changes are usually not treated as amendments but as alternative propositions.

2. Motions to consider in committee of the whole or "informally" are equivalent to motions to refer to committee, and in these cases the motions may be "I move that the house (or senate) do now resolve into committee of the whole for the purpose of considering (specifying the measure or question)," or "I move that the (specifying the measure or question) be considered informally," or "as if in committee of the whole."

3. All the rules in regard to the motion to commit or refer, except where stated to the contrary, apply equally to the motions to "go into committee of the whole," to "consider informally" and "to recommit."

Sec. 385: Hughes, Sec. 488.
Sec. 386: Sturgis, pp. 57, 58; Robert's, pp. 148, 149.

Sec. 387. Choice of Committee for Reference

1. When the motion to refer is modified and different committees are proposed, the question should be put in the following order:

(a) Committee of the whole.

(b) Standing committees.

(c) Special committees.

2. When two or more standing committees are named, the question is first put as to the last committee named unless the reverse is required by rule.

3. When it has been decided to refer a question to a committee and only two committees are proposed, or when two committees remain, a negative vote on the first proposal is equivalent to an affirmative on the second or remaining committee.

Sec. 388. Debate and Application of Subsidiary Motions to Motion to Refer

1. The motion to refer is debatable only as to the propriety of committing the main question, and does not open the main question to debate. The motion to refer with instructions is debatable as to the instructions.

2. The motion to refer to committee may not be amended, except as to the committee or as to in-

Sec. 387, Par. 1: Hughes, Sec. 337.

Sec. 387, Par. 2: Hughes, Sec. 337; Cushing, Sec. 74.

Sec. 387, Par. 3: Hughes, Sec. 337.

Sec. 388, Par. 1: Hughes, Sec. 330; Reed, Secs. 120, 201; Tilson, p. 65; U.S. House Rule XVI, Notes 787–789; Cushing, Sec. 70a; Sturgis, p. 60; Robert's, p. 143.

structions to the committee.

3. Reference of a measure to committee when amendments are pending carries the amendments to the committee with it. A motion to refer amendments to committee is not technically in order but may be accepted as referring to the main question and all pending amendments. If adopted they will carry with them the question or measure to which the amendments were proposed.

4. The motions to close, limit or extend the limits of debate may be applied to debate on the motion to refer without affecting debate on the main question.

5. The motion to refer to committee may not be laid on the table but if the main question be laid on the table, it carries a pending motion to refer or commit with it.

6. The motion to refer to committee may not be postponed to a certain time but if the main question is postponed, any pending motion to refer to committee is carried with it.

Sec. 389. Vote Required to Refer Question to Committee

1. A majority vote is required to refer a question to committee.

Sec. 388, Par. 2: Hughes, Sec. 330; Cushing, Sec. 181; Reed, Secs. 120, 165, 201; Sturgis, p. 60; Robert's, p. 143.

Sec. 388, Par. 3: Reed, Sec. 166; Sturgis, p. 60.

Sec. 388, Par. 4: Cushing, Sec. 70a; Sturgis, p. 60.

Sec. 388, Par. 5: Hughes, Sec. 330; Sturgis, p. 60.

Sec. 388, Par. 6: Jefferson, Sec. XXXIII; Sturgis, p. 60; Hughes, Sec. 330.

Sec. 389, Par. 1: Hughes, Sec. 330; Sturgis, p. 60; Robert's, p. 143.

2. Whether a question shall be referred to committee, and if so, to what committee, is usually decided by unanimous consent.

Sec. 390. Reconsideration and Renewal of Motion to Refer

1. The motion to refer may be renewed after intervening business except that a motion to refer a bill to committee may not be renewed at the same stage of the bill.

2. The motion to refer to committee may not be reconsidered but the matter referred to committee may be withdrawn.

Sec. 391. Withdrawing Questions from Committee

See also Sec. 491, Withdrawing Bills from Committee.

1. When it is desired to withdraw a question from committee a motion to that effect can be made and, if carried, brings the question back before the body. A motion to withdraw a question from committee requires a majority vote.

2. A matter withdrawn from a committee may be acted upon by the body or referred to another committee.

3. It is not in order to discuss a bill or paper on a motion to withdraw it from committee.

Sec. 390, Par. 1: Sturgis, p. 32.
Sec. 390, Par. 2: Hughes, Secs. 330, 770; Sturgis, p. 60.
Sec. 391, Par. 1: Hughes, Secs. 330, 770; Sturgis, pp. 60, 98–100.
Sec. 391, Par. 2: Sturgis, p. 59.
Sec. 391, Par. 3: Hughes, Sec. 749; Sturgis, p. 60.

CHAPTER 38

MOTION TO AMEND

See also Sec. 731, Amendment of Bills, and Sec. 669, Consideration of Committee Amendments.

Sec. 395. Test of Amendability of Question

1. The following is a convenient test to determine whether a motion or other proposition can be amended. If it could properly have been submitted in a different form, it can be amended. If the proposition could not have been stated in a different form, it cannot be amended. A motion for the previous question or to lay on the table or postpone indefinitely cannot be amended because there is no other proper form for these motions, but the motion to recess or to restrict debate or to postpone definitely can be amended because these have more than one proper form. A motion to recess for ten minutes, for example, might have been made as a motion to recess for thirty minutes or for five minutes, and so can be amended.

2. Certain questions are not of a type capable of amendment. Examples are: points of order, parliamentary inquiries, calls for division to verify a vote, requests of any kind, communications and reports. None of these are proposals for action by the body.

Sec. 395, Par. 1: Sturgis, pp. 51, 52; Hughes, Sec. 431.
Sec. 395, Par. 2: Sturgis, p. 51.

Sec. 396. What Motions May Be Amended

1. Every original main motion may be amended, and all other motions may be amended, except those contained in the following list:

(a) To adjourn (except when it is qualified, or if made when there is no provision for a future meeting).

See also Sec. 207, Amendment to Motion to Adjourn.

(b) Appeals.

See also Sec. 232, Debate on Appeals.

(c) Point of order.

See also Sec. 246, Precedence, Subsidiary Motions and Debate of Point of Order.

(d) Call for the orders of the day.

See also Sec. 259, Debate and Application of Other Motions.

(e) To object to consideration of a question.

See also Sec. 298, Debate and Application of Subsidiary Motions to Objection to Consideration.

(f) Demand for a division of a question.

See also Sec. 314, Precedence and Rules Governing Demand for a Division.

(g) To grant leave to withdraw a motion.

See also Sec. 275, Motion for Leave to Withdraw a Question.

(h) A parliamentary inquiry or request of any kind.

See also Secs. 252, Rules Governing Parliamentary Inquiries, and Sec. 254, Requests Other Than Parliamentary Inquiries.

(i) To take up a question out of its regular order.

See also Sec. 713, Taking Up Questions Out of Order; Ch. 28, Secs. 279–286, Suspension of the Rules; and Ch. 30, Secs. 302–304, Order and Manner of Considering Questions.

(j) To suspend the rules.

See also Sec. 282, Motion to Suspend the Rules.

(k) To lay on the table.

See also Sec. 335, Debate on Motion to Lay on the Table and Application of Subsidiary Motions.

(*l*) To take from the table.

See also Sec. 492, Motion to Take from the Table.

(m) The previous question.

See also Sec. 349, Previous Question—Debate and Subsidiary Motions.

(n) To amend an amendment.

See also Sec. 409, Amendment of Amendments.

(*o*) To fill a blank.

See also Sec. 417, Alternative Propositions—Filling Blanks.

(p) To postpone indefinitely.

See also Sec. 434, Application of Subsidiary Motions to Indefinite Postponement.

(q) Call for division of the house.

See also Sec. 533, Voting by Division.

(r) To reconsider.

See also Sec. 472, Application of Subsidiary Motions to Motion to Reconsider.

(s) A notice of any kind.

(t) Communications to the body.

See also Sec. 148, Communications and Petitions.

(u) Reports to the body.

See also Ch. 62, Secs. 663–678, Committee Reports.

2. An amendment to anything already adopted is not a subsidiary motion. Such a proposition is a main motion subject to amendments of the first and second degrees.

Sec. 396, Par. 1: With reference to the right of amendment, see Cushing's Legislative Assemblies, Secs. 1311–1321; Sturgis, pp. 51–53; Robert's, p. 110.

Sec. 397. Precedence of Motion to Amend and of Amendments

1. A motion to amend takes precedence over the motion to postpone indefinitely, and of main motions, and yields to all other subsidiary, privileged and incidental motions.

2. An amendment takes precedence over the original motion out of which it arises and must be voted upon before the original motion.

3. A measure should be considered in a progressive order, and amendments should be proposed in the order that they would occur in the amended measure. An exception to this occurs when a group of amendments is necessary to accomplish a general purpose. They may be proposed and voted upon as a group.

4. When a question is not being considered seriatim, the first amendment proposed will be the first amendment considered.

5. A motion to amend a paragraph takes precedence over a motion to approve, to insert or to strike out the paragraph, and a motion to amend a section takes precedence over a motion to approve, to insert or to strike out a section.

6. It is a matter of practice to consider committee amendments before amendments from the

---

Sec. 397, Par. 1: Sturgis, p. 38; Robert's, p. 109.

Sec. 397, Par. 2: Casler v. Tanzer (1929), 234 N.Y.S. 571; Robert's, p. 109.

Sec. 397, Par. 3: Cushing's Legislative Assemblies, Sec. 1305; Hughes, Sec. 373.

Sec. 397, Par. 4: Cushing's Legislative Assemblies, Sec. 1331.

Sec. 397, Par. 5: Jefferson, Sec. XXXV; Hughes, Sec. 401; N.Y. Manual, p. 471.

floor are considered.

Sec. 398. Decision on Amendment Is Final

See also Ch. 41, Secs. 450–474, Motion to Reconsider.

1. An amendment, once adopted, may not be amended. This does not prohibit the consideration of further amendments to the main proposal as amended.

2. When a proposed amendment has been defeated, the same amendment may not be proposed again without first reconsidering the vote by which the amendment lost.

3. If an amendment is inconsistent with one already adopted, it is not within the power of the presiding officer to rule it out of order. It is a matter for decision by the body.

Sec. 399. Laying Motion to Amend on the Table

1. Traditionally, an amendment may not be laid on the table by itself. The motion, if approved, has the effect of taking the principal motion and all adhering motions with it.

2. The practice of some legislative bodies is to permit amendments to be laid on the table without affecting the main question. The purpose is to pro-

Sec. 397, Par. 6: Hughes, Sec. 394.

Sec. 398, Par. 1: Cushing's Legislative Assemblies, Sec. 1307; Hughes, Sec. 375; Cushing, Secs. 98, 251.

Sec. 398, Par. 2: Cushing's Legislative Assemblies, Sec. 1308; Sturgis, p. 38; Hughes, Secs. 376, 381.

Sec. 398, Par. 3: Jefferson, Sec. XXXV; N.Y. Manual, p. 406.

Sec. 399: Hughes, Sec. 361; N.Y. Manual, p. 408; Sturgis, p. 51.

vide a simple method to dispose of amendments without debate.

Sec. 400. Form of Amendments

1. In form, amendments may be divided into the following types:

(a) To add (that is to place at the end).

(b) To insert.

(c) To strike out.

(d) To strike out and insert, or to substitute.

2. The last form is a combination of the previous two and cannot be divided, because the striking out and inserting represent one act only—to substitute.

3. Amendments to bills or resolutions must be submitted in writing.

4. Amendments to motions may be informal. When, for example, a motion to recess for ten minutes is pending, a member may properly say, "I move that the motion be amended to 'recess for thirty minutes' instead of 'ten minutes.' "

5. Under parliamentary law, after an amendment is made to a motion, the motion as amended must be put to a vote.

Sec. 401. Frivolous and Improper Amendments

1. An amendment which is frivolous or absurd is not in order, and the presiding officer may refuse to

---

Sec. 400, Par. 1: Cushing's Legislative Assemblies, Sec. 1304; Sturgis, p. 35; Reed, Sec. 132; Cushing, Sec. 94; Robert's, p. 112.

Sec. 400, Par. 5: Leonard v. School District of Cornish (1953), 98 N.H. 296, 99 A.2d 415.

state amendments which, in the presiding officer's opinion, are frivolous or absurd.

2. An amendment is not in order which would change one kind of motion into another kind or which would substitute one kind for another kind.

3. A motion striking out the enacting or resolving clause, or so changing the proposition that no rational proposition would be left before the house, is not in order.

4. An amendment identical with one previously decided on the same bill is not in order.

See also Sec. 398, Decision on Amendment Is Final.

5. The presiding officer should never rule an amendment out of order unless certain that it is. In case of doubt the presiding officer should entertain the amendment, subject to the right of a member to raise a point of order, or the presiding officer should submit to the house the question of whether the amendment is in order.

See also Sec. 242, Limitations on Use of Points of Order.

Sec. 402. Amendments Must Be Germane

1. Every amendment proposed must be germane to the subject of the proposition or to the section or paragraph to be amended.

2. To determine whether an amendment is germane, the question to be answered is whether the

---

Sec. 401, Par. 1: Hughes, Sec. 429.

Sec. 401, Par. 3: Reed, Sec. 157.

Sec. 401, Par. 4: Hughes, Sec. 421; Sturgis, p. 38.

Sec. 402, Par. 1: Sturgis, p. 51; Hughes, Sec. 380; N.Y. Manual, p. 405; Reed, Sec. 160; Cooley, Constitutional Limitations, p. 169; Heron v. Riley (1930), 209 Cal. 507, 289 P. 160.

question is relevant, appropriate, and in a natural and logical sequence to the subject matter of the original proposal.

3. To be germane, the amendment is required only to relate to the same subject. It may entirely change the effect of or be in conflict with the spirit of the original motion or measure and still be germane to the subject.

4. An entirely new proposal may be substituted by amendment as long as it is germane to the main purpose of the original proposal.

5. An amendment to an amendment must be germane to the subject of the amendment as well as to the main question.

Sec. 403. Withdrawing Amendments and Accepting Modifications

See also Ch. 27, Secs. 272–276, Withdrawal of Motions.

1. Amendments may be withdrawn prior to formal introduction by request of the member offering the amendment. After formal introduction, amendments may be withdrawn only with the consent of the body.

2. A member has the right to modify a motion or resolution that that member submitted at any time before it is stated by the presiding officer, but after it

---

Sec. 402, Par. 2: Hughes, Sec. 411; Robert's, pp. 109, 113.

Sec. 402, Par. 3: Jefferson, Sec. XXXV; Cushing's Legislative Assemblies, Secs. 1302, 1317, 1363.

Sec. 402, Par. 4: Hood v. City of Wheeling (1920), 85 W.Va. 578, 102 S.E. 259; State of Nebraska v. Cox (1920), 105 Neb. 175, 178 N.W. 913.

Sec. 402, Par. 5: Hughes, Sec. 361.

Sec. 403, Par. 1: Sturgis, p. 99; Reed, Sec. 150; Cushing, Secs. 92, 93.

is stated, it is in the possession of the body, and can be modified only with the consent of the body.

3. A member may modify an amendment only with the consent of the body.

4. A request for leave to withdraw amendments is treated the same as a motion to grant the leave, except that the request must be made by the member who proposed the amendments while the motion to grant the leave to withdraw may be made by any member.

Sec. 404. Amendment of Bills by Committees

1. A committee cannot amend a bill. That power is vested in the body alone, and a committee merely proposes amendments to the body.

2. When a measure with amendments pending is referred to a committee, it may be reported back with a substitute for the measure. In this case, the presiding officer should first put the question on the amendments which were pending when the measure was committed and then on the substitute recommended by the committee.

Sec. 405. Correction of Section Numbers and Marginal Notes

No legislative proposal may be changed in any way except to correct clearly clerical errors or by

Sec. 403, Par. 2: Sturgis, p. 99; Reed, Sec. 150.
Sec. 403, Par. 3: Sturgis, p. 99; Cushing, Secs. 92, 93.
Sec. 403, Par. 4: Sturgis, p. 98.
Sec. 404, Par. 1: N.Y. Manual, p. 405; Robert's, pp. 232, 434.

action of the body.

Sec. 406. Correction of Minutes

See also Sec. 699, Manner of Correcting the Journal.

1. Minutes are usually corrected (amended) informally by the presiding officer's directing the correction to be made when suggested. If objection is made, a formal vote is necessary for the amendment.

2. The minutes may be corrected whenever the error is noticed, regardless of the time which has elapsed, and only a majority vote is required for the adoption of the corrections or amendments, even though the minutes have previously been approved and it is too late to reconsider the vote.

3. Adoption of minutes of a previous meeting of a deliberative body is not a legislative act. The minutes may be corrected whenever the error is noticed regardless of the time which has elapsed, even though the same correction or amendment has been previously proposed and lost. This is necessary for the protection of the records, which otherwise would be subject to the risk of being tampered with by temporary majorities.

Sec. 407. Amendment of Titles of Bills

See also Sec. 731, Amendment of Bills.

Whenever amendments are prepared to a bill that call for amendments to the title, the amendments

---

Sec. 405: Jefferson, Sec. XXXV; Cushing, Sec. 91; Reed, Sec. 155; Cushing's Legislative Assemblies, Sec. 1361.

Sec. 406, Par. 1: Sturgis, pp. 118, 199, 120.

Sec. 406, Par. 3: Hornaday v. Goodman (1929), 167 Ga. 555, 146 S.E. 173; Mann v. Le Mars (1899), 109 Iowa 244, 80 N.W. 327.

should contain the necessary title amendments. A motion to amend a title of a bill being a matter of form rather than being a substantive question is not debatable.

Sec. 408. Amendments of Rules

See also Sec. 23, Rules Can Be Suspended; Sec. 24, Failure of a House of the Legislature to Conform to Its Rules Does Not Invalidate Its Acts; and Ch. 28, Secs. 279–286, Suspension of the Rules.

The amendment of rules often requires notice and a two-thirds vote, and there are sometimes other or further restrictions than on the amendment of bills, resolutions or motions. The procedure for the amendment of the rules of a house is usually provided in the rules themselves. A majority vote only is required to amend rules unless the rules require a higher vote.

Sec. 409. Amendment of Amendments

1. An amendment may be amended but an amendment to an amendment may not be amended.

2. Only one amendment to a proposition (known as an amendment of the first degree) is permitted at a time, and one amendment to that amendment (or an amendment of the second degree) is permitted at one time. An amendment of the third degree would be too complicated and is not in order.

Sec. 407: Jefferson, Sec. XLII; Hughes, Secs. 935, 936.

Sec. 408: Sturgis, pp. 206–210.

Sec. 409, Par. 1: Cushing's Legislative Assemblies, Sec. 1306; Hughes, Sec. 367; Reed, Sec. 133; Sturgis, p. 52; Cushing, Sec. 96; Robert's, pp. 111, 113.

Sec. 409, Par. 2: Jefferson, Sec. XXXIII; Hughes, Secs. 377, 378; Cushing, Secs. 96, 165; Reed, Secs. 133, 134, 165; Sturgis, pp. 52, 53; Robert's, p. 111.

3. When an amendment to an amendment may not be amended, it is proper to adopt a substitute for the amendment and the substitute may be amended.

4. An amendment of one house to an amendment adopted in the other house is an amendment only in the first degree.

Sec. 410. Transposition of Provisions by Amendment

1. In transposing parts of a proposition, the better practice is to strike out the words or provisions at one point and to insert them at the other.

2. If a section is to be transposed from one place to another in the same act, the question may be put on striking it out where it stands, and a separate question put on inserting it in the place desired. The modern legislative practice is to submit both proposals as one amendment since both are required to accomplish the single transposition.

Sec. 411. Amendment by Inserting Words

1. When a motion to insert words is lost, it does not preclude another motion to insert these words, together with other words, or in place of other words, provided the new motion presents essentially a new question.

2. When the words are inserted in the place previously occupied by the words struck out, they may

Sec. 409, Par. 3: Hughes, Secs. 379, 394; Reed, Sec. 150.

Sec. 409, Par. 4: Hughes, Sec. 431.

Sec. 410: Jefferson, Sec. XXXV; Cushing's Legislative Assemblies, Sec. 1360; Reed, Sec. 155; Cushing, Sec. 90.

Sec. 411: Cushing's Legislative Assemblies, Sec. 1332; Reed, Secs. 135, 136; Robert's, p. 117.

differ materially from the latter, provided they are germane to the subject.

3. A motion to strike out words in one place and to insert words to a different effect in another place is not in order, because it constitutes two amendments which should be submitted separately.

Sec. 412. Amendment by Striking Out Words

1. A motion to strike out certain words can be applied only to consecutive words. If it is desired to strike out separated words, it is necessary to strike out by separate motions, or a motion may be made to strike out the entire clause or line containing the words to be struck out, and to insert a new clause or line as desired.

2. If it be proposed to amend by leaving out certain words, it may be moved, as an amendment to this amendment, to leave out a part of the words of the amendment, which is equivalent to leaving them in the question or measure.

3. A motion to strike out certain words is in order after a motion to strike out the same words and insert others has been defeated, and the rejection of one proposition does not preclude the offering of a different one.

4. If the motion to strike out certain words is adopted, the same words cannot be again inserted unless the place or the wording is so changed as to make a new proposition. If the motion to strike out fails, it does not preclude a motion to strike out the

Sec. 412: Cushing's Legislative Assemblies, Secs. 1327, 1328, 1330; Jefferson, Sec. XXXV; Cushing, Secs. 111, 113; Reed, Secs. 137–139, 142; Tilson, p. 66; Hughes, Secs. 383, 384, 390; Robert's, p. 122.

same words and insert other words, nor to strike out a part of the words, nor to strike out a part and insert other words; nor to strike out these words with others, nor to do this and insert still other words if in each of these cases the new question is materially different from the old one.

Sec. 413. Amendments Striking Out and Inserting Words

1. After a motion to strike out and insert has been adopted, the inserted words cannot be struck out, nor can the words struck out be inserted, unless the words or place are so changed as to make the question a new one. When such a motion is lost, it does not preclude either of the separate motions to strike out or to insert the same words, as this would simply be equivalent to division of the question; nor does it prevent another motion to strike out and insert, when there is a material change in either the words to be struck out or the words to be inserted, so that the question is not practically identical.

2. When an amendment to strike out or to insert words, or both, is not satisfactory, the proposed amendment should be amended to make a satisfactory amendment before voting on the adoption of the amendment.

3. For purposes of correction of a proposed amendment before voting upon it, it is resolved into its constituent elements, and the words to be struck out are first corrected, after which the words to be inserted are corrected. After words have been in-

---

Sec. 413: Jefferson, Sec. XXXV; Cushing's Legislative Assemblies, Secs. 135–140; Hughes, Secs. 376, 388; Reed, Secs. 138–140, 142; Cushing, Sec. 125; N.Y. Manual, p. 471; Tilson, p. 70; Robert's, p. 128.

serted or added, they cannot be changed or struck out except by a motion to strike out the paragraph, or such a portion of it as shall make the question a different one from that of inserting the particular words, or by combining such a motion to strike out the paragraph, or a portion of it, with the motion to insert other words. The principle involved is that, when the body has voted that certain words shall form a part of a measure, it is not in order to make another motion that involves exactly the same question as the one it has decided. The only way to bring it up again is to move to reconsider the vote by which the words were inserted.

Sec. 414. Amendment by Striking Out or Inserting Paragraphs

1. A motion to insert or to strike out a paragraph is an amendment of the first degree, and, therefore, cannot be made when an amendment to strike out or insert words is pending.

2. After a paragraph has been inserted, it cannot be struck out except in connection with other paragraphs so as to make the question essentially a new one.

3. When a paragraph is struck out, it cannot be inserted afterwards, unless it is so changed in wording or place as to present an essentially new question. When a motion to insert or to strike out a paragraph is lost, it does not preclude another motion except one that presents essentially the same question.

Sec. 414: Jefferson, Sec. XXXV; Cushing, Secs. 103, 105, 106; Reed, Secs. 138, 143, 144, 148; Robert's, p. 129.

4. Although a body has refused to strike out a paragraph, it is in order to strike out a part of the paragraph or otherwise to amend it.

5. When it is proposed to insert a paragraph, or part of one, the members favorable to the paragraph may make it as nearly perfect as they can by amendments, before the question is put for inserting it. Also, when it is proposed to strike out a paragraph, the members favorable to the paragraph must first be permitted to make it as nearly perfect as they can by amendments, before the question is put on striking it out.

Sec. 415. Substitution of Paragraphs

1. A motion to substitute one paragraph for another, after being stated by the presiding officer, is resolved into its two elements for the purpose of amendment, the presiding officer at first entertaining amendments only to the paragraph to be struck out, these amendments being of the second degree. After it is perfected by the members favoring it, the presiding officer should ask if there are amendments to the paragraph to be inserted. When both paragraphs have been perfected by amendments, the question is put on substituting one paragraph for the other.

2. When a motion to substitute is lost, the body has only decided that that particular paragraph shall not replace the one specified. It may be willing to substitute that paragraph for some other paragraph, or that the paragraph retained in the resolution be

Sec. 415: Jefferson, Sec. XXXV; Cushing, Sec. 115; Reed, Sec. 145; Robert's, p. 129.

further amended, or even struck out. But no amendment is in order that presents a question substantially identical with one already decided.

Sec. 416. Consolidation and Substitution of Measures

1. When the matter contained in two propositions might be better put into one, the proper procedure is to reject one and to incorporate its provisions into the other by amendment. When the provisions would be better distributed into propositions, any part of the bill may be struck out by amendment, and put into a new proposition. When a measure is being considered by sections, a substitute for the entire measure cannot be moved until the sections have all been considered and the presiding officer has announced that the proposition is open to amendment. Even though an entire measure is substituted for another, it is necessary afterwards to vote on adopting the measure. Substitution is only a form of amendment and may be used, as long as germane, whenever amendments are in order.

2. An amendment, striking out the entire bill following the enacting clause and substituting a new bill, does not violate a constitutional provision that amendments may not change the original purpose of an act, unless the substitution changes the original purpose of the act.

Sec. 416, Par. 1: Cushing's Legislative Assemblies, Sec. 1358; Sturgis, p. 54; Jefferson, Sec. XXXV; Cushing, Sec. 88; Reed, Sec. 155; N.Y. Manual, p. 408.

Sec. 416, Par. 2: Reitzammer v. Desha Road Improvement District No. 2 (1919), 139 Ark. 168, 213 S.W. 773; State of Ohio v. Miller (1854), 3 Ohio St. 475; Nelson v. Haywood County (1892), 91 Tenn. 596,

3. The method of substituting an entirely new bill by amendment, when the changes by way of amendment are strictly germane to the original, is not unconstitutional, is in accord with universal legislative procedure, and it is not necessary that such a bill, which has been read a first and second time before amendment, be again given first and second readings before passage.

See also Sec. 722, Three Readings of Amended Bills.

Sec. 417. Alternative Propositions — Filling Blanks

Procedure on Filling Blanks

1. The method adopted in filling blanks has sometimes a great advantage over ordinary amendment. In amending, the last proposition made is the first one voted on; whereas, in filling blanks, the first proposition made, or name proposed, is voted on first, except where, from the nature of the case, another order is preferable, and then that order may be adopted.

2. When alternative propositions are submitted, they are treated, not as separate amendments, but as independent propositions, to be voted on successively.

---

20 S.W. 1; State of Nebraska v. Cox (1920), 105 Neb. 175, 178 N.W. 913; Brake v. Callison (1903), 122 F. 722.

Sec. 416, Par. 3: State of Nebraska v. Cox (1920), 105 Neb. 175, 178 N.W. 913; Hood v. City of Wheeling (1920), 85 W.Va. 578, 102 S.E. 259; Reed, Sec. 156.

Sec. 417: Cushing's Legislative Assemblies, Secs. 1354, 1355; Jefferson, Sec. XXXIII; Sturgis, p. 54; Cushing, Secs. 84–87; Hughes, Secs. 413, 414; Reed, Sec. 154; N.Y. Manual, p. 422; Robert's, pp. 135–140.

Filling Blanks with Names

3. When a name is to be selected, the presiding officer repeats the names as they are proposed so all may hear them, and finally takes a vote on each name, beginning with the first proposed, until one receives a majority vote. When several names are to be selected, and no more names are suggested than required, the names may be inserted without a vote on each name. If more names are suggested than are required, a vote is taken on each name, beginning with the first proposed, until enough to fill the blanks have received a majority vote. If the number of names is not specified, a vote is taken on each name suggested, and all that receive a majority vote are inserted.

4. Alternative propositions or the filling of blanks are also treated somewhat differently from other amendments, in that different names or numbers for filling the blanks may be proposed by any number of members, no one proposing more than one name or number for each place, except by general consent.

5. Filling blanks with names is like making nominations. Any number may be pending at the same time, not as amendments to each other, but as independent propositions, to be voted on in the order in which they were made until one of the number to be selected receives a majority vote.

Filling Blanks with Amounts or Time

6. When filling blanks with amounts or time, it should first be considered whether the greater includes the lesser. When the greater does include the

lesser, the question of the greatest number or longest time should be put first. When the greater does not include the lesser, the smallest amount or shortest time should be put first. Thus, if the purchase of specific property is under consideration, the offer of a larger sum includes a smaller sum, for if a certain sum were offered, the offer of any smaller sum would be more acceptable. The question should first be put on largest sums proposed; otherwise there could be no agreement on the amount which would be offered, for the lowest sum would be most acceptable, and its approval would preclude further effort to reach a practical offer. If, however, the question were, the price to be asked for property to be sold, the greater would not include the lesser, because if any specific amount would be acceptable, it would not mean that any lesser amount would be acceptable. In this case, the question should be first put on the smaller sum. Otherwise the largest sum proposed would be most acceptable and would be approved, and it would be impossible to reach the consensus of the body as to the proper amount.

7. The more usual practice in Congress in filling blanks, where several amounts are submitted, is to propose an amendment to an amendment, and a substitute, and an amendment to the substitute, if as many as four separate propositions are submitted.

Blanks Should First Be Filled

8. When propositions containing blanks are introduced, these must be filled before other motions to amend are entertained.

Sec. 418. Debate on Amendments

1. The motion to amend a debatable question is debatable and subject to the previous question. An amendment to a question which is not debatable is not itself debatable.

2. A member who has spoken on a main question may also speak on an amendment, because an amendment presents a new question.

3. The previous question and motions to limit or extend the limits of debate may be applied to an amendment or to an amendment of an amendment. In such case they do not affect the main question.

Sec. 419. Vote Required on Amendments

An amendment of a pending question requires only a majority vote for its adoption, even though the question may require a two-thirds or other vote greater than a majority for adoption. Thus, amendments proposed to the constitution or the rules may be amended by a majority vote, although the amendments require a two-thirds vote for adoption.

Sec. 420. Amendment After Governor's Certificate

When a certificate of necessity of immediate passage is required from the governor, in a particular case, a bill can be amended by either house after the certificate has been issued by the governor.

Sec. 418: Sturgis, p. 53; Hughes, Secs. 361, 431; Robert's, p. 111.

Sec. 419: Sturgis, p. 56; Hughes, Secs. 361, 401.

Sec. 420: People *ex rel.* Durham Realty Corporation v. La Setra (1920), 185 N.Y.S. 638.

Sec. 421. Equivalent Amendments

Where questions are equivalent, so that the negative of the one amounts to the affirmative of the other, and leaves no other alternative, the decision on the one amendment necessarily precludes the other. Thus, the negative of striking out amounts to the affirmative of agreeing, and, therefore, to put a question on agreeing after one on striking out, would in effect be to put the same question twice. This rule does not apply to the question of amendments between the two houses. A motion to recede being negatived does not amount to a positive vote to insist, because there is another alternative which is to adhere.

Sec. 421: Jefferson, Sec. XXXVIII; Cushing, Sec. 251.

CHAPTER 39

MOTION TO POSTPONE INDEFINITELY

Sec. 430. Use of Motion to Postpone Indefinitely

1. The object of this motion is not to postpone, but to reject the main motion without incurring the risk of a direct vote on it, or to avoid a recorded vote on a measure. The motion is in effect a motion to reject the main question. This motion may be applied only to main motions.

2. When a motion to postpone a question indefinitely is adopted, the effect is to prevent any further discussion of the question during the session.

3. A further effect of making this motion is to enable members who have exhausted their right to debate on the main question to speak again, since, technically, the question before the house is different.

4. A motion to postpone a question beyond the time at which it can be considered, as beyond the adjournment sine die of a legislative session, is equivalent to complete disapproval and should be

---

Sec. 430, Par. 1: Sturgis, p. 48; Hughes, Secs. 325, 326; Tilson, p. 68; Cushing, Sec. 67; Reed, Sec. 121; Robert's, p. 105; Wood v. Town of Milton (1908), 197 Mass. 531, 84 N.E. 332.

Sec. 430, Par. 2: Zeiler v. Central Railway Co. (1896), 84 Md. 304, 35 A. 932; Hughes, Sec. 322; Cushing, Secs. 67, 180; Reed, Sec. 121; N.Y. Manual (1948–49), p. 433; Tilson, p. 68; Sturgis, p. 48.

Sec. 430, Par. 3: Sturgis, p. 48.

treated as a motion to postpone indefinitely.

Sec. 431. Precedence of Motion to Postpone Indefinitely

The motion to postpone indefinitely takes precedence over nothing except the main motion to which it is applied, and yields to all privileged, incidental and other subsidiary motions.

Sec. 432. Form of Motion to Postpone Indefinitely

The usual form of the motion to postpone is "I move that consideration (or further consideration) of the question (further identifying it when necessary) be indefinitely postponed."

Sec. 433. Motion to Postpone Indefinitely Opens Main Question to Debate

The motion to postpone indefinitely is debatable and opens the main question to debate. This is because any motion, which proposes to make a final disposition of a question, opens the merits of the question to debate.

Sec. 434. Application of Subsidiary Motions to Indefinite Postponement

1. The motion to postpone indefinitely cannot be amended nor have any other subsidiary motion ap-

Sec. 430, Par. 4: Wood v. Town of Milton (1908), 197 Mass. 531, 84 N.E. 332.

Sec. 431: Sturgis, p. 49; Hughes, Sec. 322; Cushing, Sec. 67a; Tilson, p. 67; Robert's, p. 105.

Sec. 432: Sturgis, p. 47; Hughes, Sec. 322; Cushing, Sec. 70.

Sec. 433: Sturgis, p. 48; Hughes, Sec. 322; N.Y. Manual (1948–49), p. 442; Cushing, Sec. 67a; Reed, Secs. 122, 201; Tilson, p. 68; Robert's, p. 106.

plied to it, except the previous question and motions closing, limiting or extending the limits of debate. The previous question, when applied to this motion, does not affect the main question or other pending motions.

2. The motion to postpone indefinitely states a simple proposition in its simplest form and it is, therefore, not amendable. To amend such a motion as to duration, to be of any effect, would change it from a motion to suppress into a motion to defer, which is not permitted.

3. When a measure is referred to committee while a motion to postpone indefinitely is pending, the motion is defeated, as the reference to committee is incompatible with indefinite postponement.

4. When a motion to postpone indefinitely is lost, the main question is open to other motions as though the motion to postpone indefinitely had never been made.

Sec. 435. Vote Required to Postpone Indefinitely

A majority vote of the members voting is required for the adoption of the motion to postpone indefinitely.

Sec. 434, Par. 1: Sturgis, p. 49; Hughes, Sec. 322; Reed, Sec. 164; see also Cushing, Sec. 177.

Sec. 434, Par. 2: Cushing's Legislative Assemblies, Sec. 1523; Cushing, Secs. 176–178; Sturgis, p. 49; Reed, Secs. 122, 201; N.Y. Manual (1948–49), p. 433.

Sec. 434, Par. 4: Jefferson, Sec. XXXIII; Cushing, Sec. 180.

Sec. 435: Sturgis, p. 178; Hughes, Sec. 322; Robert's, p. 106.

Sec. 436. Renewal and Reconsideration of Motion to Postpone Indefinitely

1. The general practice in American legislative bodies appears to be to permit the motion to reconsider to be applied to a vote on the motion to postpone indefinitely. In Congress it was provided by rule that a question which has been indefinitely postponed could not be acted upon again at the same session and though that provision has been repealed the same practice continues.

2. In legislative bodies where the motion to postpone indefinitely is used for the final disposition of legislation it is treated as a main motion. In such bodies the motion to postpone indefinitely may not be renewed, even though the motion has been amended since the indefinite postponement was previously moved.

3. Where the motion to postpone indefinitely opens the main question to debate and where it disposes of the main question it is usually treated as a main motion and subject to reconsideration but where it is treated as a subsidiary procedural motion it may not be reconsidered. From early times, it has not been customary to permit the renewal of the motion to postpone indefinitely.

Sec. 436, Par. 1: Cushing's Legislative Assemblies, Sec. 1447; see also Hughes, Secs. 322–325.

Sec. 436, Par. 2: Cushing's Legislative Assemblies, Sec. 1447; but see Hughes, Sec. 322.

*

DIVISION 4

MAIN MOTIONS

CHAPTER 40

THE MAIN MOTION

Sec. 440. What Are Main Motions

1. The term "main motion" is used in its broad sense to include any proposition or matter of business presented to the body for its consideration. As a convenience, the term "main motion" is applied to all propositions of this type, whether they be bills in a state legislature or any question presented for the final determination of the body in any other form. A main motion presents an item of business to a deliberative body for its action or decision.

2. Main motions are distinguished from procedural motions, such as the motion to adjourn or to lay on the table or postpone, which relate to what the body will do or how it will proceed with its real business which is the consideration of main motions.

See also Sec. 488, Procedural Main Motions.

Sec. 440, Par. 1: Sturgis, pp. 36, 37.

Sec. 441. Form of Presenting Main Motions

1. The main motions may be presented in any of several forms:

(a) To adopt.

(b) To pass.

(c) To approve.

(d) To ratify.

(e) To confirm.

(f) To concur.

(g) To appoint.

(h) To elect.

(i) To reject.

(j) To repeal.

(k) To rescind.

(*l*) To annul.

(m) To remove from office.

(n) To refuse to concur.

2. For convenience in reference, main motions are occasionally classified into the ordinary main motion which presents a direct item of business or into certain other forms of main motions which are used so widely that they have acquired a special name and may have special rules applicable to them. This latter group of motions—sometimes referred to as incidental or specific main motions—have become differentiated from the regular type of main motion.

Sec. 441: Cushing's Legislative Assemblies, Secs. 1279–1281; Sturgis, pp. 35–37.

3. The most common types of incidental or specific main motions are the motion to reconsider, to rescind and to take from the table (or to resume consideration).

See also Ch. 41, Secs. 450–474, Motion to Reconsider, and Ch. 42, Secs. 480–483, Motion to Rescind.

4. Another type of classification of main motions which is used rather widely and frequently for convenience is the classification into main motions proper dealing essentially with substantive matters and into incidental main motions which are motions of a procedural nature classified as main motions only because they take precedence as main motions. Motions of this type are to:

(a) Set a future date for adjournment.

(b) Create a special order involving a question not then under consideration.

(c) Provide for future recess.

(d) Withdraw bills from committee.

(e) Take from the table.

(f) Pass on calendar or file.

(g) Dispense with constitutional readings.

(h) Suspend the rules for business not then pending.

5. These motions are procedural motions but relate to questions of procedure not having a higher precedence than main motions. While they are not main motions in the sense they present items of business, they are classified as main motions in any classification based upon precedence.

6. The motions to reconsider and to rescind, because of their complexity, require extensive treatment and are considered in separate chapters.

Sec. 442. Precedence of Main Motions

Main motions of all kinds, including incidental motions, take the lowest order of precedence. They are not in order when other business is pending. If offered out of order they need not be entertained by the presiding officer, and their consideration at that time is defeated by one objection. Any of these motions may, of course, be considered by unanimous consent when other business is pending, or they may be taken up at any time under suspension of the rules.

Sec. 443. Motion to Ratify

1. The motion to ratify is a main motion, and is used when it is desired to confirm or make valid some action which requires the approval of the body.

2. A legislative body can ratify only such actions of its officers, committees, or delegates, as it had the right to authorize in advance. It cannot ratify or make valid anything done in violation of the constitution.

3. The motion to ratify is debatable and opens the entire question to debate.

4. A motion to ratify may be amended by substituting a motion to disapprove or to censure, and vice

---

Sec. 442: Hughes, Sec. 444; Sturgis, p. 39.

versa, when the action has been taken by an officer or other representative of the body.

Sec. 444. Motion to Expunge

1. Where it is desired not only to rescind an action but to express very strong disapproval, legislative bodies have voted to rescind the objectionable action and expunge it from the record. When a record has been expunged the secretary or clerk should cross out the words or draw a line around them in the original minutes and write across them the words, "Expunged by order of the senate (or house)," giving the date of the order. This statement should be signed by the chief legislative officer. The word "expunged" must not be so blotted as not to be readable, as otherwise it would be impossible to determine whether more was expunged than ordered. When the minutes are printed or published the expunged portion is omitted.

2. This motion to expunge has no privileged status, but ranks as a main motion and follows the rules of a main motion.

Sec. 445. Motion to Adjourn Sine Die

1. When a state legislature is duly convened it cannot be adjourned sine die nor be dissolved except in the regular legal manner, and an adjournment from day to day cannot have that effect.

2. A motion or resolution to adjourn sine die or to fix the time to adjourn sine die, or any motion to adjourn which would have the effect of dissolving a

Sec. 444, Par. 1: Sturgis, p. 44; Hughes, Sec. 474.
Sec. 445, Par. 1: Cushing's Legislative Assemblies, Sec. 254.

legislative body without provision for another meeting, presents a main question and is subject to debate, amendment and all the subsidiary motions.

3. A motion to adjourn sine die has the effect of closing the session and terminating all unfinished business before the house, and all legislation pending upon adjournment sine die expires with the session. A motion to adjourn from day to day does not destroy the continuity of a session and unfinished business simply takes its place on the calendar of the succeeding day.

4. The houses of a legislature may make their records show that all their business was transacted before the time fixed for final adjournment.

5. Committees, specially authorized, may sit after adjournment sine die.

Sec. 445, Par. 2: Jefferson, Sec. LI; Reed, Sec. 170; Cushing, Secs. 137b, 139; Tilson, p. 57; N.Y. Manual, p. 403.

Sec. 445, Par. 3: Jefferson, Sec. LI; Cushing, Secs. 139, 140.

Sec. 445, Par. 4: Earnest v. Sargent (1915), 20 N.M. 427, 150 P. 1018.

Sec. 445, Par. 5: Jefferson, Sec. LI.

CHAPTER 41

MOTION TO RECONSIDER

Sec. 450. Right to Reconsider

1. With certain exceptions every legislative body has the inherent right to reconsider a vote on an action previously taken by it.

2. When not otherwise provided by law, all public bodies have a right during the session to reconsider action taken by them as they think proper and it is the final result only that is to be regarded as the thing done.

3. Unless some right of a third person intervenes, all deliberative bodies have the right to reconsider

---

Sec. 450, Par. 1: Reiff v. Connor (1849), 10 Ark. 241; McConoughey v. Jackson (1894), 101 Cal. 265, 25 P. 863; Crawford v. Gilchrist (1912), 64 Fla. 41, 59 So. 963; Red v. August (1858), 25 Ga. 386; People *ex rel.* MacMahon v. Davis (1918), 284 Ill. 439, 120 N.E. 326; Greenwood v. State of Indiana (1902), 159 Ind. 267, 64 N.E. 849; Wingert v. Snouffer & Ford (1906), 134 Iowa 97, 108 N.W. 1035; Higgins v. Curtis (1888), 39 Kan. 283, 18 P. 207; Bigelow v. Hillman (1854), 37 Me. 52; Baker v. Cushman (1879), 127 Mass. 105; Allen v. Taunton (Mass. 1837), 19 Pick. 485; Naegely v. Saginaw (1894), 101 Mich. 532, 60 N.W. 46; Witherspoon v. State of Mississippi *ex rel.* West (1925), 138 Miss. 310, 103 So. 134; State of New Jersey v. Foster (1823), 7 N.J.L. 101; State of New Jersey v. Van Buskirk (1878), 40 N.J.L. 463; Styles v. City of Lambertville (1905), 73 N.J.L. 90, 62 A. 288; *In re* Eiss (1923), 205 App. Div. 691, 199 N.Y.S. 544; Adkins v. Toledo (1905), 6 Ohio C.C.R. (n.s.) 433; Commonwealth v. Pittsburgh (1850), 14 Pa. 177; Estey v. Starr (1884), 56 Vt. 690; Tetley v. Vancouver (1897), 5 B.C. 276; Re De War (1905), 10 Ont. L.R. 463; Byron v. Timberlane Regional School Dist. (1973), 113 N.H. 449, 309 A.2d 218.

Sec. 450, Par. 2: Crawford v. Gilchrist (1912), 64 Fla. 41, 59 So. 963; State of New Jersey v. Foster (1823), 7 N.J.L. 101; People *ex rel.* MacMahon v. Davis (1918), 284 Ill. 439, 120 N.E. 326; Neill v. Ward (1931), 103 Vt. 117, 153 A. 219; Gouldey v. City Council of Atlantic City (1899), 63 N.J.L. 537, 42 A. 852; State of New Jersey v. Van Buskirk (1878), 40 N.J.L. 463; Styles v. City of Lambertville (1905), 73 N.J.L. 90, 62 A. 288.

their proceedings during a session as often as they think proper.

4. The reconsideration of a negative vote on final action is as proper as a reconsideration of a favorable vote.

5. Under general parliamentary law, all motions, whether carried or lost, can be reconsidered.

6. The statement of the rights of deliberative bodies to reconsider their actions has been broadly interpreted. Within certain limits, a vote in the affirmative or the negative may be reconsidered. Subject to the same limitations, an affirmative action can be rescinded, the essential element being the right of the body to change its mind concerning main motions or their equivalent. The action to reconsider can be taken if the question to be reconsidered is before the body and still capable of being changed. The right to rescind an action depends only on the ability of the body to reverse the action because the right to rescind is not subject to the same time limits as the motion to reconsider. Both motions are generally applied only to such substantive matters as main motions and amendments to them. In dealing with simple, nondebatable procedural motions, there is a different situation. Here if the motion is lost, it may be renewed at a proper time. To protect the body from use of renewal for dilatory purposes, there is a limit on when it can be renewed. And when such a procedural motion is

---

Sec. 450, Par. 3: Toffolon v. Zoning Board of Appeals of Town of Plainville (1967), 155 Conn. 558, 236 A.2d 96.

Sec. 450, Par. 4: Kay Jewelry Co. v. Board of Registration in Optometry (1940), 305 Mass. 581, 27 N.E.2d 1.

Sec. 450, Par. 5: Witherspoon v. State of Mississippi *ex rel.* West (1925), 138 Miss. 310, 103 So. 134.

carried, the action can be reversed by such actions as to take from the table, to withdraw from committee, to change the limitations of debate, and to reset or change the time for considering a question. This is because no finality attaches to the renewal or reversal of procedural motions. The renewal of a main motion is not available to reverse the defeat of such a motion. The principle is that the simplest and most direct procedure should be used and would require that only main motions could be reconsidered and that procedural motions could be renewed, if lost.

Sec. 451. What Actions Cannot Be Reconsidered

See also Sec. 456, Procedural Motions Generally Are Not Subject to Reconsideration But May Be Renewed; Sec. 457, Substantive Propositions Are Subject to Reconsideration But May Not Be Renewed; and Sec. 340, The Motion to Lay on the Table May Not Be Reconsidered.

1. An action cannot be reconsidered when for any reason it is not possible to cancel, nullify or void the action previously taken. In general, the action cannot be canceled or made ineffective when:

(a) Vested rights have been acquired as a result of the action.

(b) Rights cannot be constitutionally or legally taken away.

(c) The subject is beyond the control or out of reach of the body taking the original action.

(d) It may be inhibited from acting by the requirement of a notice.

Sec. 451, Par. 1: Cushing's Legislative Assemblies, Sec. 1276; Sturgis, pp. 39, 40; Reed, Sec. 204.

2. The motion to reconsider is not generally applied to procedural motions as a more direct and simple procedure is available.

3. Reconsideration cannot be applied to motions that can be renewed within a reasonable time.

Sec. 452. Vested Rights Cannot Be Affected by Reconsideration—Contracts

1. A motion to reconsider is not in order when reconsideration cannot be made effective. The following are examples of decisions of courts on the right to reconsider.

2. When an affirmative vote of a deliberative body is in the nature of a contract or has the effect of ratifying a contract, and the other party to the contract has been notified of the vote or the contract has become effective, the vote cannot thereafter be canceled or voided by reconsideration.

Sec. 453. Election or Confirmation of Officers

1. No vote on the election of an officer can be reconsidered after the acceptance and qualification of the officer. The following are instances of court decisions involving the election or confirmation of officers.

2. When a person has been elected to membership or office, if the member or officer is present and does not decline, or if absent and has learned of

---

Sec. 451, Par. 3: Robert's, p. 268; Waples, Sec. 137.

Sec. 452, Par. 2: Brown v. Winterport (1887), 79 Me. 305, 9 A. 844.

Sec. 453, Par. 1: State of Wisconsin v. Tyrrell (1914), 158 Wis. 425, 149 N.W. 280; State of Ohio v. Miller (1900), 62 Ohio St. 436, 57 N.E. 227; Regina v. Donoghue (1858), 15 Upp. Canada Q.B. 454.

the election in the usual way and has not declined, it is too late to reconsider.

3. An appointment or confirmation to office is complete on performance of the act required of the person or body vested with appointing power. But before any action is taken under a vote to confirm or elect, the vote can be reconsidered.

4. A state senate may reconsider an affirmative vote confirming or approving an appointment to office provided the motion was made at the proper time.

5. A joint meeting of delegates representing different groups can reconsider a vote on election of an officer at the same or at an adjourned meeting provided no right had vested.

6. A vote on an election is subject to reconsideration at any time before the close of the meeting at which taken.

7. Where an election is not complete until a certification of election is issued a vote on the election can be reconsidered until the issuance of the certificate.

Sec. 453, Par. 2: Wood v. Cutter (1884), 138 Mass. 149.

Sec. 453, Par. 3: Witherspoon v. State of Mississippi *ex rel.* West (1925), 138 Miss. 310, 103 So. 134; Attorney General *ex rel.* Dust v. Oakman (1901), 126 Mich. 717, 86 N.W. 151; State of Minnesota *ex rel.* Todd v. Essling (1964), 128 N.W.2d 307.

Sec. 453, Par. 4: Attorney General *ex rel.* Dust v. Oakman (1901), 126 Mich. 717, 86 N.W. 151; People *ex rel.* MacMahon v. Davis (1918), 284 Ill. 439, 120 N.E. 326; State of New Jersey v. Foster (1823), 7 N.J.L. 101; State of New Jersey v. Van Buskirk (1878), 40 N.J.L. 463; Witherspoon v. State of Mississippi *ex rel.* West (1925), 138 Miss. 310, 103 So. 134.

Sec. 453, Par. 5: Baker v. Cushman (1879), 127 Mass. 105; Reed v. Barton (1900), 176 Mass. 473, 57 N.E. 961.

Sec. 453, Par. 6: Allen v. Morton (1910), 94 Ark. 405, 127 S.W. 450.

Sec. 453, Par. 7: Conger v. Gilmer (1867), 32 Cal. 75.

8. When the rules provide specifically a time during which a motion to reconsider may be made, the confirmation does not become final and a motion to reconsider may be made until that time has passed.

9. A motion to reconsider a vote by which a nomination was confirmed is not in order after the nomination affected has passed out of the possession of the house.

10. When the appointing power has the power of removal, it may reconsider an appointment at any time and appoint a successor to the office.

Sec. 454. Subject of Reconsideration Must Be Within Control of Body

1. A measure may not be reconsidered unless it is in the possession of the body. In a bicameral legislative body a measure which has been sent to the other house must be returned before a reconsideration can be effective.

2. A vote refusing to confirm an appointment by the executive cannot be reconsidered after notice of the action has been transmitted to the executive.

3. After a bill has passed a legislative body and has become a law, it is contrary to all parliamentary law and precedent for such body to attempt to recon-

---

Sec. 453, Par. 8: Witherspoon v. State of Mississippi *ex rel.* West (1925), 138 Miss. 310, 103 So. 134.

Sec. 453, Par. 9: N.Y. Manual (1946–47), p. 693.

Sec. 453, Par. 10: State of Connecticut v. Starr (1906), 78 Conn. 636, 63 A. 512.

Sec. 454, Par. 1: Cushing's Legislative Assemblies, Sec. 1274.

Sec. 454, Par. 2: N.Y. Manual (1946–47), p. 693.

sider such final action as shown by adjournment of the body and the promulgation of its act.

4. Whatever is beyond reversal is beyond reconsideration.

Sec. 455. Reconsideration Cannot Be Used to Defeat Requirement of Notice

1. When notice is required for amendment of the rules and amendments have been made pursuant to legal notice, the body cannot reconsider its action at a subsequent meeting and take other action without complying with the rules requiring notice.

2. When a notice is required for an election, a deliberative body cannot, by reconsideration, bring the question again before itself and proceed with the election without giving the required notice.

Sec. 456. Procedural Motions Generally Are Not Subject to Reconsideration But May Be Renewed

See also Sec. 67, Renewal of Motions; Sec. 160, Procedural Motions May Be Renewed; Sec. 161, Main Motions May Not Be Renewed; and Sec. 450, paragraph 1, Right to Reconsider.

Under the rules of parliamentary law, the procedural motions such as to recess, to lay on the table and to refer to committee are not subject to reconsideration. The reason is that, where reconsideration would otherwise be justified, there is a more simple, direct way of accomplishing the purpose of reconsideration. Generally, when procedural mo-

---

Sec. 454, Par. 3: Ashton v. City of Rochester (1891), 14 N.Y.S. 855, *aff'd* 1892, 133 N.Y. 187, 31 N.E. 344; State of New Jersey v. Van Buskirk (1878), 40 N.J.L. 463.

Sec. 455, Par. 2: People v. Batchelor (1860), 28 Barb. 310, 22 N.Y. 128.

tions are not adopted, they may be renewed whenever there has been intervening business or the situation is so changed that the body might reasonably reach a different decision. When procedural motions have carried, changed conditions may be met by appropriate new motions. For example, when a motion has been laid on the table, it can be taken from the table, and when a motion has been referred to committee, it can be withdrawn.

Sec. 457. Substantive Propositions Are Subject to Reconsideration But May Not Be Renewed

See also Sec. 67, Renewal of Motions; Sec. 160, Procedural Motions May Be Renewed; Sec. 161, Main Motions May Not Be Renewed; and Sec. 450, paragraph 1, Right to Reconsider.

1. Main motions, amendments to main motions, privileged motions, when involving substantive questions, and appeals are subject to reconsideration. These all involve questions more basic than the simple procedural motions. The questions presented for determination by these motions usually require decisions of a more permanent nature. It is essential that the bodies be able to make final decisions on these questions; otherwise it would be possible for a minority to obstruct execution of the will of the majority. But, lest the action might have been taken inadvertently, without adequate information, or without mature consideration, the vote on these propositions is subject for a limited time to reconsideration.

2. To prevent abuse of the motion to reconsider, the same question cannot be reconsidered a second

---

Sec. 456: Cushing, Sec. 253; Sturgis, pp. 39, 40; Hughes, Secs. 618, 619.

time. When a motion has been so changed as to present a substantially different proposition, it can be reconsidered again in the new form.

Sec. 458. Consideration of Measures Returned by Executive Veto

When an executive returns a bill to a legislative body with objections (veto), the further consideration of the measure is not itself a reconsideration in the parliamentary sense. A vote taken on further consideration of the measure, whether in the affirmative or negative, can be reconsidered.

Sec. 459. Reconsideration in Relation to Actions of the Other House

1. In a two-house legislative body, either house has the right to reconsider its own actions provided that no rights have vested in pursuance of the first action.

2. A rule of one house of a legislature relating to reconsideration of a measure once acted upon by that house does not prevent reconsideration of the same subject matter when embodied in a bill or resolution coming from the other house.

3. Where a bill has been passed by both houses and returned to the house of its origin the other house cannot reconsider its vote passing the bill

---

Sec. 458: Nevins v. City Council of City of Springfield (1917), 227 Mass. 538, 116 N.E. 881; Kay Jewelry Co. v. Board of Registration in Optometry (1940), 305 Mass. 581, 27 N.E.2d 1; State of South Carolina *ex rel.* Coleman v. Lewis (1936), 181 S.C. 10, 186 S.E. 625.

Sec. 459, Par. 1: Adkins v. Toledo (1905), 6 Ohio C.C.R. (n.s.) 433.

Sec. 459, Par. 2: Leser v. Board of Registry (1921), 139 Md. 46, 114 A. 840; Leser v. Garnett (1922), 258 U.S. 130, 42 S. Ct. 217, 66 L. Ed. 505; Cushing's Legislative Assemblies, Sec. 1273.

unless the bill is first returned to its control, as it has no possession or control over the bill. If the house of origin refuses to return the bill the vote to reconsider will not impair the validity of the act.

4. Notwithstanding the rule that a measure defeated and not reconsidered is final for the session, a defeat of a proposition in one house does not affect actions from the other house since two proposals originating in different houses do not constitute one measure.

5. When two houses are meeting in a joint session they have the right, as long as they are in session, to reconsider any question which they have had before them or any vote which they have taken.

Sec. 460. Regulation of Motion to Reconsider by Rules

1. The right of a legislative body to make rules to govern its own proceedings includes the right to prescribe the use of and regulate the procedure applicable to the motion to reconsider.

2. When a legislative body duly determines that the passage by it of a measure has been reconsidered, such determination is binding on the courts. Such reconsideration nullifies the vote of adoption, and the measure has the status of a pending matter.

Sec. 459, Par. 3: Smith v. Mitchell (1911), 69 W.Va. 481, 72 S.E. 755.

Sec. 459, Par. 4: Leser v. Board of Registry (1921), 139 Md. 46, 114 A. 840; Leser v. Garnett (1922), 258 U.S. 130, 42 S. Ct. 217, 66 L. Ed. 505.

Sec. 459, Par. 5: State of New Jersey v. Foster (1823), 7 N.J.L. 101; Witherspoon v. State of Mississippi *ex rel.* West (1925), 138 Miss. 310, 103 So. 134.

Sec. 460, Par. 1: Nevins v. City Council of City of Springfield (1917), 227 Mass. 538, 116 N.E. 881; Cushing, Sec. 257.

Sec. 460, Par. 2: Crawford v. Gilchrist (1912), 64 Fla. 41, 59 So. 963.

3. A motion to reconsider rests exclusively in the discretion of a body whose action it is proposed to reconsider and no other body or tribunal has a right to treat a reconsideration as void.

Sec. 461. When the Motion to Reconsider May Not Be Made

1. The motion to reconsider cannot be made after the matter is:

(a) Out of the control of the body.

(b) After the action taken has gone into effect.

(c) After it is too late for any reason to reverse the action taken.

It is also customary to further limit by rule the time within which the motion to reconsider can be made. This is sometimes limited to the day on which the action was taken. Most frequently, it is limited to the day on which the action was taken or on the day following. Some legislative bodies allow the motion to be made until the second day following the vote and a few permit the motion to be made within the next three days after the vote was taken.

2. The courts do not support the statement that as a rule of parliamentary law the motion to reconsider may be made only on the day the vote was taken or on the day following. If it is desired to restrict the time within which the motion may be made, it should be done by rule. In practice, the right is closely restricted in time because the motion

---

Sec. 460, Par. 3: People v. City of Rochester Common Council (N.Y. 1871), 5 Lans. 11.

Sec. 461, Par. 1: Sturgis, p. 40; Cal. Senate Rule No. 43; N.Y. Senate Rule No. 30; Hughes, Sec. 632.

cannot be made after the subject of the vote is out of the possession of the body.

3. The rules frequently prohibit the making of a motion to reconsider on the last day of a legislative session.

4. A motion or a notice of a motion to reconsider is sometimes permitted to interrupt a speaker.

5. When an appeal has been decided and the subject matter of the appeal disposed of, it is too late to move to reconsider the vote on the appeal.

6. A vote upon a reconsideration need not be taken either at the same or the next succeeding meeting, but may be taken at any time before the rights have intervened in pursuance of the vote taken or before the status quo has been changed.

Sec. 462. Precedence of Motion to Reconsider

1. The motion to reconsider is often given a high precedence by rule following the practice in Congress. When no precedence is fixed by rule, it takes precedence as an incidental motion relating to the manner or order of considering questions. When a notice of the motion is required, the notice has the same precedence as the making of the motion.

2. The following motions, when in order, take precedence in the order stated:

Sec. 461, Par. 2: Cushing, Sec. 255a.

Sec. 461, Par. 4: Reed, Sec. 205; Hughes, Sec. 711; Cushing, Sec. 257.

Sec. 461, Par. 5: N.Y. Manual, pp. 409, 476; Reed, Sec. 204.

Sec. 461, Par. 6: Adkins v. Toledo (1905), 6 Ohio C.C.R. (n.s.) 433.

Sec. 462: Sturgis, p. 42; Cushing's Legislative Assemblies, Sec. 1266; Hughes, Sec. 635.

(a) The motion to reconsider.

(b) The motion to reconsider and enter in the journal for later consideration (when permitted by special rule).

(c) The notice of the motion to reconsider on the next day.

Sec. 463. When the Motion to Reconsider May Be Considered

See also Sec. 469, Precedence of Consideration of Motion to Reconsider.

1. Generally, a motion to reconsider may be brought up for consideration whenever the subject to which the motion relates may be considered. This is usually when new main motions may be considered. Sometimes motions to reconsider are treated as unfinished business and considered in that order of business.

2. The rules may require that a motion to reconsider be placed on calendar for the following day in order to give notice to the members.

3. A notice of one day of the making of a motion to reconsider is required by rule in some bodies. When this is the practice the notice of the motion holds up any further action as the result of the vote the same as though the motion to reconsider had been made.

Sec. 464. Who May Move to Reconsider

1. It is a common practice to provide by rule that a motion to reconsider can be made only by a member who voted on the prevailing side of the

---

Sec. 463: Sturgis, p. 40; N.Y. Manual (1948–49), p. 451; Hughes, Sec. 640.

question. This is so frequently provided by rule that it is sometimes supposed to be a rule of parliamentary law. Where it is required by rule that the motion can be made only by a member who voted on the prevailing side the purpose of the rule is regularly defeated by a member of the minority voting on the prevailing side, or changing the member's vote to that side, in order to qualify the member to move to reconsider. In any vote except a roll call vote it is impossible to determine how a member voted.

2. Some legislative bodies specifically provide by rule that the motion to reconsider may be made by any member.

3. Luther Cushing in his Law and Practice of Legislative Assemblies said: "Where there is no special rule on the subject, a motion to reconsider may be made...by any member, precisely like any other motion, and subject to no other rules."

4. Parliamentary law does not restrict the making of the motion to reconsider to a member who voted on the prevailing side of a question sought to be reconsidered.

5. The courts sustain reconsiderations made on the motion of a member who voted on the losing side.

Sec. 464, Par. 1: Sturgis, p. 41; Tilson, p. 84; N.Y. Manual (1948–49), p. 451; Reed, Sec. 207; Cushing's Legislative Assemblies, Sec. 1266; Robert's, p. 265.

Sec. 464, Par. 2: Cal. Senate Rule No. 43; N.Y. Senate Rule No. 30.

Sec. 464, Par. 3: Cushing's Legislative Assemblies, Sec. 1266.

Sec. 464, Par. 4: Sturgis, p. 41.

Sec. 464, Par. 5: Witherspoon v. State of Mississippi *ex rel.* West (1925), 138 Miss. 310, 103 So. 134; People v. City of Rochester Common Council (N.Y. 1871), 5 Lans. 11.

Sec. 465. Form of Motion to Reconsider

1. Examples of forms of making this motion are as follows: "I move to reconsider the vote whereby House (or Senate) Bill No. ___ was this day passed (or refused passage)," or, when it is desired to reconsider the vote on an amendment to a measure which has been passed, "I move to reconsider the vote on the adoption of the resolution (describing when necessary) and on the amendment to strike out ______ and insert ______." When no business is before the house, it may proceed to the consideration of the motion. When other business is before the house, the presiding officer repeats the motion and it is recorded in the minutes, and the house proceeds to the business which was interrupted by the motion.

2. When the practice is to give notice of the motion to reconsider, the form of the notice may be "I give notice that on the next legislative day I will move to reconsider the vote whereby House (or Senate) Bill No. ___ was this day passed (or refused passage)."

3. Where the notice of motion is required, the actual motion to reconsider is made in the same form as in the other case, and the motion may be considered at the time when made, if no business having a higher precedence is under consideration. Where a notice of the motion is required, it is the practice to carry notices of motions to reconsider on the calendar, and the motion may be made and considered at that place on the calendar.

4. When a member desires to call up for consideration a motion to reconsider, which was previous-

Sec. 465: Sturgis, p. 39; Hughes, Sec. 620; Robert's, p. 279.

ly made, the member may obtain the floor at the appropriate order of business, and say, "I call up (or desire to call up) for consideration the motion to reconsider the vote whereby House (or Senate) Bill No. ____ was passed (or refused passage)." When the motion is in order the presiding officer announces the question and says, "Will the House (or Senate) reconsider the vote whereby House (or Senate) Bill No. ____ was passed (or refused passage)?"

Sec. 466. Withdrawing and Renewing Motion to Reconsider

1. The motion to reconsider cannot be withdrawn after it is too late to make the motion except by unanimous consent and if the motion to reconsider is lost it may be renewed only by unanimous consent.

2. When a motion to reconsider is made but its consideration is postponed, it may be called up for consideration by another member.

Sec. 467. Effect of Making Motion to Reconsider

1. The effect of making the motion to reconsider, or of giving notice of the motion where that is the procedure, is to suspend all action on the subject of the motion until the reconsideration is acted upon.

2. When, for example, a motion to reconsider the vote on the approval of appointments was made at the same session at which it was taken and the

Sec. 466: Reed, Sec. 205; Sturgis, p. 42.

Sec. 467, Par. 1: People *ex rel.* MacMahon v. Davis (1918), 284 Ill. 439, 120 N.E. 326; Sturgis, p. 42; Hughes, Sec. 625.

question was then laid on the table to be taken up later at the convenience of the council in accordance with its rules, the question of reconsideration remained undetermined in the possession of the council awaiting its action.

3. If, however, the motion to reconsider is made and not considered, the effect terminates with the session, if not terminated earlier by waiver of the member giving the notice or making the motion, or by provisions of the rules.

4. If notice of the motion is given but the motion is not made, the effect of the notice terminates on the next legislative day.

5. As long as the motion or notice is in effect, any member may call up the motion to reconsider or make the motion and have it acted upon. But, as a matter of courtesy, no other member should call up a matter for reconsideration without the permission of the member making the motion or giving the notice, except in an emergency.

6. Where the rules permit a vote to be reconsidered at the same meeting, an adjourned meeting will be considered the same meeting and a vote taken at the originally called meeting may be reconsidered at the adjourned meeting.

7. When the motion to reconsider and have entered in the minutes for later consideration is provided for by the rules but its use is not further

---

Sec. 467, Par. 2: People *ex rel.* MacMahon v. Davis (1918), 284 Ill. 439, 120 N.E. 326.

Sec. 467, Par. 3: People *ex rel.* MacMahon v. Davis (1918), 284 Ill. 439, 120 N.E. 326.

Sec. 467, Par. 6: Delaware & Atlantic Tel. & Tel. Co. v. Mayor and Council of City of Beverly (1914), 86 N.J.L. 677, 94 A. 310.

regulated, such a motion cannot be considered the day it is made.

Sec. 468. Effect of Reconsideration

1. When a vote is reconsidered that vote is canceled as completely as though it had never been taken.

2. Where the original vote was to approve an appointment, the subsequent vote of reconsideration had the effect of disapproving the appointment.

3. Where a motion to reconsider has been passed the question immediately recurs upon the question reconsidered.

Sec. 469. Precedence of Consideration of Motion to Reconsider

1. This motion is unusual in that the making of the motion has a higher rank than its consideration, and the mere making of the motion prevents for a certain time anything being done as the result of the vote it is proposed to reconsider. While the making of the motion to reconsider has such high privilege, its consideration has only the rank of the motion to be reconsidered.

Sec. 467, Par. 7: First Buckingham Community v. Malcolm (1941), 177 Va. 710, 15 S.E.2d 54.

Sec. 468, Par. 1: Crawford v. Gilchrist (1912), 64 Fla. 41, 59 So. 963; People *ex rel.* MacMahon v. Davis (1918), 284 Ill. 439, 120 N.E. 326; Sturgis, p. 39; Cushing's Legislative Assemblies, Secs. 1277, 1278; Reed, Sec. 203; Cushing, Sec. 256; Sturgis, p. 42.

Sec. 468, Par. 2: People *ex rel.* MacMahon v. Davis (1918), 284 Ill. 439, 120 N.E. 326.

Sec. 468, Par. 3: Ashton v. City of Rochester (1891), 14 N.Y.S. 855, *aff'd* 1892, 133 N.Y. 187, 31 N.E. 344.

Sec. 469: Sturgis, pp. 40, 42; N.Y. Manual (1948–49), pp. 451–453; Hughes, Sec. 623.

2. The motion to reconsider takes precedence over any new motion of equal rank. It has the further privilege that the reconsideration of a vote may be called up at any time in the appropriate order of business, when no question is pending, and this procedure is considered as in compliance with the general orders or calendar.

3. When the reconsideration is moved while another subject is before the house, it cannot interrupt the pending business. But as soon as that business has been disposed of, the reconsideration may be called up and it takes precedence over all other main motions and general orders.

4. When the motion to reconsider is made in the proper order of business and no business is before the house, the presiding officer may at once state the question on reconsideration and it is before the house for its consideration.

5. It is permissible, when a member moves a reconsideration, to have the matter set as a special order, or, unless the rules require the consideration of the motion within a limited time, the member may have consideration of the motion postponed to a later date.

6. It is a usual practice to place pending motions to reconsider on the calendar under a special division ahead of the second and third readings of bills.

Sec. 470. Reconsideration of Amendments After Adoption of Measure

When it is desired to reconsider the vote on an amendment after the vote has been taken on the adoption of a main motion, it is necessary to reconsider the vote on the main question and on the amendment. If it is desired to reconsider an amendment to an amendment after the latter has been adopted, both must be reconsidered in order to reach the amendment it is desired to reconsider. When it is thus necessary to reconsider two or three votes, one motion should be made to cover them all, but debate is limited to the question first voted upon.

Sec. 471. Debate on Motion to Reconsider

1. The motion to reconsider is debatable except when the motion which it is proposed to reconsider is undebatable. When the question to be reconsidered is debatable, the entire question is opened to debate by the motion to reconsider. But when the motion is made after the previous question is adopted, neither the motion nor the question is debatable.

2. The previous question and the motions closing, limiting or extending the limits of debate may be applied to the motion to reconsider when the matter to be reconsidered is debatable.

3. When the rules prohibit a member speaking more than once on a question on the same day, anyone who had exhausted the right to debate the question before the vote has the right to debate the question further on the motion to reconsider.

Sec. 470: Cushing's Legislative Assemblies, Sec. 1275; Reed, Sec. 203; Hughes, Sec. 633; Robert's, p. 268.

Sec. 471, Par. 1: Sturgis, p. 42; Reed, Sec. 210.

Sec. 471, Par. 2: Sturgis, p. 42.

Sec. 471, Par. 3: Sturgis, p. 42; Reed, Sec. 210; Robert's, p. 269.

Sec. 472. Application of Subsidiary Motions to Motion to Reconsider

1. The motion to reconsider, since it is a single, invariable proposition, cannot be amended.

2. When a motion to reconsider is laid on the table or postponed definitely, the question to be reconsidered and all adhering questions go with it.

Sec. 473. Vote Required for Reconsideration

1. A majority vote of the members present and voting is necessary to reconsider an action.

2. When a measure requires more than a majority vote for passage it may still be reconsidered by a majority vote.

3. A body, under its rule-making power, can prescribe the vote required for reconsideration but, unless a different vote is prescribed, any vote can be reconsidered by a majority vote.

Sec. 474. Reconsider and Enter on the Minutes

1. Robert devised the motion to reconsider and have entered on the minutes. The motion appears in his Rules of Order, Revised and Rules of Order,

Sec. 472, Par. 1: Sturgis, p. 42; N.Y. Manual, p. 476.

Sec. 472, Par. 2: Reed, Secs. 114, 166.

Sec. 473, Par. 1: Crawford v. Gilchrist (1912), 64 Fla. 41, 59 So. 963; Wingert v. Snouffer & Ford (1906), 134 Iowa 97, 108 N.W. 1035; Naegely v. Saginaw (1894), 101 Mich. 532, 60 N.W. 46; Stockdale v. Wayland School Dist. (1881), 47 Mich. 226, 10 N.W. 349.

Sec. 473, Par. 2: Crawford v. Gilchrist (1912), 64 Fla. 41, 59 So. 963; Hughes, Sec. 642.

Sec. 473, Par. 3: Wingert v. Snouffer & Ford (1906), 134 Iowa 97, 108 N.W. 1035.

Newly Revised but not in the early printings of his Rules of Order. This motion is recognized by some writers who copy Robert. The motion, Robert says, is for the purpose of preventing "a temporary majority from taking advantage of a temporary unrepresentative attendance at the meeting to vote an action that is opposed by the majority" of the membership. The effect of the motion is to put over all action on the motion to be reconsidered until a later day, even when there is another meeting on the same day. Mr. Robert acknowledges that the motion is subject to "attempted" abuse "since it gives any two members power to hold up action taken by a meeting."

2. Robert says that the motion to reconsider and enter is to be used only when there is an unrepresentative majority. Demeter says that the motion is to be used only when a "mischievous, arrogant or unscrupulous temporary majority passes undesirable business." But who is to determine when the action is defective in any of these ways? Is it the person who has been defeated and is resentful? Those who accept this motion would hedge it with so many "safeguards" as to largely defeat the desires of its supporters. The motion has not been generally accepted by the courts as a part of parliamentary law.

3. The motion to reconsider and enter in the minutes came before a court for consideration in Rutherford v. City of Nashville in 1935. Here the City Council of Nashville had before it an act for the licensing of drivers of motor vehicles. On final reading the act passed by a majority vote. A member moved to reconsider and have entered on the

Sec. 474, Par. 1: Robert's, pp. 281–284; Demeter, pp. 160–164.
Sec. 474, Par. 2: Robert's, pp. 281–284; Demeter, pp. 160–164.

minutes. The presiding officer ruled the motion out of order and sent the act on to the mayor who signed the act and delivered it to the city clerk. At the next meeting the member who had made the motion undertook to call up the motion for disposition. The court declared that the act had been duly passed, the motion to reconsider had been properly ruled out, the law was in effect and there was nothing further before the city council concerning the driver licensing act.

Sec. 474, Par. 3: Rutherford v. City of Nashville (1935), 168 Tenn. 499, 79 S.W.2d 581.

CHAPTER 42

MOTION TO RESCIND

Sec. 480. Use of the Motion to Rescind

1. The motion to rescind has many of the same characteristics as the motion to reconsider and is used for much the same purpose. Many court decisions treat the two motions as one motion.

2. In use, the motion to rescind is ordinarily applied to actions which have been taken and are already in effect. It resembles, in many respects, the motion to repeal because it has the effect of making ineffective an action previously taken. It has also been described as being in the nature of a motion to amend by striking out the entire proposal and leaving nothing remaining.

3. A motion to rescind a vote on an action does not have the effect of suspending the action previously taken or staying it until final decision on the motion to rescind.

4. A motion to rescind is principally used to reverse a previous action after the time for consideration has passed. The motion to rescind is not in order when the question can be reached by a motion to reconsider.

Sec. 481. What Actions Can Be Rescinded

1. A legislative body can rescind an action previously taken as long as no vested rights have arisen

Sec. 480: Hughes, Sec. 469.

from the original action. In this respect the motion to rescind is in effect the same as the motion to reconsider. Instances which have been decided by the courts are stated below.

2. The motion to rescind may be made at any subsequent meeting as long as no rights have intervened and is not limited to any specific or particular time during which the motion can be made.

3. When an authorized act has been carried out the power to rescind does not exist.

4. Where a legislative body ratifies a contract the ratification completes the act and a subsequent meeting cannot rescind the ratification.

Sec. 482. Motion to Rescind

1. The motion to rescind may be made by any member whether that person voted with the prevailing side or not. The motion is debatable and opens the entire question to debate.

2. The motion to rescind yields to all privileged and incidental motions and all subsidiary motions can be applied to it, the same as any other main motion.

3. Like other main motions, the motion to rescind may not be renewed during the same meeting or session, but also may be subject to reconsideration in the same manner as a main motion.

4. In the event of the expulsion of a member the only way to reverse the action afterward is to restore

---

Sec. 481, Par. 2: McConoughey v. Jackson (1894), 101 Cal. 265, 25 P. 863; Stoddard v. Gilman (1850), 22 Vt. 568.

Sec. 481, Par. 3: Schieffelin v. Hylan (1919), 174 N.Y.S. 506.

Sec. 481, Par. 4: Brown v. Winterport (1887), 79 Me. 305, 9 A. 844.

the person to membership which requires the same procedural steps as is required for election.

5. When an action such as the enactment of legislation has been taken, and notice or three readings or like procedure would be required to repeal the action, the action is not subject to the motion to rescind.

Sec. 483. Vote Required to Rescind

The motion to rescind requires the same vote as would be required to repeal the act which it is sought to rescind. In the absence of any special rule this is a majority vote. Neither a notice nor a two-thirds vote is necessary unless expressly required in the rules.

Sec. 482, Par. 4: U.S. House Rule, 71st Cong., Pars. 71, 712.

Sec. 483: Tetley v. Vancouver (1897), 5 B.C. 276; Naegely v. Saginaw (1894), 101 Mich. 532, 60 N.W. 46; Stockdale v. Wayland School Dist. (1881), 47 Mich. 226, 10 N.W. 349; Allen v. Taunton (Mass. 1837), 19 Pick. 485; Estey v. Starr (1884), 56 Vt. 690; McConoughey v. Jackson (1894), 101 Cal. 265, 25 P. 863.

CHAPTER 43

PROCEDURAL MAIN MOTIONS

Sec. 488. Procedural Main Motions

1. In addition to main motions which are substantive propositions presented to a legislative body, there is a group of procedural motions which have the same precedence as main motions and, for that reason, are often classified with main motions.

2. These motions are often familiar types of procedural motions which differ from other procedural motions only in relating to future procedure. Motions to adjourn or to recess at some future time are examples of this class of motion.

3. Also classified with these motions are procedural motions which from their use have precedence only with main motions. Motions of this class are motions to take from the table, resume consideration, or pass on calendar.

Sec. 489. Motions Relating to Future Procedure

See also Sec. 67, Renewal of Motions.

1. Generally, motions relating to future procedure must compete with main motions for consideration, because there is no need for priority.

2. Because the urgency of immediate determination does not exist, this type of question is open to debate.

Sec. 488: Hughes, Secs. 443–452, 479–488.

3. Motions relating to future procedure are subject to the motions to postpone, to refer to committee, or to lay on the table. They are subject to amendment and motions limiting debate. These motions may be renewed after a change in the parliamentary situations but may not be reconsidered.

4. Among the motions in this class are:

(a) Motions fixing a time, or a different time, at which or to which to adjourn.

(b) Motions fixing a time for a recess or other conditions relating to a recess.

(c) Motions fixing a time or other conditions relating to committee of the whole.

(d) Motions relating to the future consideration of some matter of business.

(e) Motions relating to future meetings, program, or procedure of any kind.

Sec. 490. Procedural Motions with Precedence of Main Motions

1. Deliberative bodies make frequent use of motions in conducting their business which rank in the class of main motions. Some of these motions, like the motion to take from the table, are in order whenever no business is pending. Others, like the motion to pass on calendar, may be applied to a pending main motion.

2. Generally, these motions are subject to the same rules as other simple procedural motions. They are not debatable, except sometimes limited debate is permitted on the motion to withdraw a bill

Sec. 490: Hughes, Secs. 454–467.

from committee or discharge a committee. They are not subject to the subsidiary motions and can be renewed after a change in the parliamentary situation, but cannot be reconsidered. Unless some special rule has been adopted, they require a majority of the legal votes cast for adoption.

3. Among the more frequently used motions of this class are:

(a) Motions to withdraw from committee or discharge a committee.

(b) Motions to take from the table or resume consideration.

(c) Motions to pass on calendar or file.

(d) Motions to lay on the desk or take from the desk (sometimes used when lay on the table is restricted by rule).

(e) Cloture or making special rules concerning debate on or consideration of some pending question.

4. The motions to withdraw from committee and take from the table are the only motions in this class which require further consideration.

Sec. 491. Withdrawing Bills from Committee

1. When a legislative body wishes to give consideration to or act upon a bill or other matter which has been referred to a committee, a motion may be made to withdraw the matter from the committee, or to discharge the committee from further consideration of the matter referred to it.

Sec. 491, Par. 1: Robert's, p. 261.

2. The motion to withdraw a question or discharge a committee from further consideration is not a suspension of the rules, and may be made without previous notice.

3. The motion, in either form, takes precedence as a main motion. It is not subject to the motions to postpone, to refer to committee, to lay on the table or to amendment.

4. It is not in order to discuss the merits of a bill upon a motion to discharge a committee or withdraw the bill from committee. Debate in such cases must be confined strictly to the purpose of the motion, for if this were not true, the merits of any question could be forced under discussion merely by such a motion to withdraw.

5. A motion to discharge a committee or withdraw a bill requires a majority vote, or the action may be taken by unanimous consent.

6. A single motion to withdraw a bill from committee, amend the bill, reprint it and recommit it to committee is in order.

Sec. 492. Motion to Take from the Table

See also Ch. 33, Secs. 330–342, Motion to Lay on the Table.

Precedence of Motion

1. The motion to take from the table has no privileged status and is not in order when anything

---

Sec. 491, Par. 2: N.Y. Manual, p. 426.
Sec. 491, Par. 4: Hughes, Sec. 733.
Sec. 491, Par. 5: Hughes, Secs. 462, 463.
Sec. 491, Par. 6: N.Y. Manual, p. 411.

is before the body.

2. The motion to take from the table yields to all privileged motions and incidental motions but may be taken up in preference to new main motions at a time when business of this class, or unfinished business, or new business, is in order unless it has a privileged status.

When Motion Is in Order

3. A question is, in theory, to be laid on the table only temporarily, with the expectation of its consideration being resumed after the disposal of the interrupting question, or at a more convenient time. The motion to take from the table is not in order until after the intervening business for which it was laid on the table has been disposed of.

4. When the question laid on the table had a privileged status, a motion to take from the table is in order in the same order of business in which the matter affected was laid on the table. A motion to take from the table a motion to reconsider a vote by which a bill was defeated is in order on third reading.

Renewal and Reconsideration of Motion

5. The motion to take from the table may not be reconsidered, as it can be renewed after intervening business. A motion may be laid on the table a second time and be again taken from the table.

Application of Other Motions. Debate. Vote

6. The motion to take from the table may not be laid on the table, postponed, committed nor have

---

Sec. 492, Par. 1: Hughes, Secs. 454, 455; Reed, Sec. 114; N.Y. Manual, pp. 416, 453; U.S. House Rule XVI, Note 784.

any other subsidiary motion applied to it. It is not subject to debate. It requires for adoption a majority of the legal votes cast.

Effect of Adhering Motions

7. When taken from the table, the question, with everything adhering to it, is before the house exactly as when it was laid on the table. Thus, if a resolution had amendments and a motion to commit pending at the time it was laid on the table, when it is taken from the table, the question is first on the motion to commit and then on the amendments. If a motion to postpone to a certain time be pending when a question is laid on the table and it is taken from the table after that time, then the motion to postpone is ignored when the question is taken up.

8. If the question is taken up on the day it was laid on the table, members who have exhausted their right of debate cannot again speak on the question. But if taken up on another day, no notice is taken of speeches previously made. When the motion to lay on the table is permitted after the previous question is ordered, the previous question is not exhausted, even though the question is taken from the table on another day.

9. By a special rule, the motion to lay on the table is sometimes converted into a motion to finally dispose of questions by providing that no question may be taken from the table. This is the practice in Congress where bills are taken from the table only by suspension of the rules.

Sec. 493. Motion to Take from Desk

When there are matters at the desk concerning which no action has been taken and which a member desires to have considered, a motion may be made for that purpose. The motion may not be made when other business is before the house. A majority vote only is required, and this motion is not subject to any subsidiary motion.

Sec. 494. Motion to Pass on Calendar or File, Informally Pass or Temporarily Pass

The effect of the motion to lay aside, informally pass or temporarily pass is merely to pass the bill or measure, in the course of consideration of the calendar, without prejudice to the matter passed. Such a motion is not given any privilege by the rules. It is not subject to the subsidiary motions and is not debatable.

Sec. 495. Motion to Dispense with Constitutional Readings

1. When permitted by the constitution, the motion to dispense with constitutional readings takes precedence over no other motion than the main question on the bill for which the constitutional provision is suspended.

2. If the constitutional requirement of three readings is permitted to be suspended, a motion to dispense with constitutional readings may be applied to more than one bill.

Sec. 493: Hughes, Sec. 483.

Sec. 494: Hughes, Secs. 479–481, 715.

Sec. 495: People v. Glenn County (1893), 100 Cal. 419, 35 P. 302; Hughes, Sec. 482.

*

PART V. QUORUM, VOTING, ELECTIONS

*

PART V

QUORUM, VOTING, ELECTIONS

CHAPTER 44

QUORUM

Sec. 500. Quorum Must Be Present

See also Sec. 613, Quorum of Committees.

1. A quorum of any deliberative body, whether a legislative body, an administrative board or a court, must be present in order to transact business, and to make its acts valid.

Sec. 500, Par. 1: Cushing's Legislative Assemblies, Sec. 247; Sturgis, pp. 14–17; Reed, Sec. 9; Hughes, Sec. 644; Cushing, Sec. 17; Tilson, p. 27; Brown v. District of Columbia (1888), 127 U.S. 579, 32 L. Ed. 262; Daniels v. Bayless Stores (1935), 46 Ariz. 442, 52 P.2d 475; Downing v. Ruger (N.Y. 1899), 21 Wend. 178; Moses v. Tompkins (1888), 84 Ala. 613, 4 So. 763; State of Indiana v. Porter (1888), 113 Ind. 79, 14 N.E. 883; Logansport v. Legg (1863), 20 Ind. 315; Hamilton v. Grand Rapids etc. R. Co. (1859), 13 Ind. 347; *In re* Gunn (1893), 50 Kan. 155, 32 P. 470; Pierce v. New Orleans Building Co. (1836), 9 La. 397, 29 Am. Dec. 448; Ellsworth Woolen Mfg. Co. v. Founce (1887), 79 Me. 440, 10 A. 250; Heiskell v. City Council of Baltimore (1886), 65 Md. 125, 4 A. 116; Dingwell v. Detroit (1890), 82 Mich. 568, 46 N.W. 938; Morrill v. Little Falls Mfg. Co. (1893), 53 Minn. 371, 55 N.W. 547; Kay Jewelry Co. v. Board of Registration in Optometry (1940), 305 Mass. 581, 27 N.E.2d 1; Kimball v. Marshall (1863), 44 N.H. 465; Doughty v. Scull (1916), 96 A. 564; State of Ohio v. Wilkesville Township (1870), 20 Ohio St. 288; Commonwealth *ex rel.* Price v. Garvey (1907), 217 Pa. 425, 66 A. 652; Lockwood v. Mechanics National Bank (1869), 9 R.I. 308, 11 Am. R. 253; Boggess v. Buxton (1910), 67 W.Va. 679, 69 S.E. 367; Sharp v. Dawes (Eng. 1876), 2 Q.B.D. 26; Blacket v. Blizard (Eng. 1829), 9 B.C. 851, 109 Reprint 317; Steers Sand and Gravel Corp. v. Village Board of Northport (1954), 129 N.Y.S. 403; Bray v. Barry (1960), 91 R.I. 34, 160 A.2d 577; Davidson v. State of Indiana (1966), 248 Ind. 26, 221 N.E.2d 814, orig., 220 N.E.2d 340, *rehearing denied, cert. denied,* 387 U.S. 911, 87 S. Ct. 1696, 18 L. Ed. 2d 631 (1967); Commonwealth *ex rel.* Fox v.

2. The majority of the membership of a body constituted of a definite number of members constitutes a quorum for the purpose of transacting business.

Chace (1961), 403 Pa. 117, 168 A.2d 569; Shaughnessy v. Metropolitan Dade County (Fla. 1970), 238 So. 2d 466; Town of Smithtown v. Howell (1972), 31 N.Y.2d 365, 292 N.E.2d 10, orig., 38 App. Div. 2d 857, 330 N.Y.S.2d 164, *aff'd;* Houser v. School Dist. of South Sioux City in Dakota County (1972), 189 Neb. 323, 202 N.W.2d 621; U.S. v. Reinecke (1975), 524 F.2d 435, 173 U.S. App. D.C. 274; Chase v. Board of Trustees of Nebraska State Colleges (1975), 194 Neb. 688, 235 N.W.2d 223.

Sec. 500, Par. 2: Cushing's Legislative Assemblies, Sec. 247; Sturgis, pp. 113–115; Reed, Sec. 12; Hughes, Sec. 645; Cushing, Secs. 18–18e; Tilson, p. 27; U.S. v. Ballin (1892), 144 U.S. 1, 12 S. Ct. 507, 36 L. Ed. 321; Brown v. District of Columbia (1888), 127 U.S. 579, 32 L. Ed. 262; State of Connecticut v. Chapman (1878), 44 Conn. 595; *In re* Opinion of the Justices (1868), 12 Fla. 653; Price v. Grand Rapids etc. R. Co. (1859), 13 Ind. 58; Buell v. Buckingham (1864), 16 Iowa 284, 85 Am. Dec. 516; *In re* Gunn (1893), 50 Kan. 155, 32 P. 470; Seiler v. O'Maley (1921), 190 Ky. 190, 227 S.W. 141; Warnock v. Lafayette (1849), 4 La. Ann. 419; Cram v. Bangor House Proprietary (1835), 12 Me. 354; Heiskell v. City Council of Baltimore (1886), 65 Md. 125, 4 A. 116; Williams v. Lunenburg School Dist. (Mass. 1838), 21 Pick. 75, 32 Am. Dec. 243; *In re* Opinion of the Justices (1877), 122 Mass. 594; Kay Jewelry Co. v. Board of Registration in Optometry (1940), 305 Mass. 581, 27 N.E.2d 1; Baker v. Police Com'rs. of Port Huron (1886), 62 Mich. 327, 28 N.W. 913; Cahill v. Kalamazoo Mut. Ins. Co. (Mich. 1845), 2 Doug. 124, 43 Am. Dec. 457; State of Minnesota v. Chute (1885), 34 Minn. 135, 24 N.W. 353; State of Missouri *ex rel.* Otto v. Kansas City (1925), 310 Mo. 542, 276 S.W. 389; Despatch Line etc. v. Bellamy Mfg. Co. (1841), 12 N.H. 205, 37 Am. Dec. 203; Barnett v. City of Patterson (1886), 48 N.J.L. 395, 6 A. 15; Hutchinson v. Belmar (1898), 61 N.J.L. 443, 39 A. 643; People v. Walker (N.Y. 1856), 23 Barb. 304; Coles v. Williamsburgh (N.Y. 1833), 10 Wend. 659; *In re* Brearton (1904), 89 N.Y.S. 893; Madison Ave. Baptist Church v. Oliver St. Baptist Church (1867), 29 N.Y. Super. 649, 2 Abb. Pr. (n.s.) 254; State of North Carolina v. Ellington (1895), 117 N.C. 158, 23 S.E. 250; Hill v. Ponder (1942), 221 N.C. 58, 19 S.E.2d 5; Deglow v. Kruse (1898), 57 Ohio St. 434, 49 N.E. 477; Meyers v. Philadelphia Union League (1908), 17 Pa. Dist. 301; State of South Carolina v. Huggins (1824), 16 S.C.L. 239, 12 Rich. Law 402; State of South Carolina v. Delieseline (1821), 12 S.C.L. 52; State of Indiana v. Porter (1888), 113 Ind. 79, 14 N.E. 883; Cowan v. Murch (1896), 97 Tenn. 590, 37 S.W. 393; Commissioners Court of Limestone County v. Garrett (Tex. 1922), 236 S.W. 970; Leavitt v. Oxford etc. Silver Mfg. Co. (1883), 3 Utah 265, 1 P. 356; Booker v. Young (1855), 53 Va. 303; State of West Virginia *ex rel.* Hatfield v. Farrar (1921), 89 W.Va. 232, 109 S.E. 240; Boggess v. Buxton (1910), 67

Sec. 501. Computing a Quorum

1. The total membership of a body is to be taken as the basis for computing a quorum, but when there is a vacancy, unless a special provision is applicable, a quorum will consist of the majority of the members remaining qualified.

2. The authority which creates a body has the power to fix its quorum. The presence of all or of a certain number or proportion may be required. The body itself does not have the authority to require the presence of more than a majority to enable it to act

W.Va. 679, 69 S.E. 367; Gosling v. Veley (1847), 7 Q.B. 406, 115 Reprint 542; Blacket v. Blizard (Eng. 1829), 9 B.C. 851, 109 Reprint 317; Bray v. Barry (1960), 91 R.I. 34, 160 A.2d 577; Commonwealth *ex rel.* Fox v. Chace (1961), 403 Pa. 117, 168 A.2d 569; Davidson v. State of Indiana (1966), 248 Ind. 26, 221 N.E.2d 814, orig., 220 N.E.2d 340, *rehearing denied, cert. denied,* 387 U.S. 911, 87 S. Ct. 1696, 18 L. Ed. 2d 631 (1967); Opinion of the Justices (Del. 1969), 251 A.2d 827; Shaughnessy v. Metropolitan Dade County (Fla. 1970), 238 So. 2d 466; Town of Smithtown v. Howell (1972), 31 N.Y.2d 365, 292 N.E.2d 10, orig., 38 App. Div. 2d 857, 330 N.Y.S.2d 164, *aff'd;* U.S. v. Reinecke (1975), 524 F.2d 435, 173 U.S. App. D.C. 274; Chase v. Board of Trustees of Nebraska State Colleges (1975), 194 Neb. 688, 235 N.W.2d 223.

Sec. 501, Par. 1: Cushing's Legislative Assemblies, Secs. 246–253; Pimental v. San Francisco (1863), 21 Cal. 351; McCracken v. San Francisco (1860), 16 Cal. 591; Pollasky v. Schmid (1901), 128 Mich. 699, 87 N.W. 1030; McLean v. East St. Louis (1906), 222 Ill. 510, 78 N.E. 815; *In re* Opinion of the Justices (1868), 12 Fla. 653; People *ex rel.* Funk v. Wright (1902), 30 Colo. 439, 71 P. 365; Evanston v. O'Leary (1897), 70 Ill. App. 124; State of Indiana v. Porter (1888), 113 Ind. 79, 14 N.E. 883; State of Iowa v. Dickie (1878), 47 Iowa 629; Barry v. New Haven (1915), 162 Ky. 60, 171 S.W. 1012; Pollard v. Gregg (1914), 77 N.H. 190, 90 A. 176; Warnock v. Lafayette (1849), 4 La. Ann. 419; People v. Harshaw (1886), 60 Mich. 200, 26 N.W. 879; State of Missouri v. McBride (1836), 4 Mo. 303, 29 Am. Dec. 636; North Platte v. North Platte Water Works (1898), 56 Neb. 403, 76 N.W. 906; Mueller v. Egg Harbor City (1893), 55 N.J.L. 245, 26 A. 89; State of Ohio v. Orr (1899), 61 Ohio St. 384, 56 N.E. 14; State of South Carolina v. Delieseline (1821), 12 S.C.L. 52; State of West Virginia *ex rel.* Hatfield v. Farrar (1921), 89 W.Va. 232, 109 S.E. 240; Fisher v. Harrisburg Gas Co. (Pa. 1857), 1 Pears. 118; Rouleau v. St. Lambert (1895), 10 Que. Super. 69.

unless that authority was specifically granted to it.

3. Compliance with a constitutional provision which fixes a quorum at a stated number of members is mandatory.

4. A quorum is a majority of the number of members of a house prescribed by law, whether or not one or more vacancies have occurred by reason of death, resignation or otherwise.

Sec. 502. Who May Be Counted in Determining a Quorum

1. Ordinarily a "quorum" means a majority of all entitled to vote.

2. In determining a quorum, persons who are not at the particular time regularly qualified members of the body should not be counted.

Sec. 501, Par. 2: Ex parte Rogers (N.Y. 1821), 7 Cowp. 526; U.S. v. Ballin (1892), 144 U.S. 1, 12 S. Ct. 507, 36 L. Ed. 321; Heiskell v. City Council of Baltimore (1886), 65 Md. 125, 4 A. 116; Barnett v. City of Patterson (1886), 48 N.J.L. 395, 6 A. 15; Cleveland Cotton Mills v. Cleveland County Commissioners (1891), 108 N.C. 678, 13 S.E. 271; Borough of Florham Park v. Department of Health of State of New Jersey (1929), 7 N.J.L. 549, 146 A. 354; Hill v. Ponder (1942), 221 N.C. 58, 19 S.E.2d 5; Pinson v. Morrow (1920), 189 Ky. 291, 224 S.W. 879; Seiler v. O'Maley (1921), 190 Ky. 190, 227 S.W. 141.

Sec. 501, Par. 3: Opinion of the Justices (1959), 102 N.H. 230, 153 A.2d 409; Bezio v. Neville (1973), 113 N.H. 278, 305 A.2d 665.

Sec. 501, Par. 4: Opinion of the Justices (Del. 1969), 251 A.2d 827.

Sec. 502, Par. 1: Bedford County Hospital v. Bedford County (1957), 42 Tenn. App. 569, 304 S.W.2d 697.

Sec. 502, Par. 2: People *ex rel.* Funk v. Wright (1902), 30 Colo. 439, 71 P. 365; State of Indiana v. Porter (1888), 113 Ind. 79, 14 N.E. 883; Swan v. Indianola (1909), 142 Iowa 731, 121 N.W. 547; Commissioners v. Wachovia L. & T. Co. (1906), 143 N.C. 110, 55 S.E. 442; State of Ohio v. Orr (1899), 61 Ohio St. 384, 56 N.E. 14; State of South Carolina v. Huggins (1824), 16 S.C.L. 239, 12 Rich. Law 402; Barry v. New Haven (1915), 162 Ky. 60, 171 S.W. 1012; North Platte v. North Platte Water Works (1898), 56 Neb. 403, 76 N.W. 906; Mueller v. Egg Harbor City (1893), 55 N.J.L. 245, 26 A. 89; State of West Virginia *ex rel.* Hatfield v.

3. Every member entitled to vote should be counted in determining whether a quorum is present, but members disqualified on account of interest from voting on any question cannot be counted for the purpose of making a quorum to act on that question.

4. Where the presiding officer is a member of the body, the presiding officer is to be counted in determining a quorum. When not a member, the presiding officer is not to be counted, even though the presiding officer may vote in case of a tie.

5. In a joint meeting of legislative bodies, there being no rule to the contrary, a quorum of each

---

Farrar (1921), 89 W.Va. 232, 109 S.E. 240; Rouleau v. St. Lambert (1895), 10 Que. Super. 69.

Sec. 502, Par. 3: Cushing's Legislative Assemblies, Sec. 253; Enright v. Hecksher (1917), 240 F. 863, 153 C.C.A. 549; Curtin v. Salmon River Hydraulic Gold-Mining & Ditch Co. (1900), 130 Cal. 345, 62 P. 552; Smith v. Los Angeles Imm. Assn. (1889), 78 Cal. 289, 20 P. 677; Steele v. Gold Fissure Gold Mining Co. (1908), 42 Colo. 529, 95 P. 349; Federal Life Ins. Co. v. Griffin (1912), 173 Ill. App. 5; Jones v. Morrison (1883), 31 Minn. 140, 16 N.W. 854; Hill v. Rich Hill Coal Mining Co. (1893), 119 Me. 9, 24 S.W. 223; Metropolitan Tel. etc. Co. v. Domestic Tel. etc. Co. (1888), 44 N.J.Eq. 568, 14 A. 907; Butts v. Wood (1867), 37 N.Y. 317; Fields v. Victor Building etc. Co. (1918), 73 Okla. 207, 175 P. 529; Burton v. Lithic Mfg. Co. (1914), 73 Ore. 605, 144 P. 1149; San Antonio St. R. Co. v. Adams (1894), 87 Tex. 125, 26 S.W. 1040; Triplett v. Fauver (1904), 103 Va. 123, 48 S.E. 875; Bassett v. Fairchild (1901), 132 Cal. 637, 64 P. 1082; Star Mills v. Vontey (1910), 140 Ky. 194, 130 S.W. 1077; Seiler v. O'Maley (1921), 190 Ky. 190, 227 S.W. 141; *In re* Greymouth Pt. etc. R. Co. (Eng. 1904), 1 Ch. 32; Rouleau v. St. Lambert (1895), 10 Que. Super. 69; Cardin Building Co. v. Smith (1927), 125 Okla. 300, 258 P. 910.

Sec. 502, Par. 4: Cushing's Legislative Assemblies, Sec. 253; State of Indiana v. Porter (1888), 113 Ind. 79, 14 N.E. 883; Griffin v. Messenger (1901), 114 Iowa 99, 86 N.W. 219; Pinson v. Morrow (1920), 189 Ky. 291, 224 S.W. 879; Shugars v. Hamilton (1906), 122 Ky. 606, 92 S.W. 564; Somerset v. Smith (1899), 20 Ky. L. Rptr. 488, 49 S.W. 456; Attorney General v. Sheppard (1882), 62 N.H. 383, 13 Am. St. R. 576; People v. Harshaw (1886), 60 Mich. 200, 26 N.W. 879; McLean v. East St. Louis (1906), 222 Ill. 510, 78 N.E. 815; Reynolds County Tel. Co. v. Piedmont (1911), 152 Mo. App. 316, 133 S.W. 141; Cate v. Martin (1900), 70 N.H. 135, 46 A. 54.

branch of the body is necessary to call for and convene a joint session. Once the senate and the house have convened in joint session, the members then become a single body, with a majority of all members of both houses constituting the quorum, with each member entitled to an equal vote with every other member.

See also Sec. 655, Quorum of Joint Committees.

6. Committees are subject to the same rules concerning a quorum as are other bodies. A majority of a committee constitutes a quorum.

7. When an ex officio member of a body is a regular working member, that person is to be considered in determining a quorum, but when an officer is incidentally a member of a body as where the president is an ex officio member of all committees, that person is not to be so considered.

Sec. 503. Members Present Constitute the Quorum

1. A quorum is determined by the number of members present, not by the number voting. The fact of a quorum is not dependent upon the number who participate in the proceedings and vote. If the

---

Sec. 502, Par. 5: Guildersleeve v. Board of Education (N.Y. 1863), 17 Abb. Pr. 201; Commonwealth v. Hargest (1889), 7 P.A. County Ct. 333; State of Connecticut v. Chapman (1878), 44 Conn. 595; King v. Buller (1807), 8 East. 389; Rex v. Bellringer (Eng. 1792), 4 Term Rep. 810; Abood v. Gorsuch (Alaska 1985), 703 P.2d 1158; Willcock on Municipal Corporations, Secs. 52–54; Glover on Municipal Corporations, Sec. 148.

Sec. 502, Par. 6: Damon v. Grandy (1824), 19 Mass. 345; State of New Jersey v. Jersey City (1859), 27 N.J.L. 493; State of Missouri v. Reichmann (1911), 239 Mo. 81, 142 S.W. 304; Jefferson, Sec. XXVI.

Sec. 502, Par. 7: Horton v. Garrison (N.Y. 1856), 23 Barb. 176; Guildersleeve v. Board of Education (N.Y. 1863), 17 Abb. Pr. 201; Seiler v. O'Maley (1921), 190 Ky. 190, 227 S.W. 141.

number necessary to make a quorum is present, it makes no difference how many or how few actually participate in the discussion. A quorum is presumed to be present until the absence of a quorum is determined.

2. When a quorum is present the general rule is that a proposition may be carried by a majority of those voting or by any number, greater than a majority, that may be required by law.

3. Under the generally accepted rules of parliamentary procedure in the absence of a contrary provision, where a quorum is present, a proposition is carried by a majority of the legal votes cast even though some members present may not vote.

Sec. 504. Question of No Quorum

1. When a body has convened with a quorum present, it can continue to transact business as long as a quorum is present and it is presumed that the quorum continues to be present until the question of

---

Sec. 503, Par. 1: Hughes, Secs. 646, 649, 670; N.Y. Manual, p. 498; Reed, Secs. 15, 19; Tilson, pp. 17–20, 27; Launtz v. People (1885), 113 Ill. 137, 55 Am. R. 405; Rushville Gas Co. v. City of Rushville (1889), 121 Ind. 206, 23 N.E. 72; Meyers v. Philadelphia Union League (1908), 17 Pa. Dist. 301; State of Montana v. Yates (1897), 19 Mont. 239, 47 P. 1004; Attorney General v. Sheppard (1882), 62 N.H. 383, 13 Am. St. R. 576; Attorney General v. Remick (1902), 71 N.H. 480, 53 A. 308; *In re* Brearton (1904), 89 N.Y.S. 893; State of Ohio v. Green (1881), 37 Ohio St. 227; Booker v. Young (1855), 53 Va. 303; U.S. v. Ballin (1892), 144 U.S. 1, 12 S. Ct. 507, 36 L. Ed. 321; Auditor General v. Board of Supervisors (1891), 89 Mich. 552, 51 N.W. 483.

Sec. 503, Par. 2: Warnock v. Lafayette (1849), 4 La. Ann. 419; Southworth v. Palmyra etc. R. Co. (1851), 2 Mich. 287; State of Missouri v. Reichmann (1911), 239 Mo. 81, 142 S.W. 304.

Sec. 503, Par. 3: McCormick v. Board of Education of Hobbs Municipal School Dist. No. 16 (1954), 58 N.M. 648, 275 P.2d 299.

no quorum is raised or the lack of a quorum is disclosed by a vote.

2. Where a roll call shows that there was a quorum for the transaction of business but the roll call on a particular proposition discloses that less than a quorum voted, it will not be presumed that a quorum was not present at the time the vote was taken. When it appears that a quorum is present, and it does not appear from the records that a recess has taken place, it will be presumed that a quorum continued to be present.

3. Whenever it is observed that a quorum is not present, any member may call for the house to be counted and if found deficient, business will be suspended.

4. The suggestion of no quorum by a member is a question of order and is therefore in order at any time. The practice in governmental bodies is to permit a question of no quorum to interrupt a speech.

5. When a member desires to call attention to the fact that no quorum is present, that person should arise and address the presiding officer and without waiting to be recognized, say, "I suggest the absence of a quorum." The presiding officer may then count the members or may assume the responsibility of

Sec. 504, Par. 1: Hughes, Sec. 647; Reed, Secs. 15–17; Tilson, p. 28; *In re* Gunn (1893), 50 Kan. 155, 32 P. 470; Pollard v. Gregg (1914), 77 N.H. 190, 90 A. 176; Rolls v. Wyand (1914), 40 Okla. 323, 138 P. 158; Auditor General v. Board of Supervisors (1891), 89 Mich. 552, 51 N.W. 483.

Sec. 504, Par. 2: Cushing's Legislative Assemblies, Sec. 369; State of North Carolina v. Ellington (1895), 117 N.C. 158, 23 S.E. 250; Hughes, Sec. 663.

Sec. 504, Par. 3: Kimball v. Marshall (1863), 44 N.H. 465.

Sec. 504, Par. 4: Reed, Sec. 17; Hughes, Secs. 668, 669; Cushing, Sec. 19.

declaring a quorum present, or not present, without a count.

6. The question of no quorum is decided by the presiding officer as any other point of order, and is subject to appeal in the same manner.

See also Ch. 24, Secs. 240–246, Points of Order.

7. The point of order that no quorum is present may not be withdrawn after the absence of a quorum has been ascertained and announced by the presiding officer.

Sec. 505. Procedure on Absence of a Quorum

See also Ch. 19, Secs. 190–197, Call of the House, and Sec. 698, Reading of the Journal.

1. No question can be decided and no official action can be taken in the absence of a quorum, except to order a call or to adjourn. Even the reading of the journal of the previous day is not in order in the absence of a quorum.

2. When no quorum is present a call of the house can be ordered and the attendance of absent members compelled. The body can cancel all leaves of absence and require the attendance of all members.

3. In the absence of a quorum, two motions are in order: a call of the house to compel the attendance of absent members and the motion to adjourn,

Sec. 504, Par. 5: Sturgis, p. 114.
Sec. 504, Par. 6: Hughes, Secs. 648, 669.
Sec. 504, Par. 7: Hughes, Sec. 660.
Sec. 505, Par. 1: Hughes, Secs. 663, 667.
Sec. 505, Par. 2: N.Y. Manual, p. 422; Hughes, Sec. 655.

although motions incidental to a call may be received.

4. When the fact that a quorum is not present has been disclosed upon a question of no quorum, by roll call, or otherwise, the body is not thereby adjourned because less than a quorum can compel the attendance of absent members, although no business of a legislative character can be conducted. When a quorum is secured by the arrival of absent members, the body may continue in session for the transaction of business.

5. When a roll call has been interrupted by the absence of a quorum, the first business, when the quorum is secured, is to proceed with the roll call which was interrupted by the lack of a quorum.

6. When a vote discloses that there is not a quorum present, the vote is of no effect and the subject of the vote remains exactly as though no vote had been taken.

7. When an action has been completed, it is too late to raise a point of order that no quorum was present when the action was taken, but when an action requiring a quorum is taken after the absence of a quorum has been ascertained, the action is null and void.

Sec. 505, Par. 3: Cushing's Legislative Assemblies, Sec. 370; Hughes, Sec. 662; Reed, Sec. 21; N.Y. Manual, p. 422; Pollard v. Gregg (1914), 77 N.H. 190, 90 A. 176.

Sec. 505, Par. 4: Hughes, Sec. 671; Reed, Sec. 20; N.Y. Manual, p. 422.

Sec. 505, Par. 5: Hughes, Sec. 662.

Sec. 505, Par. 6: Jefferson, Sec. XLI; Cushing's Legislative Assemblies, Sec. 370; Cushing, Sec. 249; N.Y. Manual (1948–49), p. 372; Mass. Manual, p. 630.

Sec. 505, Par. 7: Hughes, Sec. 663; Sturgis, p. 115.

8. When the journal shows a quorum present, it will be presumed that a quorum continues to be present unless that presumption is contradicted by the journal itself.

9. Debate may continue in the absence of a quorum unless some member raises that point. A member speaking is entitled to insist on the presence of a quorum.

Sec. 506. Less Than Quorum Can Adjourn

See also Sec. 191, Right of Less Than a Quorum to Compel Attendance, and Sec. 208, Adjournment by Less Than a Quorum.

It is a general rule that less than a quorum may adjourn from day to day, though no other business can be transacted. The body, from the very nature of the situation, has the power to take an adjournment or a recess without the presence of a quorum.

Sec. 505, Par. 8: Auditor General v. Board of Supervisors (1891), 89 Mich. 552, 51 N.W. 483.

Sec. 505, Par. 9: Reed, Sec. 15.

Sec. 506: Cushing's Legislative Assemblies, Secs. 254, 255; Shelby v. Burns (1929), 153 Miss. 392, 121 So. 113.

CHAPTER 45

VOTE REQUIRED

Sec. 510. Majority of Legal Votes Is Required

1. A majority of the legal votes cast, a quorum being present, is sufficient to carry a proposition unless a larger vote is required by a constitution, charter, or controlling provision of law, and members present but not voting are disregarded in determining whether an action carried.

Sec. 510, Par. 1: St. Joseph Township v. Rogers (1872), 83 U.S. 644, 21 L. Ed. 328; Cass County v. Johnson (1877), 95 U.S. 360, 24 L. Ed. 416; U.S. v. Ballin (1892), 144 U.S. 1, 12 S. Ct. 507, 36 L. Ed. 321; Rhode Island v. Palmer (National Prohibition Cases 1920), 253 U.S. 350; Hartford Accident and Indemnity Co. v. City of Sulpher (1942), 123 F.2d 566, *cert. denied,* 315 U.S. 805, 62 S. Ct. 633, 86 L. Ed. 1204 (1942); Tayloe v. Davis (1924), 212 Ala. 282, 102 So. 433, 40 A.L.R. 1052; *In re* Opinion of the Justices (1934), 228 Ala. 140, 152 So. 901; Batesville v. Ball (1911), 100 Ark. 496, 40 S.W. 712; Smith v. Los Angeles Imm. Assn. (1889), 78 Cal. 289, 20 P. 677; State of Connecticut v. Chapman (1878), 44 Conn. 595; Martin v. Townsend (1893), 32 Fla. 318, 13 So. 887; Launtz v. People (1885), 113 Ill. 137, 55 Am. R. 405; Carrollton v. Clark (1886), 21 Ill. App. 74; Kirkpatrick v. Van Cleave (1909), 44 Ind. App. 629, 89 N.E. 913; Walden v. Vanosdal (1892), 131 Ind. 388, 31 N.E. 79; Thurston v. Huston (1904), 123 Iowa 157, 98 N.W. 637; Wheeler v. Commonwealth (1895), 89 Ky. 59, 32 S.W. 259; Barry v. New Haven (1915), 162 Ky. 60, 171 S.W. 1012; Warnock v. Lafayette (1849), 4 La. Ann. 419; Cram v. Bangor House Proprietary (1835), 12 Me. 354; Murdock v. Strange (1904), 99 Md. 89, 57 A. 628; Tudbury v. Stearns (Mass. 1838), 21 Pick. 148; Merrill v. City of Lowell (1920), 236 Mass. 463, 128 N.E. 862; Kay Jewelry Co. v. Board of Registration in Optometry (1940), 305 Mass. 581, 27 N.E.2d 1; Ten Eyck v. Pontiac etc. R. Co. (1889), 74 Mich. 226, 41 N.W. 905; State of Minnesota v. Chute (1885), 34 Minn. 135, 24 N.W. 353; Green v. Weller (1856), 32 Miss. 650; State of Missouri v. Reichmann (1911), 239 Mo. 81, 142 S.W. 304; State of Montana v. Yates (1897), 19 Mont. 239, 47 P. 1004; *In re* State Treasury (1897), 51 Neb. 116, 70 N.W. 531; Attorney General v. Sheppard (1882), 62 N.H. 383, 13 Am. St. R. 576; Edgerly v. Emerson (1851), 23 N.H. 555, 55 Am. Dec. 207; Attorney General v. Remick (1902), 71 N.H. 480, 53 A. 308; Attorney General v. Bickford (1914), 77 N.H. 433, 92 A. 835; Frost v. Hoar (1932), 85 N.H. 442, 160 A. 51;

2. Where a majority or other proportion of votes is required without specifying whether the vote refers to the entire membership or to the members

---

Mount v. Parker (1867), 32 N.J.L. 341; Hutchinson v. Belmar (1898), 61 N.J.L. 443, 39 A. 643; *Ex parte* Willcock (N.Y. 1827), 7 Cowp. 402, 17 Am. Dec. 525; Field v. Field (N.Y. 1832), 9 Wend. 395; Houseman v. Earle (1923), 98 N.J.L. 379, 120 A. 738; Abels v. McKeen (1867), 18 N.J.Eq. 462; Morris v. Cashmore (1938), 253 App. Div. 657, 3 N.Y.S.2d 624; Cashmore v. Morris (1938), 253 App. Div. 657, 3 N.Y.S.2d 624, *aff'd* 278 N.Y. 730, 17 N.E.2d 143; Madison Ave. Baptist Church v. Oliver St. Baptist Church (1867), 29 N.Y. Super. 649, 2 Abb. Pr. (n.s.) 254; *In re* Brearton (1904), 89 N.Y.S. 893; McFarland v. Crary (N.Y. 1830), 6 Wend. 297; State of North Carolina v. Ellington (1895), 117 N.C. 158, 23 S.E. 250; State of North Dakota v. Archibald (1895), 5 N.D. 359, 66 N.W. 234; Hill v. Ponder (1942), 221 N.C. 58, 19 S.E.2d 5; State of Ohio v. Green (1881), 37 Ohio St. 227; Carpenter v. Burden (Pa. 1843), 2 Pars. Eq. Cas. 24; Fisher v. Harrisburg Gas Co. (P.A. 1857), 1 Pears. 118; Granger v. Grubb (Pa. 1870), 7 Phil. 350; Commonwealth v. Fleming (1903), 23 Pa. S. Ct. 404; Meyers v. Philadelphia Union League (1908), 17 Pa. Dist. 301; Commonwealth v. Wickersham (1870), 66 Pa. 134; Lockwood v. Mechanics National Bank (1869), 9 R.I. 308, 11 Am. R. 253; State of South Carolina v. Delieseline (1821), 12 S.C.L. 52; Webb v. Carter (1914), 129 Tenn. 182, 165 S.W. 426; Lawrence v. Ingersoll (1839), 88 Tenn. 52, 12 S.W. 422; Commissioners Court of Limestone County v. Garrett (Tex. 1922), 236 S.W. 970; Leavitt v. Oxford etc. Silver Mfg. Co. (1883), 3 Utah 265, 1 P. 356; State of Vermont v. Bevins (1898), 70 Vt. 574, 41 A. 655; Booker v. Young (1855), 53 Va. 303; McMillen v. Neeley (1909), 66 W.Va. 496, 66 S.E. 635; State of Wisconsin v. Tyrrell (1914), 158 Wis. 425, 149 N.W. 280; Strathcona v. Edmonton Land Syndicate (1910), 3 Alta. 259; Austin Mining Co. v. Gemmel (1886), 10 Ont. 696; Gosling v. Veley (1847), 7 Q.B. 406, 115 Reprint 542; Grindley v. Barker (Eng. 1798), 1 B. & P. 229, 126 Reprint 875; Blacket v. Blizard (Eng. 1829), 9 B.C. 851, 109 Reprint 317, Aldknow v. Wainwright (Eng. 1760), 2 Burr. 1017, 97 Reprint 683; Cushing's Legislative Assemblies, Sec. 412; Dillon on Municipal Corporations, 4th Ed. Sec. 283; Steers Sand and Gravel Corp. v. Village Board of Northport (1954), 129 N.Y.S. 403; Bray v. Barry (1960), 91 R.I. 34, 160 A.2d 577; Commonwealth *ex rel.* Fox v. Chace (1961), 403 Pa. 117, 168 A.2d 569; Shaughnessy v. Metropolitan Dade County (Fla. 1970), 238 So. 2d 466; Ezell v. City of Pascagoula (Miss. 1970), 240 So. 2d 700; Wesley v. Board of Education of Nicholas County (Ky. 1966), 403 S.W.2d 28; Houser v. School Dist. of South Sioux City in Dakota County (1972), 189 Neb. 323, 202 N.W.2d 621; Adams v. Fort Madison Community School Dist. in Lee, Des Moines and Henry Counties (Iowa 1970), 182 N.W.2d 132; Town of Smithtown v. Howell (1972), 31 N.Y.2d 365, 292 N.E.2d 10, orig., 38 App. Div. 2d 857, 330 N.Y.S.2d 164, *aff'd;* Chase v. Board of Trustees of Nebraska State Colleges (1975), 194 Neb. 688, 235 N.W.2d 223; *In re* Opinion of the Justices (1953), 98 N.H. 530, 98 A.2d 635.

present, or to the members present and voting, the general rule is that the proportion refers to the number present and voting.

3. A fractional preponderance only is required to constitute a majority. Where votes are divided into fractions and a vote is four and five-sevenths to four and two-sevenths the larger vote is sufficient to carry a motion or elect an officer.

4. In the absence of an express regulation, a proposition is carried in legislative assemblies by a majority of the votes cast, and the exercise of law-making power is not stopped by mere silence and inaction of some who are present but do not vote.

5. In the conduct of the business of an assembly, the principle of majority rule is of the very essence. Parliamentary law is based firmly upon it. It is in fact the basis upon which popular self-government largely rests.

Sec. 511. More Than Majority of Legal Votes Cast May Be Required

1. Where a constitution, charter, or controlling provision of law requires a majority vote of the

---

Sec. 510, Par. 2: State of Iowa v. Dickie (1878), 47 Iowa 629; State of Missouri v. McBride (1836), 4 Mo. 303, 29 Am. Dec. 636; Whitney v. Village of Hudson (1888), 69 Mich. 189, 37 N.W. 184; Green v. Weller (1856), 32 Miss. 650; Morton v. Comptroller General (1873), 4 S.C. 430; Warnock v. Lafayette (1849), 4 La. Ann. 419; English v. State of Texas (1879), 7 Tex. App. 171; State of Wisconsin v. Tyrrell (1914), 158 Wis. 425, 149 N.W. 280; Doll v. Flintkote Co. (1956), 231 La. 241, 91 So. 2d 24, orig., 79 So. 2d 575, *aff'd* (1975).

Sec. 510, Par. 3: Reed v. Barton (1900), 176 Mass. 473, 57 N.E. 961.

Sec. 510, Par. 4: *In re* Opinion of the Justices (1953), 98 N.H. 530, 98 A.2d 635; Laconia Water Co. v. City of Laconia (1955), 99 N.H. 409, 112 A.2d 58; Waples, Sec. 134.

Sec. 510, Par. 5: Tilson's Manual, Sec. 19.

entire membership or of all members present or any other number or proportion to take a particular action, that vote must be obtained, and a vote of less than that number, although a majority of those present and voting, a quorum being present, is not sufficient.

2. The constitutions of many of the states require an affirmative vote of a majority of the members elected to each house of the legislature for the passage of bills.

Sec. 511, Par. 1: Pimental v. San Francisco (1863), 21 Cal. 351; McCracken v. San Francisco (1860), 16 Cal. 591; People *ex rel.* Funk v. Wright (1902), 30 Colo. 439, 71 P. 365; State of Connecticut v. Fagan (1875), 42 Conn. 32; Anniston v. Davis (1893), 98 Ala. 629, 13 So. 331; Evanston v. O'Leary (1897), 70 Ill. App. 124; McLean v. East St. Louis (1906), 222 Ill. 510, 78 N.E. 815; Logansport v. Legg (1863), 20 Ind. 315; Cascaden v. Waterloo (1898), 106 Iowa 673, 77 N.W. 333; Hansen v. Town of Anthon (1919), 187 Iowa 51, 173 N.W. 939; Warnock v. Lafayette (1849), 4 La. Ann. 419; Zeiler v. Central Railway Co. (1896), 84 Md. 304, 35 A. 932; Stockdale v. Wayland School Dist. (1881), 47 Mich. 226, 10 N.W. 349; Whitney v. Village of Hudson (1888), 69 Mich. 189, 37 N.W. 184; State of Missouri v. Reichmann (1911), 239 Mo. 81, 142 S.W. 304; Edgerly v. Emerson (1851), 23 N.H. 555, 55 Am. Dec. 207; Baker v. Police Com'rs. of Port Huron (1886), 62 Mich. 327, 28 N.W. 913; State of Ohio v. Wilkesville Township (1870), 20 Ohio St. 288; Leavitt v. Oxford etc. Silver Mfg. Co. (1883), 3 Utah 265, 1 P. 356; State of Vermont v. Bevins (1898), 70 Vt. 574, 41 A. 655; Grindley v. Barker (Eng. 1798), 1 B. & P. 229, 126 Reprint 875; Blacket v. Blizard (Eng. 1829), 9 B.C. 851, 109 Reprint 317.

Sec. 511, Par. 2: People v. DeWolf (1871), 62 Ill. 253; County Commissioners of Washington v. Baker (1922), 141 Md. 623, 119 A. 461; Kelley v. Secretary of State (1907), 149 Mich. 343, 112 N.W. 978; State of Minnesota v. Gould (1883), 31 Minn. 189, 17 N.W. 276; State of Missouri v. Mason (1900), 155 Mo. 486, 55 S.W. 636; Hull v. Miller (1876), 4 Neb. 503; State Constitutions: Ala. IV, 61, 63; Ariz. IV, Part 2, 15; Ark. V, 21, 22; Cal. IV, 8(b); Colo. V, 22; Del. II, 10; Fla. III, 7; Ga. III, Sec. V, 5; Hawaii III, 13; Idaho III, 15; Ill. IV, 8; Ind. IV, 25; Iowa III, 17; Kan. II, 8, 13, 15; Ky. 46; La. III, 15(g); Me. IV, Part III, 2, 16; Md. III, 27, 28; Mass. Part II, Ch. 1, 1, 2; Mich. IV, 26; Minn. IV, 22; Miss. IV, 59, 60; Mo. IV, 27; Mont. V, 11; Neb. III, 10, 13; Nev. IV, 18, 20; N.H. II, 20, 37; N.J. IV, Sec. IV, 6; N.M. IV, 15; N.Y. III, 14; N.C. II, 23; N.Dak. IV, 13; Ohio II, 15; Okla. V, 34; Ore. IV, 25; Pa. III, 4; R.I. IV, 2; S.C. III, 18; S.Dak. III, 17; Tenn. II, 18; Tex. III, 32, 39; Utah VI, 22; Vt. II, 6; Va. IV, 11; Wash. II, 22; W.Va. VI, 29; Wis. VIII, 8; Wyo. III, 25.

3. Constitutional provisions as to the number of votes required for the final passage of bills are mandatory.

Sec. 512. Two-Thirds Vote

1. When a two-thirds vote is required for any purpose by a constitution or charter or controlling provision of law, that vote must be obtained for the vote to be effective.

2. A two-thirds vote means that the affirmative vote must be equal to twice the negative vote. It is not necessary that it exceed a ratio of two to one.

3. The requirement of a two-thirds vote, unless otherwise specified, means two-thirds of the legal votes cast, not two-thirds of the members present, or

---

Sec. 511, Par. 3: Burlingham v. City of New Bern (1914), 213 F. 1014; Butler v. Board of Directors (1912), 103 Ark. 109, 146 S.W. 120; Rash v. Allen (1910), 24 Del. 444, 76 A. 370; Cohn v. Kingsley (1897), 5 Idaho 416, 49 P. 985; People v. DeWolf (1871), 62 Ill. 253; McCulloch v. State of Indiana (1858), 11 Ind. 424; County Commissioners of Washington v. Baker (1922), 141 Md. 623, 119 A. 461; State of Minnesota v. Gould (1883), 31 Minn. 189, 17 N.W. 276; State of Missouri *ex rel.* Schmoll v. Drabelle (1914), 261 Mo. 515, 170 S.W. 465; State of Nebraska v. Davis (1902), 66 Neb. 333, 92 N.W. 740; People v. Devlin (1865), 33 N.Y. 269; State of North Dakota v. Schultz (1919), 44 N.D. 269, 174 N.W. 81.

Sec. 512, Par. 1: State of Iowa v. Dickie (1878), 47 Iowa 629; State of Missouri v. McBride (1836), 4 Mo. 303, 29 Am. Dec. 636; Whitney v. Village of Hudson (1888), 69 Mich. 189, 37 N.W. 184; Green v. Weller (1856), 32 Miss. 650; Morton v. Comptroller General (1873), 4 S.C. 430; Warnock v. Lafayette (1849), 4 La. Ann. 419; English v. State of Texas (1879), 7 Tex. App. 171; State of Wisconsin v. Tyrrell (1914), 158 Wis. 425, 149 N.W. 280; Doll v. Flintkote Co. (1956), 231 La. 241, 91 So. 2d 24, orig., 79 So. 2d 575, *aff'd* (1975).

Sec. 512, Par. 2: (a) Daniels v. Bayless Stores (1935), 46 Ariz. 442, 52 P.2d 475, (b) Grindley v. Barker (Eng. 1798), 1 B. & P. 229, 126 Reprint 875; North Platte v. North Platte Water Works (1898), 56 Neb. 403, 76 N.W. 906, (c) Zeiler v. Central Railway Co. (1896), 84 Md. 304, 35 A. 932, (d) *In re* Opinion of the Justices (1934), 228 Ala. 140, 152 So. 901.

two-thirds of all the members.

4. Where a constitution, charter, or controlling provision of law requires a two-thirds vote of all members, a vote of less than that number, although two-thirds of a quorum, is not sufficient. Even though there are vacancies, a vote equal to two-thirds of the total membership is required.

5. A constitutional provision providing that a certain action requires a two-thirds vote of both houses means a two-thirds vote of each house and not merely an aggregate two-thirds of the members of both houses.

6. A deliberative body cannot by its own act or rule require a two-thirds vote to take any action where the constitution or controlling authority re-

---

Sec. 512, Par. 3: Rhode Island v. Palmer (National Prohibition Cases 1920), 253 U.S. 350; *In re* Opinion of the Justices (1934), 228 Ala. 140, 152 So. 901; Warnock v. Lafayette (1849), 4 La. Ann. 419; Zeiler v. Central Railway Co. (1896), 84 Md. 304, 35 A. 932; Kay Jewelry Co. v. Board of Registration in Optometry (1940), 305 Mass. 581, 27 N.E.2d 1; Southworth v. Palmyra etc. R. Co. (1851), 2 Mich. 287; State of Minnesota v. Gould (1883), 31 Minn. 189, 17 N.W. 276; Green v. Weller (1856), 32 Miss. 650; State of Missouri v. McBride (1836), 4 Mo. 303, 29 Am. Dec. 636; North Platte v. North Platte Water Works (1898), 56 Neb. 403, 76 N.W. 906; English v. State of Texas (1879), 7 Tex. App. 171; U.S. Constitution, Art. I, Sec. 7, Par. 2, Note 106 in House Manual (1947), and U.S. Constitution, Art. V, Sec. 1, Note 224 in House Manual (1947).

Sec. 512, Par. 4: Logansport v. Legg (1863), 20 Ind. 315; Griffin v. Messenger (1901), 114 Iowa 99, 86 N.W. 219; Buffington Wheel Co. v. Burnham (1883), 60 Iowa 493, 15 N.W. 282; Speed v. Crawford (1860), 60 Ky. 207; Blood v. Beal (1905), 100 Me. 39, 60 A. 427; Whitney v. Village of Hudson (1888), 69 Mich. 189, 37 N.W. 184; Stockdale v. Wayland School Dist. (1881), 47 Mich. 226, 10 N.W. 349; Pollasky v. Schmid (1901), 128 Mich. 699, 87 N.W. 1030; State of Minnesota *ex rel.* Kohlman v. Wagner (1915), 130 Minn. 424, 153 N.W. 749; Cleveland Cotton Mills v. Cleveland County Commissioners (1891), 108 N.C. 678, 13 S.E. 271; State of Missouri v. McBride (1836), 4 Mo. 303, 29 Am. Dec. 636.

Sec. 512, Par. 5: Morton v. Comptroller General (1873), 4 S.C. 430; Belote v. Coffman (1915), 117 Ark. 352, 175 S.W. 37.

quires only a majority vote. To require a two-thirds vote, for example, to take any action would be to give to any number of more than one-third of the members the power to defeat the action and amount to a delegation of the powers of the body to a minority.

See also Sec. 51, Delegation of Powers, and Sec. 518, A Legislative Body Cannot Delegate Its Powers.

7. When a constitutional provision requires more than a majority vote for the passage of certain types of bills, such bills can be amended by a majority vote and an amendment to such a bill by the other house, not involving any question itself requiring more than a majority vote, requires only a majority vote for concurrence; but it has been held in Congress that a two-thirds vote is necessary to agree on a conference report on a proposed amendment to the constitution.

8. An action requiring a two-thirds vote for passage can be repealed by a majority vote and the general rule is that an act requiring a two-thirds vote for passage can be reconsidered or rescinded by a majority vote.

See also Sec. 473, Vote Required for Reconsideration.

9. There is no rule of parliamentary law enforced by the courts or generally accepted in practice by which a two-thirds vote is required in legislative bodies for procedural questions such as: to limit

---

Sec. 512, Par. 6: Tayloe v. Davis (1924), 212 Ala. 282, 102 So. 433, 40 A.L.R. 1052; Outwater v. Borough of Carlstadt (1901), 66 N.J.L. 510, 49 A. 533.

Sec. 512, Par. 7: Wagstaff v. Central Highway Commission (1917), 174 N.C. 377, 93 S.E. 908; State of Oregon v. Boyer (1917), 84 Ore. 513, 165 P. 587; U.S. Constitution, Art. V, Note 224 in House Manual.

Sec. 512, Par. 8: Chariton v. Holiday (1883), 60 Iowa 391, 14 N.W. 775; Crawford v. Gilchrist (1912), 64 Fla. 41, 59 So. 963.

debate, to make special orders, to take up a question out of order, or even to suspend their rules. It is not unusual for such bodies, to provide by their rules for a two-thirds vote or other vote of more than a majority or to require notice. Such rules are not imposed upon them by parliamentary law.

10. Since it is a fundamental principle of parliamentary law that the deliberate will and judgment of the majority shall prevail in the decision of such questions as can properly come before the legislative body, the requirement of a two-thirds vote is exceptional. Such a vote is not required except in the particular cases in which it is prescribed by a controlling authority.

Sec. 513. Tie Votes and Casting Votes

1. When the vote for and the vote against any proposition are equal, there is a tie vote. A tie vote decides nothing but leaves the situation unchanged. The voice of the majority decides, for the lex majoris partis is the law of all legislative bodies and elections where not otherwise expressly provided. But if the body be equally divided, semper presumitur pro negante, the former law is not changed because no affirmative action can be taken except by a majority. A decision of the presiding officer is not overruled on appeal by a tie vote.

2. In some instances provisions are made to "break" a tie. This is accomplished by giving the presiding officer a vote in case of a tie. This vote is

Sec. 512, Par. 9: Cushing's Legislative Assemblies, Secs. 115, 116, 119, 412; Waples, Sec. 134; N.Y. Manual (1948–49), p. 465.

Sec. 513, Par. 1: Jefferson, Sec. XLI; Cushing's Legislative Assemblies, Sec. 412; Sturgis, p. 136.

called a "casting" vote. Such a vote can be cast only when it will decide the tie.

3. The casting vote is usually given to a presiding officer, when the presiding officer is not a regular member of the body and does not otherwise have a vote. On rare occasions, the casting vote has been given to a presiding officer who is a regular member who may first vote as a member and then may vote again to break a tie.

4. When not a member of the organization, the presiding officer can cast a vote only when expressly authorized to do so.

5. By the common law a casting vote sometimes signifies a single vote of the person who never votes except in the case of an equality and sometimes a

---

Sec. 513, Par. 2: Hansen v. Town of Anthon (1919), 187 Iowa 51, 173 N.W. 939; Merriam v. Chicago R. Co. (1908), 130 Mo. App. 247, 111 S.W. 876; City of Croswell v. Helm (1938), 284 Mich. 404, 279 N.W. 879; State of Mississippi v. Cresswell (1918), 117 Miss. 795, 78 So. 770; State of Montana *ex rel.* Easbey v. Highway Patrol Board (1960), 140 Mont. 383, 372 P.2d 930; Opinion of the Justices (1966), 225 A.2d 481; Advisory Opinion on Constitutionality of 1978 P.A. 426 (1978), 403 Mich. 631, 272 N.W.2d 495; Center Bank v. Department of Banking and Finance of State of Nebraska (1981), 210 Neb. 227, 331 N.W.2d 661.

Sec. 513, Par. 3: State of Connecticut v. Chapman (1878), 44 Conn. 595; Launtz v. People (1885), 113 Ill. 137, 55 Am. R. 405; Carroll v. Wall (1868), 35 Kan. 36, 10 P. 1; Small v. Orne (1887), 79 Me. 78, 8 A. 152; People v. Church of the Atonement (N.Y. 1866), 48 Barb. 603; Reeder v. Trotter (1919), 142 Tenn. 37, 215 S.W. 400; State of Montana *ex rel.* Easbey v. Highway Patrol Board (1960), 140 Mont. 383, 372 P.2d 930; Opinion of the Justices (1966), 225 A.2d 481; Advisory Opinion on Constitutionality of 1978 P.A. 426 (1978), 403 Mich. 631, 272 N.W.2d 495; Center Bank v. Department of Banking and Finance of State of Nebraska (1981), 210 Neb. 227, 331 N.W.2d 661.

Sec. 513, Par. 4: Reeder v. Trotter (1919), 142 Tenn. 37, 215 S.W. 400; Carrollton v. Clark (1886), 21 Ill. App. 74; People *ex rel.* Funk v. Wright (1902), 30 Colo. 439, 71 P. 365; State of Montana *ex rel.* Easbey v. Highway Patrol Board (1960), 140 Mont. 383, 372 P.2d 930; Opinion of the Justices (1966), 225 A.2d 481; Advisory Opinion on Constitutionality of 1978 P.A. 426 (1978), 403 Mich. 631, 272 N.W.2d 495; Center Bank v. Department of Banking and Finance of State of Nebraska (1981), 210 Neb. 227, 331 N.W.2d 661.

double vote of a person who votes first with the rest and then upon an equality creates a majority by casting a second vote. A presiding officer who is a member of the body and has already voted as such has no power to cast a second vote to break a tie unless such right is given by rule or statute expressly so providing.

Sec. 514. When a Casting Vote Is in Order

1. A casting vote is in order only when there is a tie vote as when the votes are equally divided between two candidates or when there is an equal number for and against a proposition.

2. A casting vote is not in order in an election to give one candidate a majority where the other votes are scattered among other candidates. A casting vote would be in order where the vote was four to four but not where the vote was three for one candidate, two for another and one for a third. A casting vote is not in order to give one candidate a plurality where two or more have an equal number of votes.

Sec. 513, Par. 5: O'Neil v. O'Connell (1945), 300 Ky. 707, 189 S.W.2d 965; People v. Church of the Atonement (N.Y. 1866), 48 Barb. 603; Reeder v. Trotter (1919), 142 Tenn. 37, 215 S.W. 400.

Sec. 514, Par. 1: Wooster v. Mullins (1894), 164 Conn. 340, 30 A. 144, 25 L.R.A. 694; Gostin v. Brooks (1892), 89 Ga. 244, 15 S.E. 361; Carrollton v. Clark (1886), 21 Ill. App. 74; Beaver Creek v. Hastings (1884), 52 Mich. 528, 18 N.W. 250; Kelley v. Secretary of State (1907), 149 Mich. 343, 112 N.W. 978; State of Minnesota v. Guiney (1879), 26 Minn. 313, 3 N.W. 977; Rich v. McLauren (1903), 83 Miss. 95, 35 So. 337; State of Montana v. Yates (1897), 19 Mont. 239, 47 P. 1004; Grant City to use of O'Neil v. Salmon (1926), 221 Mo. App. 853, 288 S.W. 88; McClain v. Church (1930), 76 Utah 170, 289 P. 88; State of Wisconsin v. Mott (1901), 111 Wis. 19, 86 N.W. 569.

Sec. 514, Par. 2: State of Montana v. Yates (1897), 19 Mont. 239, 47 P. 1004; State of Wisconsin v. Mott (1901), 111 Wis. 19, 86 N.W. 569;

3. When the presiding officer is a member of a body and entitled to vote with the other members, the fact that the member was chosen to act as the presiding officer will not deprive the presiding officer of the privilege of voting as a member, but also gives that member a second vote as presiding officer in case of a tie.

4. When voting in case of a tie, the presiding officer may explain reasons for a specific vote and have them entered in the journal the same as a regular voting member.

5. When giving a casting vote, the presiding officer should definitely cast a vote. The mere announcing of the vote, adding the presiding officer's own vote, has been held sufficient in some cases but disputed in others.

6. When voting on an appeal, although the question is "Shall the decision of the president (or speaker or chair) stand as judgment of the senate (or house, or committee)," the presiding officer, when a member, may vote, and a tie vote, even though the presiding officer's vote made it a tie, sustains the presiding officer upon the principle that the decision

---

McCourt v. Beam (1902), 42 Ore. 41, 69 P. 990; City of Croswell v. Helm (1938), 284 Mich. 404, 279 N.W. 879.

Sec. 514, Par. 3: Reeder v. Trotter (1919), 142 Tenn. 37, 215 S.W. 400.

Sec. 514, Par. 4: Cushing's Legislative Assemblies, Sec. 311; N.Y. Manual (1948–49), p. 443.

Sec. 514, Par. 5: Cases not requiring separate castings of vote are: Launtz v. People (1885), 113 Ill. 137, 55 Am. R. 405; Rushville Gas Co. v. City of Rushville (1889), 121 Ind. 206, 23 N.E. 72; Small v. Orne (1887), 79 Me. 78, 8 A. 152; State of Minnesota v. Armstrong (1893), 54 Minn. 457, 56 N.W. 97; People v. Rector (N.Y. 1866), 48 Barb. 603. Cases requiring separate castings of vote are: Hornung v. State of Indiana (1888), 116 Ind. 458, 19 N.E. 151; Lawrence v. Ingersoll (1839), 88 Tenn. 52, 12 S.W. 422; Casler v. Tanzer (1929), 234 N.Y.S. 571.

of the presiding officer can be reversed only by a majority.

Sec. 515. Presumptions as to Effect of Members Not Voting

There has been considerable discussion by the courts as to presumptions concerning the effect of members not voting. There appear to be two distinct situations:

(a) When only a majority of the legal votes cast is required, failure to vote or the casting of a blank ballot reduces the number of affirmative votes necessary to take an action. Under this situation failure to vote reduces the vote required to take the action and so has in part the same effect as a "yes" vote. The members not voting are sometimes said to be presumed to agree to abide by the decision of those voting.

(b) When a set number of votes or a majority or other proportion of the entire membership or of the members present is required, failure to vote does not reduce the vote required but reduces the pool of voters available to take the action and, therefore, has in part the same effect as a "no" vote. It would not seem to be correct to say that members not voting are presumed to be voting in the negative though in this situation that is the effect of the failure to vote.

Sec. 515: Mount v. Parker (1867), 32 N.J.L. 341; State of Ohio v. Green (1881), 37 Ohio St. 227; State of Minnesota v. Chute (1885), 34 Minn. 135, 24 N.W. 353; Wheeler v. Commonwealth (1895), 89 Ky. 59, 32 S.W. 259; Murdock v. Strange (1904), 99 Md. 89, 57 A. 628; Meyers v. Philadelphia Union League (1908), 17 Pa. Dist. 301; Caffey v. Veale (1944), 193 Okla. 444, 145 P.2d 961; State of Oklahoma *ex rel.* Hayman v. State Election Board (1938), 181 Okla. 622, 75 P.2d 861; Russell v. Murphy (1936), 177 Okla. 255, 58 P.2d 560; Redmond v. Town of

Sec. 516. Illegal Votes

1. When persons not entitled to vote have voted, or there are more ballots than persons entitled to vote, or it appears that there have been illegal votes cast, the vote should be declared void and a new vote taken.

2. When illegal votes have been cast but those votes could not have changed the result of the vote, as when two illegal votes were cast but the winning candidate won by eleven votes, an election or other vote is not invalidated by the illegal votes. When illegal votes may have changed the result of the vote, the vote is void.

3. When a majority or other proportion of the votes cast is required to take any action, the illegal votes and blank ballots are not considered in the computation. Thus when forty-eight votes were cast including three blank ballots and two ballots were illegal only forty-three legal ballots were cast and twenty-two votes were a majority and would elect a candidate or carry a motion.

Sec. 517. Action Must Be Within Power or Vote Is Ineffective

1. No motion or measure is in order that conflicts with the constitution of a state or the Constitu-

---

Sulpher (1912), 32 Okla. 201, 120 P. 262; Hartford Accident and Indemnity Co. v. City of Sulpher (1942), 123 F.2d 566, *cert. denied,* 315 U.S. 805, 62 S. Ct. 633, 86 L. Ed. 1204 (1942).

Sec. 516, Par. 1: Labourdette v. New Orleans (1847), 2 La. Ann. 527; Baker v. Cushman (1879), 127 Mass. 105; State of Connecticut v. Starr (1906), 78 Conn. 636, 63 A. 512; State of Nebraska v. Hutchens (1891), 33 Neb. 335, 15 N.W. 165.

Sec. 516, Par. 2: Commonwealth v. Green (Pa. 1839), 4 Whart. 531; Sudbury v. Stearns (Mass. 1838), 21 Pick. 148.

Sec. 516, Par. 3: Murdock v. Strange (1904), 99 Md. 89, 57 A. 628.

tion of the United States or with treaties of the United States, and if such a motion or measure be adopted, even by a unanimous vote, it is null and void.

2. No rule that conflicts with a rule of a higher order is of any authority. Thus, a legislative rule providing for the suspension, by general consent, of an article of the Constitution would be null and void.

3. Legislative acts which are irregular or void may be ratified and confirmed subsequently, provided the body had the authority originally to take the action ratified, and the procedure and vote on ratification met all requirements.

Sec. 518. A Legislative Body Cannot Delegate Its Powers

See also Sec. 51, Delegation of Powers, and Sec. 512, paragraph 6.

1. The power of any legislative body to enact legislation or to do any act requiring the use of discretion cannot be delegated to a minority, to a committee, to officers or members or to another body.

Sec. 517, Par. 1: Jefferson, Sec. XLI; Cushing's Legislative Assemblies, Sec. 370; Cushing, Sec. 249.

Sec. 517, Par. 3: Marion W. Co. v. Marion (1903), 121 Iowa 306, 96 N.W. 883; Hansen v. Town of Anthon (1919), 187 Iowa 51, 173 N.W. 939; Orange v. Clement (1919), 41 Cal. App. 497, 183 P. 189; State of Minnesota v. Hennepin Co. (1885), 33 Minn. 235, 22 N.W. 625; Jordan v. School Dist. (1854), 38 Me. 164; Curtin v. Gowan (1890), 34 Ill. App. 516; Wheat v. VanTine (1907), 149 Mich. 314, 112 N.W. 933; Brown v. Winterport (1887), 79 Me. 305, 9 A. 844.

Sec. 518, Par. 1: Ralls v. Wyand (1914), 40 Okla. 323, 138 P. 158; Attorney General v. Brissenden (1930), 271 Mass. 172, 171 N.E. 82; Coffin v. Nantucket (1850), 59 Mass. 269; Board of Excise v. Sackrider (1866), 35 N.Y. 154; State of Wisconsin v. Milwaukee (1914), 157 Wis. 505, 147 N.W. 50; Danforth v. Merrill (1975), 530 S.W.2d 290; State of Kansas *ex rel.* Schneider v. Bennett (1976), 547 P.2d 786; New York

2. A legislative body may assign ministerial or administrative duties to one of its committees to act in behalf of the body itself.

3. A legislative investigating committee may not delegate its powers of investigation to one of its members without authority granted in the resolution appointing the committee.

Public Interest Research Group, Inc. v. Carey (1976), 383 N.Y.S.2d 197, 86 Misc. 2d 329, *aff'd* 55 App. Div. 274, 390 N.Y.S.2d 236 (1976), *appeal dismissed,* 41 N.Y.2d 1072, 396 N.Y.S.2d 185, 364 N.E.2d 849 (1977).

Sec. 518, Par. 2: Gillett v. Logan County (1873), 67 Ill. 256; Dancer v. Town of Mannington (1901), 50 W.Va. 322, 40 S.E. 475.

Sec. 518, Par. 3: *In re* Leach (1922), 232 N.Y. 600, 19 N.Y.S. 135, 134 N.E. 588.

CHAPTER 46

RULES GOVERNING VOTING

Sec. 520. A Vote Is Required to Decide a Question

1. The decision of a deliberative body can be made only by the taking of a vote at a meeting. The fact that members have individually expressed opinions on a question is not a decision of the body and is of no effect.

2. The act of voting is a positive act whereby the person makes known an affirmative or negative position, and no presumption should be indulged that a voter who does not vote "yea" or "nay" is thereby to be counted.

Sec. 521. Members Must Vote Unless Excused

1. It is a general rule that a legislative body cannot only compel the attendance of its members but that it can also require them to vote unless excused by the body from voting.

Sec. 520, Par. 1: Landers v. Frank St. Methodist Episcopal Church (1889), 114 N.Y. 626, 21 N.E. 420; Mobile v. Kiernan (1910), 170 Ala. 449, 54 So. 102; Pierce v. New Orleans Building Co. (1836), 9 La. 397, 29 Am. Dec. 448; Whitney v. City of New Haven (1890), 58 Conn. 450, 20 A. 666.

Sec. 520, Par. 2: Caffey v. Veale (1944), 193 Okla. 444, 145 P.2d 961; Heimbach v. State of New York (1982), 89 App. Div. 2d 138, 454 N.Y.S.2d 993, *aff'd* 59 N.Y.2d 891, 452 N.E.2d 1264, 465 N.Y.S.2d 936, *appeal dismissed*, 464 U.S. 956, 104 S. Ct. 386, 78 L. Ed. 2d 331.

Sec. 521, Par. 1: Cushing's Legislative Assemblies, Sec. 1795; Cushing, Sec. 244; N.Y. Manual (1948–49), p. 371; Heimbach v. State of New York (1982), 89 App. Div. 2d 138, 454 N.Y.S.2d 993, *aff'd* 59 N.Y.2d 891,

2. Each house under its power to make rules for its own government has power to excuse members from voting.

3. It is the practice in the state legislatures to excuse a member from voting when that member has a personal interest in the matter voted upon or for other good cause. Ordinarily no question is raised when a member fails to vote, but, especially when a particular number of votes are required, or a certain proportion of the votes of members elected are required, one member may raise the question and insist that another member vote or state the reason for not voting and be excused.

Sec. 522. Members May Not Vote on Questions in Which They Have a Personal Interest

1. It is the general rule that no members can vote on a question in which they have a direct personal or pecuniary interest. The right of members to represent their constituencies, however, is of such major importance that members should be barred from voting on matters of direct personal interest only in clear cases and when the matter is particularly personal. This rule is obviously not self-enforcing and unless the vote is challenged members may vote as they choose. A member may vote regarding a matter when other members are included with that member in the motion, even though that

452 N.E.2d 1264, 465 N.Y.S.2d 936, *appeal dismissed,* 464 U.S. 956, 104 S. Ct. 386, 78 L. Ed. 2d 331.

Sec. 521, Par. 2: Wise v. Bigger (1884), 79 Va. 269; Heimbach v. State of New York (1982), 89 App. Div. 2d 138, 454 N.Y.S.2d 993, *aff'd* 59 N.Y.2d 891, 452 N.E.2d 1264, 465 N.Y.S.2d 936, *appeal dismissed,* 464 U.S. 956, 104 S. Ct. 386, 78 L. Ed. 2d 331.

person has a personal or pecuniary interest in the result, as where charges are preferred against a group, or the member may vote to increase salaries of all of the members.

2. One may not vote for oneself for a remunerative office such as a city marshal or a superintendent of schools, and if the member's own vote is necessary to the election, the election is void.

3. Members may not vote to give money or any direct financial benefit to themselves. They may not vote to award a contract to themselves, or renew a note in their favor or vote a salary to themselves as officers.

4. When the personal interest of a member in a question has been called to the attention of the body, even after the vote was taken, the vote has been disallowed.

5. In Congress the rules provide that no member has a right to vote on any matter in which the member is immediately or particularly interested, but the uniform present practice is to permit all

---

Sec. 522, Par. 1: Hughes, Sec. 569; Cushing, Sec. 41; Cushing's Legislative Assemblies, Sec. 1789; McQuillin on Municipal Corporations, Sec. 629; Mass. Manual, p. 652; Buffington Wheel Co. v. Burnham (1883), 60 Iowa 493, 15 N.W. 282; Coles v. Williamsburgh (N.Y. 1833), 10 Wend. 659; State of Oregon v. Hoyt (1867), 2 Ore. 246; Board of Supervisors of Oconto County v. Hall (1879), 47 Wis. 208, 2 N.W. 291; People v. Kingston (1886), 101 N.Y. 82, 4 N.E. 348; Lonbat v. LeRoy (N.Y. 1884), 15 Alb. 1.

Sec. 522, Par. 2: State of Oregon v. Hoyt (1867), 2 Ore. 246; Harmony v. State of Indiana (1888), 116 Ind. 458, 19 N.E. 151; Sturgis, p. 58.

Sec. 522, Par. 3: Smith v. Los Angeles Imm. Assn. (1889), 78 Cal. 289, 20 P. 677; Taylor County Court v. City of Grafton (1915), 77 W.Va. 84, 86 S.E. 924; Sturgis, p. 58; Mass. Manual, p. 609.

Sec. 522, Par. 4: Jefferson, Sec. XVII; Cushing's Legislative Assemblies, Sec. 1790.

members to be the judge of their own personal interest.

Sec. 523. Putting the Question to Vote

See also Ch. 14, Secs. 130–133, Closing Debate.

1. When a question is undebatable, or debate has been ordered closed, the presiding officer puts it to vote immediately after stating the question, only allowing time for members to rise if they wish to make motions of a higher rank.

2. The question is to be put first on the affirmative, and then on the negative side. After the presiding officer has put the affirmative part of the question, any member who has not spoken before to the question may rise and speak before the negative be put, because it is not a full vote until the negative part is also put. After the first member has voted on roll call, however, it is too late to resume the debate.

3. If the debate is resumed, both the affirmative and negative of the question must be put again.

4. When a vote is taken a second time, as when a division is called for, debate cannot be resumed except by unanimous consent.

5. In routine matters, such as receiving petitions, reports, withdrawing motions, reading papers, etc., the presiding officer usually assumes the consent of the body where no objection is expressed.

Sec. 522, Par. 5: U.S. House Rule VIII, Notes 658, 659.

Sec. 523, Par. 1: Sturgis, p. 127.

Sec. 523, Par. 2: Jefferson, Sec. XXXIX; Cushing's Legislative Assemblies, Secs. 1610, 1615.

Sec. 523, Par. 3: Sturgis, p. 127.

Sec. 523, Par. 4: Sturgis, p. 127.

Sec. 523, Par. 5: Jefferson, Sec. XXXIX; Sturgis, p. 143.

Sec. 524. Points of Order During Voting

See also Ch. 24, Secs. 240–246, Points of Order.

When a point of order is raised during voting which would affect the vote, the presiding officer should decide the point immediately. The presiding officer's decision is subject to appeal. If the vote is being taken by division and it would be impossible to debate the appeal because of the division, the presiding officer is not required to recognize the appeal. However, the presiding officer is subject to the censure of the body if the decision should be irregular.

Sec. 525. Announcing the Vote

1. In announcing the vote, the presiding officer should first state the vote and then announce the result and finally announce the next business.

2. In announcing a vote taken viva voce or by rising without a count, the presiding officer may announce the result as: "The yeas have it," or if the vote has been by count or on roll call, the presiding officer should announce the vote as "yeas forty—nays none."

3. Immediately following the announcement of the vote, the presiding officer should state the result as: "The resolution is adopted," "The motion is carried," "The amendments are adopted," "The appointments are confirmed," "The bill is passed" or "Mr. or Madam ________ is elected."

4. One of the principal duties of the presiding officer is to keep the body advised of the business

---

Sec. 524: 3 Hatsell 143; Jefferson, Sec. XLI; Reed, Sec. 235; Cushing, Sec. 248.

before it. The instant the business before the body is disposed of, the presiding officer should announce the next business. The announcement following a vote might be, for example, "yeas thirty—nays five, Senate (or House) Bill No. 65 is passed. The next bill on the calendar is Senate (or House) Bill No. 67, by Senator (Representative or Mr. or Madam) ________."

5. It is the duty of the presiding officer to announce the vote according to the fact. An incorrect announcement cannot nullify the effect of a vote nor can an officer be declared elected when that officer fails to receive the vote required by law.

6. Since the declaration of the presiding officer respecting a vote does not involve the exercise of judgment and discretion, it is not judicial in character and, therefore, is subject to collateral attack.

Sec. 526. Recording the Vote

See also Sec. 694, Constitutional Requirements Concerning Journal; Sec. 695, Journal Record of Proceedings; Sec. 696, What May Be Recorded in the Journal; and Sec. 697, Journal as Showing Passage and Legality of Bills.

A constitutional provision or controlling provision of law concerning the manner of recording the vote must be complied with when constitutions require the vote of each member on the passage of bills to be recorded. The bill will not be held to be duly passed unless the vote is recorded as required.

Sec. 525, Par. 5: Chariton v. Holiday (1883), 60 Iowa 391, 14 N.W. 775; Dingwell v. Detroit (1890), 82 Mich. 568, 46 N.W. 938.

Sec. 525, Par. 6: State of Connecticut v. Fagan (1875), 42 Conn. 32.

Sec. 526: State of Alabama v. Martin (1909), 160 Ala. 181, 48 So. 846; Smithee v. Garth (1878), 33 Ark. 17; Neiberger v. McCullough (1912), 253 Ill. 312, 97 N.E. 660; State of Missouri v. Mason (1900),

Sec. 527. Correcting the Vote

See also Sec. 535, paragraph 7, verifying vote by roll call.

If a mistake has been made or fraud has occurred in taking or announcing a vote and the vote is immediately questioned, it may be treated as irregular and void and the vote may be retaken or it may be corrected. A vote may not be retaken if there has been delay or other business has intervened. A legislative body always has authority to correct its records to make them state the truth.

Sec. 528. Explanation of Vote

1. In some bodies, with the consent of the body, members may make an explanation of their vote on any question and have their explanation printed in the journal.

2. In some bodies, when the presiding officer votes in case of a tie, the presiding officer has the same rights as members have to explain votes and have explanations printed in the journal.

---

155 Mo. 486, 55 S.W. 636; McClellan v. Stein (1924), 229 Mich. 203, 20 N.W. 209.

Sec. 527: Jefferson, Sec. XLI; Pevey v. Aylward (1910), 205 Mass. 102, 91 N.E. 315; Baker v. Cushman (1879), 127 Mass. 105; State of Connecticut v. Starr (1906), 78 Conn. 636, 63 A. 512.

Sec. 528, Par. 1: Cushing, Sec. 32.

Sec. 528, Par. 2: Cushing's Legislative Assemblies, Sec. 311; N.Y. Manual, p. 464.

CHAPTER 47

MANNER OF VOTING

Sec. 530. Manner in Which Votes May Be Taken

1. When the method of voting is not prescribed by controlling authority or in the rules, a vote may be taken in any of the modes by which questions are determined under the general rules of parliamentary law.

2. When a vote is required by a constitution, charter or controlling statute to be taken in a particular manner, it must be taken in that manner.

3. Except as constitutional provisions may control, votes may be taken viva voce, by show of hands or by a rising vote, upon roll call, or by ballot, and when no provision is made in the constitution, charter or controlling provision of law, the rules of each house will govern.

4. The state constitutions in most cases require the "yeas" and "nays" to be taken on the passage of bills. The "yeas" and "nays" are usually taken by roll call, but in many states mechanical voting methods have been installed. Voting by "yeas" and

---

Sec. 530, Par. 1: Richardson v. Union Congregational Soc. of Francestown (1877), 58 N.H. 187.

Sec. 530, Par. 2: Hopkins v. Mayor of Swansea (Eng. 1839), 4 N. & W. 621; Presbyterian Church v. New York City (1826), 5 Cow. 538; Hicks v. Long Branch Commission (1903), 69 N.J.L. 300, 54 A. 568; O'Neil v. Tyler (1892), 3 N.D. 47, 53 N.W. 434.

Sec. 530, Par. 3: Cushing's Legislative Assemblies, Sec. 1792; Reed, Sec. 229; Lincoln v. Haugen (1891), 45 Minn. 451, 48 N.W. 186; State of Connecticut v. Barbour (1885), 53 Conn. 76, 55 Am. R. 65.

"nays" is sometimes required in elections by the legislature and in certain other cases.

5. The state constitutions also may provide that a specified number or proportion of the legislature less than a majority can require the vote on any question to be taken by roll call and recorded in the journal.

6. A separate vote is usually required on each separate action taken by a legislative body, but the courts have held that the method of voting is an "internal" affair of the legislative body as long as there is no conflict with the constitution.

7. Where the constitution provides that on the final passage of a bill the vote shall be by "yeas" and

---

Sec. 530, Par. 4: State Constitutions: Ala. IV, 61, 63; Alaska II, 14; Ariz. IV, Part II, 12; Ark. V, 21, 22; Cal. IV, 7(b); Colo. V, 22; Del. II, 10; Fla. III, 7; Ga. III, Sec. V, 6; Hawaii III, 13; Idaho III, 15; Ill. IV, 8; Ind. IV, 1, 18; Iowa III, 17; Kan. II, 10, 13, 15; Ky. 46; La. III, 15(g); Me. IV, Part III, 2 and V, Part I, 8; Md. III, 27, 28; Mass. Part II, Ch. I, Sec. I, 2; Mich. IV, 26; Minn. IV, 16; Miss. IV, 59, 60; Mo. IV, 27; Mont. V, 11; Neb. III, 11, 13; Nev. IV, 18, 23; N.J. IV, Sec. IV, 6; N.M. IV, 17; N.Y. III, 14; N.C. II, 23; N.Dak. IV, 13; Ohio II, 9; Okla. V, 34; Ore. IV, 19; Pa. III, 4, 5; R.I. IV, 2; S.C. III, 18; S.Dak. III, 18; Tenn. II, 18; Tex. III, 32, 39; Utah VI, 22; Vt. II, 11; Va. IV, 11; Wash. II, 21, 22, 27; W.Va. VI, 29; Wis. IV, 30 and VIII, 8; Wyo. III, 25.

Sec. 530, Par. 5: Reed, Sec. 232; Cushing's Legislative Assemblies, Sec. 405; State Constitutions: Ala. IV, 55; Alaska II, 14; Ariz. IV, II, 10; Ark. V, 12; Cal. IV, 7(b); Colo. V, 13; Conn. III, 14; Del. II, 10; Fla. III, 4; Ga. III, Sec. V, 6; Hawaii III, 12; Idaho III, 13; Ill. IV, 8; Ind. IV, 12; Iowa III, 10; Kan. II, 10; Ky. 40; La. III, 15(g); Me. IV, Part III, 5; Md. III, 22; Mich. IV, 18; Minn. IV, 15; Miss. IV, 55; Mo. IV, 26; Mont. V, 12; Neb. III, 11; Nev. IV, 14; N.H. II, 24; N.J. IV, Sec. IV, 4; N.M. IV, 12; N.C. II, 19; N.Dak. IV, 13; Ohio II, 9; Okla. V, 30; Ore. IV, 13; Pa. II, 12; R.I. IV, 8; S.C. III, 22; S.Dak. III, 13; Tenn. II, 21; Tex. III, 12; Utah VI, 14; Vt. II, 9; Va. IV, 8; Wash. II, 21; W.Va. VI, 41; Wis. IV, 20; Wyo. III, 13.

C *Sec. 530, Par. 6:* Parker v. Catholic Bishop (1893), 146 Ill. 158, 34 N.E. 473; Markham v. City of Anamosa (1904), 122 Iowa 689, 98 N.W. 493; Campbell v. Cincinnati (1892), 49 Ohio St. 463, 31 N.E. 606; Ohrenstein v. Thompson (N.Y. 1983), 82 App. Div. 2d 670, 444 N.Y.S.2d 196, *appeal dismissed,* 56 N.Y.2d 537, 434 N.E.2d 1344, 449 N.Y.S.2d 966 and 56 N.Y.2d 644, 436 N.E.2d 197, 450 N.Y.S.2d 1027.

"nays," this provision is imperative and must be strictly followed.

Sec. 531. Determining Manner of Voting

See also Ch. 31, Secs. 306–308, Voting, Nominations and Elections.

1. Where not required by the constitution or the rules, a majority vote is required to order the vote to be counted, except for verification, or to be taken by roll call or by ballot, as the usual method of voting is viva voce.

2. A motion to determine the manner of taking a vote on a question that is pending ranks as an incidental question and yields only to privileged questions and other incidental questions, except motions relating to nominations or elections. Such motions may be amended but are not debatable and cannot have any subsidiary motions applied to them.

3. When different methods of voting are suggested, they should be treated as alternative propositions, the vote being taken first on the method taking the most time. In practice, the method of taking a vote is generally agreed upon without the formality of a vote.

Sec. 530, Par. 7: Burlingham v. City of New Bern (1914), 213 F. 1014; State of Alabama v. Martin (1909), 160 Ala. 181, 48 So. 846; Mech. Bldg. and Loan Assn. v. Coffman (1913), 110 Ark. 269, 162 S.W. 1090; Rash v. Allen (1910), 24 Del. 444, 76 A. 370; State of Florida v. Dillon (1900), 42 Fla. 95, 28 So. 781; Cohn v. Kingsley (1897), 5 Idaho 416, 49 P. 985; People *ex rel.* City of Springfield v. Edmands (1911), 252 Ill. 108, 96 N.E. 914; County Commissioners of Washington v. Baker (1922), 141 Md. 623, 119 A. 461; Lincoln v. Haugen (1891), 45 Minn. 451, 48 N.W. 186; State of Missouri *ex rel.* Schmoll v. Drabelle (1914), 261 Mo. 515, 170 S.W. 465; Hull v. Miller (1876), 4 Neb. 503; Debman v. Chitty (1902), 131 N.C. 657, 43 S.E. 3; State of North Dakota v. Schultz (1919), 44 N.D. 269, 174 N.W. 81.

Sec. 531, Par. 1: Cushing's Legislative Assemblies, Sec. 1792; Sturgis, p. 140; Tilson, p. 163.

4. When more than a majority vote or a majority vote of the entire membership is required, it is necessary to vote by roll call or division to ascertain that the proper number of votes has been obtained, unless such action is taken by unanimous consent.

Sec. 532. Voice Vote or Viva Voce Vote

1. The usual manner of voting, except when the constitution or rules may require a roll call, as upon the passage of a bill, is for the presiding officer to call for the "yeas" and "nays" on a question and judge the vote by the sound. This is usually known as a viva voce vote. It is the quickest and simplest manner of voting, but has the defect that if the vote is close, it is difficult to determine the prevailing side. It usually serves, however, because on most questions there is a decided majority.

2. A question is put to viva voce vote by the presiding officer after stating the question, saying, "As many as may be in favor of the motion (or other matter before the house)," or "as many as are of opinion that (stating the proposition) say 'yea,'" and then immediately stating the negative by saying, "As many as are opposed say 'nay.'" The question is often stated more briefly as "all in favor say 'yea'" and "contrary 'nay'" or "opposed 'nay.'"

3. If certain of the vote, the presiding officer may immediately announce the result, but if not certain, the presiding officer may say, "The yeas seem to have it," or "The nays seem to have it," in order to give any member an opportunity to request a verifi-

Sec. 532, Par. 2: Cushing, Sec. 238; Reed, Sec. 230; Cushing's Legislative Assemblies, Secs. 385, 403, 407; Tilson, p. 34; Sturgis, p. 141.

cation. If no member immediately requests a division or otherwise requests a further verification, the presiding officer may announce the result.

4. The presiding officer may call for the "yeas" and "nays" a second or even third time when unable to determine which side has the majority upon the taking of a viva voce vote. If considered necessary to further verify the vote, the presiding officer may count hands, have the members rise and be counted, have the vote taken by tellers or have the roll called, depending upon the judgment of the presiding officer and the practice of the body.

5. A member who doubts the accuracy of a viva voce or voice vote may demand a division or verification of the vote. A demand may be made as soon as the vote is taken when the presiding officer indicates what the determination of the vote may be, as by saying "the yeas seem to have it" or after the announcement of the vote if the demand is made promptly and before other business is taken up.

6. If made immediately, this call or demand may be made without being recognized. It is made by saying "I call for a division," or "I doubt the vote," or simply by calling out "division." It does not require a second, even when seconds are required, and can-

---

Sec. 532, Par. 3: Sturgis, p. 141; Tilson, p. 34.

Sec. 532, Par. 4: State of North Carolina v. Ellington (1895), 117 N.C. 158, 23 S.E. 250; Kimball v. Lamprey (1848), 19 N.H. 215; Cushing's Legislative Assemblies, Secs. 403, 1794; Cushing, Secs. 193, 198; Reed, Sec. 231; Tilson, p. 35; Sturgis, p. 141.

Sec. 532, Par. 5: State of North Carolina v. Ellington (1895), 117 N.C. 158, 23 S.E. 250; Kimball v. Lamprey (1848), 19 N.H. 215; Gipson v. Morris (1903), 31 Tex. Civ. App. 645, 73 S.W. 85; Hicks v. Long Branch Commission (1903), 69 N.J.L. 300, 54 A. 568; N.Y. Manual (1948–49), p. 469; Cushing's Legislative Assemblies, Secs. 1795, 1797; Hughes, Sec. 1100.

not be debated or amended nor have any subsidiary motion applied to it.

7. As soon as a division is called for, the presiding officer should proceed again to take the vote, by first having the members voting in the affirmative rise, and after they have been counted and are seated, by having the members voting in the negative rise and be counted as indicated under "voting by division," Sec. 533. Voters are sometimes verified by "show of hands" instead of rising or by roll call where voting on roll call is the usual method of voting.

8. While any member has the right to insist upon a division, the presiding officer should not permit this privilege to be abused, to the annoyance of the body, by members constantly demanding a division where there is a full vote and there is no question as to which side is in the majority. A demand for a verification is not in order when all members vote one way.

Sec. 533. Voting by Division

1. Voting by division, that is by a rising vote or by counting hands, is a satisfactory manner of voting in most organizations. It is almost as fast as a voice vote and much more accurate. This method is advantageous, and sometimes necessary, when a certain number of votes is required or more than a majority vote is required, unless voting is done by roll call. It has the disadvantages for some purposes

Sec. 532, Par. 6: Sturgis, p. 141; Cushing, Secs. 238, 240; Robert's, p. 237.
Sec. 532, Par. 7: Sturgis, p. 141; Cushing, Sec. 238.
Sec. 532, Par. 8: Hughes, Secs. 240, 241.

that it does not record the individual vote like a roll call vote, or that it is not secret, like a vote by ballot.

2. A vote by division is often used to verify a voice vote.

3. To take a vote by division the presiding officer may say, "Those in favor of the motion will rise," and then may continue, "Be seated—those opposed will rise." If unable to determine the prevailing side, the presiding officer should say, "Those in favor of the motion (or those in the affirmative) will rise and stand until counted." The presiding officer then counts those standing and says, "Be seated—those opposed (or those in the negative) rise and stand until counted." After both sides are counted, the presiding officer announces the result. If requested by the presiding officer, the secretary or clerk should also count to verify the results. In a small body a show of hands may be substituted for a rising vote.

4. The primary purpose of a call for a division of the house is to test the chair's announcement of the vote in a situation where the announcement is obviously incorrect.

Sec. 534. Voting by Tellers

1. The vote on the passage of measures in the British houses is taken by tellers, and the same

Sec. 533, Par. 3: Jefferson, Sec. XLI; Sturgis, p. 141; Cushing, Secs. 238–242; Reed, Sec. 231; Tilson, p. 35.

Sec. 533, Par. 4: Pignotti v. Local No. 3, Sheet Metal Workers Intern'l Assn. (Neb. 1973), 477 F.2d 825.

Sec. 534: Cushing's Legislative Assemblies, Secs. 404, 1801–1803; Tilson, p. 35; Cushing, Secs. 241, 242; Reed, Sec. 234.

method of voting is used for some purposes in the U.S. Congress and other legislative bodies.

2. As used in Congress, a vote by tellers may be demanded by one-fifth of a quorum, and when ordered, the Speaker appoints two tellers on each side and announces, "As many as are in favor of (stating the question) will pass between the tellers and be counted." The two tellers for the affirmative side take their position before the bar and count the members who pass between them. When the affirmative vote is taken, the Speaker announces, "As many as are opposed will pass between the tellers and be counted." The negative vote is taken and announced in the same manner. Under the old British system, separate gates were used for the affirmative and the negative votes or either those voting in the affirmative or negative left the chamber and were counted as they re-entered.

Sec. 535. Voting on Roll Call

1. The method of voting upon roll call or by "yeas" and "nays" appears to have originated in this country and to have arisen from the practice of voting by states under the Articles of Confederation. This is the method used most often in legislative bodies. It is the most accurate voting system and most easily verified. It has the further advantage of recording the individual votes of members, and since members are voting in a representative capacity, their constituents are entitled to know how their representatives voted.

Sec. 535, Par. 1: Cushing's Legislative Assemblies, Sec. 405; Sturgis, p. 142; Reed, Sec. 232; Cushing, Sec. 246.

2. As the secretary or clerk calls the roll, each member, as the member's name is called, answers "yea" or "nay," and the clerk notes the answers in separate columns. If a member is present and does not wish to vote, that person may fail to answer or may answer "present." When voting on an election, the members answer with the name of the person for whom they are voting as their names are called.

3. When a vote is to be taken by roll call, the presiding officer may put the question in a form similar to the following: "The question is on the passage of Senate (or House) Bill No. ______ by Senator (Representative or Mr. or Madam) ______. As many as are in favor of the bill will vote 'yea,' those opposed will vote 'nay.' The secretary (or clerk) will call the roll." Or, in considering a series of measures, the following is the more usual form: "The question is on the passage of Senate (or House) Bill No. ______. The secretary (or clerk) will call the roll."

4. A convenient method of recording the vote upon roll call is for the secretary or clerk, when calling the roll, to note the "yea" or "nay" votes in separate columns by writing in each case the number of "yea" or "nay" votes thus far received on the roll call. For example, the vote of the first member to vote "yea" will be recorded by writing "1" in the "yea" column opposite the member's name, and the vote of the sixth member to vote "nay" will be recorded by writing "6" in the "nay" column opposite

Sec. 535, Par. 2: Heimbach v. State of New York (1982), 89 App. Div. 2d 138, 454 N.Y.S.2d 993, *aff'd* 59 N.Y.2d 891, 452 N.E.2d 1264, 465 N.Y.S.2d 936, *appeal dismissed,* 464 U.S. 956, 104 S. Ct. 386, 78 L. Ed. 2d 331.

that member's name. By recording the vote in this manner, the secretary or clerk can state the vote to the presiding officer immediately upon the completion of the roll call.

5. Any members who have entered during the roll call or who have not voted may arise and address the presiding officer immediately following the roll call and before the vote is announced and vote as they are recognized or as their names are called by the presiding officer, the clerk repeating the name and the vote for the purpose of verification. It is not out of order for members in this case to announce their votes without waiting to be recognized.

6. After the roll call has been completed, but before the vote is announced, members may arise and address the presiding officer and, upon being recognized, may change their votes by saying, "yea to nay" or the reverse, and the secretary or clerk, upon recording the change, repeats back "Senator (Representative or Mr. or Madam) ______ 'yea to nay,'" or the reverse. It is not out of order for members to change their votes without waiting to be recognized by the presiding officer, but the best practice is to secure recognition before changing the vote. After the vote has been announced it is too late to vote or to change a vote.

7. As the members vote, the clerk calls back the vote before calling the next name in order that any mistake may be corrected. Upon the completion of the roll call, if there have been numerous changes or

---

Sec. 535, Par. 6: N.Y. Manual (1948–49), p. 469; Cushing, Sec. 247a; Mass. Manual, pp. 631, 652; Hughes, Sec. 860; State of Ohio v. Miller (1900), 62 Ohio St. 436, 57 N.E. 227.

if there appears to be need of further verification, the clerk may be directed to read the names of those, if any, who answered in the affirmative, and afterwards those in the negative, and then those, if any, who answered "present."

8. When the roll call has been completed, or verified when that has been required, the secretary or clerk then states the number voting on each side to the presiding officer who announces the result.

9. Upon the announcement of the vote by the presiding officer, the accuracy of the vote may be immediately questioned by a member, and the roll call verified, and any error in taking or announcing the vote may be corrected. This does not give a member the right to change the member's vote after the vote is announced. When the vote is unanimous, the decision may not be questioned.

10. An entry is usually made in the minutes by listing the names of all members voting in the affirmative, and of those in the negative, and the names of those who answered "present," or did not answer may also be entered. The roll upon which the vote was recorded becomes a part of the minutes.

Sec. 536. Voting by Ballot

1. Voting by ballot is rarely, if ever, used in legislative bodies, as the members vote in a representative capacity and their constituents are entitled

---

Sec. 535, Par. 8: Sturgis, p. 142; Cushing, Secs. 245, 246.

Sec. 535, Par. 9: N.Y. Manual, p. 504; State of North Carolina v. Ellington (1895), 117 N.C. 158, 23 S.E. 250; Kimball v. Lamprey (1848), 19 N.H. 215.

Sec. 535, Par. 10: Sturgis, p. 142; Reed, Sec. 232.

to know how their representatives vote. In order to insure that right, constitutions usually require that all bills be passed by roll call and that the vote be recorded in the journal, and also that a small number can require a roll call on any question and have the vote recorded in the journal.

2. Where the constitution or rules do not prohibit a vote being taken by ballot, it can be ordered by a majority vote, or by general consent. When the appointment of an officer or any other action is directed to be made by a legislative body by ballot, that action must be taken by ballot, the manner of taking a ballot being within the discretion of the body. Where an election by ballot is required, each member rising and announcing the member's choice as that person's name is called is not a compliance with the requirement.

3. In an election by ballot a majority of the valid ballots cast is necessary. A blank ballot is of no effect except to indicate the number of members present. Where four ballots are cast for one candidate, three for another and there is one blank ballot, the candidate receiving the four ballots is elected. If a greater number of ballots are cast than there are members present and entitled to vote, the vote should be retaken, and if there are enough such ballots to change the result of the election, the election is void.

Sec. 536, Par. 1: Sturgis, p. 142; Cushing's Legislative Assemblies, Secs. 103–114.

Sec. 536, Par. 2: State of Connecticut v. Starr (1906), 78 Conn. 636, 63 A. 512; Mass. Manual, p. 600.

Sec. 536, Par. 3: Murdock v. Strange (1904), 99 Md. 89, 57 A. 628; State of Connecticut v. Fagan (1875), 42 Conn. 32; Labourdette v. New Orleans (1847), 2 La. Ann. 527.

See also Sec. 516, Illegal Votes.

Sec. 537. Unanimous Consent

1. When there appears to be no opposition, the formality of voting, except where specifically required, can be avoided by the presiding officer asking if there is any objection to the proposed action, and if there be none, proceeding as though the required action were approved. The action thus taken is said to be taken by general consent or unanimous consent.

2. An action taken by unanimous consent is taken on the assumption that failure to object to the granting of a request amounts to consent or approval, but the question must be regularly presented and an opportunity to object given. Various members expressing approval and not dissenting does not constitute unanimous consent in the parliamentary sense.

3. A legislative body can take any action by unanimous consent which it is competent to take by vote, notwithstanding any rule of parliamentary law; but it would clearly be controlled by any constitutional, charter or statutory provision governing the manner of taking or recording votes.

4. Objection made with reasonable promptness, even if the presiding officer has announced the action approved, defeats the request for unanimous consent and a regular vote is required. A single

---

Sec. 537, Par. 1: Cushing's Legislative Assemblies, Sec. 1793; Sturgis, p. 143; Hughes, Sec. 615.

Sec. 537, Par. 2: Landers v. Frank St. Methodist Episcopal Church (1889), 114 N.Y. 626, 21 N.E. 420; Sturgis, p. 143; Hughes, Sec. 610; Cushing, Sec. 237.

Sec. 537, Par. 3: Reed, Sec. 24; Cushing, Sec. 237.

objection defeats a request for unanimous consent. Where the presiding officer is a member of the body, the presiding officer retains the right to object the same as any other member, and may refuse to recognize a request for unanimous consent. It is also clearly within the right of the presiding officer to put the question to a vote of the body.

5. In the absence of any constitutional or other controlling provision for the protection of absentees, unanimous consent means the unanimous consent of the members present.

6. The granting of unanimous consent may not be reconsidered or withdrawn, but the regular manner of procedure may be insisted upon at any time before that which was to have been done by unanimous consent has been completed.

Sec. 538. Absentee Voting

In a legislative body it is a rule that no member can vote who is not present when the question is put, but "pairing," which is a type of absentee voting by which a member agrees with a member who would have voted opposite to the first member not to vote, has long been used in Congress and some of the states and has been recognized by the courts. Each house of the legislature, under the authority to make rules for its own government, has power to recognize what are called "pairs." In determining the vote necessary to pass legislation when a majority

Sec. 537, Par. 4: Cushing's Legislative Assemblies, Sec. 1793; Cushing, Sec. 237; Sturgis, p. 143; Hughes, Secs. 611, 615, 617.

Sec. 537, Par. 5: Atkins v. Philips (1890), 28 Fla. 281, 8 So. 429; Zeiler v. Central Railway Co. (1896), 84 Md. 304, 35 A. 932.

Sec. 537, Par. 6: Hughes, Sec. 616.

vote of those present is required, the "paired" members may be treated as absent.

Sec. 538: Wise v. Bigger (1884), 79 Va. 269; *In re* Opinion of the Justices (1934), 228 Ala. 140, 152 So. 901.

CHAPTER 48

NOMINATIONS

See also Ch. 31, Secs. 306–308, Voting, Nominations and Elections.

Sec. 545. Manner of Making Nominations and Motions Relating to Nominations

1. Nominations are a prerequisite to an election, unless an election is by ballot or by roll call, when all members may nominate their candidates as they vote for that candidate.

2. Where no method of making nominations is designated by the rules, a motion may be made by any member describing the method of making nominations for any office to be filled. The motion may provide for nominations by the presiding officer, nominations from the floor, nominations by a nominating committee or for nominations to be made by ballot. When different methods of making nominations are proposed, they are treated as alternative propositions and are put to vote in the following order:

(a) Nomination by ballot, if voting by ballot is permitted.
(b) Nomination from the floor.
(c) Nomination by committee.
(d) Appointment by resolution or on motion.
(e) Nomination by the presiding officer.
(f) Appointment by the presiding officer.

Sec. 545: Sturgis, pp. 147–149.

3. A motion to decide the manner of making nominations for a pending election is an incidental motion and takes precedence as such, but, when no election is immediately pending, a motion relating to nominations is a main question and takes precedence in that order. When a motion relates to nominations for an immediately pending election, it is not debatable nor subject to any subsidiary motion except the motion to amend. When a motion relating to nominations is a main question, it is subject to debate and other motions as is any main question.

Sec. 546. Nominations from the Floor

1. When nominations are made from the floor, any member is entitled to nominate one candidate for a position, but no person may nominate more than one candidate if objection is raised.

2. Nominations need not be seconded, although seconds to nominations may be permitted.

Sec. 547. Nominations by Committee

1. When nominations are to be made by a committee, this committee is appointed in the same manner as any other special committee, with instructions to make nominations for certain offices.

2. A nominating committee usually submits a single list of candidates to fill the offices provided for, but it is not improper or unusual for the committee to name more than one candidate for an office.

Sec. 546: Sturgis, p. 148.
Sec. 547: Sturgis, pp. 149, 150.

3. A committee's nominations are treated the same as nominations from the floor unless a motion is made to add other candidates or to substitute candidates for those nominated by committee. No vote is required to accept the persons nominated by the committee as candidates for the offices.

Sec. 548. Nominations by the Presiding Officer

When nominations by the presiding officer have been provided for or when proceeding informally, the presiding officer may nominate candidates for a position, and in such a case, it is in order to move that names be substituted, or that names be stricken from the list nominated and that other names be added to the list. When nominations are acceptable to the body, the nominations may be approved individually or as a group.

Sec. 549. Motion to Close Nominations

1. When a sufficient number of names are proposed to fill the positions, and after allowing a reasonable time for further nominations, it is in order to move that nominations be closed. A motion to close nominations is not in order as long as a member entitled to make a further nomination desires to do so, except that a member must be reasonably prompt in claiming that right.

2. A motion to close nominations takes precedence as an incidental motion, yielding only to privileged motions when nominations are in order. The

Sec. 549: Hughes, Sec. 97; Sturgis, p. 148.

motion can have no subsidiary motions applied to it. A motion to close nominations is not debatable.

3. Before proceeding to an election, if nominations have been made from the floor or by a committee, the presiding officer should inquire if there are further nominations, and if there is no response, the presiding officer may declare the nominations closed without a motion to that effect.

Sec. 550. Reopening Nominations

If, after nominations have been closed, it is desired to make further nominations, the nominations may be opened, upon motion, by a majority vote. A motion to reopen nominations is not debatable. It can be amended but cannot have any other subsidiary motion applied to it. This motion ranks as an incidental motion yielding only to privileged motions, and to incidental motions of a higher rank.

Sec. 550: Sturgis, pp. 148, 149.

CHAPTER 49

ELECTIONS

See also Ch. 31, Secs. 306–308, Voting, Nominations and Elections.

Sec. 552. Manner of Voting in Elections

1. After nominations have been made, or in case the election is to be by roll call or ballot when nominations are not necessary, the election may be conducted in any manner provided by the rules, or if the rules do not specify the manner of election, election may be by any recognized means.

2. Where no method of election is provided, a motion specifying the manner is in order. This motion ranks as an incidental motion and when the next order of business is an election, it yields only to privileged motions and to incidental motions of a higher rank.

3. The constitutions of a large number of the states provide the manner of elections of legislative bodies, usually requiring that election be by roll call and that the vote be printed in the journal.

4. When the vote is viva voce or by division, the candidates are to be treated in the same manner as alternative propositions and their names are to be submitted to vote in the order in which they were nominated, and when more than one person is to be elected, the names are put in the order of nomination until the requisite number receive a majority vote and are declared elected.

Sec. 552: Sturgis, pp. 154–159; Hughes, Secs. 87–101.

5. When a legislative body expresses its will by ballot, its act is not complete before the result of the ballot is ascertained and made known. When this is done and it appears clearly from the announcement of the state of the vote that the number of ballots requisite to an appointment has been lawfully given to one person, and no further action is taken, the will of the body is finally expressed and the appointment is complete. It is not lawful afterwards and without any reason to revoke such an appointment and appoint another person.

6. A presiding officer cannot declare an officer elected when that person fails to receive the vote required by law.

Sec. 553. Majority Vote Required for Election

1. In the absence of a special rule, a majority vote is necessary to elect officers and a plurality is not sufficient. A vote for the election of officers, when no candidate receives a majority vote, is of no effect and the situation remains exactly as though no vote had been taken.

2. When in an election a quorum is present and a candidate receives a majority of the votes cast, although a majority of the entire body fails to vote, the election is valid.

Sec. 552, Par. 5: State of Connecticut v. Starr (1906), 78 Conn. 636, 63 A. 512.

Sec. 552, Par. 6: Dingwell v. Detroit (1890), 82 Mich. 568, 46 N.W. 938.

Sec. 553, Par. 1: Hughes, Sec. 99; Cushing's Legislative Assemblies, Secs. 118–128, 298; Sturgis, p. 134.

Sec. 553, Par. 2: Willcock on Municipal Corporations, Sec. 546; Grant on Corporations, Sec. 71; Angel and Ames on Corporations, Secs. 126 and 127; Booker v. Young (1855), 53 Va. 303; U.S. v. Ballin (1892), 144 U.S. 1, 12 S. Ct. 507, 36 L. Ed. 321.

3. When provision for election is made without specifying the proportion of the vote, a majority of a quorum duly convened is sufficient.

Sec. 554. Effective Date of Election

1. An election takes effect immediately:

(a) If the candidate is present and does not decline the election.

(b) If the candidate is absent but has consented to candidacy.

2. When the person elected is absent and has not consented to candidacy, the election takes effect immediately on notification to the candidate of that person's election, provided the candidate does not immediately decline.

3. If a member does not immediately decline upon learning of election to an office, by silence the member is deemed to accept the office and is under obligation to perform the duty until there has been a reasonable opportunity for the member's resignation to be accepted.

4. When an officer or member has been notified of election and has not declined, the election has taken effect and it is too late to reconsider the vote on election.

5. An officer takes possession of office immediately upon that person's election and acceptance,

Sec. 553, Par. 3: Cadmus v. Farr (1885), 47 N.J.L. 208.

Sec. 554, Par. 1: Sturgis, p. 159.

Sec. 554, Par. 2: Sturgis, p. 159.

Sec. 554, Par. 3: Sturgis, p. 159.

Sec. 554, Par. 4: State of Wisconsin v. Tyrrell (1914), 158 Wis. 425, 149 N.W. 280; State of Ohio v. Miller (1900), 62 Ohio St. 436, 57 N.E. 227; Regina v. Donoghue (1858), 15 Upp. Canada Q.B. 454.

unless the law or rules specify a different time and no formal initiation is necessary.

6. The election of an officer by a legislative body by ballot is not complete until the result of the ballot is ascertained and announced, and where fraud or error occurs in the election, as where there are more ballots than members present and entitled to vote, the vote must be retaken.

See also Sec. 516, Illegal Votes.

7. Statutes usually require that public officers must take an oath of office and often that they file a bond to qualify for office.

Sec. 555. Declining to Accept Elective Position

1. When a candidate for office is present at the election and declines the position, the vacancy is filled as if no election had taken place. When a person declines an office or appointment, no resignation and acceptance of the resignation are necessary unless the law or rules make the performance of the duties of the office obligatory.

2. An office is vacated by the refusal of the person elected to accept it, communicated to the proper authorities.

3. When a person is not present at the election and that person's refusal to take office is announced

---

Sec. 554, Par. 5: Sturgis, p. 159.

Sec. 554, Par. 6: State of Connecticut v. Starr (1906), 78 Conn. 636, 63 A. 512; Gouldey v. City Council of Atlantic City (1899), 63 N.J.L. 537, 42 A. 852.

Sec. 555, Par. 2: Cushing's Legislative Assemblies, Secs. 471–478; State of West Virginia *ex rel.* Hatfield v. Farrar (1921), 89 W.Va. 232, 109 S.E. 240.

by the presiding officer, the election to fill the vacancy may take place at once, unless some other provision to fill vacancies is provided by the rules.

Sec. 556. Vacancies in Office

1. Ordinarily having accepted an office of responsibility, one cannot immediately relieve oneself of responsibility by resigning, and one's responsibility continues until one's resignation is accepted, or at least until there has been a reasonable time for its acceptance.

2. If a member is elected to office or appointed to a committee or has any other duty imposed upon the member which that person is unable or unwilling to accept, that person should immediately decline the office or appointment if present, or if absent, should notify the presiding officer or clerk immediately that the member cannot accept the position or responsibility.

3. In case of a resignation presented to a legislative body, the presiding officer may immediately state the question on accepting it, or a motion may be made to that effect. A motion to accept is debatable and may have any subsidiary motion applied to it. Such a motion yields to privileged and other incidental motions.

4. The assumption that a member of a legislative body is no longer eligible to office by having moved from the district does not in itself create a vacancy, and the majority of those in office at the time including such member is required to constitute a quorum.

Sec. 556, Par. 2: In re Opinion to the Governor (1918), 41 R.I. 79, 102 A. 802.

There is no vacancy until the fact of a disqualification of a member has been ascertained and determined and the vacancy declared.

5. When offices are held without fixed terms, the electing authority can replace the officeholders by a majority vote.

Sec. 556, Par. 4: State of West Virginia *ex rel.* Hatfield v. Farrar (1921), 89 W.Va. 232, 109 S.E. 240.

Sec. 556, Par. 5: State of Missouri v. Reichmann (1911), 239 Mo. 81, 142 S.W. 304.

PART VI. LEGISLATIVE AND ADMINISTRATIVE BODIES

*

PART VI

LEGISLATIVE AND ADMINISTRATIVE BODIES

CHAPTER 50

ELECTION AND QUALIFICATION OF MEMBERS

Sec. 560. Each House of a Legislature Is the Judge of the Election and Qualification of Its Members

1. By constitutional provision, each house of the legislature is made the judge of the election, qualifications and returns of its members.

2. Under constitutional provisions to the effect that each house shall have the power to judge the

Sec. 560, Par. 1: Corbett v. Naylor (1904), 25 R.I. 550, 579 A. 303; Burge v. Tibor (1964), 88 Idaho 149, 397 P.2d 235; Harris v. Shanahan (1963), 192 Kan. 183, 387 P.2d 771; Rogers v. Shanahan (1976), 221 Kan. 221, 565 P.2d 1384; Hiett v. Brier (1978), 2 Kan. App. 2d 610, 586 P.2d 55; State Constitutions: Ala. IV, 46, 47, 53; Alaska II, 12; Ariz. IV, Part II, 8; Ark. V, 11; Cal. IV, 5; Colo. V, 10; Conn. III, 13; Del. II, 7, 8; Fla. III, 2; Ga. III, Sec. IV, 7; Hawaii III, 12; Idaho II, 9; Ill. IV, 14; Ind. IV, 10; Iowa III, 7; Kan. II, 8; Ky. 34, 38; La. III, 7(a); Me. IV, Part I, 7, Part II, 8, Part III, 3; Md. III, 19; Mass. Part II, Ch. I, Sec. II, 4, 7, Sec. III, 10; Mich. IV, 16; Minn. IV, 6; Miss. IV, 38; Mo. IV, 18; Mont. V, 10; Neb. III, 10; Nev. IV, 6; N.H. II, 14, 29; N.J. IV, Sec. IV, 2, 3; N.M. IV, 7, 9; N.Y. III, 9; N.C. II, 20, 22; N.Dak. IV, 12; Ohio II, 6; Okla. V, 28, 30; Ore. IV, 11; Pa. II, 9; R.I. V, 2, IV, 6; S.C. III, 11, 12; S.Dak. III, 9; Tenn. II, 11; Tex. III, 8; Utah VI, 10, 12; Vt. II, 14, 19; Va. IV, 7; Wash. II, 8; W.Va. VI, 24; Wis. IV, 7; Wyo. III, 10.

qualifications and elections of its members, each branch of a state legislature has the sole and exclusive power to judge the election and qualifications of its own members.

3. When a legislative body is made the sole judge of the election and qualifications of its members, its determination is conclusive and not subject to review even by the state supreme court.

4. The provisions of the constitution relating to the eligibility of members of the legislature, of course, must be complied with.

5. The exclusive power to judge the qualifications and elections of its members is fixed in each house and cannot by its own consent or by legislative action be vested in any other tribunal or office.

Sec. 560, Par. 2: Young v. Boles (1909), 92 Ark. 242, 122 S.W. 496; Allen v. Lelande (1912), 164 Cal. 56, 127 P. 643; Mills v. Newell (1902), 30 Colo. 377, 70 P. 405; Rainey v. Taylor (1928), 166 Ga. 476, 143 S.E. 383; State of Kansas v. Tomlinson (1878), 20 Kan. 692; State of Louisiana v. Judges Civ. Dist. Ct. (1888), 40 La. Ann. 598, 4 So. 482; Price v. Ashburn (1914), 122 Md. 514, 89 A. 410; Attorney General v. 7th Senatorial District Board (1908), 155 Mich. 44, 118 N.W. 584; State of Minnesota v. Peers (1885), 33 Minn. 81, 21 N.W. 860; State of Montana v. Porter (1919), 55 Mont. 471, 178 P. 832; Bingham v. Jewett (1890), 66 N.H. 382, 29 A. 694; Sherrill v. Pendleton (1907), 188 N.Y. 185, 81 N.E. 124; Petition of Knowles (1897), 25 R.I. 522, 57 A. 303; State of Wyoming v. Schnitger (1908), 16 Wyo. 479, 95 P. 698.

Sec. 560, Par. 3: Allen v. Lelande (1912), 164 Cal. 56, 127 P. 643; Corbett v. Naylor (1904), 25 R.I. 550, 579 A. 303; Reif v. Barrett (1934), 355 Ill. 104, 188 N.E. 889; Auditor General v. Board of Supervisors (1891), 89 Mich. 552, 51 N.W. 483; Rainey v. Taylor (1928), 166 Ga. 476, 143 S.E. 383.

Sec. 560, Par. 4: People v. Chicago Election Commissioners (1906), 221 Ill. 9, 77 N.E. 321; State of Minnesota v. Scott (1908), 105 Minn. 513, 117 N.W. 1044; People v. Markham (1892), 96 Cal. 262, 31 P. 102; Opinion of the Justices (1877), 122 Mass. 594.

Sec. 560, Par. 5: State of Kansas v. Gilmore (1878), 20 Kan. 551, 27 Am. R. 189; Watson v. Medical Society of New Jersey (1876), 38 N.J.L. 377; Bingham v. Jewett (1890), 66 N.H. 382, 29 A. 694.

6. The courts will not entertain a proceeding to determine the rights of one who has been seated by a legislative body.

7. When specifically authorized by statute, courts may take evidence in legislative election contests, but only so far as specifically authorized.

8. A legislative body which is the sole judge of the election of its members, upon a contest respecting election of one of its members, may appoint a committee to take testimony and report the facts and the evidence to the body.

9. A member of a legislature cannot be removed from office under a general law relating to the removal of "any officer." But a person who holds a seat in the legislature and thereafter accepts an appointment to an incompatible office, thereby vacates that person's seat in the legislature.

10. The authority of a house of a legislature to pass upon its membership is a continuing power and the question of the election and qualification of members is never finally decided, in the sense that a decision is conclusive upon the house, until final adjournment. A member at any time may be seated or unseated upon the same facts.

Sec. 560, Par. 6: State of Montana v. Cutts (1917), 53 Mont. 500, 163 P. 470.

Sec. 560, Par. 7: State of Minnesota v. Nelson (1919), 141 Minn. 499, 169 N.W. 788; State of Minnesota v. Peers (1885), 33 Minn. 81, 21 N.W. 860.

Sec. 560, Par. 8: State of New Jersey v. Haynes (1887), 50 N.J.L. 97, 11 A. 151.

Sec. 560, Par. 9: State of Kansas v. Gilmore (1878), 20 Kan. 551, 27 Am. R. 189; State of New Jersey v. Parkhurst (1802), 9 N.J.L. 427.

Sec. 560, Par. 10: State of Montana v. Porter (1919), 55 Mont. 471, 178 P. 832; State of Kansas v. Gilmore (1878), 20 Kan. 551, 27 Am. R. 189.

11. A member of a legislature has the right to resign the member's office providing that person adopts the proper procedure to that end, such procedure being that the member's resignation should be tendered to the office or body having power to order a new election.

12. Unless the constitution so provides, when the president pro tempore of the senate becomes lieutenant governor by reason of the lieutenant governor's becoming governor to fill a vacancy in that office, the president pro tempore does not cease to be a senator.

Sec. 561. Power of Legislatures to Discipline Members

1. Whatever is spoken in the house is subject to the censure of the house; and offenses of this kind have been severely punished by calling the person to the bar to make submission, committing the person to prison, expelling the person from the house or inflicting other punishment.

2. A member who is absent without leave of the house is in contempt and may be punished as the house may direct.

3. The right of a house to compel the attendance of absent members is usually guaranteed by the constitution. In order to compel attendance, mem-

Sec. 560, Par. 11: *In re* Opinion to the Governor (1918), 41 R.I. 79, 102 A. 802; Braddom v. Three Point Coal Corp. (1941), 288 Ky. 734, 157 S.W.2d 349.

Sec. 560, Par. 12: State of Minnesota v. Stearns (1898), 72 Minn. 200, 75 N.W. 210.

Sec. 561, Par. 1: Jefferson, Sec. III.

Sec. 561, Par. 2: N.Y. Manual, p. 423.

bers may be arrested and, when arrested, they continue in the custody of the arresting officer until discharged by the house.

4. The constitutional power of a house to arrest and compel the attendance of members is not confined to the time when a call is in effect nor to when there is no quorum. To deprive a house of its power to compel the attendance of any or all members would destroy its function as a legislative body. The majority of the members of a house may compel the presence of all members.

5. When a member is absent during the session, and a sufficient excuse is not rendered, those present may take steps necessary to secure the member's attendance and may suspend the member from service of the house for a given period. They also may inflict such censure or pecuniary penalty as may be deemed just.

6. A requirement that a member of the legislature disclose the member's personal or private interest in any measure or bill may be enforced under the power of each house to judge the election and qualifications of its own members.

Sec. 562. Right of Legislatures to Expel Members

1. Most state constitutions provide that each house, with the concurrence of two-thirds of all the

Sec. 561, Par. 3: Hughes, Sec. 655.
Sec. 561, Par. 4: Hughes, Sec. 655.
Sec. 561, Par. 5: N.Y. Manual (1948–49), p. 372.
Sec. 561, Par. 6: Melland v. Johanneson (N.D. 1968), 160 N.W.2d 107.

members elected, may expel a member.

2. If these constitutional provisions were omitted and there were no other constitutional limitations, the power to expel would nevertheless exist and could be exercised by a majority. The only effect of the constitutional provisions is to make the concurrence of two-thirds of the members elected necessary to expel a member. In all other respects the power is absolute.

3. A house, in passing upon the question of expelling a member, has power to adopt any procedure and to change it at any time and without notice.

4. The oath of each individual member of a house, and that member's duty under it to act conscientiously for the general good, is the only safeguard to the fellow members against an unjust and causeless expulsion. This is the only practical rule that can be adopted as to those unrestricted governmental powers which are necessary to the exercise of governmental functions and which must be lodged somewhere. Each department of the state is necessarily vested with some power which is beyond the supervision of any other department, and in such

---

Sec. 562, Par. 1: State Constitutions: Ala. IV, 53; Alaska II, 12; Ariz. IV, II, 11; Ark. V, 12; Cal. IV, 5; Colo. V, 12; Conn. III, 13; Del. II, 9; Fla. III, 4; Ga. III, Sec. IV, 7; Idaho III, 11; Ill. IV, 14; Ind. IV, 14; Iowa III, 9; Kan. II, 8; Ky. 39; La. III, 7(a); Me. IV, Part III, 4; Md. III, 19; Mass. Part II, Ch. I, Sec. II, 7, Sec. III, 10; Mich. IV, 16; Minn. IV, 7; Miss. IV, 55; Mo. IV, 18; Mont. V, 10; Neb. III, 10; Nev. IV, 6; N.H. II, 22, 35; N.J. IV, Sec. IV, 3; N.M. IV, 11; N.Dak. IV, 9, 12; Ohio II, 6; Okla. V, 30; Ore. IV, 15; Pa. II, 11; R.I. IV, 7; S.C. III, 12; S.Dak. III, 9; Tenn. II, 12; Tex. III, 11; Utah VI, 10; Vt. II, 14, 19; Va. IV, 7; Wash. II, 9; W.Va. VI, 25; Wis. IV, 8; Wyo. III, 12.

Sec. 562, Par. 2: French v. Senate (1905), 146 Cal. 604, 80 P. 1031, 69 L.R.A. 556.

Sec. 562, Par. 3: French v. Senate (1905), 146 Cal. 604, 80 P. 1031, 69 L.R.A. 556.

cases the only protection against abuse is the conscience of the individual in whom the power is vested.

5. A house having expelled members in the mode prescribed by the constitution, its action is not a deprivation of office without due process of law, within the meaning of the Fourteenth Amendment to the Federal Constitution. The sovereign power which created the office can prescribe the terms upon which it is to be held and the conditions under which it can be taken away.

6. The provision for the disfranchisement of a member upon conviction for crime has no effect upon the power to expel members nor does expulsion operate as a bill of attainder in violation of the state or Federal constitutions.

7. The constitutional provision that relates to expulsion of members deals only with expulsion for misconduct.

8. A member of a state legislature may resign.

Sec. 563. Courts Have No Power Concerning Expulsion of Members

1. The power conferred upon a house of the legislature by the constitution to determine the rule of its proceeding, and with the concurrence of two-

Sec. 562, Par. 4: French v. Senate (1905), 146 Cal. 604, 80 P. 1031, 69 L.R.A. 556.

Sec. 562, Par. 5: French v. Senate (1905), 146 Cal. 604, 80 P. 1031, 69 L.R.A. 556.

Sec. 562, Par. 6: French v. Senate (1905), 146 Cal. 604, 80 P. 1031, 69 L.R.A. 556.

Sec. 562, Par. 7: Sincock v. Gately (Del. 1967), 262 F. Supp. 739.

Sec. 562, Par. 8: State of Indiana *ex rel.* Black v. Burch (1948), 226 Ind. 445, 80 N.E.2d 560, *rehearing denied,* 81 N.E.2d 850 (1948).

thirds of the members elected, to expel a member is exclusive; and the judicial department has no power to revise even the most arbitrary and unfair action of the legislative department taken in pursuance of the power committed exclusively thereto by the constitution.

2. There is no authority for courts to control, direct, supervise or forbid the exercise by either house of the power to expel a member. These powers are functions of the legislative department, and therefore in the exercise of the power thus committed to it, the house is supreme. An attempt by a court to direct or control the legislature, or either house thereof, in the exercise of the power, would be an attempt to exercise legislative functions, which it is expressly forbidden to do.

3. A legislative house, in a proceeding to expel a member, has power to adopt any procedure, and to change it at any time without notice. There is no constitutional provision giving persons who have been expelled the right to have a trial and opportunity to be heard in the house.

4. The courts will not entertain a proceeding to determine the rights of one who has been unseated by a legislative body.

5. In view of the constitutional provision that each house shall be the judge of the qualifications,

---

Sec. 563, Par. 1: French v. Senate (1905), 146 Cal. 604, 80 P. 1031, 69 L.R.A. 556.

Sec. 563, Par. 2: French v. Senate (1905), 146 Cal. 604, 80 P. 1031, 69 L.R.A. 556.

Sec. 563, Par. 3: French v. Senate (1905), 146 Cal. 604, 80 P. 1031, 69 L.R.A. 556.

Sec. 563, Par. 4: State of Montana v. Cutts (1917), 53 Mont. 500, 163 P. 470.

elections and returns of its members, the courts are without authority to determine whether a legislator had the right to hold office.

Sec. 564. Investigation of Charges Against Members

See also Sec. 796, Investigations Respecting Members.

1. When a charge of bribery or corruption is made against members of a house, the house has power to investigate the charge and to summon the person making the charge before its bar as a witness, and to commit that person for contempt for refusing to testify without sufficient legal cause. This power does not admit doubt, and a house in following this course in no respect exceeds its jurisdiction.

2. When charges of bribery are made by any person against members of either branch of the legislature, without giving their names, and a resolution is adopted by the branch to which the members accused are said to belong, reciting the charge, and resolving to investigate it, and witnesses are summoned before it, an issue is made within the meaning of the statute against perjury.

3. The appointment of a committee by a house, with power to investigate charges of bribery made against members of that body, does not preclude the house from afterwards summoning the witnesses and making the investigation before the bar of the house.

Sec. 563, Par. 5: English v. Bryant (Fla. 1963), 152 So. 2d 167; Raney v. Stovall (Ky. 1962), 361 S.W.2d 518.

Sec. 564, Par. 1: *Ex parte* D.O. McCarthy (1866), 29 Cal. 395.

Sec. 564, Par. 2: *Ex parte* D.O. McCarthy (1866), 29 Cal. 395.

Sec. 564, Par. 3: *Ex parte* D.O. McCarthy (1866), 29 Cal. 395.

See also Sec. 799, Legislative Investigating Committees.

4. A common understanding or belief concerning improper conduct of a member is a sufficient ground for the house to proceed by inquiry concerning the member and even to make an accusation.

Sec. 564, Par. 4: Jefferson, Sec. XIII.

CHAPTER 51

PRIVILEGE OF MEMBERS FROM ARREST

Sec. 568. Constitutional Basis of Privilege from Arrest

1. It was considered so necessary that the normal functioning of the legislative bodies should not be interfered with by charges against individual members that the guarantee of freedom of members from arrest during and immediately before and following sessions was placed in almost all of the state constitutions.

2. The doctrine of legislative immunity is applicable, though not absolutely, to officers and employees of legislative bodies.

3. Both legislators and judges are immune from suit when acting in their official capacity.

Sec. 568, Par. 1: State Constitutions: Ala. IV, 56; Alaska II, 6; Ariz. IV, Part II, 6; Ark. V, 15; Cal. IV, 14; Colo. V, 16; Conn. III, 15; Del. II, 13; Ga. III, Sec. IV, 9; Hawaii III, 7; Idaho III, 7; Ill. IV, 12; Ind. IV, 8; Iowa III, 11; Kan. II, 22; Ky. 43; La. III, 8; Me. IV, Part III, 8; Mass. Part II, Ch. 1, Sec. III, 10; Mich. IV, 11; Minn. IV, 10; Miss. IV, 48; Mo. IV, 19; Mont. V, 8; Neb. III, 15; Nev. IV, 11; N.H. II, 21; N.J. IV, Sec. IV, 9; N.M. IV, 13; N.Dak. IV, 15; Ohio II, 12; Okla. V, 22; Ore. IV, 9; Pa. II, 15; R.I. IV, 5; S.C. III, 14; S.Dak. III, 11; Tenn. II, 13; Tex. III, 14; Utah VI, 8; Va. IV, 9; Wash. II, 16; W.Va. VI, 17; Wis. IV, 15; Wyo. III, 16.

Sec. 568, Par. 2: State of Wisconsin v. Beno (1984), 116 Wis. 2d 122, 341 N.W.2d 668.

Sec. 568, Par. 3: Krause v. Rhodes (Ohio 1972), 471 F. Supp. 430; Gravel v. U.S. (1972), 408 U.S. 606, 92 S. Ct. 2614, 33 L. Ed. 2d 583.

Sec. 569. Present Rule Concerning Privilege from Arrest

1. The courts by a series of decisions have explained away almost every essential feature of the privilege from arrest as it once existed. The usual exemption from arrest granted a member of the legislature by the provisions of the constitutions is now held to be a personal privilege which is waived unless claimed by plea or motion, and it is waived when one goes to trial upon the plea of not guilty of the offense charged.

2. The constitutional exemptions are now interpreted to relate only to civil process, and a member of the legislature is not entitled to exemption from arrest where the member is charged with a traffic violation or other offense of a criminal nature. Furthermore freedom from arrest does not confer immunity on a member of a legislature from service of process as a defendant in civil matters, or as a witness in a criminal case.

3. Any arrest of a member of the legislature in violation of the member's constitutional privilege is merely voidable and not void. A member of the legislature has no right to physically resist an officer attempting to make such an arrest to the extent of assaulting such officer.

Sec. 569, Par. 1: Ex parte Emmett (1932), 120 Cal. App. 349, 7 P.2d 1096; Kallock v. Elward (1919), 118 Me. 346, 108 A. 256; State of Wisconsin v. Polacheck (1898), 101 Wis. 727, 77 N.W. 78; Johnson's Executors v. Johnson (1785), 7 Cal. 38.

Sec. 569, Par. 2: Ex parte Emmett (1932), 120 Cal. App. 349, 7 P.2d 1096; Gravel v. U.S. (1972), 408 U.S. 606, 92 S. Ct. 2614, 33 L. Ed. 2d 583.

Sec. 569, Par. 3: Ex parte Emmett (1932), 120 Cal. App. 349, 7 P.2d 1096.

4. The privilege from arrest provision in the national Constitution as well as in many of the state constitutions is limited by interpretation to civil suits. It affords no protection from arrest in any criminal case.

5. However, one should be aware of Article I, Section 6 of the U.S. Constitution (Speech and Debate Clause) which recognizes the need for protection of legislative independence in a governmental system of separation of powers. There is an entire body of case law that interprets and lays out applicable guidelines of appropriate conduct. For example: Privilege from arrest as implicitly contained in the Speech and Debate Clause applies in a civil action if the activity of the legislator is within the sphere of legitimate legislative activity.

Sec. 570. When Privilege from Arrest Applies

1. Privilege from arrest, insofar as it still exists, takes effect by force of the election, as before a return is made a member elected may be named on a committee and is to every extent a member except that the member cannot vote until sworn.

2. Privilege from arrest applies in a civil action if the activity of the legislator is within the sphere of legitimate legislative activity. The standard for determining if the activity falls within the legitimate legislative sphere is a two-part test. First, the activity must be an integral part of the deliberative and

Sec. 569, Par. 4: Williamson v. U.S. (1908), 207 U.S. 425, 28 S. Ct. 163.

Sec. 569, Par. 5: Gravel v. U.S. (1972), 408 U.S. 606, 92 S. Ct. 2614, 33 L. Ed. 2d 583; Eastland v. U.S. Servicemen's Fund (1975), 421 U.S. 491, 95 S. Ct. 1813, 44 L. Ed. 2d 324.

Sec. 570, Par. 1: Jefferson, Sec. III.

communicative process by which members participate in committee and house proceedings and second, the activity addresses proposed legislation or some other subject within the legislature's constitutional jurisdiction. The scope of the privilege prohibits inquiry into these legislative acts or the motivation for performance of such acts and the context and the circumstançes regarding such motivation.

3. A former legislator is not immune from prosecution for bribery charges because taking a bribe is not a legislative act. But when the plaintiff's cause of action focuses on a legislator's attempt to use the legislator's position to influence the regulation of currency exchanges, this was deemed a legitimate legislative activity and therefore prohibited prosecution of the legislator on grounds of immunity. A presiding officer accused of conspiracy and violation of a legislator's civil rights was deemed immune from liability when the presiding officer compelled the legislator's presence at a legislative session with the assistance of state troopers because this was within the presiding officer's legitimate legislative sphere.

4. However, the privilege does not immunize a state legislator from a federal criminal prosecution in connection with that person's legislative acts to the extent that a subpoena required disclosure of

---

Sec. 570, Par. 2: U.S. v. Brewster (1972), 408 U.S. 501, 92 S. Ct. 2531, 33 L. Ed. 2d 507; Gravel v. U.S. (1972), 408 U.S. 606, 92 S. Ct. 2614, 33 L. Ed. 2d 583; Abercrombie v. McClung (1974), 55 Hawaii 595; Eastland v. U.S. Servicemen's Fund (1975), 421 U.S. 491, 95 S. Ct. 1813, 44 L. Ed. 2d 324; State of Alaska v. Dankworth (1983), 672 P.2d 148.

Sec. 570, Par. 3: U.S. v. Brewster (1972), 408 U.S. 501, 92 S. Ct. 2531, 33 L. Ed. 2d 507; Thillens, Inc. v. Community Currency Exchange (1984), 729 F.2d 1128, *cert. dismissed,* 469 U.S. 976, 105 S. Ct. 375, 83 L. Ed. 2d 342; Schultz v. Sundberg (Alaska 1985), 759 F.2d 714.

certain information such as documents or exhibits authored by witnesses testifying before a legislative committee and which were in the legislator's possession and could not be obtained by any other means.

5. Common law doctrine does not immunize state legislators from federal criminal prosecution in connection with their legislative acts. The legislator charged with a federal crime or who is the target of a criminal investigation cannot claim the privilege.

6. A member of a legislature is not privileged from arrest in a civil action after the member has been expelled from the house.

7. If an offense is committed by a member in the house of which the house has cognizance, it is an infringement of that body's right for any person or court to take notice of it until the house has punished the offender or referred the matter to other authorities.

Sec. 570, Par. 4: U.S. v. Brewster (1972), 408 U.S. 501, 92 S. Ct. 2531, 33 L. Ed. 2d 507; Schultz v. Sundberg (Alaska 1985), 759 F.2d 714; *In re* Grand Jury Subpoena (M.D. Pa. 1986), 626 F. Supp. 1319.

Sec. 570, Par. 5: U.S. v. Gillock (1980), 445 U.S. 360, 100 S. Ct. 1185, 63 L. Ed. 2d 454.

Sec. 570, Par. 6: Hiss v. Bartlett (1855), 69 Mass. 473, 63 Am. Dec. 768.

Sec. 570, Par. 7: Jefferson, Sec. III, and notes in U.S. House Manual.

CHAPTER 52

THE PRESIDING OFFICER

Sec. 575. Duties of Presiding Officer

See also Sec. 523, Putting the Question to Vote.

1. The duties of the presiding officer of each house are, in general, as follows:

(a) To open the session at the time at which the body is to meet by taking the chair and calling the members to order.

(b) To announce the business before the body in the order in which it is to be acted upon.

(c) To recognize the members entitled to the floor.

(d) To state and put to vote all questions which are regularly moved or which necessarily arise in the course of the proceedings and to announce the result of the vote.

(e) To preserve order and decorum.

(f) To restrain the members when engaged in debate within the rules of order.

(g) To decide all points of order, subject to appeal, unless when in doubt the presiding officer prefers to submit the question to the decision of the body.

(h) To inform the body when necessary, or when any question is raised, on any point of order or practice pertinent to the pending business.

(i) To sign or authenticate all acts, proceedings or orders of the body.

(j) To receive all messages and communications and, when applicable, to announce them to the body.

(k) To guide and direct the proceedings of the body, subject to the control and will of the body.

(*l*) To enforce all laws and regulations applicable to the body.

(m) To have general charge and supervision of the legislative chamber, galleries, committee rooms and adjoining and connecting hallways and passages.

2. It is in order for the presiding officer to suggest the proper form of propositions or motions and the proper course of procedure or order of business.

3. When a presiding officer is required to sign a bill to authenticate its passage, the act of signing is simply ministerial and not an exercise of legislative discretion; therefore, mandamus will lie to compel its performance. To hold otherwise would give the presiding officer, in effect, a veto upon the acts of the legislative body. But the courts should not require the presiding officer to sign a legislative proposal which that officer had ruled had not passed, because, in this instance, the presiding officer was exercising discretion. When required to certify as to the number of votes and that a quorum was present

Sec. 575, Par. 1: In re Sawyer (1887), 124 U.S. 200, 31 L. Ed. 402; Cockran v. McCleary (1867), 22 Iowa 75; Reynolds v. Baldwin (1846), 1 La. Ann. 162; Rex v. Williams (Eng., circa 1760), 1 Burr 402; Willcock on Municipal Corporations, Sec. 456; Sturgis, p. 162; Cushing's Legislative Assemblies, Sec. 291; Cushing, Sec. 27; Reed, Secs. 34, 221; Tilson, pp. 28–39; U.S. House Rule I, Pars. 1–6.

Sec. 575, Par. 2: Sturgis, p. 13; N.Y. Manual, p. 443.

the presiding officer can rely on personal observations or consult the records.

4. When there has been no provision for a clerk or secretary to keep the minutes of the proceedings, the presiding officer may appoint someone to act as clerk or secretary. The fact that the person who presides at a meeting also acts as its clerk does not invalidate the proceedings.

Sec. 576. Refusal of Presiding Officer to Perform Duties

1. Whenever the presiding officer attempts to thwart the purpose of the office, the power resides in the assembly to pass the presiding officer by and proceed to action otherwise. This right is but a branch of the power which assemblies exert in choosing temporary officers when the permanent officers are absent. It is not their absence which justifies the exercise of the power, but the fact they are not performing duties necessary to the proper fulfillment of the functions of the assembly. Inability or refusal to perform those duties has the same effect as actions in suspending the ordinary functions of the meeting and equally warrants the selection of the temporary chair. The power is inherent or inseparably attached to the right of the body to convene and act.

Sec. 575, Par. 3: Pevey v. Aylward (1910), 205 Mass. 102, 91 N.E. 315; State of Missouri v. Bolte (1899), 151 Mo. 362, 52 S.W. 262; N.Y. Manual (1948–49), p. 449.

Sec. 575, Par. 4: Parsons v. Brainard (N.Y. 1837), 17 Wend. 522; Budd v. Walla Walla Printing and Publishing Co. (1885), 2 Wash. 347, 7 P. 896.

Sec. 576, Par. 1: Hicks v. Long Branch Commission (1903), 69 N.J.L. 300, 54 A. 568; similarly, State of Connecticut v. Lasher (1899), 71 Conn. 540, 42 A. 636.

2. When the presiding officer refuses to put a motion which is properly before the body, the proper procedure is to select, at once, a temporary presiding officer to put the motion to vote. It is not legal or proper procedure for the member making the motion to put the motion to vote.

3. The presiding officer cannot prevent the transaction of business by leaving the chair or leaving the meeting. In either instance the members can elect a temporary presiding officer and proceed. If a member properly questions the presiding officer's ruling on a motion to adjourn, it is the presiding officer's duty to resolve the question or take a division before declaring an adjournment and, upon the presiding officer's failure to do so, a temporary presiding officer can be elected and the business can proceed in proper order.

Sec. 577. Emergency Power of Presiding Officer

In case of fire, riot or other great emergency, the presiding officer has the right, when, in the presiding officer's opinion, it is impractical or dangerous to delay action for a vote, to declare the body adjourned to some other time and, if necessary, to some other place. When, through some emergency or through inadvertence, the body is adjourned without provision for the next meeting, the presiding

Sec. 576, Par. 2: State of Connecticut v. Lasher (1899), 71 Conn. 540, 42 A. 636; Hicks v. Long Branch Commission (1903), 69 N.J.L. 300, 54 A. 568; Finley Coal Co. v. Proctor (1895), 98 Ky. 405, 33 S.W. 188; Ostrom v. Greene (1897), 45 N.Y.S. 852; State of North Dakota v. Archibald (1895), 5 N.D. 359, 66 N.W. 234.

Sec. 576, Par. 3: Ostrom v. Greene (1897), 45 N.Y.S. 852; Chariton v. Holiday (1883), 60 Iowa 391, 14 N.W. 775; Pevey v. Aylward (1910), 205 Mass. 102, 91 N.E. 315.

officer can issue a call specifying the time and, if an emergency requires, the presiding officer may specify a different place. When conditions permit, however, the call should be issued only after consultation with available members. Such actions are to be taken only in real emergencies and become valid legal actions only upon acceptance and approval by the body.

Sec. 578. Limitations on Presiding Officer

1. Under ordinary conditions, the authority of the presiding officer is derived wholly from the body itself. The presiding officer is the servant of the body to declare its will and to obey its commands.

2. The presiding officer may not refuse to put any motion which is in order.

3. The presiding officer may not limit or close debate except as authorized by the rules, or as required by the previous question, or by a motion duly approved by the body.

4. The presiding officer may not prevent the making of any legitimate motions by hurrying through the proceedings or by other means. Members must be reasonably prompt in order to exercise their right to speak or to make motions.

5. The presiding officer may not interrupt a member who has the floor, except for deciding points of order, considering questions of privilege or

---

Sec. 578, Par. 1: Cushing's Legislative Assemblies, Sec. 294; 2 Hatsell 242; Hicks v. Long Branch Commission (1903), 69 N.J.L. 300, 54 A. 568; Casler v. Tanzer (1929), 234 N.Y.S. 571.

Sec. 578, Par. 2: Jefferson, Sec. III.

Sec. 578, Par. 3: Sturgis, pp. 126, 127.

Sec. 578, Par. 4: Sturgis, p. 27.

other matters requiring immediate attention, as long as the member does not transgress the rules.

6. It is not the right of the presiding officer to rule upon the constitutionality of bills as that authority belongs to the house.

Sec. 579. Selection of Presiding Officer

1. Under the constitutions of all the states, each house has the right to choose its own presiding officer, except in those cases where the presiding officer of the senate acts ex officio.

2. When the officer whose legal right and duty it is to preside over the meeting is necessarily or willfully absent or no provision has been made for a presiding officer, the members at the meeting are of necessity authorized to elect a temporary presiding officer from their members to conduct the deliberations.

3. When it is necessary for the presiding officer to vacate the chair, the president pro tempore, the speaker pro tempore or the vice chair should take the chair, and in the absence of the pro tempore or vice chair, the presiding officer next in order, if there be one.

4. Practice, based on convenience and courtesy, permits the appointment of another member by the presiding officer to act as a replacement when it is

Sec. 578, Par. 6: Hughes, Sec. 28; Cushing, Sec. 102.

Sec. 579, Par. 1: Cushing's Legislative Assemblies, Sec. 283.

Sec. 579, Par. 2: Billings v. Fielder (1882), 44 N.J.L. 381; Commonwealth v. Vandegrift (1911), 232 Pa. 53, 81 A. 153; Woodruff v. Stewart (1879), 63 Ala. 206; Mills v. Gleason (1860), 11 Wis. 493; Cockran v. McCleary (1867), 22 Iowa 75; Ostrom v. Greene (1897), 45 N.Y.S. 852.

Sec. 579, Par. 3: Reed, Secs. 36, 37; Cushing, Sec. 28.

necessary for the presiding officer to vacate the chair and there is no presiding officer pro tempore or vice chair present. The body can at any time terminate such an appointment by electing a presiding officer pro tempore. In any event, the right of a person so appointed to preside terminates with the next adjournment.

5. In houses of the state legislatures where the presiding officer serves ex officio, the houses appear to have the right to elect a presiding officer pro tempore. There can be no question as to this right when the presiding officer is elected by the house.

Sec. 580. Motions Affecting Presiding Officer

1. When a motion is made which complements the presiding officer with others, it may, as a matter of courtesy, be put to vote by a vice chair or a presiding officer pro tempore or by the secretary. The presiding officer should not hesitate to put a question or a motion to appoint a committee of which the presiding officer is to be a member or any motion of like purpose.

2. The presiding officer should leave the chair during the discussion of any business concerning the presiding officer. When a member is censured for use of improper references to the presiding officer, the presiding officer should leave the chair and call another to preside until any action is taken against the offender.

Sec. 579, Par. 4: Reed, Secs. 37–39.
Sec. 579, Par. 5: Cushing's Legislative Assemblies, Sec. 314.
Sec. 580, Par. 1: Sturgis, p. 164.
Sec. 580, Par. 2: Hughes, Secs. 74, 571.

3. Complaint of the conduct of the presiding officer should be presented directly for the action of the house and not by way of debate on other matters.

Sec. 581. Removal of Presiding Officer

1. A presiding officer who has been elected by the house may be removed by the house upon a majority vote of all the members elected, and a new presiding officer pro tempore elected and qualified.

2. When there is no fixed term of office, an officer holds office at the pleasure of the organization or until a successor is elected and qualified.

Sec. 582. Rights of Presiding Officer to Debate, Vote and Introduce Business

1. The presiding officer may speak to a point of order in preference to members or to other members. The presiding officer may also state facts, which are particularly within the presiding officer's knowledge, for the benefit of the body. The presiding officer should be seated during debate and may read or state a question seated, but should rise to put a question to vote, to decide a point of order, when speaking on an appeal or when otherwise addressing the body.

2. When the presiding officer is a member of the body, it is the presiding officer's privilege to call

---

Sec. 580, Par. 3: Jefferson, Sec. XVII.

Sec. 581, Par. 1: *In re* Speakership of the House of Representatives (1890), 15 Colo. 520, 25 P. 707; Jefferson, Sec. IX; Reed, Sec. 36; Malone v. Meekins (Alaska 1982), 650 P.2d 351.

Sec. 581, Par. 2: Ostrom v. Greene (1897), 45 N.Y.S. 852.

Sec. 582, Par. 1: Tilson, p. 58; U.S. House Rule I, Par. 5; Cushing, Sec. 202; Hughes, Secs. 48, 536; Demeter, p. 190.

another member to the chair and participate in debate without requesting permission of the body to do so.

3. When a member of the body, the presiding officer has the same right to explain a vote as other members. Also when permitted to vote only in case of a tie, the presiding officer may still give the reasons for a specific vote.

4. When a member of the body, the presiding officer is entitled to vote the same as any other member and may vote with the minority to produce a tie vote and thus defeat a motion.

5. When not a member of a legislative body, the presiding officer may vote only as authorized by the constitution, which usually gives the presiding officer a vote in the senate in case of a tie.

See also Sec. 513, Tie Votes and Casting Votes, and Sec. 514, When a Casting Vote Is in Order.

6. The presiding officer, when a member, retains the same rights as other members to introduce business but does not make motions from the chair.

Sec. 582, Par. 2: Hughes, Sec. 74; Reed, Sec. 40; Marsh v. Chambers (1983), 463 U.S. 783, 103 S. Ct. 3330, 77 L. Ed. 2d 1019.

Sec. 582, Par. 3: N.Y. Manual, p. 464.

Sec. 582, Par. 4: Cushing, Sec. 243b.

Sec. 582, Par. 5: Cushing, Sec. 243b; N.Y. Manual, p. 464; State of Montana *ex rel.* Easbey v. Highway Patrol Board (1960), 140 Mont. 383, 372 P.2d 930; Opinion of the Justices (1966), 225 A.2d 481; Advisory Opinion on Constitutionality of 1978 P.A. 426 (1978), 403 Mich. 631, 272 N.W.2d 495; Center Bank v. Department of Banking and Finance of State of Nebraska (1981), 210 Neb. 227, 313 N.W.2d 661.

Sec. 582, Par. 6: Hughes, Sec. 42.

CHAPTER 53

LEGISLATIVE OFFICERS

Sec. 584. Chief Legislative Officers

In most states the chief legislative officers are the secretary of the senate and the chief clerk of the house. In some states they are called "chief clerk" in the senate as well as the house.

General Duties

Duties of these officers vary widely from state to state. In many legislatures they are the chief administrative officers of each house, managing all staff and fiscal matters, as well as procedural matters. In others, they direct research, bill drafting, personnel and the sergeant at arms. In most, they are the publishers of the journals and calendars.

1. Almost universally, chief legislative officers manage the session proceedings and record-keeping of the legislature which includes the following specific duties:

(a) To keep, or supervise the keeping of, a correct journal and other records of the proceedings of the house.

(b) To call the roll.

(c) To read all bills, resolutions, amendments and other papers ordered read by the house or the presiding officer.

(d) To notify the other house of all acts of the house on all matters originating in the other house.

(e) To certify to and transmit to the other house all bills, resolutions and papers requiring the concurrence of the other house immediately upon their passage or adoption.

(f) To secure the proper authentication of bills of the chief legislative officer's house which have passed both houses and to see that they are transmitted to the executive.

(g) To have supervision over all clerical work to be done for the house and to supervise all employees.

2. The chief legislative officers have other similar duties depending upon the circumstances in each case. Their principal duties are usually stated in the rules and the chief legislative officers are always subject to the direction of the bodies they serve.

3. In the absence of the chief legislative officer, that officer's duties devolve upon the legislative officer next in rank or, in case of more than one assistant of the same rank, then upon the assistant first selected.

Custody of Records

4. The chief legislative officer must not permit any records or papers to be taken from the desk or from that officer's custody, except as required by the rules and except as such papers or records are necessary or appropriate to the work of a committee, in which case such papers may be placed in the custody of the chair or staff director of the committee.

Sec. 584, Par. 1: Tandy v. Hopkinsville (1917), 174 Ky. 189, 192 S.W. 46; Rouleau v. St. Lambert (1895), 10 Que. Super. 69; Hill v. Goodwin (1876), 56 N.H. 441; Cushing, Secs. 31–35; Reed, Sec. 43.

Sec. 584, Par. 3: Reed, Sec. 44.

Sec. 584, Par. 4: Jefferson, Sec. XVI; Cushing, Sec. 33.

5. All records of the house are open to inspection by any member at all reasonable times and any records or papers necessary or useful to a committee in the performance of its duties should be turned over to the chair or staff director of the committee upon request.

6. When a committee is appointed, the chief legislative officer should give to the chair or staff director of the committee, or other of its members, a list of the names of the members of the committee and all papers referred to it.

7. The chief legislative officer should receive and preserve reports of committees until they can be acted upon by the house, and it is not necessary to vote that a report be placed on file in order for reports of regular committees to be received by the chief legislative officer.

Correction of Reports

8. The rule that the same legislature may correct its journals so as to make them speak the truth, and that when corrected the journals will stand as if so originally made, is applicable to the amendment of legislative records.

9. The right of legislative bodies to amend records does not depend upon statutes but is an inherent right.

Sec. 584, Par. 5: Sturgis, p. 180.

Sec. 584, Par. 6: Sturgis, p. 180; Cushing, Sec. 272.

Sec. 584, Par. 7: Sturgis, p. 189.

Sec. 584, Par. 8: Richmond County Commissioners v. Farmers Bank (1910), 152 N.C. 387, 67 S.E. 969; Hughes, Sec. 82.

Sec. 584, Par. 9: People *ex rel.* Stewart v. Chicago M. & St. P. Railway Co. (1927), 326 Ill. 179, 145 N.E. 200.

10. It is the right of the secretary of the senate or the chief clerk of the house, without direction from the body, to correct any errors which may be discovered that have resulted from the work of the office of the senate secretary or the chief clerk of the house, and this right extends even to papers which have been sent to the other house.

Access to Records

11. Upon proper request, the chief legislative officer must make public records available for public inspection during normal business hours.

12. It is the duty of the chief legislative officer to ensure that public records are protected from deterioration, alteration, mutilation, loss, removal or destruction and are repaired, renovated or rebound as necessary.

Parliamentarian

13. Most legislative bodies have a parliamentarian and in many states the secretary of the senate or chief clerk of the house serves in that capacity. It is particularly advisable to have a parliamentarian when the presiding officer is not trained in parliamentary law and experienced in presiding over the body.

Sec. 584, Par. 10: Hughes, Sec. 82.

Sec. 584, Par. 11: Westinghouse Broadcasting Company, Inc. v. Sergeant at Arms of the General Court of Massachusetts (1978), 375 N.E.2d 1205; Nero v. Hyland (1978), 386 A.2d 846; Union Leader Corporation v. Chandler, Clerk of the New Hampshire House (1979), 402 A.2d 914; State of Florida v. Kaufman (1983), 430 So. 2d 904; Abercrombie v. The Senate, Regular Session of 1983, Twelfth State Legislature, State of Hawaii (May 23, 1983), No. 9451, Slip op.; Legislative Joint Auditing Committee v. Woosley (January 26, 1987), No. 86–140, Slip op.

Sec. 584, Par. 13: Sturgis, pp. 230–232.

14. It is the duty of the parliamentarian to advise and assist the presiding officer. The relationship is similar to that of an attorney and a client. The parliamentarian should be thoroughly trained in parliamentary law and in the rules, precedents and practices of the body and be a ready source of accurate information and advice for the presiding officer.

15. The parliamentarian serves as the presiding officer's adviser on matters of procedure. The parliamentarian's responsibility is to the presiding officer rather than the body. The parliamentarian works under the direction of the presiding officer and is an adviser only. The parliamentarian's advice can be disregarded by the presiding officer and the body.

16. The parliamentarian should unobtrusively call the attention of the presiding officer to serious errors in procedure. As far as possible, the parliamentarian should anticipate difficult parliamentary situations and keep the presiding officer advised of questions that may arise and of the rules and precedents or practices concerning those questions. The parliamentarian should be ready to give the presiding officer assistance in any matter requested by the presiding officer. The parliamentarian can, for example, if the presiding officer wishes, keep the presiding officer advised as to what committees are ready to report or what is the status of any particular business.

Sec. 584, Par. 14: Sturgis, pp. 230–232.
Sec. 584, Par. 15: Sturgis, pp. 230–232.
Sec. 584, Par. 16: Sturgis, pp. 230–232.

Sec. 585. Other Officers

1. *The Sergeant at Arms.* Most legislative bodies have a sergeant at arms, who is either elected or appointed. The sergeant at arms must, under the direction of the presiding officer, maintain order on the floor of the house, in the lobby and adjoining rooms and see that no person remains on the floor unless entitled to the privilege of the same and the sergeant at arms should be constantly in attendance during the sessions of the house except when absent in the discharge of duty.

2. *The Chaplain.* It is the general practice in the houses of the state legislatures to select a chaplain who attends each day and offers prayer at the beginning of each day's session.

3. *Clerks.* Some legislative bodies elect a minute clerk, an engrossing clerk and other officers and assistants, but in most legislatures these officers are appointed by and under the direction of the secretary of the senate or chief clerk of the house.

Sec. 586. Selection of Officers

1. It is an almost invariable rule in legislative bodies of the United States that the bodies have full authority concerning the selection of their officers. They can select their officers in the manner they choose and remove them at any time without notice or hearing. The constitutions provide that state legislatures shall select their own officers and usually

Sec. 585, Par. 1: U.S. House Rule IV and House Rule XIV, Par. 7; Reed, Sec. 47.

specify presiding officers, chief clerk of the house and secretary of the senate.

2. Officers of legislative bodies are usually qualified by taking an oath of office.

3. The authority of legislative officers expires with the authority of those from whom the authority was derived. It is usually required by statute or rules or precedent that the principal officers return at the next session and perform their duties until the houses are organized.

Sec. 587. Officers Are Responsible Only to Their House

See also Sec. 760, The Other House and Its Members.

1. The officers of a house are not officers of the members individually but of the entire house. They may be given orders only by the house through the presiding officer. The secretary or clerk and other officers are without authority to execute an order of an individual member that would in any way affect the entire house.

2. No officer has any right to interfere with the duties of another officer unless requested to do so by such officer or unless directed by a superior officer.

Sec. 586, Par. 1: Cliff v. Parson (1894), 90 Iowa 665, 57 N.W. 599; Cushing's Legislative Assemblies, Sec. 331.

Sec. 586, Par. 2: Cushing's Legislative Assemblies, Sec. 331.

Sec. 586, Par. 3: Cushing's Legislative Assemblies, Sec. 331; U.S. House Rule III, Note 637.

Sec. 587, Par. 1: Hughes, Sec. 83.

CHAPTER 54

SELECTION OF COMMITTEES

See also Ch. 48, Secs. 545–550, Nominations, and Ch. 49, Secs. 552–556, Elections.

Sec. 600. Manner of Selecting Committees

1. In the absence of any controlling provision, committees may be selected in any manner the body may determine.

2. The rules usually provide for the appointment of standing committees by the presiding officer. The usual method of appointing special committees is for a motion to be adopted stating the purpose of the committee, the number of members and directing the presiding officer to appoint the members.

3. A motion for the selection of a committee should always state the purpose of the committee, the number of members and the manner of their selection. When the motion does not specify the number of members, the number is left to the discretion of the presiding officer or persons selecting the members.

4. It is in order in a motion for a committee to name members proposed as the committee, and the adoption of such a motion constitutes the members named as the committee. A resolution of this type is subject to amendment.

Sec. 600, Par. 2: Hughes, Secs. 752, 754; Cushing, Sec. 266; Reed, Sec. 65.

Sec. 600, Par. 3: Hughes, Sec. 752.

Sec. 600, Par. 4: Reed, Secs. 64, 66; Hughes, Sec. 752.

5. Where different methods for the selection of a committee are proposed, the proposals are regarded as alternative propositions and put to vote in the following order:

(a) Nomination from floor and election.

(b) Nomination by committee and election.

(c) Nomination by presiding officer and election.

(d) Appointment by resolution.

(e) Appointment by presiding officer.

6. When different numbers of members of committees are proposed, the question should first be put to vote on the largest number, and then on the next largest until a particular number receives a majority vote.

7. When a committee is to be selected and no other method of selecting has been proposed, the body may proceed to nominate and elect the members, without a motion to that effect, in the same manner as any other election is conducted.

8. It is a general rule of parliamentary procedure that the appointing authority has the right to remove a chair or a committee member.

Sec. 600, Par. 5: Hughes, Secs. 750–753.
Sec. 600, Par. 6: Cushing, Sec. 264.
Sec. 600, Par. 7: Cushing, Sec. 265.

Sec. 601. Nomination of Members of Committees

See also Ch. 48, Secs. 545–550, Nominations, and Ch. 49, Secs. 552–556, Elections.

1. The members of a committee may be selected by nomination from the floor and formal election by the body in the same manner as any other election.

2. Another method of selecting a committee is for the presiding officer to suggest names, putting the question: "Shall these members constitute the committee?" and before a vote is taken on the group, it is in order to move to strike out names, and if any names are stricken out, to move the names of others to replace those so removed. This is in effect a confirmation of appointments by the presiding officer.

Sec. 602. Appointment by the Presiding Officer

1. When the presiding officer has been authorized to appoint a committee, no confirmation of the appointments is required. The presiding officer may delay the announcement of the appointments until a later time to take time to consider appointments and to consult with members if the presiding officer wishes; but the names of the committee members must be officially announced, and until the announcement is made, the committee is not formally appointed.

Sec. 601, Par. 1: Sturgis, p. 178; Reed, Sec. 67; Cushing, Sec. 268.
Sec. 601, Par. 2: Cushing, Sec. 268.
Sec. 602, Par. 1: Hughes, Sec. 753.

2. When a motion for the appointment of a special committee does not state the number of members to be appointed to the committee, the presiding officer may use personal discretion.

3. It is a common practice in some bodies, based on courtesy, to appoint the person making the motion for the appointment of a committee as chair of the committee if that person will accept the appointment. This practice is based on courtesy only, and it is not even necessary that the person making the motion for the committee should be appointed a member.

Sec. 602, Par. 2: Hughes, Sec. 752.
Sec. 602, Par. 3: Hughes, Sec. 762; Reed, Sec. 64.

CHAPTER 55

OFFICERS AND QUORUM OF COMMITTEES

Sec. 608. Selection of Committee Chairs and Vice Chairs

1. It is the usual practice for the authority appointing a committee to designate the chair and vice chair. When a committee is elected it is the proper procedure following the election to designate the chair by a motion.

2. The power to appoint a committee carries with it, if there is no rule to the contrary, the inherent power to appoint the chair or the vice chair of the committee. A chair and vice chair are usually designated by the appointing power.

Sec. 609. Acting Chair

See also Sec. 626, Calls for Committee Meetings.

When no chair has been designated, the committee has the right to select one of its members to be chair, but the first member appointed should in every case call the committee together and act until a chair has been elected by the committee. That person continues to act as chair unless the committee chooses a different chair. When the chair is not designated by the appointing power, if the first person named fails or refuses to call the committee together, the second

---

Sec. 608: Jefferson, Secs. XI, XII; Hughes, Sec. 761; N.Y. Manual, p. 325; Cushing, Sec. 273; Sturgis, p. 177; Cushing's Legislative Assemblies, Sec. 1910.

member appointed should act, and each member in succession may act in the absence, or refusal to act, of those appointed before.

Sec. 610. Resignation of Chair

The chair of a committee may resign as chair with the consent of the body and still retain membership on the committee. When the chair resigns, the presiding officer, if the presiding officer appointed the committee, may appoint another chair, or the committee may make its own selection and notify the body of its action.

Sec. 611. Duties of Committee Chairs

The principal duties of the chair of a committee are:

(a) To call the committee together to properly perform its functions.

(b) To preside over meetings of the committee and to put all questions.

(c) To maintain order and decide all questions of order subject to appeal.

(d) To supervise and direct the clerical staff and other employees of the committee.

(e) To prepare, or supervise the preparation of reports of the committee and submit the same to the body.

(f) To have custody of all papers referred to the committee, and to transmit them to the chief

---

Sec. 609: Jefferson, Sec. XI; Hughes, Sec. 763; Reed, Sec. 71.
Sec. 610: Hughes, Secs. 835, 845.

legislative officer of the house as required.

Sec. 612. Appointment or Election of Other Committee Officers

1. If not designated by an appointing authority, a committee has the authority by a majority vote to elect other committee officers.

2. If a regular secretary is not employed for the committee, it is customary to elect a secretary whose duties shall be to keep a record of the actions of the committee, to prepare reports and to perform other duties as shall be directed by the chair or the committee. In a small committee the chair may act as secretary.

Sec. 613. Quorum of Committees

See also Ch. 44, Secs. 500–506, Quorum, and Sec. 625, Committees Can Act Only When Properly Assembled.

Requirement of Quorum

1. The presence of a quorum is required in order for a committee to act legally and officially. A committee cannot legally transact business, and it is irregular to proceed to the consideration of business, in the absence of a quorum. The quorum of a committee must meet formally to transact business, and opinions of members of a committee cannot be taken separately, nor should a report be circulated securing signatures of a majority of the members of

---

Sec. 611: (a) Reed, Sec. 73, (b) Jefferson, Sec. XI; Hughes, Sec. 764; Reed, Sec. 73, (c) Hughes, Sec. 764, (d) Reed, Sec. 73, (e) Jefferson, Sec. XI, (f) Reed, Sec. 73.

Sec. 612, Par. 1: Jefferson, Sec. XI.

Sec. 612, Par. 2: Reed, Secs. 71, 73.

a committee and this report be submitted as a report of the committee.

What Constitutes a Quorum

2. The quorum of a committee is a majority of the members of the committee unless the rules of the body otherwise provide. A quorum of a committee may transact business and, unless provided by the rules, a majority of the quorum, even though it is a minority of the committee, may authorize a report.

3. Since a committee is an agency of the body, the body has authority to fix a quorum of the committee which may be more or less than a majority, or may fix the number necessary to take any official action.

Sec. 613, Par. 1: Jefferson, Sec. XXVI; Hughes, Sec. 765; Reed, Sec. 72; Cushing, Sec. 266; N.Y. Manual, p. 427.

Sec. 613, Par. 2: Jefferson, Sec. XXVI; Sturgis, p. 113; Hughes, Secs. 754, 772, 806; Reed, Sec. 72; Damon v. Grandy (1824), 19 Mass. 345; State of New Jersey v. Jersey City (1859), 27 N.J.L. 493; State of Missouri v. Reichmann (1911), 239 Mo. 81, 142 S.W. 304.

CHAPTER 56

POWERS OF LEGISLATIVE COMMITTEES

Sec. 615. Committees Are Agencies of the House

1. The method of performing a part of the work of a deliberative body through committees is not forbidden and has been sanctioned by judicial decisions.

2. A legislative body cannot delegate its powers to a committee, but when it ratifies the act of a committee in due form the act of the committee becomes the act of the body.

3. Committees are instruments or agencies of the body appointing them, and their function is to carry out the will of that body.

4. The functions of a legislative committee are purely advisory. All its acts are subject to review by

---

Sec. 615, Par. 1: Whitney v. City of New Haven (1890), 58 Conn. 450, 20 A. 666; Holland v. State of Florida (1887), 23 Fla. 123, 1 So. 521; Gillett v. Logan County (1873), 67 Ill. 256; Duncan v. The Board of Commissioners of Lawrence County (1884), 101 Ind. 403; Stewart v. Council Bluffs (1882), 58 Iowa 624, 12 N.W. 718; Keys v. Westford (Mass. 1835), 17 Pick. 273; *In re* Holman (1917), 270 Mo. 696, 195 S.W. 711; Burlington v. Denison (1880), 42 N.J.L. 165; Gilmore v. Utica (1892), 131 N.Y. 26, 29 N.E. 841; Commonwealth v. Pittsburgh (1850), 14 Pa. 177; Dancer v. Town of Mannington (1901), 50 W.Va. 322, 40 S.E. 475; State of Wisconsin v. Milwaukee (1914), 157 Wis. 505, 147 N.W. 50; Bullitt County v. Washer (1889), 130 N.S. 142.

Sec. 615, Par. 2: Milford Town School v. Powner (1891), 126 Ind. 528, 26 N.E. 484; Hannibal & St. Joseph R.R. v. Marion County (1865), 35 Mo. 294; Salmon v. Haynes (1887), 50 N.J.L. 97, 11 A. 151.

Sec. 615, Par. 3: Hughes, Sec. 751; Sturgis, p. 179; State of Louisiana *ex rel.* Guste v. Legislative Budget Committee (1977), 347 So. 2d 160.

the body and may be approved or rejected. Committee acts are recommendations only and except as especially authorized have no force until approved by the body.

5. A committee may make a report concerning any bill before it as it sees fit, but the body is not limited by the report and can take action as it chooses.

6. If authorized by the legislature, a committee may employ the necessary staff needed to accomplish its lawful purpose.

Sec. 616. Proposing Amendments to Bills

See also Sec. 669, Consideration of Committee Amendments.

1. A committee can only propose amendments to the bills referred to it and cannot actually amend or modify them. The sole power of the committee is to make recommendations to the body, and no recommendation becomes effective until adopted by the body.

2. A committee should never alter a bill or other document referred to it, but should submit any proposed amendments to the body on a separate paper.

3. It is within the power of a committee to which a bill has been referred to report it back with or without amendments. There is no limit to the number of amendments which may be made to a bill as long as the amendments are germane to the original

Sec. 615, Par. 4: Hughes, Secs. 751, 755.

Sec. 615, Par. 5: N.Y. Manual, p. 431; Cushing, Sec. 276.

Sec. 615, Par. 6: Terrell v. King (1929), 118 Tex. 237, 14 S.W.2d 786.

Sec. 616, Par. 1: N.Y. Manual, p. 405; Reed, Sec. 76; Jefferson, Sec. XXVI.

Sec. 616, Par. 2: Reed, Sec. 76; Cushing, Sec. 283.

purpose of the bill. Amendments may be so numerous as to amount to a substitution of the bill.

4. A committee has full power with reference to proposing amendments to measures submitted to it, except that it cannot change the subject. All amendments must be germane to the subject of the measure. The body may refuse to receive or consider amendments proposed by a committee which are not relevant to the general subject of the bill. A committee may properly propose any amendments within the general scope of the bill, and in case amendments are numerous, the committee may offer a substitute for the bill instead of a series of amendments to it.

5. If amendments are pending on a measure when referred to a committee, the amendments go with the bill to the committee and the committee may recommend concerning the adoption or rejection of the amendments already proposed and make such further recommendations and propose such other amendments as it may choose.

Sec. 617. Substitute Bills

See also Sec. 416, Consolidation and Substitution of Measures.

1. A committee may recommend that every clause in a bill be changed and that entirely new matter be substituted as long as the new matter is relevant to the title and subject of the original bill.

Sec. 616, Par. 3: State of Alabama v. Buckley (1875), 54 Ala. 599; Reitzammer v. Desha Road Improvement Dist. No. 2 (1919), 139 Ark. 168, 213 S.W. 773.

Sec. 616, Par. 4: Jefferson, Sec. XXVI; Hughes, Sec. 423; Reed, Sec. 77.

A substitute bill is considered as an amendment and not as a new bill.

2. The proper form of reporting a substitute bill by a committee is to propose amendments to strike out all of the bill following the enacting clause and to substitute the new bill, recommending also any necessary changes in the title.

Sec. 618. Introduction of Bills by Committee

1. Committees have authority to introduce bills respecting any matters referred to them and standing committees may introduce bills within their general scope.

2. Where the rules require that all bills be referred to committee, a bill which has been introduced by a committee is not required to be referred to a committee for further consideration.

Sec. 619. Committees Cannot Discipline Members

1. A committee has no power to punish its members for disorderly conduct, but may notify the body for its action.

2. The absence of members from committee meetings may be brought to the attention of the body.

Sec. 617, Par. 1: Hughes, Sec. 877; Cushing, Sec. 284.
Sec. 617, Par. 2: Hughes, Sec. 870.
Sec. 618, Par. 1: Hughes, Sec. 853.
Sec. 618, Par. 2: N.Y. Manual, p. 416.
Sec. 619, Par. 1: Cushing, Sec. 278.
Sec. 619, Par. 2: Hughes, Sec. 702.

3. When a committee is charged with an inquiry and finds that one of its members is involved, it cannot take any action against that member, but must make a special report to the body, which may take action concerning that person or give special authority to the committee to investigate concerning the member.

Sec. 620. Instructions to Committees

1. When a question is referred to committee it may be referred with instructions or without. The committee may be left without restrictions or may be partly or completely restricted. The rules usually contain instructions governing the consideration of bills in committee and their return to the houses.

2. When a committee receives specific instructions, they must be accurately carried out.

3. A particular section of a bill may not be referred to a committee, but the entire bill may be referred to the committee with instructions confining the consideration of the committee to a particular section or paragraph. When a bill is referred to a committee with instructions relating to a part only of the bill, the committee may not recommend with reference to other parts.

4. A motion to refer a bill to committee may be amended by adding instructions, and such instructions may also be amended as long as they are germane to the subject of the bill, unless amend-

---

Sec. 619, Par. 3: Jefferson, Sec. XI.
Sec. 620, Par. 1: Cushing, Sec. 75.
Sec. 620, Par. 2: Hughes, Sec. 859.
Sec. 620, Par. 3: Hughes, Secs. 863, 882.

ments or further amendments are prevented by the previous question.

Sec. 621. Papers and Information for Committees

1. The chief legislative officer should furnish the chair of the committee, or in the chair's absence, some other member of the committee with the notice of the appointment of the committee, the names of members, papers or other matters referred to it, and such instructions as may have been decided upon.

2. If a chair has not been designated or has not yet been elected by the committee, bills may be delivered by the officers to any member of the committee, but it is usual to deliver them to the first named on a committee.

3. All papers or books necessary for the information of a committee in the proper performance of its duties should be turned over to it by the legislative officers upon its request.

4. When the work of a committee has been completed, it is the duty of the chair to return to the chief legislative officer all documents or papers which were referred to it.

Sec. 620, Par. 4: Hughes, Secs. 857, 858.
Sec. 621: Jefferson, Sec. XXIII; Sturgis, p. 180.

Sec. 622. Committees Functioning During Recess or After Adjournment

See also Sec. 803, Right of Investigating Committees to Sit Between Sessions.

1. The courts have upheld the legislature's authority to empower committees to sit during the interim, and conduct public hearings, gather information and work on proposed legislation.

2. When there is no special authority for committees continuing to act after the adjournment of the current body, the committees still have the authority to make a report following adjournment of the session at which they were appointed. The constitutional provision limiting pay of members to a certain period does not deprive the legislature of the power to appoint committees to serve after the expiration of the session, to complete its records.

Sec. 622, Par. 1: State of Washington *ex rel.* Hamblen v. Yelle (1947), 29 Wash. 2d 68, 185 P.2d 723; State of Washington *ex rel.* Robinson v. Fluent (1948), 30 Wash. 2d 194, 191 P.2d 241, *cert. denied,* Washington Pension Union v. State of Washington *ex rel.* Robinson, 335 U.S. 844, 69 S. Ct. 66, 93 L. Ed. 394; Hagaman v. Andrews (1970), 232 So. 2d 1.

Sec. 622, Par. 2: Russell v. Cone (1925), 168 Ark. 989, 272 S.W. 678; Commercial and Farmers Bank v. Worth (1895), 117 N.C. 146, 23 S.E. 160; Marshall v. Harwood (1855), 7 Md. 466.

CHAPTER 57

COMMITTEE MEETINGS

Sec. 625. Committees Can Act Only When Properly Assembled

1. A committee can act only at a meeting and not by separate consultation and consent, and a committee has no authority to report anything not agreed upon when actually assembled. Everything done by a committee must have been submitted to the committee in actual session, and an opportunity must have been given for consideration and discussion. Any exception to this rule should not be recognized unless clearly authorized by the rules.

2. When no meeting of a committee has been held, a report of the committee cannot properly be presented to the body. It is irregular for a committee to report on any matter which has not been considered by it in a formal meeting and the report authorized. The presiding officer should reject any report which has not been considered in committee.

3. An action formally taken by a committee cannot be altered thereafter by a committee or its members except by further formal action of the committee.

Sec. 626. Calls for Committee Meetings

See also Sec. 609, Acting Chair.

Sec. 625, Par. 1: Jefferson, Secs. XI, XXVI; Hughes, Sec. 765; N.Y. Manual, p. 427; Reed, Sec. 79; Cushing, Sec. 276.

Sec. 625, Par. 2: Hughes, Sec. 765; N.Y. Manual, p. 428.

Sec. 625, Par. 3: Jefferson, Sec. XXVI.

1. A committee should meet at the time and place officially set for its meetings when a time and place has been provided, but when no regular time or place has been provided, it may meet at such times and places as its members may decide.

2. When a meeting is called for a specific time but the meeting does not commence until a later time, the delay does not invalidate the meeting. However, when a meeting is called for a specific time and the meeting commences prior to that, business transacted before the scheduled time may be declared void and of no effect.

3. When a regular time and place is fixed for a committee meeting, the chair may, after consultation with and upon the consent of a majority of the members, change the time of the meeting in extraordinary cases.

4. It is the duty of the chair to call the committee together, but if the chair is absent or neglects or declines to call a meeting of the committee, a meeting may be held on the call of the majority of its members.

5. A special notice of a recessed committee meeting is not necessary if the meeting involves a continuation of the original meeting and resumes on the same day or before the passage of a specified period of time.

Sec. 626, Par. 1: Jefferson, Sec. XXVI; N.Y. Manual, p. 427; Cushing, Secs. 274–277; Reed, Sec. 70.

Sec. 626, Par. 2: North v. Cary (1874), 4 N.Y. 357; People v. Albany etc. Railroad Co. (N.Y. 1869), 1 Lans. 308, 55 Barb. 344.

Sec. 626, Par. 3: Hughes, Sec. 745.

Sec. 626, Par. 4: Hughes, Sec. 745.

Sec. 626, Par. 5: Hughes, Sec. 743.

6. When committees adjourn without provision for future meetings, they adjourn subject to call of the chair.

Sec. 627. Special Meetings

1. A special committee meeting is one called to transact definite specified business and in this particular differs from a regular or adjourned meeting.

2. When a special committee meeting is called, notice of the meeting must be given to each member.

3. Business to be transacted at a special committee meeting must be set out in the call for the meeting and no business is in order except as specified in the call.

Sec. 628. Committee Meetings While House Is in Session

1. Committees, except conference committees, may not meet during the sessions of the house without the consent of the house. To secure consent, the chair of the committee should present a motion requesting the consent.

2. Whenever the house goes into session, it is the duty of a committee, upon receiving notice, to immediately discontinue its meetings, and attend in the house. Committees may not continue in session when the time for convening of the house has arrived.

3. Legislative committees, in the absence of a special authority, can act only while the legislature is

---

Sec. 627: Hughes, Sec. 744.

Sec. 628, Par. 1: Hughes, Sec. 817.

Sec. 628, Par. 2: Jefferson, Sec. XI; Hughes, Sec. 875; Reed, Sec. 70; Cushing, Sec. 275.

in session, but it is within the power of a legislature, in the absence of constitutional restrictions, to appoint committees to sit after adjournment.

Sec. 629. Attendance of Members at Committee Meetings

1. Any member of a legislative body has the right, ordinarily, to be present at committee meetings and to express an opinion, but the member cannot vote and must give way to any member of the committee. Committee meetings are generally open to persons who are interested in the business before the committee and to the press and the public.

2. The general rule is that a committee cannot exclude other members of the body from its deliberations. Unless the practice of committees to hold closed or secret sessions is clearly established, the committee should secure the definite authority from the legislative body whenever it desires to hold closed sessions.

Sec. 630. Committee Meetings Open to the Public

Historically it was quite common for committees to hold some meetings in private, without notice.

Sec. 628, Par. 3: Russell v. Cone (1925), 168 Ark. 989, 272 S.W. 678; Fergus v. Russel (1915), 270 Ill. 304, 110 N.E. 130; Branham v. Lange (1861), 16 Ind. 497; Marshall v. Harwood (1855), 7 Md. 466; Commercial and Farmers Bank v. Worth (1895), 117 N.C. 146, 23 S.E. 160; *Ex parte* Caldwell (1906), 61 W.Va. 49, 55 S.E. 910.

Sec. 629, Par. 1: Jefferson, Sec. XXVI; Reed, Sec. 78; Hughes, Sec. 810.

Sec. 629, Par. 2: Hughes, Sec. 846; Sturgis, p. 182; Reed, Sec. 78, states that a committee has authority to exclude all but members of the committee.

Most states now have provisions in their constitutions, statutes or rules which require legislative committee meetings to be open to all members and the public, subject to public notice, except when considering certain strictly specified subjects where secrecy is required.

Sec. 630: Coggin v. Davey (1975), 233 Ga. 407, 211 S.E.2d 708; Moffitt v. Willis (Fla. 1984), 459 So. 2d 1018.

CHAPTER 58

PROCEDURE IN COMMITTEES

Sec. 632. Committee Procedure Less Formal

1. The rules of procedure in the committee are the same as the rules of the body insofar as such rules are applicable to committee procedure. But insofar as the conditions permit, the rules limiting debate should be relaxed in order to give free discussion and not to handicap the work of the committee. The principal rules which are thus not vigorously enforced are the following:

(a) That no motions to close or limit debate are allowed.

(b) That it is not necessary to arise and address the body before making a motion.

(c) That the chair does not rise to put a question.

(d) That the chair does not leave the chair to speak or to make motions.

(e) That motions are not required to be seconded even though this requirement may still be retained by the body.

(f) That a member may speak more than once at the same stage of consideration of a question.

2. Committee members cannot appeal to the presiding officer of the full body any decisions on points of order made by the committee chair.

Sec. 632, Par. 1: Hughes, Sec. 780; N.Y. Manual, p. 428; Reed, Sec. 74; Cushing, Sec. 279.

Sec. 632, Par. 2: Hughes, Sec. 764.

Sec. 633. Order of Consideration of Measures

1. It is customary for a committee to take up business referred to it in the order in which it was referred unless a schedule of hearings has been prepared, but measures may, upon motion or upon general consent, be taken up out of order.

2. The business of committees can be expedited by the chair preparing a schedule of measures to be heard and giving notice some time in advance.

Sec. 634. Manner of Considering Measures

1. The usual manner of considering a paper of any kind in committee, when copies are not available for the members, is for the chair to read the paper by sections or paragraphs and give opportunity for discussion and amendment of each section before proceeding to the next. When measures are considered in this manner, the question is not put on each section separately, unless a division is requested, but reserved until the paper is completed and the question is put on the whole document.

2. In a committee all questions must be put to a vote unless agreed to by general consent.

Sec. 635. Reconsideration by Committee

1. A legislative committee has a right to reconsider any action taken by it as long as the subject matter remains in the possession of the committee.

Sec. 633: Hughes, Sec. 780.
Sec. 634, Par. 1: Reed, Sec. 74.
Sec. 635, Par. 1: Hughes, Sec. 878.

2. Reconsideration in a committee is generally subject to the same rules as in the body. The principal variations are that even when there is a time limit on the motion to reconsider in the main body a reconsideration can be moved at any time while the matter still remains before the committee, and that a reconsideration may be moved by any member, even though that person was absent when the vote was taken.

Sec. 636. Authority of Committee with Reference to Measures

1. Where a paper or document is referred to a committee, no action considering or proposing the whole need be taken, because the document already stands as a measure before the body. The sole authority of the committee with reference to such measures is to propose such changes as the committee desires to recommend, and to make its recommendation concerning the action to be taken on the measure by the body.

2. If a committee is opposed to the whole bill or document, it cannot reject it, but should report it back to the body. The measure may be reported without recommendation or the committee may recommend the disapproval of the measure. The committee may, of course, propose to the body any change by amendment as long as the amendments are germane to the subject of the measure.

3. The practice of preventing the passage of measures by leaving them in committee without taking

Sec. 636, Par. 1: Jefferson, Sec. XXVI.
Sec. 636, Par. 2: Jefferson, Sec. XXVI.

action on them, or laying them on the table in committee, is well established in some legislatures.

Sec. 637. Recessing and Adjournment of Committee Meetings

1. A regular or special committee meeting may be recessed but never beyond the time for the next regular meeting. If a recessed meeting does not complete its business, it may recess again to a time not beyond the next regular meeting, and any business that might be conducted at the regular meeting may be conducted at the recessed meeting.

2. All committees, upon the completion of the regular business of the meeting, should be adjourned upon motion or on general consent.

3. The motion to rise is never used in standing committees except when the work of the committee is completed and the committee will not meet again. This motion in a committee is equivalent to the motion to adjourn sine die in the house.

Sec. 636, Par. 3: Hughes, Sec. 880.
Sec. 637, Par. 1: Hughes, Sec. 743.
Sec. 637, Par. 2: Hughes, Sec. 745.

CHAPTER 59

SPECIAL OR SELECT COMMITTEES

Sec. 640. Membership of Special Committees

1. As a matter of policy, a committee for action should be small and consist only of those in favor of the proposed action, and if one not at sympathy is appointed, that person should ask to be released.

2. A committee for deliberation or investigation should represent all the important factions in the body, so that its opinion will carry as great weight as possible. Such a committee should also consist of representatives on both sides of a question, where there is a clear division, as the committee will also be subject to charges of bias if any important faction is not represented.

3. Where a committee is appointed to study some particular measure or matter, persons opposed to the whole project should not be appointed, for such persons may attempt to destroy the matter referred to the committee, rather than to place it in condition to be better considered by the body.

Sec. 640, Par. 1: Sturgis, pp. 176, 177.
Sec. 640, Par. 2: Sturgis, p. 177; Reed, Sec. 69.
Sec. 640, Par. 3: Jefferson, Sec. XXVI.

Sec. 641. Instructions to Special Committees

See also Sec. 620, Instructions to Committees.

1. Instructions to a special committee may be agreed to or stated before the vote is taken on the motion to commit or they may be given afterwards.

2. Even after a select committee has been chosen, it is in order to move to discharge the order referring the subject matter and thereafter to appoint a different committee with different instructions.

Sec. 642. Meeting of Special Committees

See also Ch. 57, Secs. 625–630, Committee Meetings.

A meeting of a special committee may be called at any time by the chair or by a majority of the members of the committee by notifying every member of the meeting. When a special committee adjourns or recesses to meet at another time, it is advisable, though not necessary, that absent members be notified of the adjourned or recessed meeting. When a special committee adjourns or recesses without fixing a time for the next meeting, it is regarded as having adjourned or recessed at the call of the chair.

Sec. 643. Procedure in Special Committees

See also Ch. 58, Secs. 632–637, Procedure in Committees.

1. Procedure in special committees is the same in all important particulars as procedure in standing committees.

Sec. 641: Hughes, Sec. 752; Cushing's Legislative Assemblies, Secs. 2161–2166.

Sec. 642: Cushing's Legislative Assemblies, Secs. 1895–1899; Hughes, Sec. 752.

2. Most of the routine consideration of bills is done by standing committees, but the matters which require some special consideration are often referred to special or select committees. The selection of special committees, therefore, differs from that of standing committees, and because of the different nature of their duties they have no regular meetings, and when their special work is completed they are discharged. Their reports, usually on special matters, receive special consideration, while the recommendations of standing committees on bills accompany the bills to second and third readings without the reports themselves receiving any separate consideration.

Sec. 644. Reports of Special Committees

When a report by a special committee on some special question is received, it may require special consideration. When such a report has been received from committee and presented to the body, the next business is the appropriate disposition of the report. This depends largely on the nature of the report and the urgency of the matter reported. When there is no special urgency the report may be placed on calendar for consideration in the usual course.

Sec. 645. Discharge or Dissolution of Special Committees

1. When a special committee is appointed for a special purpose, it continues to exist until the purpose assigned to it has been fulfilled, unless sooner discharged. When the final or complete report of a special or select committee has been received by the

house, the committee is thereby dissolved or ceases to exist without any motion to that effect being made. When the report is only partial, the committee is not discharged until the final report is received.

2. A special or select committee may be dissolved by discharging or rescinding the order or motion providing for it.

3. A special or select committee which has expired is revived by a vote or by the reference of any matter to it.

4. A special committee expires at the end of a session of the legislature unless continued by resolution.

5. When a committee is discharged, the chair should promptly return to the secretary or chief clerk all papers that have been entrusted to the committee.

Sec. 646. Appointment Should Immediately Follow Reference

It is in order to refer a matter to a committee not yet appointed. When a motion to refer a matter to a special committee is adopted, the committee should be selected as promptly thereafter as is reasonably possible.

Sec. 645, Par. 1: Keys v. Westford (Mass. 1835), 17 Pick. 273; Jefferson, Sec. XXVII; Hughes, Sec. 760; Reed, Sec. 85; Cushing, Secs. 290, 291.

Sec. 645, Par. 2: Hughes, Sec. 758.

Sec. 645, Par. 3: Jefferson, Sec. XXVI; Hughes, Secs. 759, 760; Cushing, Sec. 290.

Sec. 645, Par. 4: Hughes, Sec. 759.

CHAPTER 60

SUBCOMMITTEES

Sec. 650. Appointment, Powers, Etc. of Subcommittees

1. Any committee, except a committee of the whole, may appoint a subcommittee. The subcommittee can make such investigation or exercise such authority of the committee as may be delegated to it by the committee. A subcommittee reports to the committee from which it was appointed and not to the house. A subcommittee can consist only of members of the committee from which appointed.

2. In cases demanding special investigation or inquiry, it is proper for a committee to appoint subcommittees, referring certain matters to their particular consideration, and to receive and consider the reports of the subcommittees.

3. A special investigation committee may not delegate its powers to any of its members, except as may be authorized by the house.

4. It is also proper for a legislative body to divide committees into subcommittees and to give certain power directly to subcommittees.

Sec. 650, Par. 1: Hughes, Sec. 813.

Sec. 650, Par. 2: Hughes, Sec. 812.

Sec. 650, Par. 3: *In re* Leach (1922), 232 N.Y. 600, 19 N.Y.S. 135, 134 N.E. 588.

Sec. 650, Par. 4: Hughes, Sec. 841.

CHAPTER 61

JOINT COMMITTEES

See also Sec. 764, Conferences Between the Houses, and Ch. 71, Secs. 766–775, Conferences Concerning Amendments.

Sec. 653. Joint Committees Defined

A joint committee is a committee made up of committees appointed by each house.

Sec. 654. Chairs of Joint Committees

In the absence of a designation by the appointing authority, a joint committee has the right to select its own chair.

Sec. 655. Quorum of Joint Committees

See also Sec. 502, paragraph 5, for quorum of joint meetings, and Sec. 658, Voting in Joint Committees.

A quorum of a joint committee is a majority of its combined membership and when a quorum is present, a majority of that quorum is capable of transacting business. The quorum of a committee on conference is a quorum of the committees of each house.

Sec. 653: Cushing's Legislative Assemblies, Sec. 2043; Hughes, Sec. 747; Reed, Secs. 62, 238.

Sec. 654: Hughes, Sec. 747.

Sec. 655: Hughes, Sec. 747.

Sec. 656. Instructions to Joint Committees

See also Sec. 620, Instructions to Committees.

A joint committee may be instructed by either house acting independently or both houses acting concurrently.

Sec. 657. Reports of Joint Committees

The report of a joint committee should be made to each house by the members of the house represented on the committee.

Sec. 658. Voting in Joint Committees

In voting in joint committees, except in conference committees, the members vote individually and not by houses. Conference committees are in fact joint meetings of separate committees; consequently, in conference committees, the committees from each house vote separately, and a majority vote of each committee is required to take any action.

Sec. 659. Joint Meetings of Standing Committees

A house may authorize or direct two standing committees to sit as one committee for the consideration of a specified bill or subject.

Sec. 656: Hughes, Sec. 864.
Sec. 657: Hughes, Sec. 856.
Sec. 658: Hughes, Sec. 747.
Sec. 659: Hughes, Sec. 839.

CHAPTER 62

COMMITTEE REPORTS

Sec. 663. Preparation of Committee Reports

1. In other than simple, routine reports, when the general nature of the report to be made has been agreed upon, some member of the committee should be directed to prepare the report. No one has authority to make a report for a committee except as authorized by the committee.

2. Usually the committee chair prepares a draft of the report and submits it for approval by the full committee. The chair is never justified in making a report which has not been approved by the committee.

Sec. 664. Form of Committee Reports

1. Every bill reported by a committee must be accompanied by a written report. The bill should be returned with its report but should not be permanently attached to it.

2. A committee should report only such recommendations as have been agreed upon by a majority vote at a meeting to which all members were invited, and at which a quorum was present.

3. A committee report should make distinct recommendations concerning each bill or question reported by it.

Sec. 663: Hughes, Secs. 764–770; Sturgis, pp. 185–189; Reed, Sec. 80.
Sec. 664: Hughes, Secs. 772, 773, 820, 825–833; Reed, Sec. 76; Sturgis, pp. 185, 186.

4. When a committee is unable to reach agreement on a bill, it may report the bill back without recommendation.

5. When a bill is referred to a committee with amendment(s), the committee should make a recommendation on the amendment. But when a motion to postpone consideration indefinitely is pending, it may be regarded as defeated by the reference and so may be ignored.

6. When resolutions are required to carry into effect the recommendations of a committee on matters submitted to it, the appropriate resolutions should be prepared by the committee and submitted with its report.

7. A committee report does not necessarily contain a recommendation but may simply report facts.

8. The report of a committee appointed to investigate or report upon any matter should be accompanied by formal resolutions covering all recommendations concerning the matter referred to it, so that when the report is made, no motion is necessary except to adopt the resolutions.

Sec. 665. Authentication of Committee Reports

1. Committee reports must be authorized by a majority of a quorum meeting as a committee, but it is not necessary that the report be signed by all members agreeing to it.

2. In cases where the rules require that a majority of the members of a committee sign the report,

Sec. 665, Par. 1: Hughes, Sec. 771; Reed, Sec. 79.

the signatures of members not in agreement with the report may not be questioned.

3. If a committee report be sustained by a majority vote of a committee, it is not impeached by the fact that a lesser number signed or that more than a majority of a committee signed a further or different report.

4. A member's signature may not be withdrawn from a committee report which that member has regularly signed, since the signing of a report is the act of the committee itself and not of the members with the consent of the committee.

Sec. 666. Presentation of Committee Reports

1. In general practice, committees on enrollment, engrossment, calendar or rules and committees on conference may report at any time when no other business is pending. All other committees should report at the proper place in the order of business.

2. Under the appropriate order of business, reports of committees are presented when called for by the presiding officer. When called upon, the chair of the committee, unless another member is appointed to make the report, rises and addresses the presiding officer, and when recognized, reads the report and sends or delivers it to the desk, and when necessary, moves its adoption or acceptance. Currently, in most states, the committee report is sub-

Sec. 665, Par. 2: Hughes, Sec. 780.
Sec. 665, Par. 3: Hughes, Sec. 800.
Sec. 665, Par. 4: Hughes, Sec. 883.
Sec. 666: Hughes, Secs. 820, 856, 861, 869; Cushing, Secs. 287, 289; Reed, Secs. 63, 80; Sturgis, p. 187.

mitted to the secretary or clerk for reading or publication under the proper order of business.

3. If it is desired to receive a report earlier than the rules provide, it can be done by unanimous consent or by suspending the rules.

4. The right given to a committee to report at any time carries with it the right to consider the matter when reported.

5. Committee reports are sometimes received out of order by unanimous consent or by suspension of the rules. When a bill is so reported, it may be taken up for immediate consideration without a motion to that effect.

6. The report of a joint committee should be made to each house by the members of the house represented on the committee.

Sec. 667. Committee Recommendations Concerning Bills

The regular reports of committees, particularly the reports of standing committees concerning bills referred to them, usually follow a simple routine. The reports, after being received from the committee with the bills, are read under the appropriate order of business and the bills are ordered to second reading where any amendments proposed by the committee shall be considered. Any other amendments may be proposed on second reading. From second reading the bills are ordered to engrossment and third reading where the question of passage is considered. The reports of the committees as such receive no special or independent consideration, but

Sec. 666, Par. 6: Hughes, Sec. 856.

the recommendation of amendments proposed by committees are considered on second reading. The recommendation concerning passage is considered when the bills receive consideration on third reading.

Sec. 668. Amendments Proposed by Committees

See also Ch. 38, Secs. 395–421, Motion to Amend, and Sec. 404, Amendment of Bills by Committees.

1. Amendments proposed by a committee are not binding on a legislative body in any sense but are recommendations. The body may adopt or reject any or all of the amendments and may add other amendments or take such other action as it may choose.

2. When committee amendments are presented it is in order to offer amendments to such amendments, or to offer other amendments. However, amendments proposed by the committee are given priority consideration.

3. The previous question may be ordered on amendments submitted by a committee and thus prevent the submission of further amendments as well as prevent debate or motions concerning the amendments submitted by the committee.

Sec. 669. Consideration of Committee Amendments

See also Sec. 616, Proposing Amendments to Bills; Sec. 617, Substitute Bills; and Ch. 38, Secs. 395–421, Motion to Amend.

Sec. 668, Par. 1: Jefferson, Sec. XI; Hughes, Sec. 797; N.Y. Manual, p. 431; Reed, Sec. 81.

Sec. 668, Par. 2: Hughes, Sec. 795; Reed, Sec. 84.

Sec. 668, Par. 3: Hughes, Sec. 795.

1. When a committee reports back a bill or resolution previously referred to it, with amendments, the amendments proposed by the committee may be treated in the same manner as if proposed from the floor. The first question should be on the adoption of the amendments of the committee followed by amendments from the floor and the final question being on the passage of the bill or adoption of the resolution. The offering of any amendments can, of course, be prevented by the adoption of the previous question.

2. The question may be put on the adoption of all amendments proposed by a committee to a measure, at the same time, unless a separate vote is ordered on any amendment or group of amendments.

Sec. 670. Consideration of Committee Reports

1. The report of a committee consists only of recommendations and has no force or effect until agreed to by the house.

2. When the report of a committee is agreed to, the recommendation of the committee becomes the action of the house.

3. When a committee report is agreed to, if any motions are necessary to carry out the purpose of the report, they should be submitted immediately.

4. When the house desires more time to consider a committee report, it is in order to move that

Sec. 669, Par. 1: Sturgis, pp. 187, 188.

Sec. 670: Jefferson, Sec. XI; Hughes, Secs. 795–799; N.Y. Manual, pp. 421, 488; Reed, Secs. 80–83; Sturgis, p. 187.

further consideration be postponed until a later time.

5. It is the usual procedure not to consider bills reported by committees when the report is received by the house, but to order the bill to second reading. The bill and the recommendation of the committee is considered when the bill comes up for second or third reading.

6. The action of the house in considering committee recommendations on measures is always directed to the bill or resolution, as, to adopt amendments or to pass the bill; and the action of the house is not directed to accepting or approving the report of the committee, except in the case of adopting reports of conference committees.

7. Members of a special committee may vote on the question of receiving their own report.

Sec. 671. Presenting Committee Recommendations

When a report contains recommendations, they should be summarized at the end so that they may be conveniently given special or separate consideration. When the committee proposes that some action be taken by the legislative body, the proper resolutions should be prepared and submitted with the report. The proper procedure is for the member making the report to move the adoption of the resolutions. When the body desires to approve these recommendations, the proper motion is to adopt the recommendations.

Sec. 671: Sturgis, p. 187; Cushing, Secs. 294–296.

Sec. 672. Reports of Committees for Information

1. When a report contains only a statement of facts or a statement for the information of the body, no action is necessary. In such cases, it is usually received and the presiding officer may order it filed or printed in the journal without a motion to that effect.

2. Where a partial report is received which reports progress only and does not contain any recommendations, it is treated the same as a report for information only.

3. The report of a nominating committee does not require any action or other consideration by the body, but the nominations upon receipt of the report are treated as if they had been made by members from the floor.

See also Ch. 48, Secs. 545–550, Nominations.

Sec. 673. Motion to "Adopt" Committee Reports

1. When a report makes any statement of policy which the body desires to approve, the proper motion is to "adopt" or "approve" the report, which has the effect of endorsing the statement or expressing its approval by the body.

2. When the body desires to take no action on the report, the motion should not be made to "accept" the report, as this motion has the effect of expressing approval or endorsing the findings or recommendations.

Sec. 673: Sturgis, p. 188; Hughes, Secs. 134, 676.

3. It is in order for the presiding officer, upon the consideration of a report or recommendation made by a committee, to put the question on adoption of the report, amendment, or substitution, without waiting for a motion from the floor. The report of the committee may be regarded as proposing any matter to the body which is contained or recommended in the report.

Sec. 674. Minority Committee Reports

1. The receipt of a minority report of a committee is a mere matter of courtesy, as the report must be made by the committee as such, and no minority need be officially recognized. It is customary to permit the minority to submit a report following the submission of the regular committee report.

2. The minority members of a committee may, collectively or individually, present views with the committee report. However, unless they are filed with the report, they may be presented only by consent of the body.

3. It is proper for a single member to dissent from the report of the majority or to agree to the report with certain exceptions.

4. A member of a committee who does not agree with the report may be permitted to state that person's views following the filing of the committee report.

5. A minority of a committee may, with permission, submit a report in which those members make recommendations opposed to all or part of the rec-

Sec. 674, Par. 1: Hughes, Secs. 787–789; N.Y. Manual, pp. 428, 485; Reed, Sec. 75; Sturgis, p. 189.

ommendations of the majority, or they may make recommendations concerning matters within the consideration of the committee which were not covered by the majority report.

6. A regular committee report or a minority report may be laid on the table without the other report adhering to or being affected by the action.

Sec. 675. Improper Committee Reports

1. It is not in order for a committee to report a bill or other matter which was not considered at a regular committee meeting. It is the duty of the presiding officer to refuse to accept any report on a bill or other question when the presiding officer has knowledge that it was not considered and acted upon at a regular meeting.

2. A committee consists of a quorum of the membership of that committee meeting together as a committee. A paper circulated and signed by a majority of the members of the committee reporting a bill or authorizing a certain committee action to be taken, in the absence of a rule authorizing that procedure, is ineffective and cannot be regarded as a report of the committee because a committee can act only when convened as such.

3. A bill not properly reported from a committee is not entitled to its place on the calendar and should be referred back to the committee.

Sec. 675, Par. 1: Hughes, Sec. 815.
Sec. 675, Par. 2: Hughes, Secs. 741, 742.
Sec. 675, Par. 3: Hughes, Sec. 798.

Sec. 676. Questioning Validity of Committee Reports

1. Neither the right of a committee to consider and report a bill, nor the validity of any action reported by a committee may be questioned after the house has begun its consideration of the bill or other matter reported.

2. If a question is raised concerning whether a committee report is sufficient, or has been properly authorized, the question should be submitted to the body itself for a decision rather than being decided by the presiding officer.

3. After the report on a bill has been filed and the bill is no longer in the possession of the committee, the committee has no authority to present a supplemental report.

Sec. 677. Records of Actions in Committees

1. It is not in order for minutes of the meetings of a committee to be produced in the body and made public, but the chair may make a statement regarding action taken on a pending bill.

2. It is not in order in debate to refer to proceedings of a committee unless the committee has formally reported its proceedings. Members may not allude to, nor relate in debate, what was done or said in committee, or by any members of the committee, except such as is contained in the written report made to the body by authority of the committee.

Sec. 677, Par. 1: Reed, Sec. 51; Hughes, Secs. 694, 748.

Sec. 677, Par. 2: Hughes, Secs. 694, 850.

3. No member of a committee nor any other person has a right to publish any portion of the proceedings of a committee that is not public until it has been reported by the committee to the body. Any publication of a committee report before it is presented to the body is a breach of the privilege of the body.

4. The ancient rule that committees must report all matters referred to them back to the body is treated with such laxity as to standing committees that its observance is almost obsolete. In Congress, the motion to indefinitely postpone is permitted in standing and select committees.

Sec. 678. Substitute Measures Proposed by Committee

When a committee recommends a substitute resolution, the question must first be put on any amendments pending when the resolution was referred to the committee. Opportunity should be given for amendment to both the original measure and the substitution proposed by the committee before the question on the substitution is put, because if the substitute measure is adopted, it is not subject to further amendment.

Sec. 677, Par. 3: Hughes, Sec. 850.
Sec. 677, Par. 4: Hughes, Sec. 880.
Sec. 678: Hughes, Secs. 134, 795.

CHAPTER 63

COMMITTEE OF THE WHOLE AND INFORMAL CONSIDERATION

Sec. 683. Purpose of Committee of the Whole

The purpose of the committee of the whole is to permit more free and informal discussion of any question than could be had in a deliberative body acting under its ordinary rules of procedure.

Sec. 684. Chair of Committee of the Whole

1. When the house resolves itself to the committee of the whole, the presiding officer may appoint a chair of the committee and leave the chair. When a member, the presiding officer may join the other members.

2. The appointment of the chair of the committee of the whole by the presiding officer is usually accepted.

3. If a message to the house is announced during a committee of the whole, the presiding officer takes the chair and receives the message, relinquishing the meeting again to the chair of the committee of the whole.

4. The secretary or clerk does not record in the minutes the proceedings of the committee of the

Sec. 684, Par. 1: Jefferson, Sec. XII; Cushing, Secs. 297, 298; Reed, Sec. 87.

Sec. 684, Par. 2: Jefferson, Sec. XII; Reed, Sec. 87.

Sec. 684, Par. 3: Jefferson, Sec. XII.

whole, but should keep a record of the proceedings for the use of the committee.

5. In case of disorder in committee of the whole, the presiding officer of the house may resume the chair without formality, and after the disturbance subsides, may again relinquish the meeting to the chair of the committee of the whole.

Sec. 685. Going into Committee of the Whole

1. When it is desired to go into the committee of the whole, the motion is made "that the senate (or house) do now resolve itself into a committee of the whole to consider," or "for the purpose of considering," the subject which it is desired to consider more freely.

2. The motion to resolve into a committee of the whole is equivalent to the motion to commit and takes precedence in the same order.

Sec. 686. Quorum of Committee of the Whole

1. The quorum of the committee of the whole is the same as the quorum of the house, and in case a quorum is not present or other defect is observed, the committee can take no other action than to rise.

2. A motion to rise may be carried by less than a quorum in committee of the whole.

Sec. 684, Par. 4: Cushing, Sec. 301; Reed, Sec. 88.

Sec. 684, Par. 5: N.Y. Manual, p. 433; Cushing, Sec. 300a.

Sec. 685: Cushing, Sec. 297.

Sec. 686, Par. 1: Jefferson, Sec. XII; Cushing's Legislative Assemblies, Sec. 1995; Reed, Secs. 18, 89; Cushing, Sec. 299.

Sec. 686, Par. 2: Hughes, Sec. 651.

Sec. 687. Procedure in Committee of the Whole

See also Ch. 58, Secs. 632–637, Procedure in Committees.

1. Except for the greater leeway offered for debate and discussion, the procedure in committee of the whole is subject to the same rules as the house. The rules of the house should be observed so far as they are applicable.

2. After resolving into committee of the whole, it is permissible on motion to limit the debate to a certain length of time, to close at a certain time, to limit the length of speeches, or to otherwise limit debate.

3. Unless debate is limited, any member may speak as often as that person can get the floor, and as long as the rules permit, although the member cannot speak a second time should another member who has not spoken wish the floor.

4. The motion for the previous question cannot be put in committee of the whole, and a vote taken in committee of the whole may not be reconsidered.

5. The motions permitted in committee of the whole are considerably restricted, the only regular motions available being: to limit debate, to propose amendments, to recommend and to rise.

6. Likewise, the committee of the whole cannot take any final action but its power is limited to recommendation to the house, the same as any other committee.

Sec. 687: Concerning procedure in committee of the whole, see: Cushing's Legislative Assemblies, Secs. 1987–2022; Jefferson, Sec. XII; N.Y. Manual, p. 435; Reed, Secs. 86–99; Cushing, Secs. 302–309.

7. An appeal from a decision of the chair can be made but must be taken directly as it cannot be laid on the table nor postponed, since neither of these motions is permitted.

8. When the house has fixed the duration of the committee of the whole, the time cannot be extended even by unanimous consent; however, when the work of the committee is incomplete, at the expiration of the time available, the chair of the committee of the whole may ask leave to sit again.

Sec. 688. Limitations on Committee of the Whole

1. The committee of the whole, like other committees, derives its authority solely from the body and is confined strictly to the powers delegated to it.

2. Also, being but a committee, it is limited in other matters.

3. A committee of the whole:

(a) Cannot order a vote by roll call taken on any matter.

(b) Cannot entertain any question of priority.

(c) Cannot entertain any matter of privilege.

(d) Cannot lay a question on the table.

(e) Cannot postpone the consideration of any question.

(f) Cannot reconsider a vote on a proposal no longer in the possession of the committee of the whole.

Sec. 688, Par. 1: N.Y. Manual, p. 435.
Sec. 688, Par. 2: N.Y. Manual, p. 434.

(g) Has no authority to appoint a subcommittee.

(h) Cannot punish members for disorderly conduct, but must report any misconduct to the body for its action.

(i) Is dissolved by the absence of a quorum, but may proceed when a quorum is obtained.

4. Seconds to motions were not required in committee of the whole even before they became obsolete in legislative bodies generally.

Sec. 689. Returning from Committee of the Whole to Proceeding as Body

1. When it is decided to revert to proceedings as the body, the motion is made that "The committee rise and report," or that "The committee do now rise." This motion is equivalent to the motion to adjourn in the body and is always in order, except while voting or while a member has the floor. It is likewise undebatable and cannot be amended nor have any subsidiary motions applied to it.

2. The motion to adjourn is not in order in committee of the whole. The proper procedure is to adopt the motion to "rise," restoring the committee to the status of the body when the motion to adjourn is in order.

Sec. 688, Par. 3: (a) Reed, Sec. 90; Cushing's Legislative Assemblies, Sec. 2000, (b) N.Y. Manual, p. 435, (c) Cushing's Legislative Assemblies, Sec. 2000; N.Y. Manual, p. 434, (d) Tilson, p. 61; Cushing's Legislative Assemblies, Sec. 2000, (e) Cushing's Legislative Assemblies, Sec. 2000, (f) Cushing's Legislative Assemblies, Sec. 2000, (g) Reed, Sec. 97; Cushing, Sec. 306; N.Y. Manual, p. 435, (h) Reed, Sec. 94; Cushing, Sec. 308; N.Y. Manual, p. 433, (i) Cushing, Sec. 299; N.Y. Manual, p. 436.

Sec. 688, Par. 4: Cushing's Legislative Assemblies, Sec. 2000.

Sec. 689, Par. 1: Jefferson, Sec. XXVI; Cushing, Sec. 310; Reed, Sec. 92.

3. The motion to rise in committee of the whole may be carried by less than a quorum.

4. Upon the adoption of the motion to rise, the presiding officer resumes the chair and the committee chair submits the report of the committee of the whole.

5. Reports of a committee of the whole are usually made to the body.

6. Recommendations of the committee of the whole may be considered and treated in the same manner as reports of other committees.

Sec. 690. Informal Consideration

As a matter of convenience in considering measures by a legislative body, in lieu of resolving into committee of the whole, the rules may be materially relaxed by the presiding officer to allow much greater freedom of discussion. Under this condition, the greater freedom allowed is by general consent, and compliance with any of the rules of procedure may be insisted upon by any member at any time.

Sec. 691. Meetings of Committee of the Whole Open to the Public

See also Sec. 630, Committee Meetings Open to the Public, and Sec. 784, Sessions Open to the Public.

The provisions of state constitutions, statutes or rules which require that the doors of each house shall be open to the public during its session also apply when the body is meeting in committee of the whole.

Sec. 689, Par. 3: Hughes, Sec. 651.

Sec. 689, Par. 5: Cushing's Legislative Assemblies, Sec. 2011.

Sec. 690: Reed, Sec. 219.

CHAPTER 64

JOURNALS AND RECORDS

Sec. 694. Constitutional Requirements Concerning Journal

1. Each house must keep and publish a journal of its proceedings and the houses are also required, in many cases, upon the demand of a certain number or proportion of the members, to take a "yea" and "nay" vote on any question and publish the same in the journal.

2. The usual constitutional requirement that each house must keep a journal does not require that every step in the passage of bills or amendments be recorded in the journals of the houses or endorsed on the bills. In the absence of a constitutional requirement, it is not essential that the journal should show the adoption of amendments.

3. Where the constitution authorizes each house to determine the rules of its proceedings and pro-

Sec. 694, Par. 1: Cushing's Legislative Assemblies, Sec. 423; State Constitutions: Ala. IV, 55; Alaska II, 12; Ariz. IV, II, 10; Ark. V, 12; Cal. IV, 7(b); Colo. V, 13; Conn. III, 14; Del. II, 10; Fla. III, 4; Ga. III, Sec. V, 1; Hawaii III, 12; Idaho III, 13; Ill. IV, 7; Ind. V, 12; Iowa III, 9, 10, 17; Kan. II, 10; Ky. 40; La. III, 10(b); Me. IV, Part III, 5; Md. III, 22; Mich. IV, 18; Minn. IV, 15; Miss. IV, 55; Mo. IV, 26; Mont. V, 10; Neb. III, 11, 13; Nev. IV, 14; N.H. II, 24; N.J. IV, Sec. IV, 4; N.M. IV, 12; N.Y. III, 10; N.C. II, 17; N.Dak. IV, 13; Ohio II, 9; Okla. V, 30; Ore. IV, 13; Pa. II, 12; R.I. IV, 8; S.C. III, 22; S.Dak. III, 13; Tenn. II, 21; Tex. III, 12; Utah VI, 14; Vt. II, 9; Va. IV, 10; Wash. II, 11, 21; W.Va. VI, 41; Wis. IV, 10, 20; Wyo. III, 13.

Sec. 694, Par. 2: Perry v. State of Arkansas (1919), 139 Ark. 227, 214 S.W. 2; State of Nebraska v. Cox (1920), 105 Neb. 175, 178 N.W. 913; School District No. 11, Dakota County, Neb. v. Chapman (1907), 152 F. 887; West v. State of Florida (1905), 50 Fla. 154, 39 So. 412.

vides that it shall keep a journal, the journal must refer to those matters required by the constitution.

4. Where there is no provision requiring the entry in a journal of either house of the time when a bill was returned by the governor with the governor's objections, a recital in the journal that a bill vetoed by the governor was returned on a particular day is not conclusive as to the date of its return. The return of a bill by the governor without the governor's approval is not a proceeding of either house within the constitutional provision requiring each house to keep a journal of its proceedings.

5. The duty of keeping a journal is imposed by constitutional provisions upon the house and not upon the presiding officer. The duty of keeping the journal, imposed by the rules upon the secretary or chief clerk, is not a delegation of the control of the journal and only such matters as the body determines shall be placed thereon.

Sec. 695. Journal Record of Proceedings

See also Sec. 723, Journal Record of Readings.

1. The journal is the official record of the acts of a legislative body. It should be a true record of the proceedings arranged in chronological order. It should be a record of what is done rather than what is said.

2. The journal should be a clear, concise, unembellished statement of all proposals made and all actions taken complying with all requirements of

---

Sec. 694, Par. 3: Jefferson, Sec. XVIII.

Sec. 694, Par. 4: Parkinson v. Johnson (1911), 160 Cal. 756, 117 P. 1057.

Sec. 694, Par. 5: Turnbull v. Giddings (1893), 95 Mich. 314, 54 N.W. 887.

Sec. 695, Par. 1: Cushing's Legislative Assemblies, Sec. 415; Jefferson, Sec. XLIX; Sturgis, p. 200; Reed, Sec. 46; Hughes, Sec. 193.

constitutions, statutes or rules concerning what is to be recorded and how it is to be recorded. It should record all procedural motions such as: to recess, to lay on the table and to postpone; and the action taken on them, the same as upon bills or other main motions. When a motion is reversed, the original action and the one reversing it should both be in the record.

3. While legislative journals are printed and published for the convenience and information of the public, the official journal is the original or certified copy and it governs where there is any discrepancy between it and the printed journal. The manuscript prevails over the printed journal.

4. Every member of the house has the right to see the minutes and to take notes from them, and the approved journal being a public record, everyone may see and publish it.

5. In determining from its journal what was or was not done by the house, the journal must be considered as a whole as any other record would be.

Sec. 696. What May Be Recorded in the Journal

1. There is nothing in the constitutional requirements for keeping a journal which prevents the recording in the journal of any matter considered by the house, though it may have no relation to legislation or the constitutional duties of the house.

Sec. 695, Par. 3: State of Alabama v. Martin (1909), 160 Ala. 181, 48 So. 846; Stewart v. Wilson Printing Co. (1924), 210 Ala. 624, 99 So. 92; Chicot County v. Davies (1882), 40 Ark. 200.

Sec. 695, Par. 4: Jefferson, Sec. XLIX.

Sec. 695, Par. 5: State of South Carolina v. Tollison (1915), 100 S.C. 165, 84 S.E. 819.

2. The houses of the legislature may make their journals show that all their business was transacted before the time fixed for final adjournment. The statement of the legislative journals that a bill was read by sections on final passage will be accepted as true although it was physically impossible for all bills passed at such session to have been read by sections on final passage.

3. A member of a legislative body may not vote or change a vote, when the vote was properly taken, after the result has been announced by the presiding officer. The member may, however, upon permission, have a statement concerning the vote printed in the journal. In having a protest against the passage of a bill printed in the journal, a member merely exercises a personal privilege and the protest does not destroy the conclusive effect of the journal.

4. A house of a state legislature can speak only through its journal. For the confirmation of an appointment of the governor to be effective it must be set forth in the journal.

Sec. 697. Journal as Showing Passage and Legality of Bills

Mandatory Requirements Must Be Complied With

1. All requirements of the constitution concerning the passage of bills must be complied with, but

---

Sec. 696, Par. 2: Earnest v. Sargent (1915), 20 N.M. 427, 150 P. 1018; State of Florida *ex rel.* Buford v. Carley (1925), 89 Fla. 361, 104 So. 577.

Sec. 696, Par. 3: City of Ensley v. Simpson (1909), 166 Ala. 366, 52 So. 61; Cushing, Sec. 32; N.Y. Manual, p. 504.

Sec. 696, Par. 4: Witherspoon v. State of Mississippi *ex rel.* West (1925), 138 Miss. 310, 103 So. 134.

there are several distinct rules as to the evidence which will be accepted by the courts to establish compliance with the mandatory requirements of the constitution. The principal rules are set forth in the footnotes below.

Sec. 697, Par. 1: Following is a list of the jurisdictions with the rule applied in each:

U.S. Congress—The enrolled bill cannot be impeached by the journals: Field v. Clark (1891), 143 U.S. 649, 36 L. Ed. 294.

Alabama—Journal and bill both accepted as evidence but no other evidence will be considered. Entry of votes in journal mandatory. Robertson v. State of Alabama (1901), 130 Ala. 164, 30 So. 494; State of Alabama v. Martin (1909), 160 Ala. 181, 48 So. 846.

Arizona—Appears to follow the enrolled bill rule. Graves v. Alsap (1876), 1 Ariz. 274, 25 P. 836; Harwood v. Wentworth (1895), 4 Ariz. 378, 42 P. 1025.

Arkansas—Enrolled bill is prima facie evidence but may be disputed by journals and records of the secretary of state. Hodges v. Keel (1913), 108 Ark. 84, 159 S.W. 21; Mech. Bldg. and Loan Assn. v. Coffman (1913), 110 Ark. 269, 162 S.W. 1090; Rice v. Lonoke-Cabot Road Improvement Dist. (1920), 142 Ark. 454, 221 S.W. 179; Ewing v. McGehee (1925), 169 Ark. 448, 275 S.W. 766; Ricarte v. State of Arkansas (1986), 290 Ark. 100, 717 S.W.2d 488.

California—Enrolled bill rule strictly followed. Journal record not permitted to dispute the enrolled bill. Parkinson v. Johnson (1911), 160 Cal. 756, 117 P. 1057; People v. Taft (1919), 42 Cal. App. 411, 183 P. 845.

Colorado—Enrolled bill is prima facie evidence but may be disputed by the journal. Mass. Mutual Life Insurance Co. v. Colorado Loan & Trust Co. (1894), 20 Colo. 1, 36 P. 793; Robertson v. People (1894), 20 Colo. 279, 38 P. 326; In re House Bill No. 250 (1899), 26 Colo. 234, 57 P. 49; Andrews v. People (1905), 33 Colo. 193, 79 P. 1031.

Connecticut—The enrolled bill rule is followed. Eld v. Gorham (1849), 20 Conn. 8; State of Connecticut v. Savings Bank of New London (1906), 79 Conn. 141, 64 A. 5.

Delaware—Journals are conclusive as to matters required to be recorded. Rash v. Allen (1910), 24 Del. 444, 76 A. 370.

Florida—Enrolled bill is prima facie evidence of passage of bill but may be disputed by showing, by journals only, that the mandatory provisions of the constitution were not complied with. State of Florida *ex rel.* Buford v. Carley (1925), 89 Fla. 361, 104 So. 577; Gwynn v. Hardee (1926), 92 Fla. 543, 110 So. 343; Volusia County v. State of Florida (1929), 98 Fla. 1166, 125 So. 375; State of Florida v. Kaufman (1983), 430 So. 2d 904.

Georgia—The court will look to the journal to determine whether a bill passed. Carswell v. Wright (1910), 133 Ga. 714, 66 S.E. 905.

Idaho—Enrolled bill may be disputed by journals. Journals must show that mandatory requirements of constitution were complied with. Cohn v. Kingsley (1897), 5 Idaho 416, 49 P. 985.

Illinois—Enrolled bill is prima facie evidence but may be impeached by the journals. Illinois Central R. Co. v. People (1892), 143 Ill. 434, 33 N.E. 173; Neiberger v. McCullough (1912), 253 Ill. 312, 97 N.E. 660; People *ex rel.* Dezettel v. Lueders (1918), 283 Ill. 287, 119 N.E. 339.

Indiana—The journals cannot be used to impeach the enrolled bill. Bender v. State of Indiana (1876), 53 Ind. 254; Edger v. Board of Commissioners (1886), 70 Ind. 331.

Iowa—The courts will look to the journals to determine whether the constitutional requirements were complied with in the passage of an act. State of Iowa v. Livermore (1921), 192 Iowa 626, 185 N.W. 1.

Kansas—Enrolled bill is prima facie evidence but may be disputed by journal entries. Weyand v. Stover (1886), 35 Kan. 545, 11 P. 355; State of Kansas *ex rel.* Bradford v. Robertson (1889), 41 Kan. 200, 21 P. 382.

Kentucky—(No court decisions have been found which are directly in point but municipal corporations must rely upon their records.) County Board of Education of Warren County v. Durham (1923), 198 Ky. 732, 249 S.W. 1028.

Louisiana—Courts look to the journals to determine whether a bill was properly enacted. State of Louisiana *ex rel.* Caillouet v. Laiche (1901), 105 La. 84, 29 So. 700.

Maine—Enrolled bill is best evidence and may be disputed by journals only if incomplete. Weeks v. Smith (1889), 81 Me. 538.

Maryland—Reliance is placed on journal entries rather than on the enrolled bill. County Commissioners of Washington v. Baker (1922), 141 Md. 623, 119 A. 461.

Massachusetts—(No court decisions found on this question.)

Michigan—Courts look to the journals. Journals are conclusive evidence of recitals but presumptions favor regularity. City of Lansing v. Michigan Power Co. (1914), 183 Mich. 400, 150 N.W. 250; McClellan v. Stein (1924), 229 Mich. 203, 20 N.W. 209.

Minnesota—Enrolled bill is prima facie evidence but may be overcome by journal record. Ellis v. Ellis (1893), 55 Minn. 401, 56 N.W. 1056; State of Minnesota *ex rel.* Kohlman v. Wagner (1915), 130 Minn. 424, 153 N.W. 749.

Mississippi—Enrolled bill rule is followed. Green v. Weller (1856), 32 Miss. 650; *Ex parte* Wren (1886), 63 Miss. 512, 56 Am. R. 825; Witherspoon v. State of Mississippi *ex rel.* West (1925), 138 Miss. 310, 103 So. 134.

Missouri—Enrolled bill raises presumption that provisions not required to be entered in the journal have been complied with but the presumption may be rebutted and the courts will look to journals. State of Missouri v. Mason (1900), 155 Mo. 486, 55 S.W. 636; State of Missouri *ex rel.* Schmoll v. Drabelle (1914), 261 Mo. 515, 170 S.W. 465; *Ex parte* Seward (1923), 299 Mo. 385, 253 S.W. 356, *error dismissed sub nom.* Seward v. Brady, 264 U.S. 599, 44 S. Ct. 335, 68 L. Ed. 869.

Montana—The courts look to the journals to determine whether a bill has passed. Johnson v. City of Great Falls (1909), 38 Mont. 369, 99 P. 1059.

Nebraska—Enrolled bill is prima facie evidence and may be disputed by the journals. State of Nebraska v. Burlington N.R.R. Co. (1900), 60 Neb. 741, 84 N.W. 254; State of Nebraska v. Davis (1902), 66 Neb. 333, 92 N.W. 740; State of Nebraska v. Ryan (1912), 92 Neb. 636, 139 N.W. 235; State of Nebraska v. Cox (1920), 105 Neb. 175, 178 N.W. 913.

Nevada—Enrolled bill may not be disputed by the journal. State of Nevada v. Rogers (1875), 10 Nev. 250; State of Nevada v. Glenn (1883), 18 Nev. 34, 1 P. 186.

New Hampshire—Courts will look to the journals to determine whether a bill passed. *In re* Opinion of the Justices (1857), 35 N.H. 579; *In re* Opinion of the Justices (1864), 45 N.H. 607; *In re* Opinion of the Justices (1873), 52 N.H. 622.

New Jersey—The courts will look to the journals to determine in what form a bill passed. *In re* Jaegle (1912), 83 N.J.L. 313, 85 A. 214.

New York—Enrolled bill cannot be impeached by the journals. People v. Chenango County Supervisors (1853), 8 N.Y. 317; People v. Marlborough Highway Commissioners (1873), 54 N.Y. 276.

North Carolina—The courts look to the journals which must affirmatively show that the bill was properly passed. Smathers v. Commissioners of Madison County (1899), 125 N.C. 480, 34 S.E. 554; Debman v. Chitty (1902), 131 N.C. 657, 43 S.E. 3; Burlingham v. City of New Bern (1914), 213 F. 1014.

North Dakota—Enrolled bill is presumed to have been legally passed but may be disputed by journals. State of North Dakota v. Schultz (1919), 44 N.D. 269, 174 N.W. 81; State of North Dakota *ex rel.* Sorlie v. Steen (1927), 55 N.D. 239, 212 N.W. 843.

Ohio—Journals prevail over the enrolled bill. Herron v. Smith (1886), 44 Ohio St. 348; State of Ohio v. Kiesewetter (1887), 45 Ohio St. 254.

Oklahoma—Would seem that courts will look to journals. Rolls v. Wyand (1914), 40 Okla. 323, 138 P. 158.

Oregon—Journals control over the enrolled act. State of Oregon v. Wright (1887), 14 Ore. 365.

Pennsylvania—Great weight is placed on the enrolled bill. Apparently it will not be disputed by the journals. Kilgore v. Magee (1877), 85 Pa. 401; Commonwealth v. Martin (1884), 107 Pa. 185.

Rhode Island—Language in enrolled bill controls, but passage is established by journal. State of Rhode Island v. Septon (1855), 3 R.I. 119; O'Neil v. Remers (1922), 44 R.I. 504.

South Carolina—The enrolled bill rule prevails. The courts do not look to the journals. State of South Carolina *ex rel.* Coleman v. Lewis (1936), 181 S.C. 10, 186 S.E. 625.

Tennessee—Courts look to the journals and will not permit the journals to be impeached by other evidence. State of Tennessee *ex rel.* Thompson v. Dixie Finance Co. (1925), 152 Tenn. 306, 278 S.W. 59.

Texas—Enrolled bill is best evidence and not controlled by the journals. Usener v. State of Texas (1880), 8 Tex. App. 177; *Ex parte* Tipton (1890), 28 Tex. App. 438.

Utah—The enrolled bill is prima facie, but not conclusive evidence of its constitutional enactment and of what the law is. Ritchie v. Richards (1896), 14 Utah 345, 47 P. 670.

Enrolled Bill Rule

2. Any act of the legislature which has been properly enrolled, authenticated by the signatures of the proper officers of both houses, signed by the governor, and deposited with the secretary of state is conclusive evidence as to the act and of its passage which will not be impeached by resort to the journals of the legislature or outside evidence of any sort.

3. The enrolled bill rule appears to be based on the opinion that the certificate of the officers of the legislature made at the time of passage of the act is more reliable than evidence from the journals or other sources which might be presented to the courts at a later time.

Vermont—Enrolled bill rule appears to prevail. In the Matter of Welman (1844), 20 Vt. 653.

Virginia—Presumption favors the enrolled bill but may be defeated by the journal record. Wise v. Bigger (1884), 79 Va. 269.

Washington—A regularly enrolled bill is conclusively presumed to have been passed. State of Washington v. Jones (1893), 6 Wash. 452, 34 P. 201, 23 L.R.A. 343.

West Virginia—Courts look to the journals. Price v. City of Moundsville (1897), 43 W.Va. 522, 27 S.E. 218.

Wisconsin—Journal controls over the enrolled bill as to procedure but presumption favors content of law as in enrolled bill. State of Wisconsin v. Wendler (1896), 94 Wis. 369, 68 N.W. 759; Milwaukee County v. Isenring (1901), 109 Wis. 9, 85 N.W. 131.

Wyoming—Courts will look at the entire record to determine whether a bill has properly passed. Arbuckle v. Pflaeging (1912), 20 Wyo. 351, 123 P. 918.

Sec. 697, Par. 2: Sherman v. Story (1866), 30 Cal. 253; Hale v. McGettigan (1896), 114 Cal. 112, 45 P. 1049; Yolo County v. McColgan (1901), 132 Cal. 265, 64 P. 403; Parkinson v. Johnson (1911), 160 Cal. 756, 117 P. 1057; People v. Taft (1919), 42 Cal. App. 411, 183 P. 845; De Loach v. Newton (1910), 134 Ga. 739, 68 S.E. 708; Green v. Weller (1856), 32 Miss. 650; State of Nevada v. Glenn (1883), 18 Nev. 34, 1 P. 186; People v. Chenango County Supervisors (1853), 8 N.Y. 317; State of South Carolina *ex rel.* Coleman v. Lewis (1936), 181 S.C. 10, 186 S.E. 625; State of Washington v. Jones (1893), 6 Wash. 452, 34 P. 201, 23 L.R.A. 343.

Presumptions Favor Enrolled Bill

4. A regularly enrolled bill will be presumed to have been duly passed and legal, in the absence of evidence in the journal alone or in the journal and other records that the bill was not legally passed, and any omissions in the record except as to those matters required to be recorded will be overcome by the presumption.

Journal Must Show Passage of Bill

5. The journal alone or the journals and other records are required to show all necessary steps in the passage of bills. Unless questioned, the enrolled bill will stand, but no further presumptions favor its passage or regularity.

Sec. 697, Par. 4: City of Ensley v. Simpson (1909), 166 Ala. 366, 52 So. 61; Smithee v. Garth (1878), 33 Ark. 17; Mech. Bldg. and Loan Assn. v. Coffman (1913), 110 Ark. 269, 162 S.W. 1090; Ewing v. McGehee (1925), 169 Ark. 448, 275 S.W. 766; Mass. Mutual Life Insurance Co. v. Colorado Loan & Trust Co. (1894), 20 Colo. 1, 36 P. 793; State of Florida *ex rel.* Buford v. Carley (1925), 89 Fla. 361, 104 So. 577; Larrison v. Peoria etc. R.R. (1875), 77 Ill. 11; Markham v. City of Anamosa (1904), 122 Iowa 689, 98 N.W. 493; Weyand v. Stover (1886), 35 Kan. 545, 11 P. 355; People *ex rel.* Hart v. McElroy (1889), 72 Mich. 446, 40 N.W. 750, State of Minnesota v. City of Hastings (1877), 24 Minn. 78; State of Minnesota *ex rel.* Kohlman v. Wagner (1915), 130 Minn. 424, 153 N.W. 749; State of Missouri v. Mason (1900), 155 Mo. 486, 55 S.W. 636; State of Nebraska v. Cox (1920), 105 Neb. 175, 178 N.W. 913; State of North Dakota *ex rel.* Sorlie v. Steen (1927), 55 N.D. 239, 212 N.W. 843; State of Oregon v. Boyer (1917), 84 Ore. 513, 165 P. 587.

Sec. 697, Par. 5: Rash v. Allen (1910), 24 Del. 444, 76 A. 370; Volusia County v. State of Florida (1929), 98 Fla. 1166, 125 So. 375; Cohn v. Kingsley (1897), 5 Idaho 416, 49 P. 985; Auditor General v. Board of Supervisors (1891), 89 Mich. 552, 51 N.W. 483; City of Lansing v. Michigan Power Co. (1914), 183 Mich. 400, 150 N.W. 250; *In re* Opinion of the Justices (1873), 52 N.H. 622; Smathers v. Commissioners of Madison County (1899), 125 N.C. 480, 34 S.E. 554; State of Tennessee *ex rel.* Thompson v. Dixie Finance Co. (1925), 152 Tenn. 306, 278 S.W. 59; Milwaukee County v. Isenring (1901), 109 Wis. 9, 85 N.W. 131; Arbuckle v. Pflaeging (1912), 20 Wyo. 351, 123 P. 918.

Sec. 698. Reading of the Journal

See also Sec. 505, Procedure on Absence of a Quorum.

1. When a quorum is present, no business is in order until after the reading of the journal, except that the motion to dispense with the reading and the simple motion to adjourn are sometimes permitted.

2. The reading of the journal may not be interrupted, even by a highly privileged question, other than the question of no quorum, or the motion to dispense with the further reading of the journal.

3. The presiding officer should ascertain the presence of a quorum before directing the reading of the journal, for if a question of no quorum is raised, the reading of the journal is not permitted until the fact that a quorum is present has been ascertained by count.

4. In the absence of a quorum, a call of the house may be moved before the journal is read.

Sec. 699. Manner of Correcting the Journal

1. Journals are usually corrected informally, the presiding officer directing the correction to be made when suggested. But if objection be made, a formal vote is necessary for the approval of the correction or amendment. In approving the journals, the usual procedure is for the presiding officer to inquire if there are any corrections. If any are suggested, they are made, providing there is no objection. If there

---

Sec. 698, Par. 1: Hughes, Secs. 663, 668; N.Y. Manual, p. 423.

Sec. 698, Par. 2: Hughes, Sec. 668.

Sec. 698, Par. 3: Cushing's Legislative Assemblies, Sec. 369; Hughes, Secs. 663, 668, 673.

Sec. 698, Par. 4: N.Y. Manual, p. 422.

are no corrections or when there are no further corrections, the presiding officer may say, "There being no corrections (or no further corrections), the journal stands approved." No particular form of approving the journal is required.

2. The more usual manner of correcting the journals is to move at intervals that the journals of certain days be approved as corrected by a committee assigned that responsibility or by the journal clerk or other officer charged with that duty, the corrected journals being at the same time submitted to the body so that they may be inspected and corrections questioned or further corrections made.

Sec. 700. Authority to Correct Journal

1. The right of a legislative body to correct its journal is an inherent right which does not depend upon the constitution nor upon statute.

2. Each house of the legislature has power to correct its journals prior to final adjournment.

3. Where, through inadvertence, the clerk of the senate failed to enter in the journal the passage of a bill and the yea and nay votes thereon as required by the constitution, the same legislature at a special session could correct the journal to show that a quorum was present and that all the members voted for the bill and the journal when so corrected

Sec. 700, Par. 1: People *ex rel.* Stewart v. Chicago M. & St. P. Railway Co. (1927), 326 Ill. 179, 145 N.E. 200; State of South Carolina v. Tollison (1915), 100 S.C. 165, 84 S.E. 819.

Sec. 700, Par. 2: Stewart v. Wilson Printing Co. (1924), 210 Ala. 624, 99 So. 92; State of South Carolina v. Tollison (1915), 100 S.C. 165, 84 S.E. 819.

showed a compliance with the constitution and made the statute valid.

4. The legislature may even at a subsequent session correct its journals by amendments which show the true facts as they actually occurred when it is satisfied that by neglect or design the truth has been omitted or suppressed.

5. The rule that the legislature may correct its journals and that when corrected the journals will stand as if so originally made is applicable to an amendment of legislative records, especially where no adversary rights of innocent third persons have intervened.

6. The house itself is the only tribunal authorized to correct an error in the legislative journal. On information that an error or omission has been made in the journal, a committee may be appointed to examine and correct it and report to the house.

7. Where the secretary is authorized to correct the journal, the record with any corrections by the secretary is to be accepted as the true record. When it is not affirmatively shown at what time the clerk made corrections in the daily journal, they will be presumed to have been made on or before the time of certification.

Sec. 700, Par. 3: Richmond County Commissioners v. Farmers Bank (1910), 152 N.C. 387, 67 S.E. 969.

Sec. 700, Par. 4: Turley v. Logan Co. (1855), 17 Ill. 151.

Sec. 700, Par. 5: Richmond County Commissioners v. Farmers Bank (1910), 152 N.C. 387, 67 S.E. 969.

Sec. 700, Par. 6: Jefferson, Sec. XLIX; State of Tennessee *ex rel.* Thompson v. Dixie Finance Co. (1925), 152 Tenn. 306, 278 S.W. 59.

Sec. 700, Par. 7: People v. Burch (1891), 84 Mich. 408, 47 N.W. 765.

8. The record contained in the journals of the houses of the legislature is binding on all persons.

Sec. 701. The Corrected Journal

1. The action of the house in approving a corrected journal makes such journal the only authorized journal of the day's proceedings.

2. The regular printed journals of the legislature are competent evidence of their content and their effect as evidence will not be destroyed by clerical errors or omissions shown to have occurred in writing up the records to complete the written journals.

3. Clerical errors in the journal, where the facts can be ascertained do not invalidate the bill.

Sec. 702. The Enrolled Bill

See also Sec. 738, Enrollment of Bills, and Sec. 697, Journal as Showing Passage and Legality of Bills.

1. The enrolled bill is a copy of the bill in the form it has passed both houses, which has been proofread and corrected, usually under the direction of the secretary and chief clerk, and printed with blanks for the certification of passage and accuracy and signature by the governor. This bill is certified by the presiding officers and chief legislative officers of both houses as being correct and as having duly

---

Sec. 700, Par. 8: Dowling v. W.R. Hodges & Son (1938), 131 Fla. 672, 179 So. 702.

Sec. 701, Par. 1: State of Minnesota *ex rel.* Kohlman v. Wagner (1915), 130 Minn. 424, 153 N.W. 749; Mann v. Le Mars (1899), 109 Iowa 244, 80 N.W. 327.

Sec. 701, Par. 2: Lincoln v. Haugen (1891), 45 Minn. 451, 48 N.W. 186.

Sec. 701, Par. 3: Desha-Drew Road Improvement Dist. v. Taylor (1917), 130 Ark. 503, 197 S.W. 1152; Marshall v. Baugh (1918), 133 Ark. 64, 201 S.W. 808; Thrift v. Towers (1915), 127 Md. 54, 95 A. 1064; Price v. City of Moundsville (1897), 43 W.Va. 522, 27 S.E. 218.

passed both houses and sent by messenger to the governor's office for consideration and approval. If the governor approves the bill, the governor signs it and delivers it to the office of the secretary of state who assigns it a chapter or statute number and files it with the legislation of the session.

2. Under the "enrolled bill rule," an enrolled bill, properly authenticated, approved by the governor and deposited with the secretary of state as a part of the records of that office, is conclusive as to regularity of its enactment, and the courts cannot look beyond the duly authenticated bill to the journals of either house to ascertain whether the constitutional requirements were complied with in its passage.

3. Ordinarily the courts will not go behind the enrolled bill to determine its validity. The supreme court can look behind the enrolled bill only to determine whether the constitutional mandate relative to vote and journal entry upon the final passage have been complied with.

4. The failure of legislative journals to show that certain acts were read in full in each house and signed by the proper officers in open session did not invalidate the acts under the enrolled bill rule.

Sec. 702, Par. 2: Thompson v. Saunders (1947), 52 N.M. 1, 189 P.2d 87.

Sec. 702, Par. 3: Standard Oil Co. v. State Board of Equalization (1940), 110 Mont. 5, 99 P.2d 229; Vaughn & Ragsdale Co. v. State Board of Equalization (1939), 109 Mont. 52, 96 P.2d 420.

Sec. 702, Par. 4: Thompson v. Saunders (1947), 52 N.M. 1, 189 P.2d 87.

Sec. 703. The Journal and the Enrolled Bill

See also Sec. 697, Journal as Showing Passage and Legality of Bills; Sec. 702, The Enrolled Bill; and Sec. 738, Enrollment of Bills.

1. There does not appear to be agreement between the states concerning whether to rely on the journal record or the enrolled bill record to determine whether a bill has been duly passed and what the provisions of the bill are when there are conflicts in the records.

2. It appears that the enrolled bill as certified on the bill itself by the presiding officers and the legislative officers of both houses is more likely to be correct than the record maintained by the journal clerk. The state constitutions contain provisions concerning the journal and the records that must be kept and some have rules concerning the enrollment of bills. These requirements vary widely from state to state. It is sometimes difficult to reconcile the different rules for even one state and apparently impossible to reconcile the law on the subject generally. It appears that the law in each state must be arrived at from a consideration of the constitution, court decisions and rules in that state.

Sec. 703: See notes following Sec. 697 for law and practice of the different states concerning engrossment and journal records.

CHAPTER 65

THE LEGISLATIVE CHAMBER

Sec. 705. Admission to Legislative Chambers

1. When the place of meeting of a legislative body has been designated by law, it may be changed only on legal authority, and no valid meeting can be held nor business conducted at any other than the legally designated place.

2. When the legislative body adjourns without any previous order or resolution, it is to reconvene on the next legislative day at the usual place of sitting and at the usual hours.

3. A legislative body has absolute control of its chambers and may exclude therefrom, at its pleasure, all persons who are not members, even though they are members of a coordinate branch or other offices of the government.

4. Of right, the door of the house ought not to be shut, but to be kept by porters or sergeants at arms, assigned for that purpose.

5. It is a matter of practice that legislative bodies are open to the public, galleries usually being provided for visitors.

6. No persons except the members of the house and the officers when engaged in their duties are

---

Sec. 705, Par. 1: Cushing's Legislative Assemblies, Sec. 343.
Sec. 705, Par. 2: Cushing's Legislative Assemblies, Sec. 510.
Sec. 705, Par. 3: Cushing's Legislative Assemblies, Sec. 343.
Sec. 705, Par. 4: Jefferson, Sec. XVIII.

permitted upon the floor of the chamber while the house is in session except as may be permitted by the rules or by the house. The rules frequently provide that ex-members, certain state officers and accredited representatives of the press may be admitted to the floor.

Sec. 706. Use of Legislative Chambers

1. A committee may not occupy the legislative chamber for the purpose of meetings without the consent of the house.

2. The fact that persons who are not members are permitted to sit on the floor of the chamber and consult with members does not invalidate acts passed.

Sec. 705, Par. 6: Cushing's Legislative Assemblies, Sec. 346.

Sec. 706, Par. 1: Hughes, Sec. 858.

Sec. 706, Par. 2: State of Michigan v. Iron Cliffs County (1884), 54 Mich. 350, 20 N.W. 493.

*

PART VII. CONDUCT OF BUSINESS

*

PART VII

CONDUCT OF BUSINESS

CHAPTER 66

GENERAL ORDER OF BUSINESS

Sec. 710. Usual Order of Business

It is customary for each house of a legislature to provide in its rules for a regular daily order of business. This order of business varies in different legislatures but the order of the essential procedure established by usage, and therefore the general order when no rule to the contrary has been adopted, is as follows:

(a) Call to order.

(b) Roll call.

(c) Invocation. (In recent years some states have changed the order of business, placing the invocation before the call to order and/or roll call to avoid the conflict of church and state and to allow those who do not wish to be present for the prayer to answer roll call in a timely manner.)

(d) Reading and approval of the journal of the previous day.

(e) Presentation of petitions and papers.

(f) Messages from the governor.

(g) Messages from the other house.

(h) Reports of standing committees.
(i) Reports of special or select committees.
(j) Special orders.
(k) Unfinished business.
(*l*) Introduction and first reading of bills.
(m) Consideration of daily calendar.
(n) Announcement of committee meetings.
(*o*) Adjournment.

Sec. 711. Motions Relating to Business Under Regular Order

Where reports are submitted in the proper order of business, motions that these be received, read or adopted are unnecessary, unless there is objection.

Sec. 712. When Certain Motions Are in Order

1. A motion to take from the table is in order in the same order of business in which the matter affected was laid on the table. The motion to take from the table a motion to reconsider the vote by which a bill was defeated may be made on the order of business "third reading of bills."

2. A motion to discharge a committee from further consideration of a bill is in order only under reports of committees or motions and resolutions.

3. Motions affecting bills on third reading are not in order, even under that order of business, until the particular bill is reached on the calendar.

Sec. 710: Reed, Secs. 260–264; Sturgis, p. 116; U.S. House Rule XXIV; Marsh v. Chambers (1983), 463 U.S. 783, 103 S. Ct. 3330, 77 L. Ed. 2d 1019.

Sec. 711: Hughes, Secs. 134, 676.

Sec. 712: N.Y. Manual, pp. 419, 425, 453, 459, 462; Hughes, Secs. 454, 455.

4. A motion to suspend the rules may be made, either under the order of business of motions and resolutions, or under the order of business to which the matter proposed to be considered relates.

Sec. 713. Taking Up Questions Out of Order

See also Ch. 28, Secs. 279–286, Suspension of the Rules.

1. A motion to take up a question out of order suspends the rules, and therefore requires the same vote as is required to suspend the rules. Such a motion may be renewed after intervening business, but may not be debated, amended, laid on the table, postponed nor committed. The motion to take up a question out of order is in order whenever any main motion is in order.

2. An order of the day may be discharged at any time, and a new one made for a different time or day.

Sec. 714. Unfinished Business

1. When the consideration of a question regularly on the calendar is interrupted by adjournment, it does not come up for further consideration as unfinished business, but comes up in its proper place on the daily calendar.

2. A motion relating to the order of business, when not disposed of, does not recur as unfinished business on the succeeding day, as such motions expire with the completion of the day's business to which they relate.

Sec. 713: Hughes, Sec. 517; Jefferson, Sec. XVIII.
Sec. 714: Jefferson, Sec. XXXVII; Hughes, Sec. 270.

CHAPTER 67

REQUIRED READING OF BILLS

Sec. 720. Bills Must Be Read on Three Separate Days

1. Ancient parliamentary practice and the constitutions of most of the states require that bills be read three separate times on three separate days in each house of a legislature before final passage.

2. The requirement that each bill be read on three separate days, prescribed by the constitution, legislative rules or statutes, is one of the many restrictions imposed upon the passage of bills to prevent hasty and ill-considered legislation, surprise or fraud, and to inform the legislators and the public of the contents of the bill.

3. A substantial compliance with the constitutional requirement as to the reading of bills is generally sufficient, although it has been held that the requirement of reading the bill on different days is mandatory. Mandatory requirements must

Sec. 720, Par. 1: Jefferson, Sec. XVIII; Cushing's Legislative Assemblies, Sec. 2123; State Constitutions: Ala. IV, 61, 63; Alaska II, 14; Ariz. IV, Part II, 12; Ark. V, 21, 22; Cal. IV, 8(b); Colo. V, 22; Fla. III, 7; Ga. III, Sec. V, 7; Hawaii III, 15; Idaho III, 15; Ill. IV, 8; Ind. IV, 1, 18; Kan. II, 15; Ky. 46; La. III, 24; Md. III, 27; Mass. II, Ch. I, Sec. I, 2; Mich. IV, 26; Minn. IV, 19; Miss. IV, 59, 60; Mo. IV, 21; Neb. III, 14; Nev. IV, 18, 23; N.J. IV, Sec. IV, 6; N.M. IV, 15; N.Y. III, 14; N.C. II, 22; N.Dak. IV, 13; Ohio II, 15; Okla. V, 34; Ore. IV, 19; Pa. III, 4; R.I. IV, 2; S.C. III, 18; S.Dak. III, 17; Tenn. II, 18; Tex. III, 32; Utah VI, 22; Va. IV, 11; Wash. II, 18; W.Va. VI, 29; Wyo. III, 20.

Sec. 720, Par. 2: State of Alabama v. Buckley (1875), 54 Ala. 599; State of Florida *ex rel.* Buford v. Carley (1925), 89 Fla. 361, 104 So. 577.

be complied with.

4. A reading of a bill by title is considered a reading of the bill, unless it is specifically required by the constitution that the bill be read at length or in full.

5. The requirement that bills be read on different days in each house does not prevent the reading of a bill the first time in one house on the same date that it was given third reading and passed in the other.

6. The official reading of bills is not invalid or ineffective because it takes place on Sunday.

Sec. 721. Suspension of Requirement of Three Readings

1. The constitutions of many of the states provide that the requirement of reading a bill on three several days may be suspended by a two-thirds vote in case of emergency. It has been held that the legisla-

Sec. 720, Par. 3: State of Arkansas v. Crawford (1879), 35 Ark. 237; Smith v. Mitchell (1911), 69 W.Va. 481, 72 S.E. 755; Tarr v. Western Savings and Loan (1909), 15 Idaho 741, 99 P. 1049; Smathers v. Commissioners of Madison County (1899), 125 N.C. 480, 34 S.E. 554; City of Charlotte v. Shepard (1898), 122 N.C. 602, 29 S.E. 842; State of Minnesota *ex rel.* Kohlman v. Wagner (1915), 130 Minn. 424, 153 N.W. 749; Wagstaff v. Central Highway Commission (1917), 174 N.C. 377, 93 S.E. 908; Aurora Water Co. v. City of Aurora (1895), 129 Mo. 540, 31 S.W. 946; Nelson v. City of South Omaha (1909), 84 Neb. 434, 121 S.W. 453.

Sec. 720, Par. 4: Saunders v. Board of Liquidation (1903), 110 La. 313, 34 So. 457; People *ex rel.* Hart v. McElroy (1889), 72 Mich. 446, 40 N.W. 750; McClellan v. Stein (1924), 229 Mich. 203, 20 N.W. 209.

Sec. 720, Par. 5: Skipper v. Street Improvement Dist. No. 1 (1920), 144 Ark. 38, 221 S.W. 866; Chicot County v. Davies (1882), 40 Ark. 200; Smithee v. Garth (1878), 33 Ark. 17; State of Tennessee v. Persica (1914), 130 Tenn. 48, 168 S.W. 1056; Smith v. Mitchell (1911), 69 W.Va. 481, 72 S.E. 755.

Sec. 720, Par. 6: Ex parte Seward (1923), 299 Mo. 385, 253 S.W. 356, *error dismissed sub nom.* Seward v. Brady, 264 U.S. 599, 44 S. Ct. 335, 68 L. Ed. 869.

tive body is the exclusive judge as to when a case of emergency arises or exists.

2. In suspending the requirement for reading bills on three separate days, when suspension is permitted by the constitution, the suspension may be effected by a resolution naming the bill and approved by the prescribed vote without any other formality. It is not material that bills other than the one in question are included in the resolution suspending the provision.

Sec. 722. Three Readings of Amended Bills

1. The constitutional requirement that bills be read three times is not generally interpreted to apply to amendments, so that bills are required to be read the specified number of times after amendment, although in some jurisdictions material amendments are excluded from this rule. When amended bills are required to be read, this requirement can be suspended the same as for other readings.

Sec. 721, Par. 1: People v. Glenn County (1893), 100 Cal. 419, 35 P. 302; Weyand v. Stover (1886), 35 Kan. 545, 11 P. 355; Hull v. Miller (1876), 4 Neb. 503; McCulloch v. State of Indiana (1858), 11 Ind. 424; Brown v. Lutz (1893), 36 Neb. 527, 54 N.W. 860.

Sec. 721, Par. 2: State of Minnesota *ex rel.* Kohlman v. Wagner (1915), 130 Minn. 424, 153 N.W. 749; People v. Glenn County (1893), 100 Cal. 419, 35 P. 302.

Sec. 722, Par. 1: School District No. 11, Dakota County, Neb. v. Chapman (1907), 152 F. 887; People v. Thompson (1885), 2 Cal. unreported 481, 7 P. 142; State of Florida v. Dillon (1900), 42 Fla. 95, 28 So. 781; People *ex rel.* Brady v. LaSalle St. Trust & Savings Bank (1915), 269 Ill. 518, 110 N.E. 38; Allopathic St. Board v. Fowler (1898), 50 La. Ann. 1358, 24 So. 809; State of Missouri v. Field (1892), 119 Mo. 593, 24 S.W. 752; State of Nebraska v. Ryan (1912), 92 Neb. 636, 139 N.W. 235; People v. Chenango County Supervisors (1853), 8 N.Y. 317; Miller v. State of Ohio (1854), 3 Ohio St. 475; Evanhoff v. State Industrial Accident Commission (1915), 78 Ore. 503, 154 P. 106; State of South Carolina v. Brown (1890), 35 S.C. 151, 11 S.E. 641; Tennessee Coal, Iron & R. Co. v. Hooper (1915), 131 Tenn. 611, 175 S.W. 1146; Nelson v. Haywood

2. When a bill which has been passed by one house has been materially amended in the other, and there passed as amended, it has been held that the constitutional provision with reference to reading three times does not require the bill as amended to be read three times in the house of origin before concurring in the amendments of the other house. The same rule applies when a bill has been recalled and reconsidered and again passed.

3. Where a substituted bill may be considered as an amendment, the rule with reference to reading a bill on three several days does not require the bill to be read three times after substitution. One house may substitute an identical bill of its own for the bill of the other house without the rereading of the substitute bill being required.

4. A bill already read one or two times is not required to be reread because of a change in the title.

5. A bill which is amended or redrafted by a conference committee is not a new bill in the sense

---

County (1892), 91 Tenn. 596, 20 S.W. 1; Capito v. Topping (1909), 65 W.Va. 587, 64 S.E. 845. Re suspension of readings of amended bills, see Tarr v. Western Savings and Loan (1909), 15 Idaho 741, 99 P. 1049.

Sec. 722, Par. 2: State of Florida v. Dillon (1900), 42 Fla. 95, 28 So. 781; Brake v. Callison (1903), 122 F. 722; State of Arkansas v. Crawford (1879), 35 Ark. 237.

Sec. 722, Par. 3: People *ex rel.* Brady v. LaSalle St. Trust & Savings Bank (1915), 269 Ill. 518, 110 N.E. 38; State of Nebraska v. Cox (1920), 105 Neb. 175, 178 N.W. 913; Edwards v. Nash County Board of Commissioners (1922), 183 N.C. 58, 110 S.E. 600; Brown v. Road Commissioners (1917), 173 N.C. 598, 92 S.E. 502; Tennessee Coal, Iron & R. Co. v. Hooper (1915), 131 Tenn. 611, 175 S.W. 1146; State of Tennessee v. Persica (1914), 130 Tenn. 48, 168 S.W. 1056; Hood v. City of Wheeling (1920), 85 W.Va. 578, 102 S.E. 259; Smith v. Mitchell (1911), 69 W.Va. 481, 72 S.E. 755; see also State of Alabama v. Buckley (1875), 54 Ala. 599; Worthen v. Badgett (1877), 32 Ark. 496.

Sec. 722, Par. 4: State of Nebraska v. Cronin (1904), 72 Neb. 636, 101 N.W. 325; State of Missouri v. Field (1892), 119 Mo. 593, 24 S.W. 752.

that it requires three readings thereafter.

Sec. 723. Journal Record of Readings

See also Ch. 64, Secs. 694–703, Journals and Records.

1. Where the constitution or controlling statutory provision does not expressly require the journal to show three readings of bills, or the reading thereof at length before final passage, or the suspension of rules by a particular number of votes or that a case of emergency exists, it will be presumed that the legislature observed the constitutional requirements, nothing affirmatively appearing to the contrary.

2. Provisions of the constitution as to the reading of bills are generally considered as not requiring these matters to be entered in the journal, unless there are express words to that effect.

Sec. 722, Par. 5: Nelson v. Haywood County (1892), 91 Tenn. 596, 20 S.W. 1.

Sec. 723, Par. 1: Illinois Central R. Co. v. State of Illinois (1892), 33 F. 730, 146 U.S. 387, 13 S. Ct. 110; Clifton v. State of Alabama (1928), 22 Ala. App. 559, 118 So. 235; State of Alabama v. Buckley (1875), 54 Ala. 599; Chicot County v. Davies (1882), 40 Ark. 200; Worthen v. Badgett (1877), 32 Ark. 496; State of Florida *ex rel.* Buford v. Carley (1925), 89 Fla. 361, 104 So. 577; Andrews v. People (1905), 33 Colo. 193, 79 P. 1031; Illinois Central R. Co. v. People (1892), 143 Ill. 434, 33 N.E. 173; McCulloch v. State of Indiana (1858), 11 Ind. 424; Weyand v. Stover (1886), 35 Kan. 545, 11 P. 355; Mass. Mutual Life Insurance Co. v. Colorado Loan & Trust Co. (1894), 20 Colo. 1, 36 P. 793; State of Minnesota *ex rel.* Kohlman v. Wagner (1915), 130 Minn. 424, 153 N.W. 749; Ellis v. Ellis (1893), 55 Minn. 401, 56 N.W. 1056; Hull v. Miller (1876), 4 Neb. 503; Miller v. State of Ohio (1854), 3 Ohio St. 475; Supervisors of Schuyler Co. v. People (1860), 25 Ill. 181.

Sec. 723, Par. 2: Illinois Central R. Co. v. State of Illinois (1892), 33 F. 730, 146 U.S. 387, 13 S. Ct. 110; State of Alabama v. Buckley (1875), 54 Ala. 599; Worthen v. Badgett (1877), 32 Ark. 496; Vinsant v. Knox (1871), 27 Ark. 266; Mass. Mutual Life Insurance Co. v. Colorado Loan & Trust Co. (1894), 20 Colo. 1, 36 P. 793; State of Florida *ex rel.* Buford v. Carley (1925), 89 Fla. 361, 104 So. 577; Weyand v. Stover (1886), 35 Kan. 545, 11 P. 355; Ellis v. Ellis (1893), 55 Minn. 401, 56 N.W. 1056; Miller v. State of Ohio (1854), 3 Ohio St. 475.

3. When a provision of a constitution or statute requires that the journal show three readings on separate days, or show the vote on each legislative proposal or make other like affirmative provisions, these provisions must be complied with or the proposed legislation does not become effective.

4. When the enrolled bill rule is followed, the absence from the journal of an entry showing that a particular thing was done is no evidence that it was not done.

5. When a bill is read by title and passed and the journal is silent as to the suspension of the rule, the court, to uphold the act, will presume that the rules were suspended when the constitution does not require that the journal affirmatively show the suspension.

6. When an act is read at length the required number of times but certain amendments to the act are not so read, the act nevertheless retains its identity and the reading of the entire act for the required number of times is sufficient.

7. The mere fact that the house journals disclosed that a bill had been read as required by law and that the title in each case in the record was correct but that the number of the bill was erroneously set down

---

Sec. 723, Par. 3: Tarr v. Western Savings and Loan (1909), 15 Idaho 741, 99 P. 1049; State of Iowa v. Livermore (1921), 192 Iowa 626, 185 N.W. 1; County Commissioners of Washington v. Baker (1922), 141 Md. 623, 119 A. 461; City of Charlotte v. Shepard (1898), 122 N.C. 602, 29 S.E. 842; Debman v. Chitty (1902), 131 N.C. 657, 43 S.E. 3.

Sec. 723, Par. 4: Ellis v. Ellis (1893), 55 Minn. 401, 56 N.W. 1056.

Sec. 723, Par. 5: Chicot County v. Davies (1882), 40 Ark. 200.

Sec. 723, Par. 6: People *ex rel.* Brady v. LaSalle St. Trust & Savings Bank (1915), 269 Ill. 518, 110 N.E. 38.

on its third reading did not invalidate the enactment, such error being a clerical misprision.

8. Whether an emergency is such as will permit a legislative body to suspend the provision requiring bills be read three times on separate days in each house is a question within the exclusive judgment of the house as to when a case of emergency arises or exists, and it is not necessary in order that the reading of the bill be considered valid that the emergency be stated in the journal.

Sec. 723, Par. 7: Marshall v. Baugh (1918), 133 Ark. 64, 201 S.W. 808.
Sec. 723, Par. 8: Weyand v. Stover (1886), 35 Kan. 545, 11 P. 355.

CHAPTER 68

PROCEDURE ON CONSIDERATION OF LEGISLATION

Sec. 726. Introduction of Legislation

See also Ch. 16, Secs. 155–165, Presentation of Motions.

1. The regular formal manner of introducing bills and other measures is for the member, in the appropriate order of business, to rise at the member's desk and secure recognition and to then present the measure, giving it to a page to be presented at the desk. When there is a regular order of business, any business properly coming up under the appropriate order requires no special consent. When such business is in the nature of submitting bills or other measures, it is the established practice in many legislative bodies to permit the documents to be sent to the desk in advance of the order of business. It is the duty of the chief legislative officers to keep all such papers in their possession and not to permit them to be removed, even by members. When the proper order of business is reached, the bills or other documents are presented from the desk without the special request of the person submitting them, and receive consideration in regular order.

2. A bill is not regarded as having been introduced until it has been delivered to the clerk, read and given a number.

Sec. 726, Par. 1: Cushing's Legislative Assemblies, Sec. 2120; Hughes, Sec. 134.

Sec. 726, Par. 2: Jefferson, Sec. XXXIII.

3. Bills are introduced in the form in which it is desired that the law will read.

4. There is nothing to prevent the introduction of identical bills in both houses.

5. When a bill has been rejected at any stage in the house in which it originated, it may not be reintroduced in the same house; but a new bill, presenting the same question or the same question in a modified form, or a bill presenting substantially the same question, may be introduced.

6. When a bill has been passed in one house and defects are discovered, it is within the established practice to permit the introduction of a new bill in the same house with the corrections desired.

7. State constitutions sometimes provide that bills may not be introduced after a certain time or period except by consent of the house or by unanimous consent. It is the practice of many legislatures to place stringent limitations upon the introduction of bills after a particular date or period. Such limitations are of an entirely different nature than the general rule concerning the objection to consideration, and where such rules are adopted, measures or motions may be submitted only as authorized by the rules.

8. When a bill has been introduced into the legislature within the time limit prescribed by the constitution for the introduction of bills, amendments

Sec. 726, Par. 3: Cushing's Legislative Assemblies, Sec. 2055.
Sec. 726, Par. 4: Cushing's Legislative Assemblies, Secs. 2321, 2322.
Sec. 726, Par. 5: Cushing's Legislative Assemblies, Sec. 2321.
Sec. 726, Par. 6: Cushing's Legislative Assemblies, Sec. 2323.
Sec. 726, Par. 7: Jefferson, Sec. XVIII.

which are germane to the purpose of the bill may be made after that limit has expired and bills may be consolidated after that date.

9. When amendments are required to be made only by setting out the section or law to be amended in full as amended, new sections can be added to an act without setting out the entire act.

Sec. 727. Withdrawal of Bills

See also Sec. 272, Right to Withdraw Motions.

1. A bill may be withdrawn prior to introduction, which consists of giving it a number and reading it by title. A bill may not be withdrawn, after introduction, in the absence of a special rule, without the consent of the body. Many legislative bodies have provided by rule that a bill may be withdrawn without consent before decision or amendment. Under such a rule a bill may be withdrawn after a motion is made concerning it, or after an amendment is proposed, but before the adoption of either. As long as no rule is violated, a bill may be withdrawn, with the consent of the body, at any time prior to passage.

2. When a bill is withdrawn, the situation is as though the bill had never been before the house, and the same bill or a similar bill may

---

Sec. 726, Par. 8: State of Nebraska v. Ryan (1912), 92 Neb. 636, 139 N.W. 235; People *ex rel.* Hart v. McElroy (1889), 72 Mich. 446, 40 N.W. 750; Hale v. McGettigan (1896), 114 Cal. 112, 45 P. 1049.

Sec. 726, Par. 9: People *ex rel.* City of Springfield v. Edmands (1911), 252 Ill. 108, 96 N.E. 914.

Sec. 727, Par. 1: Cushing's Legislative Assemblies, Secs. 1235, 1240, 1241, 1477; Hughes, Secs. 205, 206; U.S. House Rule XVI, Par. 2.

be again introduced.

Sec. 728. Bill Numbers

1. The number of a bill is not part of the act but is a convenient device for identifying bills in legislative procedure.

2. When there is a discrepancy between the number and the title of a bill, the title will control.

3. When a bill is identified only by number and the number could refer to a different bill, it will not be presumed that a wrong number was erroneously used.

Sec. 729. Titles to Legislation

1. The main object of a provision requiring that every act shall embrace but one subject which shall be expressed in its title is to prevent a legislative body and the public from being entrapped by misleading titles, whereby legislation relating to one subject might be obtained under the title of another; and in the accomplishment of this object the provision is not to receive narrow or technical construction.

2. Discrepancies and irregularities in the title of legislation as it appears in various places in the journal will not invalidate the legislation as long as

---

Sec. 727, Par. 2: State of Nebraska v. Ryan (1912), 92 Neb. 636, 139 N.W. 235; State of Nebraska v. Cronin (1904), 72 Neb. 636, 101 N.W. 325; Price v. City of Moundsville (1897), 43 W.Va. 522, 27 S.E. 218.

Sec. 728, Par. 1: Volusia County v. State of Florida (1929), 98 Fla. 1166, 125 So. 375.

Sec. 728, Par. 3: State of Wisconsin v. Wendler (1896), 94 Wis. 369, 68 N.W. 759.

Sec. 729, Par. 1: Heron v. Riley (1930), 209 Cal. 507, 289 P. 160; Liffeau v. Metropolitan Sports Facilities Commission (1977), 270 N.W.2d 749.

there is no question of identity and the legislation is properly enrolled.

3. When the object of an act as passed is fully expressed in the title, the form or status at its introduction, or during the stages of legislation before it becomes a law, is immaterial.

4. It is not necessary that an act retain the same title through all its stages in both houses. The title of the bill as it is adopted by the legislature controls, not the title by which the bill may have been introduced or which it may have carried in reports of committees.

Sec. 730. Emergency Clauses—Legislation Immediately Effective

1. Courts will not ordinarily inquire into existence of an emergency nor question a provision

Sec. 729, Par. 2: Weyand v. Stover (1886), 35 Kan. 545, 11 P. 355; Clifton v. State of Alabama (1928), 22 Ala. App. 559, 118 So. 235; Ewing v. McGehee (1925), 169 Ark. 448, 275 S.W. 766; Desha-Drew Road Improvement Dist. v. Taylor (1917), 130 Ark. 503, 197 S.W. 1152; State of Florida v. Bethea (1911), 61 Fla. 60, 55 So. 550; Volusia County v. State of Florida (1929), 98 Fla. 1166, 125 So. 375; Ellis v. Parsell (1894), 100 Mich. 170, 58 N.W. 839; *Ex parte* Seward (1923), 299 Mo. 385, 253 S.W. 356, *error dismissed sub nom.* Seward v. Brady, 264 U.S. 599, 44 S. Ct. 335, 68 L. Ed. 869; Tyson v. City of Salisbury (1909), 151 N.C. 418, 66 S.E. 532; Nelson v. Haywood County (1892), 91 Tenn. 596, 20 S.W. 1; State of Wisconsin v. Wendler (1896), 94 Wis. 369, 68 N.W. 759; Walnut v. Wade (1880), 103 U.S. 683.

Sec. 729, Par. 3: Common Council of Detroit v. Schmid (1901), 128 Mich. 379, 87 N.W. 383; People *ex rel.* Hart v. McElroy (1889), 72 Mich. 446, 40 N.W. 750; State of Nebraska v. Cronin (1904), 72 Neb. 636, 101 N.W. 325.

Sec. 729, Par. 4: Walnut v. Wade (1880), 103 U.S. 683; Cantini v. Tillman (1893), 54 F. 969; Illinois Central R. Co. v. People (1892), 143 Ill. 434, 33 N.E. 173; *Ex parte* Seward (1923), 299 Mo. 385, 253 S.W. 356, *error dismissed sub nom.* Seward v. Brady, 264 U.S. 599, 44 S. Ct. 335, 68 L. Ed. 869; State of Missouri v. Field (1892), 119 Mo. 593, 24 S.W. 752; Milwaukee County v. Isenring (1901), 109 Wis. 9, 85 N.W. 131; Nelson v. Haywood County (1892), 91 Tenn. 596, 20 S.W. 1; Chicago B. & Q. R. Co. v. Smyth (1900), 103 F. 376.

passed by the requisite vote declaring the existence of an emergency, providing that legislation shall by reason thereof become immediately effective.

2. The failure of one house to pass a bill on the first vote by a majority necessary to make certain provisions of the act effective does not amount to an amendment striking out these provisions. When a bill passed one house but did not receive sufficient votes to make the emergency clause effective and was sent to the other house, there amended, passed with a vote sufficient to make the emergency clause effective, was returned to the first house where the amendments were concurred in by a vote sufficient to make the emergency clause effective and the speaker declared the emergency clause carried, both houses adopted the emergency clause by the constitutional vote necessary to make the clause effective.

3. When, on the original passage of a bill, one house voted that the bill should take effect immediately and the other house, after amending the bill, passed it by a like vote, the bill took effect immediately although the first house, when it concurred in the amendments, did not vote again to make the bill effective immediately.

4. When a bill was passed by one house with an emergency clause which was omitted in the other and the journals did not show that it had been amended, the statute was invalid as not being passed by both houses.

Sec. 730, Par. 1: Hill v. Taylor (1936), 264 Ky. 708, 95 S.W.2d 566.

Sec. 730, Par. 2: State of North Dakota *ex rel.* Sorlie v. Steen (1927), 55 N.D. 239, 212 N.W. 843.

Sec. 730, Par. 3: People v. Burch (1891), 84 Mich. 408, 47 N.W. 765.

Sec. 730, Par. 4: People v. Knopf (1902), 188 Ill. 340, 64 N.E. 843.

5. The constitutional provision that no act can go into effect until 90 days after adjournment, except acts calling elections, providing for tax levies and certain other purposes and emergency measures, which require a two-thirds vote, did not prevent a sales tax act from going into effect immediately though passed by only a majority vote.

Sec. 731. Amendment of Bills

See also Ch. 38, Secs. 395–421, Motion to Amend, and Sec. 407, Amendment of Titles of Bills.

1. It is competent for the legislature to correct defects or imperfections or to amend a bill at any time before the final passage as long as the subject of the bill is not essentially changed.

2. A bill is open to amendment on second reading and upon third reading. Amendments to bills are frequently proposed in committee but can be adopted only upon second and third readings or upon the adoption of a conference report.

3. A bill, after passing a house, may be materially amended in the other and passed as amended, this practice being in accordance with common legislative procedure; and the amendments may take the form of the substitution of an entirely new bill for the bill introduced, as long as the subject of the bill is not changed.

4. The right of amendment, in the absence of constitutional restrictions, may be exercised with

---

Sec. 730, Par. 5: Roth Drugs v. Johnson (1936), 13 Cal. App. 2d 720, 57 P.2d 1022.

Sec. 731, Par. 2: Cushing's Legislative Assemblies, Sec. 2328; N.Y. Manual, p. 405; Hughes, Sec. 795.

Sec. 731, Par. 3: State of Florida v. Dillon (1900), 42 Fla. 95, 28 So. 781; Thrift v. Towers (1915), 127 Md. 54, 95 A. 1064.

equal freedom by either house irrespective of the house in which the bill originated.

5. It is not proper for any member or officer to make any change in a legislative proposal except as may be ordered by the body. Unless the rules so provide, it is not proper even to correct a clerical error in a measure after its introduction, the proper procedure being to present an amendment to accomplish that purpose.

Sec. 732. Printing of Bills

1. The constitutional provisions requiring the printing of bills are mandatory.

2. A constitutional provision requiring a bill to be printed with amendments before passage is mandatory, and acquiescence in a failure to comply with the provision for a long period of time will not be permitted by the courts to defeat the requirement.

3. When the constitution requires a printed bill to be before the house before it is voted upon for passage, the bill must be printed in the form required by the rules. When the rules require amendatory or amended bills to be printed in a particular manner, the bill is not properly on the files or before

---

Sec. 731, Par. 4: In re Amendments of Legislative Bills (1894), 19 Colo. 356, 35 P. 917.

Sec. 732, Par. 1: In re House Bill No. 250 (1899), 26 Colo. 234, 57 P. 49; Cohn v. Kingsley (1897), 5 Idaho 416, 49 P. 985; Neiberger v. McCullough (1912), 253 Ill. 312, 97 N.E. 660; State of Nebraska v. Burlington N.R.R. Co. (1900), 60 Neb. 741, 84 N.W. 254; People *ex rel.* Hatch v. Reardon (1906), 184 N.Y. 431, 77 N.E. 970.

Sec. 732, Par. 2: Neiberger v. McCullough (1912), 253 Ill. 312, 97 N.E. 660; People *ex rel.* Hatch v. Reardon (1906), 184 N.Y. 431, 77 N.E. 970.

the house until it is printed in conformity with the rules.

4. A constitutional requirement that a bill be printed before it shall be considered or become a law does not necessitate the printing of the bill before it is read, but it is sufficient if it is printed before it is taken up for debate or amendment.

5. It is not necessary that the journal affirmatively show that bills were printed before consideration or passage unless the constitution contains that requirement, as it will be presumed that the bills were printed in compliance with the requirement.

6. When a constitutional provision requires that all substantial amendments to a bill be printed, the question as to what is a substantial amendment is a judicial question.

7. The object of the requirement for the printing of bills is to prevent fraud and trickery, deceit and subterfuge in the enactment of bills and to prevent hasty and ill-considered legislation.

Sec. 732, Par. 3: N.Y. Manual, pp. 405, 454.

Sec. 732, Par. 4: Mass. Mutual Life Insurance Co. v. Colorado Loan & Trust Co. (1894), 20 Colo. 1, 36 P. 793.

Sec. 732, Par. 5: People *ex rel.* Brady v. LaSalle St. Trust & Savings Bank (1915), 269 Ill. 518, 110 N.E. 38; Mass. Mutual Life Insurance Co. v. Colorado Loan & Trust Co. (1894), 20 Colo. 1, 36 P. 793; State of Missouri v. Field (1892), 119 Mo. 593, 24 S.W. 752; *Ex parte* Seward (1923), 299 Mo. 385, 253 S.W. 356, *error dismissed sub nom.* Seward v. Brady, 264 U.S. 599, 44 S. Ct. 335, 68 L. Ed. 869; State of Nebraska v. Cox (1920), 105 Neb. 175, 178 N.W. 913. In Illinois where the constitution specifically requires that bills be printed with amendments before passage and where "the journals must show on their face a compliance with every requirement of the constitution," failure of the journals to show that conference amendments were printed in the bill before the adoption of a conference report was held to invalidate a bill.

Sec. 732, Par. 6: *In re* House Bill No. 250 (1899), 26 Colo. 234, 57 P. 49.

Sec. 732, Par. 7: *In re* House Bill No. 250 (1899), 26 Colo. 234, 57 P. 49.

Sec. 733. First Reading of Bills

1. The usual procedure on introduction of a bill is for the bill to be given a number, read the first time by title and referred by the presiding officer to the appropriate committee.

2. Amendments may not be proposed to a bill at the first reading nor before reference to committee unless the bill is considered without reference to committee.

3. It is not usual for a bill to be opposed on first reading but it may be opposed and rejected at this stage unless this action is prevented by some rule of the house.

4. When the rules require that all bills be referred to committee or make other like provisions, the introduction of a bill may not be objected to without first suspending the rules.

Sec. 734. Second Reading of Bills

1. When bills are required to be read on three several days, the second reading must, of course, be on a day following the day upon which the bill was read the first time, unless the rule may be suspended and the proper steps to suspend the rule have been taken.

2. Upon second reading of a bill it is open to amendment.

Sec. 733, Par. 2: Hughes, Sec. 203; Jefferson, Sec. XXIV.

Sec. 733, Par. 3: Jefferson, Sec. XXIV.

Sec. 734, Par. 1: Jefferson, Sec. XXV.

Sec. 734, Par. 2: Hughes, Sec. 795; Cushing's Legislative Assemblies, Sec. 2328; N.Y. Manual, p. 405.

3. On taking up a bill reported by a committee with amendments, the committee amendments are disposed of before any other amendments are admitted, except an amendment to a committee amendment. When the amendments proposed by the committee are disposed of, the presiding officer should pause and give time for amendments to be proposed from the floor, as is also done when a bill has been reported without amendments. When the bill has been read the second time, and any amendments disposed of, it is ordered to engrossment and third reading, or to print, engrossment and third reading.

4. When a bill is favorably reported by a committee and an identical bill from the other house is on third reading, the rules of many of the legislatures provide that a motion is in order that the bill reported from committee, when read the second time, be substituted for the bill on the third reading calendar, and if this action is taken, the effect is to indefinitely postpone the bill already on the calendar.

Sec. 735. Engrossment of Bills

1. All bills must be engrossed prior to third reading, and when a bill is amended on third reading, it must be re-engrossed before it can be considered again for passage.

2. An engrossment is a proofreading and verification in order to be certain that the bill before the house is identical with the original bill as introduced with all amendments which have been adopted cor-

Sec. 734, Par. 3: Jefferson, Sec. XXIX.

Sec. 734, Par. 4: Hughes, Sec. 872.

Sec. 735, Par. 1: Cushing's Legislative Assemblies, Sec. 2133; N.Y. Manual, p. 419.

rectly inserted. The engrossment is usually done under the direction of a clerk or secretary or a committee on engrossment and enrollment. The engrossed bill is also usually reprinted, omitting the means of indicating the amendments, when bills are printed in this manner. The copy of the bill, when reported by the committee as correctly engrossed, is substituted for the official original bill on the files.

Sec. 736. Third Reading of Bills

1. On third reading, a bill is presented for consideration and passage.

2. Amendments on third reading of a bill are not favored but are permitted. After passage, the title of a bill may be amended to conform to the body, but the body of a bill is no longer subject to amendment, except upon reconsideration.

3. Motions affecting bills on third reading are not in order, even under that order of business until the particular bill is reached upon the calendar.

4. A motion or request for the reading of a bill for the information of the members is not in order after the roll call has been ordered.

Sec. 737. Passage of Bills

1. The word "passage," used in connection with legislation, refers to the compliance with all the

Sec. 735, Par. 2: Cushing's Legislative Assemblies, Sec. 2284.
Sec. 736, Par. 1: Jefferson, Sec. XL.
Sec. 736, Par. 2: Jefferson, Sec. XL.
Sec. 736, Par. 3: N.Y. Manual, p. 419.
Sec. 736, Par. 4: N.Y. Manual, p. 448.

forms necessary to give force and effect to the legislation.

2. A bill is not duly enacted until it has been voted on affirmatively by both houses in its final form.

3. Under the U.S. system of government, the house and senate are separate and independent bodies, and their votes are to be taken and counted separately.

4. The fact that there is agreement between the houses as to the contents of a bill should appear with certainty, but it is sufficient if it be clear from the record as a whole that the bill, as finally passed by both houses, was identical.

Sec. 737, Par. 1: People v. Coffin (1917), 279 Ill. 401, 117 N.E. 185.

Sec. 737, Par. 2: Chicago B. & Q. R. Co. v. Smyth (1900), 103 F. 376; Jefferson County v. Crow (1904), 14 Ala. 126, 37 So. 469; Rogers v. State of Arkansas (1904), 72 Ark. 565, 82 S.W. 169; State of Connecticut v. Savings Bank of New London (1906), 79 Conn. 141, 64 A. 5; Volusia County v. State of Florida (1929), 98 Fla. 1166, 125 So. 375; People v. Knopf (1902), 188 Ill. 340, 64 N.E. 843; Norman v. Ky. Board of Managers (1892), 93 Ky. 537, 20 S.W. 901; State of Louisiana *ex rel.* Caillouet v. Laiche (1901), 105 La. 84, 29 So. 700; County Commissioners of Washington v. Baker (1922), 141 Md. 623, 119 A. 461; Ellis v. Parsell (1894), 100 Mich. 170, 58 N.W. 839; Johnson v. City of Great Falls (1909), 38 Mont. 369, 99 P. 1059; State of Nebraska v. Cox (1920), 105 Neb. 175, 178 N.W. 913; *In re* Opinion of the Justices (1857), 35 N.H. 579; *In re* Jaegle (1912), 83 N.J.L. 313, 85 A. 214; Tyson v. City of Salisbury (1909), 151 N.C. 418, 66 S.E. 532; State of North Dakota v. Schultz (1919), 44 N.D. 269, 174 N.W. 81; State of Oregon v. Boyer (1917), 84 Ore. 513, 165 P. 587; State of Tennessee v. Persica (1914), 130 Tenn. 48, 168 S.W. 1056; Wilson v. Young County Hardware & Furniture Co. (Tex. Civ. App. 1924), 262 S.W. 873; Smith v. Mitchell (1911), 69 W.Va. 481, 72 S.E. 755; State of Wisconsin v. Wendler (1896), 94 Wis. 369, 68 N.W. 759; Arbuckle v. Pflaeging (1912), 20 Wyo. 351, 123 P. 918.

Sec. 737, Par. 3: Belote v. Coffman (1915), 117 Ark. 352, 175 S.W. 37.

Sec. 737, Par. 4: Perry v. State of Arkansas (1919), 139 Ark. 227, 214 S.W. 2; Walnut v. Wade (1880), 103 U.S. 683; Butler v. Board of Directors (1912), 103 Ark. 109, 146 S.W. 120; State of Florida v. Bethea (1911), 61 Fla. 60, 55 So. 550; City of Lansing v. Michigan Power Co. (1914), 183 Mich. 400, 150 N.W. 250.

5. When a house has passed a bill, and it is out of that body's possession, as when it has been returned to the other house which has refused to return the bill, jurisdiction of the bill has been lost and it has been finally passed.

6. When a bill has been voted upon favorably by both houses, but a motion to reconsider its action in passing the bill is pending in the house last acting on the bill and the bill is still in its possession, the bill has not been finally passed by both houses.

7. The fact that legislative action in the passage of a bill is taken on Sunday does not render the action ineffective.

8. Concurrence by one house in amendments of the other to a bill is "final passage" within the meaning of the requirements of passage by roll call.

Sec. 738. Enrollment of Bills

See also Sec. 702, The Enrolled Bill (Sec. 697, Enrolled Bill Rule and Presumptions Favor Enrolled Bill and notes to Sec. 697).

1. An enrolled bill, in legislative parlance, is a reproduction or copy of the identical bill passed by both houses.

Sec. 737, Par. 5: Smith v. Mitchell (1911), 69 W.Va. 481, 72 S.E. 755.

Sec. 737, Par. 6: State of Connecticut v. Savings Bank of New London (1906), 79 Conn. 141, 64 A. 5; Crawford v. Gilchrist (1912), 64 Fla. 41, 59 So. 963.

Sec. 737, Par. 7: *Ex parte* Seward (1923), 299 Mo. 385, 253 S.W. 356, *error dismissed sub nom.* Seward v. Brady, 264 U.S. 599, 44 S. Ct. 335, 68 L. Ed. 869.

Sec. 737, Par. 8: Cox v. Stults Eagle Drug Co. (1933), 42 Ariz. 1, 21 P.2d 914.

Sec. 738, Par. 1: Rice v. Lonoke-Cabot Road Improvement Dist. (1920), 142 Ark. 454, 221 S.W. 179.

2. After passage a bill is enrolled, authenticated by the signatures of the presiding officers and chief legislative officers of both houses and presented to the governor for signature.

3. The enrolling clerk or committee has no power or authority to modify in any respect a bill passed by the legislature, but a correction may be made by concurrent resolution prior to enrollment.

4. A bill as enrolled and presented to the governor should be to the same effect as the bill passed by both houses of the legislature. A bill presented to the governor in a form different from that in which it was passed, if the change is material, is void even if signed. Correction of purely typographical errors or errors in form only, apparently, will not invalidate legislation.

5. The governor, in signing an enrolled bill, approves the bill as passed by the legislature, the enrolled bill being merely a reproduction thereof and the act not being impaired by additions, omissions or misprisions of the enrolling clerk in copying the bill.

Sec. 738, Par. 3: Rice v. Lonoke-Cabot Road Improvement Dist. (1920), 142 Ark. 454, 221 S.W. 179; Katerndahl v. Daugherty (1917), 30 Idaho 356, 164 P. 1017; Davis v. State (1920), 88 Tex. Crim. 183, 225 S.W. 532; State of Wisconsin *ex rel.* Pollard v. Wisconsin Board of Medical Examiners (1920), 172 Wis. 317, 177 N.W. 910.

Sec. 738, Par. 4: Gwynn v. Hardee (1926), 92 Fla. 543, 110 So. 343; People *ex rel.* Dezettel v. Lueders (1918), 283 Ill. 287, 119 N.E. 339; Katerndahl v. Daugherty (1917), 30 Idaho 356, 164 P. 1017; Davis v. State (1920), 88 Tex. Crim. 183, 225 S.W. 532; State of Wisconsin *ex rel.* Pollard v. Board of Medical Examiners (1920), 172 Wis. 317, 177 N.W. 910.

Sec. 738, Par. 5: Ewing v. McGehee (1925), 169 Ark. 448, 275 S.W. 766; Rice v. Lonoke-Cabot Road Improvement Dist. (1920), 142 Ark. 454, 221 S.W. 179.

Sec. 739. Authentication of Passage of Bills

1. After a bill has been passed by both houses and enrolled, it is signed by the presiding officer and chief legislative officer of the house where it originated and then sent to the other house, where it is signed by the presiding officer and chief legislative officer. Procedure for the authentication of legislation prescribed by the constitution or other controlling authority must be complied with.

2. Where a bill has duly passed a legislative body, the presiding officer must sign it. When there is no prescribed procedure to determine whether legislation has been duly passed, that decision is made by the presiding officer subject to appeal and decision by the body.

3. When a state constitution designates certain officers to sign bills, the signature of an assistant, acting in the capacity of the principal, is substantial and sufficient compliance with the requirement of the provision.

4. The duty of the presiding officer to sign legislation, properly passed by the body over which that person presides, is a legislative act and not a ministerial one, and a writ of mandate or an injunction will not lie to compel the presiding officer to sign or to restrain that person from signing legislation. If a presiding officer should refuse to sign legislation which has been duly passed, that person could be

---

Sec. 739, Par. 1: Jefferson, Sec. XLVIII; Amos v. Gunn (1922), 84 Fla. 285, 94 So. 615.

Sec. 739, Par. 2: Amos v. Gunn (1922), 84 Fla. 285, 94 So. 615; State of Missouri v. Meier (1898), 143 Mo. 439, 45 S.W. 306; Allbright v. Fisher (1901), 164 Mo. 56, 64 S.W. 106.

Sec. 739, Par. 3: Robertson v. State of Alabama (1901), 130 Ala. 164, 30 So. 494; State of Nevada v. Glenn (1883), 18 Nev. 34, 1 P. 186.

required to do so or be deposed from office and another presiding officer elected who would have authority and whose duty it would be to sign the legislation.

Sec. 740. Presentation of Bills to the Governor

See also Sec. 755, Procedure on Veto of Legislation.

1. After being authenticated, an enrolled bill must be presented by the committee on enrollment, or officer charged with this duty, to the governor and that fact is reported to the house.

2. The procedure for the presentation of legislation to the executive for approval is usually prescribed in detail by the constitution and rules.

3. In presenting legislation to the executive for approval, constitutional or other controlling provisions must, of course, be strictly followed.

4. When a bill has passed both branches of the legislature and has been signed by the appropriate officers and sent to the governor for approval, it has passed beyond the control of either house and cannot be recalled except by the joint action of both houses.

Sec. 739, Par. 4: Amos v. Gunn (1922), 84 Fla. 285, 94 So. 615; *Ex parte* Echols (1866), 39 Ala. 698. In Kansas, the failure of the lieutenant governor, as the presiding officer of the senate, to certify to the passage of a bill as required by the constitution, was held not to render the act invalid. It was argued in the opinion that if such a failure invalidated the act it would, in effect, give the lieutenant governor veto power. State of Wyoming v. Cahill (1904), 12 Wyo. 225, 75 P. 433.

Sec. 740, Par. 1: People v. Devlin (1865), 33 N.Y. 269; Amos v. Gunn (1922), 84 Fla. 285, 94 So. 615.

Sec. 740, Par. 4: People v. Devlin (1865), 33 N.Y. 269.

5. When a bill is presented to the governor without amendments adopted in the legislature and is signed by the governor, the bill is void.

Sec. 741. Effective Date of Legislation

1. A statute speaks from the time it commences to take effect.

2. Different parts of the same statute may go into effect at different times unless prohibited by constitutional provisions.

3. A statute may be in effect in the sense that it is a valid subsisting law but not become operative until a later or future date.

4. The time a particular statute shall take effect may be fixed by another statute passed at the same legislative session.

Sec. 740, Par. 5: In re Jaegle (1912), 83 N.J.L. 313, 85 A. 214.
Sec. 741, Par. 1: State of Missouri *ex rel.* Otto v. Kansas City (1925), 310 Mo. 542, 276 S.W. 389.

PART VIII. RELATIONS WITH THE EXECUTIVE AND WITH THE OTHER HOUSE

*

Part VIII

RELATIONS WITH THE EXECUTIVE AND WITH THE OTHER HOUSE

CHAPTER 69

RELATIONS WITH THE EXECUTIVE

Sec. 750. Messages from the Governor

Messages from the governor relating to the bills or measures of one house need be sent only to that house, but messages relating to general matters should be communicated to both houses. Where the subject of a message is of such a nature that it should be communicated to both houses of the legislature, it should be communicated to both on the same day and as nearly at the same hour as conditions reasonably permit.

Sec. 751. Confirmation of Appointments of the Governor

1. It is not in order for the presiding officer to question the legality of an appointment by the governor which is regularly before the house for confirmation.

Sec. 750: Jefferson, Sec. XLVII.

Sec. 751, Par. 1: N.Y. Manual, p. 454; State of Minnesota *ex rel.* Todd v. Essling (1964), 128 N.W.2d 307.

2. A motion to reconsider a vote confirming or refusing to confirm an appointment of the governor is not in order after the notice of the action of the house has been transmitted to the governor.

See also Ch. 41, Secs. 450–474, Motion to Reconsider, and particularly Sec. 453, Election or Confirmation of Officers.

Sec. 752. Reference to Executive in Debate

It is inappropriate for a member in debate to use the name of the executive for the purpose of influencing votes of the members.

Sec. 753. Communications with Executive

1. Upon the organization of the houses of a legislature, each should notify the governor of its organization. This notice is usually sent by committee, but in some states the notice is sent by message.

2. A constitutional provision requiring the governor to certify to the necessity of immediate passage of a bill is supplied by a message to one house and no certification to the other is necessary.

3. If either house desires to revise an enacted bill, concurrent action of the two houses should be taken, and the motion should be one providing that a message be sent by the two houses requesting the governor to return the bill. It is the practice in some states for one house to request the return of the bill without the concurrence of the other house.

Sec. 751, Par. 2: N.Y. Manual, p. 454.

Sec. 752: Cushing's Legislative Assemblies, Sec. 738.

Sec. 753, Par. 1: Cushing's Legislative Assemblies, Sec. 277.

Sec. 753, Par. 2: People *ex rel.* Durham Realty Corporation v. La Setra (1920), 185 N.Y.S. 638.

Sec. 753, Par. 3: Mass. Manual, p. 594.

Sec. 754. Executive Approval or Rejection of Legislation

1. There are three ways in which a bill may become a law:

(a) By signature of the governor after passage by the legislature.

(b) By the governor's retention of the bill for a specified period or beyond a specified period without action on the bill while both houses are in session.

(c) By passage of the bill over the veto of the governor.

2. The approval of the executive to legislation must be in writing.

3. When legislation is approved by the governor, it is signed and transmitted to the secretary of state who assigns a chapter number to each law, files it in the secretary of state's office and makes such publication as the law requires.

4. It is not necessary to the validity of a law that the governor should inform the legislative body of approval. However, it is common practice in most states that the governor communicate approval to the legislative body.

5. When the recitals of a legislative journal show that a bill was not returned by the governor with a

Sec. 754, Par. 1: Parkinson v. Johnson (1911), 160 Cal. 756, 117 P. 1057.
Sec. 754, Par. 2: Martindale v. Palmer (1876), 52 Ind. 411.
Sec. 754, Par. 4: U.S. Constitution, Art. I, Sec. 7, Par. 2, Note 106 in House Manual.

veto within the time prescribed by the constitution, it became a law.

6. The constitutional provisions with reference to the time within which a governor must veto a bill or have it go into effect without the governor's signature is mandatory with respect to both the time and manner of exercising the veto power.

7. A constitutional provision relating to legislative consideration of vetoed bills is construed in connection with the constitutional provision authorizing each house to determine its rules of procedure.

8. A constitutional provision may require that when a governor vetoes a bill the governor must return it to the house where it originated, and if that house passes over the governor's objection, it is then sent to the other for consideration. If the house of origin fails to pass the bill by the required majority, the bill is not transmitted to the other body for consideration.

9. In most states, when the governor returns a bill to either house without approval, the objections of the governor are entered upon the journal of its proceedings. However, unless specifically required by the constitution, it is not necessary that the journal of the house to which the bill is returned contain an entry of the time when it was returned.

Sec. 754, Par. 5: State of Tennessee *ex rel.* Thompson v. Dixie Finance Co. (1925), 152 Tenn. 306, 278 S.W. 59; Parkinson v. Johnson (1911), 160 Cal. 756, 117 P. 1057.

Sec. 754, Par. 6: Capito v. Topping (1909), 65 W.Va. 587, 64 S.E. 845.

Sec. 754, Par. 7: State of South Carolina *ex rel.* Coleman v. Lewis (1936), 181 S.C. 10, 186 S.E. 625.

Sec. 754, Par. 8: Webb v. Carter (1914), 129 Tenn. 182, 165 S.W. 426.

Sec. 754, Par. 9: Parkinson v. Johnson (1911), 160 Cal. 756, 117 P. 1057.

10. When legislation is passed so late in the session that the session ends prior to the expiration of the time the governor is given to act on bills, the governor has the power to withhold action on the bill and let it die from failure to approve it. This is called the pocket veto.

11. The executive may sign legislation within the time allowed for consideration, even though the legislature may have adjourned or taken a recess.

12. While engaged in considering bills which have passed both houses of the legislature and are before the governor for approval or disapproval, the governor acts in a legislative and not in an executive capacity.

Sec. 755. Procedure on Veto of Legislation

1. It is permissible to reconsider a vote refusing to pass a bill over the executive veto, notwithstanding that the first vote is described in the constitution as a reconsideration of the bill.

2. Legislation which is not approved by the executive is returned to the house in which it originated by the executive within the time allowed the executive to consider and act upon legislation. It is first considered by this house and, if approved by the required vote, sent to the other house, where it is considered. If approved by the second house by the required vote, it is transmitted with a certificate of

---

Sec. 754, Par. 11: Edwards v. U.S. (1931), 286 U.S. 482.

Sec. 754, Par. 12: Lukens v. Nye (1909), 156 Cal. 498, 105 P. 593.

Sec. 755, Par. 1: U.S. Constitution, Art. I, Sec. 7, Par. 2, Notes 108 and 109 in House Manual; Mass. Manual, p. 596; N.Y. Manual (1948–49), p. 453.

passage notwithstanding the objections of the executive.

3. Legislation returned by the executive with objections is usually considered promptly but may be referred to committee or laid on the table.

Sec. 756. Recalling Legislation from the Executive

1. Legislation incorrectly enrolled may be recalled from the executive for correction.

2. Legislation is also sometimes recalled from the executive for further consideration. Legislation is usually recalled by a resolution but sometimes a committee is sent to the executive for that purpose.

3. The vote upon final passage of a bill recalled from the governor may be reconsidered at any time after its return in the house having such bill in its possession.

Sec. 757. Legislative Oversight of the Executive Branch

1. Legislatures have undertaken significant responsibilities for overseeing the operations of the executive branch. Ensuring the effective implementation and operation of state government programs is a legitimate responsibility of the legislature.

Sec. 755, Par. 2: U.S. Constitution, Art. I, Sec. 7, Par. 2, Notes 108 and 109 in House Manual; Mass. Manual, p. 596; N.Y. Manual (1948–49), p. 453.

Sec. 755, Par. 3: U.S. Constitution, Art. I, Sec. 7, Par. 2, Notes 108 and 109 in House Manual; Mass. Manual, p. 596; N.Y. Manual (1948–49), p. 453.

2. Legislatures use several mechanisms to oversee the operation of the executive branch. These include program evaluation and performance auditing units, review and analysis of agency budgets and the review of administrative regulations.

3. To better monitor and maintain control over state expenditures when the legislature is not in session, several legislatures have delegated authority to adjust appropriations to a committee of the legislature. Some state courts have determined that such delegation of budget authority to legislative committees is an unconstitutional delegation of the legislatures' powers.

4. Legislative committees may be created to investigate any subject legitimately within the scope of functions, powers and duties of the legislature. The legislature may continue its investigatory function between sessions. The legislature may require information from other branches of government as is reasonably necessary to complete the work of the committees.

Sec. 758. Legislative Review of Regulations

1. To provide for the effective oversight of state agencies, legislatures have established procedures

Sec. 757, Par. 3: State of Montana *ex rel.* Judge v. Legislative Finance Committee and Its Members (1975), 168 Mont. 470, 543 P.2d 1317; State of Kansas *ex rel.* Schneider v. Bennett (1976), 547 P.2d 786; State of Louisiana *ex rel.* Guste v. Legislative Budget Committee (1977), 347 So. 2d 160; *In re* Opinion of the Justices (1982), 305 N.C. No. 1; Legislative Research Commission by and through Prather v. Brown, Governor (1984), 664 S.W.2d 907.

Sec. 757, Par. 4: State of Montana *ex rel.* Judge v. Legislative Finance Committee and Its Members (1975), 168 Mont. 470, 543 P.2d 1317; State of Washington *ex rel.* Robinson v. Fluent (1948), 30 Wash. 2d 194, 191 P.2d 241, *cert. denied,* Washington Pension Union v. State of Washington *ex rel.* Robinson, 335 U.S. 844, 69 S. Ct. 66, 93 L. Ed. 394.

for reviewing administrative rules and regulations. Generally, this review considers whether the agencies have statutory authority to promulgate the regulations and whether the regulations are consistent with the legislature's intent when granting rule-making authority. Over 40 legislatures review rules and regulations.

2. Some legislatures have established procedures to veto regulations that do not meet certain requirements. Legislatures have adopted different procedures for vetoing regulations including vote by committee, passage of a resolution by one chamber, passage of a resolution by both chambers and passage of a statute.

3. State courts have held that to veto administrative regulations by any means short of passage by both chambers and presentment to the governor is unconstitutional. In four states, legislative veto of regulations by other means is specifically authorized by the state constitution.

Sec. 758, Par. 3: State of Alaska v. A.L.I.V.E. Voluntary (1980), 606 P.2d 769; State of West Virginia *ex rel.* Barker v. Manchin (1981), 167 W.Va. 155, 279 S.E.2d 622; Opinion of the Justices (1981), 49 Md. App. 300, 431 A.2d 783; General Assembly of New Jersey v. Byrne (1982), 488 A.2d 438; Legislative Research Commission by and through Prather v. Brown, Governor (1984), 664 S.W.2d 907; State of Kansas *ex rel.* Stephan v. Kansas House of Representatives (1984), 236 Kan. 45, 687 P.2d 622; Connecticut Constitution Art. II; Iowa Constitution Art. III, Sec. 40; Michigan Constitution Art. IV, Sec. 37; South Dakota Constitution Art. III, Sec. 30.

CHAPTER 70

RELATIONS WITH THE OTHER HOUSE

Sec. 760. The Other House and Its Members

1. Neither house can exercise any authority over a member or officer of the other, but when some action appears advisable, one house may complain to the other concerning the conduct of a member or officer and leave any punishment to that house.

2. The members or officers of one house have no right to attempt to direct the members or officers of the other house, but either house may request the other house to instruct its officers or members concerning any matter of interest to the first house.

3. When there is complaint of words disrespectfully spoken by a member of the other house, it is difficult to obtain punishment, because of the rules supposed necessary to be observed, that the objectionable words must be immediately noted down, for the security of members. It is, therefore, the duty of the house, and more particularly of the presiding officer, to interfere immediately and not to permit expressions to go unnoticed which may give a ground of complaint to the other house and introduce proceedings and mutual accusations between the two houses.

Sec. 760, Par. 1: Jefferson, Sec. XVII; Hughes, Secs. 83, 84, 694.
Sec. 760, Par. 2: Hughes, Sec. 85.
Sec. 760, Par. 3: Jefferson, Sec. XVII; Hughes, Sec. 694.

4. It is a breach of order in debate to notice what has been said on the same subject in the other house, or the particular votes or majorities on it there, because the opinion of each house should be independent and not be influenced by the proceedings of the other, and the quoting of them might cause reflections leading to a misunderstanding between the two houses.

5. A record of a vote in the journal of one house is sufficient ground for the other house to take official notice of the action of that house.

6. It is not within the province of one house to question any action taken by a committee of the other house in reporting a bill to that branch.

Sec. 761. Communications Between the Houses

1. Communications between houses may take place by messages or by conference committees. The usual form of communication is by written message.

2. Messages may relate to passage of bills, to amendments, to questions of privilege, to recall for further consideration or to any other business between the houses.

3. Upon the organization of the houses of the legislature, each should notify the other of its orga-

---

Sec. 760, Par. 4: Jefferson, Sec. XVII; Reed, Sec. 224; Cushing's Legislative Assemblies, Sec. 739.

Sec. 760, Par. 5: Jefferson, Sec. XLIX.

Sec. 760, Par. 6: Mass. Manual, p. 697.

Sec. 761, Par. 1: Cushing's Legislative Assemblies, Sec. 804.

nization. Notice of organization may be transmitted by committee or by written message.

4. When a bill has passed one house, that fact should be noted on the bill itself with such other record as the rules or practice may require, and it should be authenticated by the signature of the secretary or chief clerk. It is usually provided by rule in U.S. legislative bodies that a bill sent from one house to the other should bear a statement of the action taken by the house, authenticated by the signature of the clerk or secretary. In the absence of any such rule, however, it appears that the passage of a bill is sufficiently authenticated by the message which accompanies it.

5. When one house has passed upon a matter and forwarded it to the other in the form provided by rule, the latter, as a rule, is bound to receive it.

6. It is a practice in some legislatures that each house notify the other of the passage of bills of the other house. When this practice is followed, the bills are returned with a message noting their passage. When a bill of one house is rejected by the other, the house in which the bill originated is notified of the action.

7. When a bill is returned from one house to the house of its origin with amendments, it is sent with a message noting the passage of the bill with amend-

---

Sec. 761, Par. 3: Cushing's Legislative Assemblies, Sec. 277.

Sec. 761, Par. 4: Cushing's Legislative Assemblies, Secs. 2276, 2285, 2293.

Sec. 761, Par. 5: Mass. Manual, p. 696.

Sec. 761, Par. 6: Jefferson, Sec. XLVII; Reed, Sec. 237; Cushing's Legislative Assemblies, Sec. 2292.

ments and requesting its concurrence in the amendments.

8. It is not within the authority of a legislative body or its committees to proceed with consideration of a bill not in its possession.

Sec. 762. Request for Return of Bill

1. When a bill is sent from one house to the other by mistake, or when the originating house wants the bill returned for the purpose of reconsideration or for correcting an error discovered after the bill was sent to the other house, it may request its return by message. Upon receipt of the message, the other house, on motion, may return the bill.

2. When a bill has been sent to one house by the other without its passage being authenticated by the signature of the secretary or clerk, the bill may be returned upon the receipt of a message requesting its return, or the signature of the secretary or clerk may be permitted to be affixed to the bill in the other house.

3. If a mistake occurs in a message accompanying a bill, the mistake may be corrected by means of a new message from the house which sent the message or by a message from the other suggesting the correction.

Sec. 761, Par. 7: Cushing's Legislative Assemblies, Secs. 2233, 2287.
Sec. 761, Par. 8: Cushing's Legislative Assemblies, Sec. 2396.
Sec. 762, Par. 1: Cushing's Legislative Assemblies, Secs. 2393, 2394.
Sec. 762, Par. 2: Cushing's Legislative Assemblies, Sec. 2393.
Sec. 762, Par. 3: Cushing's Legislative Assemblies, Sec. 2392.

Sec. 763. Delivery of Messages

1. In some legislatures, messages between the houses are sent only while both houses are sitting. In other legislatures, in lieu of the formal presentation of messages to the house, they may be presented by a messenger of one house to the appropriate officer of the other. When messages are not formally presented to the house, a receipt should be signed by an officer of the house receiving the message.

2. It is customary for messages to be received in any state of business except:

(a) While a question is being put.

(b) While roll is being called.

(c) While the ballots are being counted.

3. When a message is received while debate is in progress, the debate may be suspended long enough for the delivery of the message and the speaker is permitted to resume.

4. When a house is in committee of the whole when a message arrives, the business may be interrupted while the presiding officer takes the chair and receives the message. The business of the committee of the whole is then resumed without any motion being made or question being put.

5. When a messenger from the other house appears, that person may be announced by the sergeant at arms to the presiding officer, and the mes-

---

Sec. 763, Par. 1: Jefferson, Sec. XXVIII.
Sec. 763, Par. 2: Jefferson, Sec. XLVII.
Sec. 763, Par. 3: Jefferson, Sec. XLVII; Reed, Sec. 237.
Sec. 763, Par. 4: Jefferson, Sec. XLVII; Reed, Sec. 237.

senger may state the message and either deliver or send the message to the desk by a page.

Sec. 764. Conferences Between the Houses

See also Ch. 61, Secs. 653–659, Joint Committees.

1. It is proper for either house to request a conference with the other on any matter of difference or dispute between them. When a conference is requested, the subject of the conference should always be stated. One house may request a conference to inquire or protest concerning an offense or default on the part of a member or officer of the other house. When there is a question concerning procedure, or when an unparliamentary message has been sent, instead of replying directly, a conference should be requested. When there are questions as to procedure between the two houses, the proper procedure is to discuss the matter by a conference committee; also, where one house desires to formally present a question to the other, the question should be submitted through a conference committee.

2. Conference committees are used for this purpose in order to discuss matters between the houses in a more confidential and direct manner than they could be conducted by a message transmitted in the usual manner. The common present practice in ordinary cases appears to be for the conferences to be entirely informal and to be between the presiding officers or members without formal designation as committees, but in cases of particular importance,

Sec. 763, Par. 5: Reed, Sec. 237.
Sec. 764, Par. 1: Jefferson, Secs. XLVI, XLVII; Reed, Sec. 241.

committees may be appointed or existing committees designated for that purpose.

3. Any difference between the two branches can be submitted to a committee of conference.

Sec. 765. Coordination Through Committees

When houses have Committees on Rules or Committees on Organization or other committees with important management responsibilities, these committees, either by joint meetings or by forming a joint committee, can and do provide the means of cooperation by the leadership of the two houses and communication between the houses. Within this group, activities between the houses can be coordinated, disputes largely avoided and cooperation promoted on a very informal basis.

Sec. 764, Par. 2: Reed, Sec. 241.
Sec. 764, Par. 3: Mass. Manual, p. 682.

CHAPTER 71

CONFERENCES CONCERNING AMENDMENTS

Sec. 766. Concurrence in Amendments

See also Ch. 61, Secs. 653–659, Joint Committees, and Sec. 764, Conferences Between the Houses.

1. When a bill has been amended in the second house and passed with the amendment, it is returned by that house to the house of its origin with a message stating the facts and requesting the house where the bill originated to concur in the amendment.

2. When a message is received by one house from the other requesting it to concur in amendments, the message, upon being received, may be immediately considered or consideration may be had at some more convenient time.

3. It is proper for a house, upon receiving an amended bill with a request to concur, to refer the message with the bill to a committee for consideration and a report upon concurrence.

4. When acting upon a request for concurrence in amendments of the other house, the question should be placed upon the concurrence in the amendments, either individually or as a whole, and not upon the adoption of the report of a committee.

5. When the house of origin concurs in amendments of the other house, a message should be sent

---

Sec. 766: Cushing's Legislative Assemblies, Secs. 2233, 2334, 2337.

informing the other house of the concurrence. The bill is not returned with this message but is order enrolled.

6. When the house of origin passes a bill and sends it to the other body, parliamentary procedures which extend the amendment process possibilities include:

(a) The other body amends and passes the bill and returns it to the house of origin.

(b) The house of origin then may amend the amendment adopted by the other house and return the bill to said house; (first degree amendment).

(c) The other house again may amend the amendment and return the bill to the house of origin; (second degree amendment).

(d) Because amendments to the third degree are prohibited, the house of origin at this point must either concur and pass the bill or refuse to concur and may request a conference.

At any point during this process, either house has the option to concur and pass the bill or refuse to concur and request a conference to resolve the differences.

7. When one house is considering the question of concurrence in the amendments of the other house, amendments to the amendments of the other house only are in order. Amendments to portions of the bill already agreed to by both houses are not proper. Attempts to alter text of the bill agreed to by both houses under the guise of an amendment to the other house's amendment are not in order during

the consideration of concurrence in the amendments of the opposite house.

8. A refusal of one house to concur in amendments of the other does not have the same effect as if the bill had been passed by the latter without the amendments.

Sec. 767. Receding from Amendments

1. When one house refuses to concur in amendments of the other, the bill is not thereby lost as the house which originally adopted the amendments may be willing to recede from them.

2. A vote to recede from amendments constitutes a final passage of the bill without the amendments from which the house has receded, since both houses have then agreed to the bill in its form prior to amendment.

3. When a house which amended a bill of the other recedes from its amendments, a message to that effect is sent to the house where the bill originated and, as both houses have then agreed to the bill in the identical form, the bill has been passed in its form prior to amendment and is thereupon sent to enrollment.

4. The ancient practice in Parliament was to communicate a refusal to concur by means of a

---

Sec. 766, Par. 8: Robertson v. People (1894), 20 Colo. 279, 38 P. 326; People *ex rel.* City of Springfield v. Edmands (1911), 252 Ill. 108, 96 N.E. 914; Loomis v. Callahan (1928), 196 Wis. 518, 220 N.W. 816.

Sec. 767, Par. 1: Cushing's Legislative Assemblies, Sec. 2239.

Sec. 767, Par. 2: Robertson v. People (1894), 20 Colo. 279, 38 P. 326; People *ex rel.* City of Springfield v. Edmands (1911), 252 Ill. 108, 96 N.E. 914; Loomis v. Callahan (1928), 196 Wis. 518, 220 N.W. 816.

Sec. 767, Par. 3: Cushing's Legislative Assemblies, Sec. 2242.

conference committee. The modern U.S. practice is to communicate such a matter through an ordinary message delivered by the staff of one house to the staff of the other stating that the house has refused to concur in the amendments of the other and may request that house to recede from its amendments.

Sec. 768. Insisting and Adhering in Amendments

1. When one house refuses to recede from its amendments, the bill is not thereby lost as the house may vote to insist upon its amendments. A message is sent to the other house stating that the house has insisted upon its amendments and is usually accompanied by a request for conference.

2. When one house insists upon its amendments, the other house may then insist upon its nonconcurrence in the amendments and request a conference or recede from its nonconcurrence and concur in the amendments which would constitute a final passage of the bill with the amendments.

3. When both houses have insisted without a request for conference, it is also in order to move to adhere. Adoption of a motion to adhere represents an unyielding attitude of the adopting house.

4. It is unparliamentary for an adhering house to request a conference; however, the other house may continue to insist and request a conference. It is in order for an adhering house to recede from its adherence and agree to a conference.

Sec. 767, Par. 4: Cushing's Legislative Assemblies, Secs. 2240, 2241.

5. The motion to recede takes precedence over the motion to adhere, and the motion to adhere takes precedence over the motion to insist. All present a debatable question, only as to the amendments at issue.

Sec. 769. Appointment of Conference Committee

1. When a house refuses to recede from its amendments, the generally accepted procedure is for it to request a conference. The procedure in requesting a conference is for the house making the request to appoint its committee on conference and to send a message to the other house requesting a conference and informing the other house of the conferees.

2. Upon receiving a message requesting a conference, the house may appoint a conference committee and notify the other house of the appointment and the names of the members of the committee.

3. It is the usual practice for each house to appoint a conference committee of three members, but if the rules do not otherwise regulate the matter, either house can fix the size of its committee on conference.

4. According to the earlier practice, the same member could not be appointed to more than one conference or free conference committee on the

Sec. 769, Par. 1: Jefferson, Sec. XLVI; Cushing's Legislative Assemblies, Secs. 2243, 2265.

Sec. 769, Par. 2: Jefferson, Sec. XLVI; Cushing's Legislative Assemblies, Sec. 2243.

Sec. 769, Par. 3: Jefferson, Sec. XLVI; Cushing's Legislative Assemblies, Sec. 2267.

same subject. This practice is still rigidly adhered to in some legislatures but in Congress and some of the states this rule has been relaxed or abolished.

5. If no special provisions exist in the rules for the appointment of conference committees, they are appointed pursuant to the provisions applicable to other committees.

6. Where there was a division in the house with reference to a bill, it is the established practice to appoint a majority of the committee from the prevailing side in the controversy, but to also appoint a representative from the minority. In committees of three, two will represent the majority and one, the minority, if any.

7. The bill, concerning which the dispute as to amendments exists, should be referred to the conference committee of the house in which the bill originated and will thereafter remain in the possession of the house of origin or its conference committee.

Sec. 770. Conference Committees

1. Conference committees are usually small committees consisting of the same number of persons from each house. It is the practice in some legislative bodies to appoint the author or sponsor of the measure at issue to the conference committee.

Sec. 769, Par. 4: Jefferson, Sec. XLVI.

Sec. 769, Par. 5: Cushing's Legislative Assemblies, Sec. 2267.

Sec. 769, Par. 6: Jefferson, Sec. XLVI; Cushing's Legislative Assemblies, Sec. 2267.

Sec. 769, Par. 7: Cushing's Legislative Assemblies, Sec. 2269.

Sec. 770, Par. 1: Jefferson, Sec. XLVI; Cushing's Legislative Assemblies, Sec. 2267.

2. A committee on conference from each of the two houses meeting together is not a joint committee but a joint meeting of two committees. The quorum of a committee on conference is a majority of the members of each committee. In voting in a conference committee, the committee of each house votes separately. The committee on conference from each house submits its report to the house from which it was appointed. The report, upon being received, may be treated like other reports, except that the report of a conference committee is usually given a higher precedence. Under no condition, including suspension of the rules, may the house alter or amend the report of the committee, but must adopt or refuse to adopt the report in the form submitted.

3. As the two houses have equal authority, it is not proper for either to appoint the time and place for a conference. The custom is for no specific provision to be made by either house but for the committees to meet at a time arranged among themselves at the usual or a convenient place for the meeting of conference committees. It is usual for the chair of the conference committee of the house of origin to take the principal responsibility for arranging the conference.

Sec. 771. Reports of Conference Committees

1. When the conference committee has agreed on its report, an identical report is made to each house by the committee from that house. The reports are

Sec. 770, Par. 2: Jefferson, Sec. XLVI; Hughes, Sec. 754; Reed, Secs. 63, 240–243; Cushing's Legislative Assemblies, Sec. 2267; N.Y. Manual, p. 430.

Sec. 770, Par. 3: Cushing's Legislative Assemblies, Sec. 2267.

signed by the members or a majority of the members of each committee, the committee of either house signing first on the report which is made to its house.

2. The report of a conference committee is objectionable in form if the committee has not confined itself to differences of opinion between the houses. Objection to form must be made at the time the report is introduced, and if not made at that time is not in order at a later period.

3. Reports of conference committees are highly privileged and may be made at any time except when the journal is being read or a vote is being taken.

4. The report of a committee on conference may be taken up immediately, or consideration may be delayed and it may be referred to a select committee or considered in committee of the whole.

5. When the report of the committee on conference is adopted by either house, a message to that effect is sent to the other. When both houses have adopted the report, they have both approved the bill in its final form and it is ordered to enrollment.

6. When the conference committees are unable to agree that the amendments in dispute be concurred in by the house of origin, or that they be receded from or not insisted upon by the house making

---

Sec. 771, Par. 1: Jefferson, Sec. XLVI; Cushing's Legislative Assemblies, Sec. 2269; Reed, Sec. 244.

Sec. 771, Par. 2: Cushing's Legislative Assemblies, Sec. 2270.

Sec. 771, Par. 3: Jefferson, Sec. XLVI; Reed, Sec. 246; Cushing's Legislative Assemblies, Sec. 2270.

Sec. 771, Par. 4: Cushing's Legislative Assemblies, Sec. 2270.

Sec. 771, Par. 5: Cushing's Legislative Assemblies, Secs. 2244, 2247.

them, that fact should be reported to the houses. The committee should then be discharged and committees on free conference may be appointed in the same manner as the original committee. Also when, for any reason, either house refuses to adopt the report of the committee, the committees should be discharged and new committees on conference or free conference appointed.

7. During conference procedure, it is in order for one house if in possession of the bill to reconsider a vote previously taken on the measure.

8. It is unparliamentary, but within the power of a house, to indefinitely postpone the consideration of a report of the committee on conference.

9. When amendments to a bill are adopted by the second house and returned to the house of origin and there concurred in, the clerk in that house should immediately insert or have the amendments inserted in the bill; and when conference committee amendments are adopted, these amendments are inserted in the bill in the same manner as though they had been adopted by either house in the usual manner.

Sec. 772. Vote on Report of Conference Committee

1. The final passage of a bill upon which the vote is required to be taken by "yeas" and "nays" is the

Sec. 771, Par. 6: Jefferson, Sec. XLVI; Cushing's Legislative Assemblies, Sec. 2244.

Sec. 771, Par. 7: Jefferson, Sec. XLVI; Cushing's Legislative Assemblies, Sec. 2273.

Sec. 771, Par. 8: Cushing's Legislative Assemblies, Sec. 2274.

Sec. 771, Par. 9: Cushing's Legislative Assemblies, Secs. 2275, 2283.

vote by which each house adopts it after final reading, and not the vote by which the house in which it originated may subsequently concur in amendments made by the other house. The constitutional provision requiring a "yea" and "nay" vote on final passage of bills does not apply to concurrence in amendments of the other house.

2. When more than a majority vote is required for the passage of certain types of bills, an amendment by the other house, not involving any question requiring more than a majority vote, requires only the majority vote for concurrence.

Sec. 773. Free Conference

1. When a conference committee is unable to reach an agreement, or either house refuses to approve the recommendation of its committee, it is in order to commit the bill to free conference at which the committee on conference has authority to propose any amendments within the scope of the issue between the houses.

2. When the free conference committee is unable to agree or either house refuses to adopt its recommendations, the bill may be ordered to a second or

---

Sec. 772, Par. 1: Ewing v. McGehee (1925), 169 Ark. 448, 275 S.W. 766; State of Arkansas v. Crowe (1917), 130 Ark. 272, 197 S.W. 4; Brown v. Road Commissioners (1917), 173 N.C. 598, 92 S.E. 502; Wilson v. Young County Hardware & Furniture Co. (Tex. Civ. App. 1924), 262 S.W. 873; but see the following case which holds that the same vote is required to concur in amendments as to pass the bill: State of Oregon v. Boyer (1917), 84 Ore. 513, 165 P. 587.

Sec. 772, Par. 2: Wagstaff v. Central Highway Commission (1917), 174 N.C. 377, 93 S.E. 908; State of Oregon v. Boyer (1917), 84 Ore. 513, 165 P. 587.

Sec. 773, Par. 1: Cushing's Legislative Assemblies, Sec. 2245.

successive committee on free conference.

3. Procedure in a committee on free conference is the same as a committee on conference, except that such a committee has authority to propose amendments in addition to recommending that one house concur in the amendments of the other, or that the house proposing the amendments recede from its amendments. A committee on free conference has authority to recommend concerning all matters of dispute on a particular bill between the two houses.

4. Conference procedure between the houses is usually controlled by joint rules.

5. Some legislatures have shortened and simplified conference procedure by sending a bill directly to free conference upon refusal to concur or refusal to recede.

Sec. 774. Journal Records of Conference Procedure

In general, the rules relating to journal records and votes applicable to the passage of legislation apply to conference procedure. When the "enrolled bill rule" is not in effect, the journal must show the essential steps in the procedure and account for the concurrence or nonconcurrence of all amendments adopted by the second house. It has been held in Arkansas and Montana that the vote on concurrence is not required to meet the technicalities of vote on final passage and the vote may be viva voce and the names of those voting need not be entered in the

---

Sec. 773, Par. 2: Cushing's Legislative Assemblies, Secs. 2246, 2247.
Sec. 773, Par. 3: Cushing's Legislative Assemblies, Secs. 2245, 2269.

journal. The best practice would require that the vote on concurrence be taken with the same formalities as the vote on final passage.

Sec. 775. Trends in Conference Procedure

The procedure for conference and free conference on amendments followed above is the ancient procedure developed in Parliament and used with some changes in Congress and state legislatures. There are distinct trends toward simplification of the procedure and modern practice proves that many of the old technicalities are not necessary. The houses may provide for such procedure as they may agree upon unless constitutional requirements prevent. For example, a bill may be sent directly to a conference committee with broad authority to recommend any changes in a bill upon the house of origin's refusal to concur in amendments.

Sec. 774: Mech. Bldg. and Loan Assn. v. Coffman (1913), 110 Ark. 269, 162 S.W. 1090; Johnson v. City of Great Falls (1909), 38 Mont. 369, 99 P. 1059; Ewing v. McGehee (1925), 169 Ark. 448, 275 S.W. 766; State of Alabama v. Martin (1909), 160 Ala. 181, 48 So. 846; Robertson v. State of Alabama (1901), 130 Ala. 164, 30 So. 494; Jefferson County v. Crow (1904), 14 Ala. 126, 37 So. 469; State of Louisiana *ex rel.* Caillouet v. Laiche (1901), 105 La. 84, 29 So. 700; County Commissioners of Washington v. Baker (1922), 141 Md. 623, 119 A. 461; People v. Chenango County Supervisors (1853), 8 N.Y. 317; State of Oregon v. Boyer (1917), 84 Ore. 513, 165 P. 587; Dakota School Dist. v. Chapman (1907), 152 F. 887.

*

PART IX. SESSIONS AND MEETINGS

*

PART IX

SESSIONS AND MEETINGS

CHAPTER 72

SESSIONS OF STATE LEGISLATURES

Sec. 780. Calls for Special Sessions

1. A constitutional provision forbidding the enactment of laws at a special session, other than those specified in the proclamation by the governor, is mandatory.

2. In issuing a call for a special session of the legislature, the governor may confine legislation to the subjects specified in the governor's proclamation.

3. The governor may limit the consideration of a special session to a special phase of a general subject, but the governor cannot restrict the details

Sec. 780, Par. 1: Long v. State of Texas (1910), 58 Tex. Cr. 209, 127 S.W. 208; State of Missouri *ex rel.* Rice v. Edwards (1922), 241 S.W. 945.

Sec. 780, Par. 2: Devereaux v. City of Brownsville (1887), 29 F. 742; Denver & Rio Grande R. Co. v. Moss (1911), 50 Colo. 282, 115 P. 696; Bunger v. State of Georgia (1917), 146 Ga. 672, 92 S.E. 72; State of Missouri *ex rel.* Rice v. Edwards (1922), 241 S.W. 945; State of Montana v. Clancy (1904), 30 Mont. 529, 77 P. 312; People v. Parker (1873), Tennant's Case, 3 Neb. 409; State of Oklahoma *ex rel.* Swirczynski v. Key (1926), 121 Okla. 64, 247 P. 656; *In re* Likens Petitions (1909), 223 Pa. 456, 72 A. 858; State of Tennessee *ex rel.* National Conservation Exposition Co. v. Woollen (1913), 128 Tenn. 456, 161 S.W. 1006; *Ex parte* Fulton (1919), 86 Tex. Cr. 149, 215 S.W. 331.

springing from that subject.

4. While a legislature cannot go beyond the business specified in a call for an extra session, yet within such limits, it can act freely, in whole or in part or not at all.

5. A special message need not be addressed by the governor to the legislature as a whole and, if addressed to the respective houses, it is a message to the legislature within the meaning of the constitution. The governor is not limited to any precise form, manner or time in presenting recommendations.

6. In determining whether a given act is germane to the subject stated in the proclamation, the entire proclamation should be considered and should be reasonably construed to bring the act within its meaning if possible.

Sec. 780, Par. 3: State of Tennessee *ex rel.* National Conservation Exposition Co. v. Woollen (1913), 128 Tenn. 456, 161 S.W. 1006; Sims v. Weldon (1924), 165 Ark. 13, 263 S.W. 42; *In re* Likens Petitions (1909), 223 Pa. 456, 72 A. 858; *Ex parte* Fulton (1919), 86 Tex. Cr. 149, 215 S.W. 331; Devereaux v. City of Brownsville (1887), 29 F. 742; State of Missouri *ex rel.* Rice v. Edwards (1922), 241 S.W. 945; State of Montana v. Clancy (1904), 30 Mont. 529, 77 P. 312.

Sec. 780, Par. 4: *In re* Governor's Proclamation (1894), 19 Colo. 333, 35 P. 530; State of Oklahoma *ex rel.* Swirczynski v. Key (1926), 121 Okla. 64, 247 P. 656; State of Missouri *ex rel.* Rice v. Edwards (1922), 241 S.W. 945; Denver & Rio Grande R. Co. v. Moss (1911), 50 Colo. 282, 115 P. 696; *Ex parte* Davis (1919), 86 Tex. Cr. 168, 215 S.W. 341; *In re* Opinion of the Justices (1934), 94 Colo. 215, 29 P.2d 705; Hagaman v. Andrews (1970), 232 So. 2d 1.

Sec. 780, Par. 5: Lauck v. Reis (1925), 310 Mo. 184, 274 S.W. 827; State of Utah v. Tweed (1924), 63 Utah 176, 224 P. 443; State of Oklahoma *ex rel.* Swirczynski v. Key (1926), 121 Okla. 64, 247 P. 656; State of Missouri *ex rel.* Rice v. Edwards (1922), 241 S.W. 945.

Sec. 780, Par. 6: Wells v. Missouri Pacific Railway Co. (1892), 110 Mo. 286, 19 S.W. 530; State of Montana v. Clancy (1904), 30 Mont. 529, 77 P. 312; City of Rockwood v. Rodgers (1927), 154 Tenn. 638, 290 S.W. 381; *Ex parte* Davis (1919), 86 Tex. Cr. 168, 215 S.W. 341; State of West Virginia v. Shores (1888), 31 W.Va. 491, 7 S.E. 413.

7. As a general rule, after the legislature has been convened pursuant to proclamation by the governor, subjects in addition to those specified in the proclamation may be submitted by special message.

8. A proclamation by a governor calling a special session may be revoked by the governor or the governor's successor, and when revoked, the legislature is without authority to act.

9. When the constitution prohibits passage of legislation not included in the governor's call, legislation passed at a special session not within the call is not valid, even if it is subsequently signed by the governor.

10. The governor is invested with the authority to call an extraordinary or special session of the legislature and in the exercise of such power, neither the legislature nor the judicial department has any power to call the governor to account.

11. Some state constitutions or statutes include provisions whereby a legislature may call itself into special session.

12. A statute passed at a special or extraordinary session of the legislature will be held by the courts to

---

Sec. 780, Par. 7: State of Oklahoma *ex rel.* Swirczynski v. Key (1926), 121 Okla. 64, 247 P. 656; State of Utah v. Tweed (1924), 63 Utah 176, 224 P. 443; Jaksha v. State of Nebraska (1986), 222 Neb. 690, 385 N.W.2d 925.

Sec. 780, Par. 8: People v. Parker (1873), Tennant's Case, 3 Neb. 409.

Sec. 780, Par. 9: Long v. State of Texas (1910), 58 Tex. Cr. 209, 127 S.W. 208; Wells v. Missouri Pacific Railway Co. (1892), 110 Mo. 286, 19 S.W. 530; Jaksha v. State of Nebraska (1986), 222 Neb. 690, 385 N.W.2d 925.

Sec. 780, Par. 10: Farrelly v. Cole (1899), 60 Kan. 356, 56 P. 492; Bunger v. State of Georgia (1917), 146 Ga. 672, 92 S.E. 72; Jaksha v. State of Nebraska (1986), 222 Neb. 690, 385 N.W.2d 925.

be within the scope of the governor's call if it can be done so under any reasonable construction.

13. It is only when both houses are lawfully assembled that they constitute the legislature of the state.

14. The governor has the power to call a special session while the legislature is in general session.

15. When the constitution requires the governor in calling a special session to specify the subjects that the legislature is to act upon, a call can be invalidated by an overly broad specification of purposes.

Sec. 781. Adjournment of Legislative Sessions

See also Sec. 445, Motion to Adjourn Sine Die.

1. When a state legislature is duly convened, it cannot be adjourned sine die or dissolved except in a manner provided by law, and an adjournment from day to day can have no other effect than to enable those present to determine whether a quorum is present.

2. The date of adjournment of the legislature as shown by its journals is not contradicted or rendered uncertain by record evidence therein of the transaction of a large amount of business within a short period of time. When the records of the

---

Sec. 780, Par. 12: City of Rockwood v. Rodgers (1927), 154 Tenn. 638, 290 S.W. 381.

Sec. 780, Par. 13: *In re* Hague (1929), 105 N.J.Eq. 134, 147 A. 220.

Sec. 780, Par. 14: State of Wisconsin *ex rel.* Groppi v. Leslie (1969), 44 Wis. 2d 282, 171 N.W.2d 192.

Sec. 780, Par. 15: Denver & Rio Grande R. Co. v. Moss (1911), 50 Colo. 282, 115 P. 696.

Sec. 781, Par. 1: Cushing's Legislative Assemblies, Sec. 254.

legislature show the time of adjournment and are clear and unambiguous, they are conclusive, and extraneous evidence cannot be admitted to show a different date of adjournment.

3. The two houses of the legislature have the right and power to make their respective journals show that all their business was transacted before the arrival of the moment of time for their adjournment as fixed by the constitution and, at least in the absence of a gross and flagrant violation of the constitutional restriction as to the length of the session, evidence is inadmissible to contradict the journal.

4. In the past it was fairly common for legislatures to continue their session beyond the fixed time for adjournment, and they often stopped the clock before the hour for adjournment had arrived. A legislative body has the power and right to determine for itself when the moment of time has arrived for adjournment, and it has the power to make its journals conform to what it determines to be that moment of time.

5. A legislative session is the period of time between the initial convening and adjournment sine die. During that time, a legislature sits "in session" from day to day. Committee meetings are also an integral part of a legislative session and are held on an almost daily basis during the session. Days on which committee meetings only are held are also considered legislative days in many states. Some

Sec. 781, Par. 2: Capito v. Topping (1909), 65 W.Va. 587, 64 S.E. 845.
Sec. 781, Par. 3: Earnest v. Sargent (1915), 20 N.M. 427, 150 P. 1018.
Sec. 781, Par. 4: Earnest v. Sargent (1915), 20 N.M. 427, 150 P. 1018; Davis v. Thompson (Okla. 1986), 721 P.2d 789.

states "recess" from daily sessions for the purpose of holding committee meetings or conducting other legislative business.

6. Though the legislative power continues perpetually, the legislative body ceases to exist on the moment of adjournment or periodic dissolution.

7. On the expiration of the terms of office of a legislative body, the body is adjourned.

8. An extraordinary session of the legislature is terminated on the date provided for the convening of the regular session.

Sec. 782. Joint Sessions

1. The two houses of a legislature may have the right to sit in joint session for certain purposes, but the right so to sit is a limited constitutional right and cannot be augmented by the legislature.

2. Once the senate and the house have convened in joint session, the members then become a single body, with a majority of all members of both houses constituting the quorum, with each member entitled to an equal vote with every other member.

3. When the two houses meet in a joint session, they in effect merge into one house where the quorum is a majority of the members of both houses,

---

Sec. 781, Par. 5: Cushing's Legislative Assemblies, Sec. 495.

Sec. 781, Par. 6: Petition of the Special Assembly Interim Committee on Public Morals of California Legislature (1939), 13 Cal. 2d 497, 90 P.2d 304.

Sec. 781, Par. 7: Opinion of the Justices (1965), 54 Del. 222, 210 A.2d 852.

Sec. 781, Par. 8: Opinion of the Justices (1963), 275 Ala. 102, 152 So. 2d 427.

Sec. 782, Par. 1: *In re* Hague (1929), 105 N.J.Eq. 134, 147 A. 220.

Sec. 782, Par. 2: Anderson v. Krupsak (1976), 386 N.Y.S.2d 859, 353 N.E.2d 822; Abood v. Gorsuch (Alaska 1985), 703 P.2d 1158.

where the votes of members of each house have equal weight and where special rules can be adopted to govern joint sessions or they can be governed by the parliamentary common law.

Sec. 783. Adjournment for More Than Three Days

See also Sec. 271, Legislative Day.

1. Under the constitutional provision that neither house, without the consent of the other, shall adjourn for more than three days, a particular mode of manifesting such consent is not required.

2. When both houses agree to an adjournment of more than three days, the days when neither is in session nor holding committee meetings are not legislative days.

3. When the senate or house is in lawful session on a certain day, that day is a legislative day whether the other house meets or not.

Sec. 784. Sessions Open to the Public

See also Sec. 705, paragraph 5, Admission to Legislative Chambers.

Most states have provisions in their constitutions, statutes or rules which require that the doors of each house shall be open to the public during its session, other than when secrecy is required.

Sec. 782, Par. 3: Anderson v. Krupsak (1976), 386 N.Y.S.2d 859, 353 N.E.2d 822; Abood v. Gorsuch (Alaska 1985), 703 P.2d 1158.

Sec. 783, Par. 1: Opinion of the Justices (1972), 288 Ala. 89, 257 So. 2d 336.

Sec. 783, Par. 2: Opinion of the Justices (1972), 288 Ala. 89, 257 So. 2d 336.

Sec. 783, Par. 3: Opinion of the Justices (1972), 288 Ala. 89, 257 So. 2d 336.

*

PART X. INVESTIGATIONS AND PUBLIC ORDER

*

PART X

INVESTIGATIONS AND PUBLIC ORDER

CHAPTER 73

INVESTIGATIONS BY LEGISLATIVE BODIES

Sec. 795. Right of a Legislative Body to Make Investigations

1. The right of a legislative body to make investigations in order to assist it in the preparation of wise and timely laws must exist as an indispensable incident and auxiliary to the proper exercise of legislative power. This has been recognized from the earliest times in the history of U.S. legislation, both federal and state, and from even earlier epochs in the development of British jurisprudence.

2. The legislature has the power to investigate any subject regarding which it may desire informa-

Sec. 795, Par. 1: Marshall v. Gordon (1917), 243 U.S. 521, 37 S. Ct. 448, 61 L. Ed. 881; Burnham v. Morrissey (Mass. 1859), 14 Gray 226, 74 Am. Dec. 676; Wilckens v. Willet (1878), 40 N.Y. 521, 4 Abb. App. Dec. 596; Briggs v. MacKellar (N.Y. 1855), 2 Abb. Pr. 30; Robertson v. Peeples (1919), 120 S.C. 176, 115 S.E. 300; Anderson v. Dunn (U.S. 1821), 6 Wheat. 204, 5 L. Ed. 242; Federal Trade Commission v. American Tobacco Co. (1924), 264 U.S. 298, 44 S. Ct. 336, 68 L. Ed. 696; Harriman v. Interstate Commerce Commission (1908), 211 U.S. 407, 29 S. Ct. 115, 53 L. Ed. 253; *In re* Chapman (1897), 166 U.S. 661, 17 S. Ct. 677, 41 L. Ed. 1154; Kilbourn v. Thompson (1880), 103 U.S. 168, 26 L. Ed. 377; *In re* Battelle (1929), 207 Cal. 227, 277 P. 725; Goldman v. Olson (Wis. 1968), 268 F. Supp. 35; Murphy v. Collins (1974), 20 Ill. App. 3d 181, 312 N.E.2d 772.

tion in connection with the proper discharge of its function to enact, amend or repeal statutes or to perform any other act delegated to it by the constitution.

3. The power and duty reposed in the legislature and in each and every member of both houses thereof is that of preparing and proceeding to enact wise and well-formed and needful laws, and in the preparation of such laws, the necessity of investigation of some sort must exist as an indispensable incident.

4. Legislatures in enacting laws, like courts in interpreting such laws when enacted, must have in mind the former law, if any; the wrong or defect requiring remedial action; and the nature and extent of the needed and appropriate remedy; and, in the application of this principle, the power of these coordinate branches of government.

5. The inherent and auxiliary power reposed in legislative bodies to conduct investigations in aid of prospective legislation carries with it the power in proper cases to compel the attendance of witnesses and the production of books and papers by means of legal process. Also the legislature has the power to institute and carry to the extent of punishment, contempt proceedings in order to compel the attendance of such witnesses and the production of such

---

Sec. 795, Par. 2: Ex parte D.O. McCarthy (1866), 29 Cal. 395; Greenfield v. Russel (1920), 292 Ill. 392, 127 N.E. 102; Attorney General v. Brissenden (1930), 271 Mass. 172, 171 N.E. 82; Briggs v. MacKellar (N.Y. 1855), 2 Abb. Pr. 30; People v. Keeler (1885), 99 N.Y. 463, 2 N.E. 615; Simpson v. Hill (1927), 128 Okla. 269, 263 P. 635; Commonwealth v. Costello (1912), 21 Pa. Dist. 232; State of Wisconsin v. Frear (1909), 138 Wis. 173, 119 N.W. 894.

Sec. 795, Par. 3: In re Battelle (1929), 207 Cal. 227, 277 P. 725; Briggs v. MacKellar (N.Y. 1855), 2 Abb. Pr. 30.

Sec. 795, Par. 4: In re Battelle (1929), 207 Cal. 227, 277 P. 725.

documentary evidence as may be legally called for in the course of such proceedings, whether conducted by the legislative body or a branch thereof, directly or through its properly constituted committees.

6. The legislature has power to investigate any subject where there is a legitimate use that the legislature can make of the information sought, and an ulterior purpose in the investigation or an improper use of the information cannot be imputed.

7. The legislature or a committee of the legislature cannot be enjoined from investigating a matter which is under litigation in the courts.

8. The ascertainment of pertinent facts as a basis for legislation is within the power of a legislative body.

9. A legislature, in conducting whatever inquisitions the proper exercise of its proper functions requires, must be as broad as the subject to which the inquiry properly entered upon has relation.

10. An investigation into the management of the various institutions of the state and the departments of the state government is at all times a legitimate function of the legislature.

Sec. 795, Par. 5: In re Battelle (1929), 207 Cal. 227, 277 P. 725; Petition of the Special Assembly Interim Committee on Public Morals of California Legislature (1939), 13 Cal. 2d 497, 90 P.2d 304.

Sec. 795, Par. 6: Robertson v. Peeples (1919), 120 S.C. 176, 115 S.E. 300.

Sec. 795, Par. 7: Robertson v. Peeples (1919), 120 S.C. 176, 115 S.E. 300.

Sec. 795, Par. 8: Attorney General v. Brissenden (1930), 271 Mass. 172, 171 N.E. 82.

Sec. 795, Par. 9: In re Battelle (1929), 207 Cal. 227, 277 P. 725.

Sec. 795, Par. 10: Dickinson v. Johnson (1915), 117 Ark. 582, 176 S.W. 116.

11. The right to investigate any lawful matter is a right separate and distinct in each house and may be exercised through a committee.

12. Authority to obtain information for its determination concerning the exercise of power to make laws may be conferred on nonlegislative bodies.

13. In the exercise of its power to make investigations, a legislature may incur reasonable, necessary expenses payable out of the public funds.

14. The legislature and each house thereof has the inherent and implied power to appoint investigation committees and conduct investigations to obtain information concerning proposed or future legislation and to report back its findings to the body that appointed it.

Sec. 796. Investigations Respecting Members

See also Sec. 564, Investigation of Charges Against Members.

1. The legislature of either house has the power to investigate and institute an inquiry into the truth of an alleged bribery of any of its members or the members of a previous legislature connected with its legislative functions. In the exercise of such power, it must necessarily have the same power to compel the attendance of witnesses before it or before a

---

Sec. 795, Par. 11: In re Hague (1929), 105 N.J.Eq. 134, 147 A. 220; Simpson v. Hill (1927), 128 Okla. 269, 263 P. 635; Robertson v. Peeples (1919), 120 S.C. 176, 115 S.E. 300.

Sec. 795, Par. 12: Attorney General v. Brissenden (1930), 271 Mass. 172, 171 N.E. 82.

Sec. 795, Par. 13: State of Wisconsin v. Frear (1909), 138 Wis. 173, 119 N.W. 894; Goldman v. Olson (Wis. 1968), 268 F. Supp. 35.

Sec. 795, Par. 14: Petition of the Special Assembly Interim Committee on Public Morals of California Legislature (1939), 13 Cal. 2d 497, 90 P.2d 304; Masset Bldg. Co. v. Bennett (1950), 4 N.J. 53, 71 A.2d 327.

committee and compel them to testify as in any other investigation.

2. A legislative body has the right in an election contest concerning one of its members to conduct an investigation before the body or one of its committees and to compel the attendance of witnesses and take testimony.

3. Knowledge or information acquired by a witness, though at the instance of and in connection with and under the direction of a prosecuting attorney to use in the trial of indictment against members of the legislature for bribery, is not privileged and furnishes a witness lawfully summoned no legal ground for refusing to respond to legitimate questions by a legislative committee appointed to investigate the matter.

4. When a house is investigating the conduct of its members upon a public charge that some of them whose names are not given have taken bribes and have called as witnesses the editor and reporter of the paper which published the charge, it is a contempt of the authority of the house for the witnesses to refuse to give the names of those from whom they have received information concerning the charge of bribery and of the nature of that information.

5. When a committee is charged with an inquiry into any matter, and during that inquiry, it appears that a member of that committee or of either house is involved, the committee cannot proceed against

Sec. 796, Par. 1: In re Falvey (1856), 7 Wis. 528; Briggs v. MacKellar (N.Y. 1855), 2 Abb. Pr. 30.

Sec. 796, Par. 2: In re Gunn (1893), 50 Kan. 155, 32 P. 470.

Sec. 796, Par. 3: Sullivan v. Hill (1913), 73 W.Va. 49, 79 S.E. 670.

Sec. 796, Par. 4: Ex parte Lawrence (1897), 116 Cal. 298, 48 P. 124.

that member but must make a special report to the house; whereupon the member is heard in place or at the bar, or a special authority is given to the committee to inquire concerning the member.

Sec. 797. Limitations on Right of a Legislative Body to Investigate

1. It is a general rule that the legislature has no power through itself or any committee or any agency to make inquiry into the private affairs of a citizen except to accomplish some authorized end.

2. The legislature has no right to conduct an investigation for the purpose of laying a foundation for the institution of criminal proceedings, for the aid and benefit of grand juries in planning indictments, for the purpose of intentionally injuring such persons or for any ulterior purpose.

3. A state legislature in conducting any investigation must observe the constitutional provisions relating to the enjoyment of life, liberty and property.

4. An investigation instituted for political purposes and not connected with intended legislation or with any of the matters upon which a house should

---

Sec. 796, Par. 5: Jefferson, Sec. XI.

Sec. 797, Par. 1: Greenfield v. Russel (1920), 292 Ill. 392, 127 N.E. 102; Attorney General v. Brissenden (1930), 271 Mass. 172, 171 N.E. 82; *In re* Hague (1929), 105 N.J.Eq. 134, 147 A. 220; *In re* Barnes (1912), 204 N.Y. 108, 97 N.E. 508.

Sec. 797, Par. 2: Kilbourn v. Thompson (1880), 103 U.S. 168, 26 L. Ed. 377; Greenfield v. Russel (1920), 292 Ill. 392, 127 N.E. 102; *In re* Hague (1929), 105 N.J.Eq. 134, 147 A. 220; Attorney General v. Brissenden (1930), 271 Mass. 172, 171 N.E. 82.

Sec. 797, Par. 3: Attorney General v. Brissenden (1930), 271 Mass. 172, 171 N.E. 82.

act is not a proper legislative proceeding and is beyond the authority of the house or legislature.

5. When a committee is appointed by resolution to make an investigation and the object of the investigation, as shown by the resolution, is not a proper legislative object but is to establish an extraordinary tribunal for the trial of judicial and other officers, the duties imposed on the commission being strictly judicial and not ancillary to legislation, the committee has no legal status.

6. A governmental "fishing expedition" into the papers of a private corporation on the possibility that they may disclose evidence of crime is contrary to the first principles of justice and an intention to grant the power must be expressed in most explicit language.

7. The investigatory power of a legislative body is limited to obtaining information on matters which fall within its proper field of legislative action.

Sec. 798. Method of Investigation by a Legislative Body

1. The legislative arm of government is not to be restricted in the exercise of the power of inquiry by the fact that methods and processes, judicial or quasi-judicial in character, are employed in the course of the inquiry. It is immaterial whether the power of inquiry is to be exercised by a state or federal legislative body, or whether in the exercise of that

Sec. 797, Par. 4: Keeler v. McDonald (1885), 99 N.Y. 463, 2 N.E. 615.

Sec. 797, Par. 5: Commonwealth v. Costello (1912), 21 Pa. Dist. 232.

Sec. 797, Par. 6: Federal Trade Commission v. American Tobacco Co. (1924), 264 U.S. 298, 44 S. Ct. 336, 68 L. Ed. 696.

Sec. 797, Par. 7: U.S. v. Owlett (1936), 15 F. Supp. 736.

power the legislative arm of the government is acting under or by virtue of granted or reserved authority, or what the particular constitutional limitations may be which separate legislative from judicial functions of government and which forbid the trespass of the one on the domain of the other.

2. Legislative bodies, by the mere employment of methods of procedure which resemble those employed or required in judicial proceedings, are not to be held to be engaged in the exercise of a judicial function and to be thereby trenching upon the area exclusively assigned to the judicial department of the state government.

3. Where the legislature has constitutional power to institute an investigation, the manner of conducting such investigation rests on the sound discretion of the legislature.

Sec. 799. Legislative Investigating Committees

See also Sec. 564, Investigation of Charges Against Members.

1. In legislatures, the investigation of public matters before committees, preliminary to legislation or with the view of advising the house which appointed the committee, is a parliamentary usage as well established as it is in England, and the right of either house to compel witnesses to appear and testify

---

Sec. 798, Par. 1: In re Battelle (1929), 207 Cal. 227, 277 P. 725; Briggs v. MacKellar (N.Y. 1855), 2 Abb. Pr. 30; Kilbourn v. Thompson (1880), 103 U.S. 168, 26 L. Ed. 377.

Sec. 798, Par. 2: In re Battelle (1929), 207 Cal. 227, 277 P. 725.

Sec. 798, Par. 3: In re Falvey (1856), 7 Wis. 528.

before its committees and to punish for disobedience has been frequently enforced.

2. The legislature may proceed to make any investigations within its authority, by authorized committees of one or both houses. The houses can act jointly in appointing a committee, or either house can act alone.

3. The legislative power of a state being vested in the two houses of the legislature, such bodies may create committees or even commissions by concurrent resolutions as well as by act and may confer upon them such power as they are not prohibited by express provision of the constitution from conferring.

4. Powers delegated by the legislature or either house to a committee by a simple resolution cease with the adjournment sine die of the legislature. But a legislature may invest its committees with power to function after the adjournment of the session; and where each house can act separately, the joint act of both houses is not required to set up a committee which can continue to function after adjournment.

Sec. 799, Par. 1: Briggs v. MacKellar (N.Y. 1855), 2 Abb. Pr. 30.

Sec. 799, Par. 2: *Ex parte* Bunkers (1905), 1 Cal. App. 61, 81 P. 748; Dickinson v. Johnson (1915), 117 Ark. 582, 176 S.W. 116; Attorney General v. Brissenden (1930), 271 Mass. 172, 171 N.E. 82; People v. Keeler (1885), 99 N.Y. 463, 2 N.E. 615; *Ex parte* Dalton (1886), 44 Ohio St. 142, 5 N.E. 136; Robertson v. Peeples (1919), 120 S.C. 176, 115 S.E. 300; Terrell v. King (1929), 118 Tex. 237, 14 S.W.2d 786; State of Wisconsin v. Frear (1909), 138 Wis. 173, 119 N.W. 894.

Sec. 799, Par. 3: People v. Backer (1920), 185 N.Y.S. 459; Terrell v. King (1929), 118 Tex. 237, 14 S.W.2d 786; People *ex rel.* Bender v. Milliken (1906), 185 N.Y. 35, 77 N.E. 872.

Sec. 799, Par. 4: Fergus v. Russel (1915), 270 Ill. 304, 110 N.E. 130; People *ex rel.* Hastings v. Hofstadter (1932), 258 N.Y. 425, 180 N.E. 106; *In re* Impeachment (1913), 22 Pa. Dist. 833; see also *Ex parte* Caldwell

5. A legislative investigating committee may not delegate its powers of investigation to one of its members without authority granted in the resolution appointing the committee.

6. Testimony before a committee should be taken down for the information of the house.

7. A legislator's service on an interim committee appointed pursuant to a statute duly passed for the purpose of investigating and reporting to the next legislature would not be violative of a constitutional prohibition against occupation by legislators of any other office, trust or employment.

Sec. 800. Witnesses in Legislative Investigations

See also Sec. 797, Limitations on Right of a Legislative Body to Investigate.

1. By the common parliamentary law, a legislative body may compel the attendance of all persons as witnesses in regard to any subject on which it has power to act, and into which it has instituted an investigation.

(1906), 61 W.Va. 49, 55 S.E. 910; State of Washington *ex rel.* Hamblen v. Yelle (1947), 29 Wash. 2d 68, 185 P.2d 723; State of Washington *ex rel.* Robinson v. Fluent (1948), 30 Wash. 2d 194, 191 P.2d 241, *cert. denied,* Washington Pension Union v. State of Washington *ex rel.* Robinson, 335 U.S. 844, 69 S. Ct. 66, 93 L. Ed. 394; Hagaman v. Andrews (1970), 232 So. 2d 1.

Sec. 799, Par. 5: In re Leach (1922), 232 N.Y. 600, 19 N.Y.S. 135, 134 N.E. 588.

Sec. 799, Par. 6: Jefferson, Sec. XIII.

Sec. 799, Par. 7: Petition of the Special Assembly Interim Committee on Public Morals of California Legislature (1939), 13 Cal. 2d 497, 90 P.2d 304.

Sec. 800, Par. 1: Ex parte D.O. McCarthy (1866), 29 Cal. 395; *Ex parte* Bunkers (1905), 1 Cal. App. 61, 81 P. 748; Hendricks v. Carter (1918), 21 Ga. App. 527, 94 S.E. 807; *In re* Gunn (1893), 50 Kan. 155, 32 P. 470; Attorney General v. Brissenden (1930), 271 Mass. 172, 171 N.E. 82; State of New Jersey v. Brewster (1916), 89 N.J.L. 658, 99 A. 338; Briggs v.

2. The power of a state legislative body to compel witnesses to testify in aid of investigations is an attribute of the power to legislate and follows as an essential implication.

3. When witnesses are brought before either branch of the legislature, they may be compelled to testify by process of contempt, when without legal cause they refuse to do so.

4. Witnesses before a legislative body or its committee need not be sworn, unless there is some provision of law or of the constitution requiring it, but give their testimony under the penalty of being adjudged guilty of contempt and punished if they testify falsely.

5. When any person is examined before a committee, or at the bar of the house, any member wishing to ask the person a question must address it to the presiding officer, who puts the question to the person. If the propriety of the question be objected to, the presiding officer should direct the witness, counsel and parties to withdraw, for no question can be moved or put or debated while they are there. Sometimes the questions are previously settled in writing before the witness enters.

MacKellar (N.Y. 1855), 2 Abb. Pr. 30; *Ex parte* Dalton (1886), 44 Ohio St. 142, 5 N.E. 136; Sullivan v. Hill (1913), 73 W.Va. 49, 79 S.E. 670.

Sec. 800, Par. 2: Attorney General v. Brissenden (1930), 271 Mass. 172, 171 N.E. 82.

Sec. 800, Par. 3: *Ex parte* D.O. McCarthy (1866), 29 Cal. 395; Attorney General v. Brissenden (1930), 271 Mass. 172, 171 N.E. 82; Briggs v. MacKellar (N.Y. 1855), 2 Abb. Pr. 30; *In re* Gunn (1893), 50 Kan. 155, 32 P. 470; *Ex parte* Dalton (1886), 44 Ohio St. 142, 5 N.E. 136; Sullivan v. Hill (1913), 73 W.Va. 49, 79 S.E. 670.

Sec. 800, Par. 4: *Ex parte* D.O. McCarthy (1866), 29 Cal. 395.

Sec. 800, Par. 5: Jefferson, Sec. XIII.

6. A member, in place, may give information to the house of what the member knows of any matter under hearing at the bar.

7. Either house may request, but not command, the attendance of a member of the other. In case a member refuses to attend or testify, the house desiring the member's testimony may make the request by message to the other house, expressing clearly the purpose of the attendance.

8. If either house has occasion for the presence of a person in custody of the other, it may ask the other house for the custody of the person.

Sec. 801. Compelling Witnesses to Attend and Testify. Power to Punish for Contempt

1. Each house of the legislature may punish breaches of its authority when they are committed in its presence and may equally punish a witness for contempt of the house for the witness' refusal to appear or testify before a properly empowered committee or to produce books and papers.

2. The power of a house of a state legislature to punish a person for contempt can be exercised only in strict conformity with the rules of procedure

Sec. 800, Par. 6: Jefferson, Sec. XIII.

Sec. 800, Par. 7: Jefferson, Sec. XIII.

Sec. 800, Par. 8: Jefferson, Sec. XIII.

Sec. 801, Par. 1: *Ex parte* D.O. McCarthy (1866), 29 Cal. 395; *In re* Gunn (1893), 50 Kan. 155, 32 P. 470; Burnham v. Morrissey (Mass. 1859), 14 Gray 226, 74 Am. Dec. 676; Lowe v. Summers (1897), 69 Mo. App. 637; *In re* Barnes (1912), 204 N.Y. 108, 97 N.E. 508; Keeler v. McDonald (1885), 99 N.Y. 463, 2 N.E. 615; *Ex parte* Dalton (1886), 44 Ohio St. 142, 5 N.E. 136; *In re* Impeachment (1913), 22 Pa. Dist. 833; *In re* Falvey (1856), 7 Wis. 528; *In re* Battelle (1929), 207 Cal. 227, 277 P. 725.

which the laws of the state provide as a prerequisite to the validity of an adjudication of contempt.

3. A statute empowering either house to imprison a contumacious witness is not in excess of legislative power. Where a witness refuses to answer proper questions propounded by an investigating committee, it has been held to be criminal contempt.

4. Witnesses cannot be punished for contempt before a legislature unless the matters inquired into are within the jurisdiction of the legislature. A witness before a court or any other inquisitorial body who is otherwise orderly and respectful cannot be adjudged guilty of contempt committed in the presence of such tribunal for the witness' failure or refusal to answer any question or to produce any record, book or paper, unless the order so adjudging the witness guilty of contempt contains an express recital of the facts affirmatively showing not only the precise question which the witness has declined to answer, or the precisely specified books or papers which that person has refused to produce, but also affirmatively setting forth the facts which show the materiality and pertinency of each of these forms of evidence to the issue before the court or tribunal.

5. In order to authorize a conviction under a statute making it a misdemeanor for a witness in an investigation before a legislative committee to refuse to produce documents in the witness' possession, it

Sec. 801, Par. 2: In re Battelle (1929), 207 Cal. 227, 277 P. 725.

Sec. 801, Par. 3: People v. Keeler (1885), 99 N.Y. 463, 2 N.E. 615; *Ex parte* Wolters (1912), 64 Tex. Cr. 238, 144 S.W. 531.

Sec. 801, Par. 4: Ex parte Hague (1930), 123 N.J.Eq. 475, 150 A. 322; *In re* Battelle (1929), 207 Cal. 227, 277 P. 725.

must appear that the documents demanded are material to the inquiry.

6. The right to compel a witness to produce books and papers before a legislative committee is determined by whether their production is necessary to the inquiry which it is conducting, and the production of papers material to an inquiry cannot be refused merely because they are private.

7. An examination of the history of the English Parliament and the decisions of the English courts show that the power of the House of Commons, under the law and customs of Parliament, to punish for contempt rests upon principles peculiar to it and not upon any general rule applicable to all legislative bodies.

8. No expressed power to punish for contempt was granted to the houses of Congress except the power to deal with contempt submitted by its own members (U.S. Constitution Article I, Section 5). The houses have implied power to deal directly with contempt so far as necessary to preserve and exercise legislative authority especially granted, it being, however, a power of self-preservation. It is a power to prevent acts which inherently prevent or obstruct the discharge of legislative duty.

Sec. 801, Par. 5: People v. Foster (1923), 236 N.Y. 610, 142 N.E. 304; *In re* Battelle (1929), 207 Cal. 227, 277 P. 725; Federal Trade Commission v. American Tobacco Co. (1924), 264 U.S. 298, 44 S. Ct. 336, 68 L. Ed. 696.

Sec. 801, Par. 6: *In re* Barnes (1912), 204 N.Y. 108, 97 N.E. 508; Burnham v. Morrissey (Mass. 1859), 14 Gray 226, 74 Am. Dec. 676; People v. Foster (1923), 236 N.Y. 610, 142 N.E. 304.

Sec. 801, Par. 7: Kilbourn v. Thompson (1880), 103 U.S. 168, 26 L. Ed. 377; Lowe v. Summers (1897), 69 Mo. App. 637; Marshall v. Gordon (1917), 243 U.S. 521, 37 S. Ct. 448, 61 L. Ed. 881.

Sec. 801, Par. 8: Marshall v. Gordon (1917), 243 U.S. 521, 37 S. Ct. 448, 61 L. Ed. 881.

9. A legislative house may refuse the aid of counsel to a party, summoned before it as a witness charged with contempt in not answering questions.

Sec. 802. Summons, Subpoenas and Warrants

1. A legislative body or a committee, when acting within the scope of its authority to conduct an investigation, may summon and examine witnesses, require the production and examination of books, records and papers.

2. The law may make it a penal offense for a person to fail to appear before a legislative committee on process, regular on its face, issued by the chair of the committee under general authority conferred upon the chair by the committee, either expressly or by parliamentary usage, either with or without specific authority in the particular case.

3. When a committee is authorized to subpoena witnesses, the chair of the committee, in conjunction with its counsel, may select the names and number of witnesses for attendance at each session, and the chair may sign the summons for each witness. Subpoenas should not be issued in blank.

4. A summons by the committee ordering a witness to appear before a joint committee of the two

Sec. 801, Par. 9: Ex parte D.O. McCarthy (1866), 29 Cal. 395.

Sec. 802, Par. 1: Ex parte Bunkers (1905), 1 Cal. App. 61, 81 P. 748; *Ex parte* Dalton (1886), 44 Ohio St. 142, 5 N.E. 136; Hagaman v. Andrews (1970), 232 So. 2d 1.

Sec. 802, Par. 2: State of New Jersey v. Brewster (1916), 89 N.J.L. 658, 99 A. 338; People v. Foster (1923), 236 N.Y. 610, 142 N.E. 304; Sullivan v. Hill (1913), 73 W.Va. 49, 79 S.E. 670; *In re* Chapman (1897), 166 U.S. 661, 17 S. Ct. 677, 41 L. Ed. 1154.

Sec. 802, Par. 3: State of New Jersey v. Scott (1916), 89 N.J.Eq. 726, 99 A. 342; Jefferson, Sec. XIII.

houses may be signed by the chair of the committee.

5. A subpoena for attendance of a witness is not vitiated as to the necessity of the attendance of a witness by the inclusion of illegal requirements for the production of documents.

6. When a subpoena duces tecum has been issued under statutory authority showing that the purpose of the examination was within the scope of the inquiry authorized, the court cannot cancel the subpoena nor enjoin the issuance of any further subpoena.

7. When a witness lawfully summoned refuses to appear, a warrant may be issued to compel the witness' attendance.

8. No affidavit charging contempt need be filed before a house to authorize it to issue its warrant to arrest a contumacious person who refuses to testify before one of its committees. The written report of the committee is sufficient authority for the issuance of the warrant.

9. A person disobeying a subpoena of a legislative committee may be apprehended and brought before the committee by a sheriff under a warrant issued to the sheriff, and either prosecuted for a misdemeanor under a statute for failure to obey the subpoena or punished for contempt by the legislature, but that

Sec. 802, Par. 4: Sullivan v. Hill (1913), 73 W.Va. 49, 79 S.E. 670.

Sec. 802, Par. 5: *In re* Hague (1929), 104 N.J.Eq. 369, 145 A. 618.

Sec. 802, Par. 6: *In re* Martens (1919), 180 N.Y.S. 171.

Sec. 802, Par. 7: *In re* Hague (1929), 105 N.J.Eq. 134, 147 A. 220; Wilckens v. Willet (1878), 40 N.Y. 521, 4 Abb. App. Dec. 596; *Ex parte* Caldwell (1906), 61 W.Va. 49, 55 S.E. 910.

Sec. 802, Par. 8: Lowe v. Summers (1897), 69 Mo. App. 637.

person cannot be punished by the judiciary for contempt.

10. A writ of prohibition cannot be used to prevent an administrative or legislative body from proceeding with an investigation.

11. Service of a subpoena or the execution of a warrant requiring attendance before a legislative committee is not "an arrest" within statute exempting members of the legislature from arrest.

12. Warrants, subpoenas, etc. issued during recess of Congress are signed only by authority specially given. The Speaker also certifies cases of contumacious witnesses for action by the court.

Sec. 803. Right of Investigating Committees to Sit Between Sessions

See also Sec. 622, Committees Functioning During Recess or After Adjournment, and Sec. 799, Legislative Investigating Committees.

1. A legislative committee may be created by statute or concurrent resolution, authorized to sit during the interim between sessions for any proper purpose, empowered to take testimony, compel attendance of witnesses and punish for contempt and report its findings to the next session.

Sec. 802, Par. 9: People *ex rel.* Hastings v. Hofstadter (1932), 258 N.Y. 425, 180 N.E. 106.

Sec. 802, Par. 10: People *ex rel.* Bender v. Milliken (1906), 185 N.Y. 35, 77 N.E. 872.

Sec. 802, Par. 11: People *ex rel.* Hastings v. Hofstadter (1932), 258 N.Y. 425, 180 N.E. 106.

Sec. 802, Par. 12: U.S. House Rule I, Note 626.

Sec. 803, Par. 1: State of Washington *ex rel.* Hamblen v. Yelle (1947), 29 Wash. 2d 68, 185 P.2d 723; State of Washington *ex rel.* Robinson v. Fluent (1948), 30 Wash. 2d 194, 191 P.2d 241, *cert. denied,* Washington Pension Union v. State of Washington *ex rel.* Robinson, 335 U.S. 844, 69 S. Ct. 66, 93 L. Ed. 394; Hagaman v. Andrews (1970), 232 So. 2d 1.

2. A committee for the purpose of obtaining information concerning proposed legislation and reporting back its findings, with the power to sit during a session or during a constitutional recess between parts of the session, may be authorized by a single house resolution or by concurrent resolution.

3. Unless authorized by the constitution, neither house of the legislature can lawfully appoint by single house resolution a committee with power to sit after adjournment sine die.

4. A fact-finding committee which was appointed by a single house resolution during a regular session of the legislature has no legal authority to sit after the adjournment of the legislature sine die.

5. The fact that interim committees had been appointed by single house resolutions and had theretofore carried on without objection was not determinative of whether the legislature by single house resolution might lawfully create an investigating fact-finding committee with power to function after adjournment sine die.

Sec. 803, Par. 2: Petition of the Special Assembly Interim Committee on Public Morals of California Legislature (1939), 13 Cal. 2d 497, 90 P.2d 304.

Sec. 803, Par. 3: Petition of the Special Assembly Interim Committee on Public Morals of California Legislature (1939), 13 Cal. 2d 497, 90 P.2d 304.

Sec. 803, Par. 4: Petition of the Special Assembly Interim Committee on Public Morals of California Legislature (1939), 13 Cal. 2d 497, 90 P.2d 304.

Sec. 803, Par. 5: Petition of the Special Assembly Interim Committee on Public Morals of California Legislature (1939), 13 Cal. 2d 497, 90 P.2d 304.

CHAPTER 74

PUBLIC ORDER

Sec. 805. Maintaining Order in Public Bodies

1. An official charged with the responsibility of presiding over a public body has the discretion or implied authority to maintain the order and dignity becoming that body.

2. The power of the houses to vindicate their authority and processes by punishing acts of contempt committed in their presence is inherent in the legislative function.

3. It is within the discretionary capacity of a presiding officer of a public body to insist upon the orderly recognition of speakers, and to make quick judgments as to what method to use to maintain order at emotionally charged meetings.

4. A state legislative body possesses inherent power of self-protection going to process of qualifications of its members as well as to expulsion of members.

5. A legislative body has the right to regulate its own halls.

Sec. 805, Par. 1: Arrington v. Moore (1976), 31 Md. App. 448, 358 A.2d 909.

Sec. 805, Par. 2: Commissioner *ex rel.* Carcari v. Brandamore (1974), 459 Pa. 48, 327 A.2d 1.

Sec. 805, Par. 3: Arrington v. Moore (1976), 31 Md. App. 448, 358 A.2d 909.

Sec. 805, Par. 4: Bond v. Floyd (Ga. 1966), 251 F. Supp. 333.

Sec. 805, Par. 5: Davidson v. Common Council of City of White Plains (1963), 244 N.Y.S.2d 385.

Sec. 806. Use of Contempt Power in Maintaining Public Order

1. A constitutional provision that each house may punish for contempt and disorderly conduct is not a grant of contempt power but recognition and affirmation of historic and inherent contempt power possessed by the legislative branch.

2. Statutes relating to punishment of contempt of either house of the legislature are not a grant, but a regulation, of contempt power.

3. A resolution of a legislative body finding that action by a protester was disorderly conduct and imprisoning him for contempt committed in its presence is not a bill of attainder nor a bill of pains and penalties.

4. A "bill of attainder" and a "bill of pains and penalties" are the same in nature, a special act of the legislature inflicting punishment upon a person supposed to be guilty of a severe offense without trial or conviction in the course of judicial proceedings. The penalty in "bill of attainder" is death and in a "bill of pains and penalties" is a milder degree of punishment less than death.

Sec. 806, Par. 1: State of Wisconsin *ex rel.* Groppi v. Leslie (1969), 44 Wis. 2d 282, 171 N.W.2d 192.

Sec. 806, Par. 2: State of Wisconsin *ex rel.* Groppi v. Leslie (1969), 44 Wis. 2d 282, 171 N.W.2d 192.

Sec. 806, Par. 3: State of Wisconsin *ex rel.* Groppi v. Leslie (1969), 44 Wis. 2d 282, 171 N.W.2d 192.

Sec. 806, Par. 4: State of Wisconsin *ex rel.* Groppi v. Leslie (1969), 44 Wis. 2d 282, 171 N.W.2d 192.

Sec. 807. Procedure in Maintaining Public Order

1. In contempt cases, punishment for the sake of punishment is not provided and is not the object of the confinement. Incarceration by the legislature is not an end in itself but a means to an end, the freedom to perform its public duties which could be obtained only by imprisonment of intruders during the session.

2. A question of order takes precedence over the pending question, may be raised when another has the floor, requires no second, may be amended and must be decided by the presiding officer unless in doubtful cases the question is submitted to the assembly.

Sec. 807, Par. 1: State of Wisconsin *ex rel.* Groppi v. Leslie (1969), 44 Wis. 2d 282, 171 N.W.2d 192.

Sec. 807, Par. 2: Ryan v. Grimm (1964), 22 App. Div. 2d 171, 254 N.Y.S.2d 462.

*

TABLE OF CASES CITED

A

TABLE OF CASES

TABLE OF CASES

TABLE OF CASES

TABLE OF CASES

TABLE OF CASES

C

TABLE OF CASES

TABLE OF CASES

TABLE OF CASES

TABLE OF CASES

D

TABLE OF CASES

TABLE OF CASES

TABLE OF CASES

TABLE OF CASES

TABLE OF CASES

TABLE OF CASES

TABLE OF CASES

J

K

TABLE OF CASES

L

TABLE OF CASES

TABLE OF CASES

TABLE OF CASES

N

TABLE OF CASES

TABLE OF CASES

TABLE OF CASES

TABLE OF CASES

R

TABLE OF CASES

S

TABLE OF CASES

TABLE OF CASES

TABLE OF CASES

TABLE OF CASES

TABLE OF CASES

TABLE OF CASES

TABLE OF CASES

TABLE OF CASES

TABLE OF CASES

TABLE OF CASES

V

W

TABLE OF CASES

*

ALPHABETICAL INDEX BY SUBJECT

(References are to sections and paragraphs.)

A

INDEX

(References are to sections and paragraphs.)

B

C

INDEX

(References are to sections and paragraphs.)

D

INDEX

(References are to sections and paragraphs.)

E

F

INDEX

(References are to sections and paragraphs.)

G

H

INDEX

(References are to sections and paragraphs.)

J

L

INDEX

(References are to sections and paragraphs.)

INDEX

(References are to sections and paragraphs.)

M

INDEX

(References are to sections and paragraphs.)

INDEX

(References are to sections and paragraphs.)

N

INDEX

(References are to sections and paragraphs.)

INDEX

(References are to sections and paragraphs.)

INDEX

(References are to sections and paragraphs.)

Q

(References are to sections and paragraphs.)

R

INDEX

(References are to sections and paragraphs.)

(References are to sections and paragraphs.)

INDEX

(References are to sections and paragraphs.)

S

INDEX

(References are to sections and paragraphs.)

W

Y

*

BRIEF INDEX

(See general index, pp. 631–672.)

BRIEF INDEX

LIST OF MOTIONS

The following is a list of the more common questions or motions, arranged according to the usual classification, in the order of their precedence in relation to main motions.

Privileged Motions

1. Call of the house.
2. To make, or to give notice of, a motion to reconsider (usual precedence established by rule).
3. To adjourn.
4. To recess.
5. Questions of privilege.
   - (a) Privilege of the house
     - (1) Presence of members. (When a quorum is present, a call ranks as a question of privilege.)
     - (2) Organization of the house.
     - (3) Comfort of the members.
     - (4) Freedom from disturbance.
     - (5) Disorderly conduct of members.
     - (6) Conduct of officers or employees.
     - (7) Conduct of reporters or the press or the accuracy of published reports.
     - (8) Accuracy of the journal and records of the house.
   - (b) Personal privilege

     Questions relating to the reputation or conduct of members in their representative capacity.

Incidental Motions

6. Appeals.
7. Points of order.
8. Parliamentary inquiry and like requests for information.
9. Orders of the day.
10. Requests or motions for leave to withdraw a motion or question which is under consideration.
11. Suspension of rules for some immediate purpose.
12. Objection to consideration of a question.
13. Manner or order of consideration of questions.
14. Motions relating to voting.
15. Motions relating to nominations and elections.
16. Motions relating to division of a question.

LIST OF MOTIONS

Subsidiary Motions

17. To lay on the table (postpone temporarily).
18. The previous question (vote immediately).
19. Close, limit or extend limits of debate.
20. Postpone definitely or to a certain time.
21. To refer or commit.
22. To amend.
23. To postpone indefinitely.

Main Motions

24. The main motion.

The main question presents a bill, resolution or other substantive proposition, for the passage, adoption, approval or rejection.

Incidental Main Motions

The following motions, though they have procedural elements, have the principal characteristics of main motions and take precedence in the same order.

25. To consider motion to reconsider.
26. To rescind.
27. To dissolve or adjourn sine die when no hour has previously been fixed.
28. To fix the time for final adjournment or adjournment sine die.
29. To fix a different time to which to adjourn when a regular time is fixed.
30. To fix the time at which or to which to recess.
31. To withdraw a bill from committee or discharge the committee.
32. To take from the table.
33. To take from desk.
34. To lay aside or pass on calendar.
35. Motion to change the order of consideration of questions not then under consideration.
36. To withdraw papers not under consideration.
37. To suspend the rules with reference to business not immediately pending.
38. To close debate in committee of the whole.
39. To expunge.
40. To consider petitions when no other provision for consideration of petitions is made by rules.

See Chapter 18, Sec. 187.

†